A HUSTLER'S DREAM I

GRINDING IN ATLANTA'S HIP HOP UNDERWORLD

By

Chauncey "Chino Dolla" Stevens

and

Antoine "Don Twan" Robinson

MASTERMIND
PUBLISHING

MasterMind Publishing Company

Atlanta, GA

Cover Design by Chino Dolla

Graphic Design by Derek Peacock
dpeacockstudios@gmail.com

Editing by the staff at Eagle Eye Editing
eagleye713@gmail.com

ISBN 978-0-9888210-0-2

Library of Congress Control Number 2013941826

Published by:
MasterMind Publishing
P.O. Box 3197
Loganville, GA 30052
www.chinodollar.com ©

Dedicated

to

Willie Sue Stevens

&

Blondeen Mahalia Stevens

Acknowledgements

First off, I would like to give thanks to the Father for giving me the gift of life and all that follows.

I'd like to thank everybody that influenced my story and a special "Thank You" goes out to Norma and Nancy Stevens, Nikkia Moon, Toya Thornton, Tracey Willis, Marquet Watkins, Jeffrey Wooten and Antoine Robinson for your part in bringing this masterpiece to fruition.

Foreword by Don Twan

As a self-proclaimed hip hop connoisseur, I, Don Twan, have been enthralled with the hip hop culture since I was a child. Hip hop is a culture that was once birthed from an inner city community just like the one I was raised in. Having grown up inside an era filled with so much charisma and international influence, it was no surprise that hip hop's artists would have such a strong impact on my life. From the Boogie Down Bronx of New York to the notorious streets of Compton, California, hip hop communities in America and abroad watched as street poets brought the ins and outs of their environments--raw reporters giving us the ghetto news.

We watched as the rise of this industry brought us face to face with incredible success stories. Soon the voices of hip hop could be heard depicting exotic tales masterfully crafted from artists across the U.S. These men and women would bring their gifted messages to all of us while finding fame and fortune in the process. This would soon open doors for others who would find their way into the industry, mastering both the art and the business. Unknowingly, they were carving out paths that others would follow in the years to come. Hip hop-bred hood entrepreneurs.

Vinyl records, tapes, mix tapes, CDs and mix CDs would be the new products being pushed to eagerly waiting fans who would fiend for that next satisfying hit. The rise of independently owned labels and indestructible crews led by platinum-selling artists became the new thing. Money and power fueled brand-named rappers to collide--as beef was born--with us fans cheering for the teams we formed alliances with. Most of the time we never really knew the "real deal" behind the animosity our favorite artists had with their opposition. And to be honest, we couldn't be sure if the "beef" was authentic or simply something staged to promote record sales. All we knew was that we were interested, and it made for the best entertainment money could buy.

I found myself after years of being hooked on hip hop following the culture all over the nation; I really enjoyed what each region had to offer. But it was in the south where I became acquainted with a city that showcased a plethora of acts, all unique in their own way. This place soon became recognized as the mecca of hip hop for the bottom of the map: Atlanta, Georgia.

From Outkast to Goodie Mob and from Ludacris to T.I., I witnessed laid back rap and snap and was soon put up on new terminology describing the drug-infested communities and the activities of the dealers in them.
They called it Trap Musik.

Atlanta became the one-stop-shop for hip hop heads to get a variety of flavors. The city had grown so successful in the business of music that even major companies and our favorite artists began relocating to be closer to the action. Atlanta was on fire and us as fans were basking in its warmth.

One act in particular that made me a true believer in this interesting city came by the way of an independent label by the name of Block Entertainment. Though I had been acquainted with the Organized Noizes and the So-So Defs of The ATL, Block Entertainment stood out as unique because it gained the co-sign from a music mogul out of New York. Bad Boy Records CEO Sean "P. Diddy" Combs attached himself to this company, and, to me, this was incredible as it happened at a time when most East Coasters were expressing their distaste for the Southern sound. But Mr. Combs, being the true visionary he is, saw the potential in this label and placed his star power behind it, a move that would prove to be ingenious.

Block Entertainment CEO Russell "Big Block" Spencer would release a group bearing a name inner city fans worldwide already associated as legendary: Boys N Da Hood. The name alone went platinum in our minds and the artists had the look and street cred needed to carry the moniker in an appropriate manner. By the time their first single, "Dem

Boys," was released, their sound proved worth the praise, as the group
brought us that heat we'd been waiting for. Mr. Combs was the shit, Big
Block had a hit, and we fans were getting high off their venture via a new
division called Bad Boy South. The ATL had done it again!

With the pendulum and momentum swinging in his favor, Big
Block rode the high waves and made it his business to capitalize off his
new found success. We fans sat and watched as he seemingly dug into his
bag of tricks and *Poof*, out of nowhere, produced yet another hit artist,
one who would end up surpassing the success of his initial super group.

Big Block hooked up with Chauncey "Chino Dolla" Stevens, the
CEO of MasterMind Music, to form a joint venture that introduced us
to a charismatic rapper by the name of Yung Joc armed with the hit single, "It's Going Down," and a signature body rock dance move. America
watched as actors such as Tom Cruise got a fix of the *Joc Mania* invading
the mainstream airwaves. Then, to show that this new artist wasn't a one
hit wonder, MasterMind and Block Entertainment released Joc's second
single titled, "I Know U See It." This also reached Number 1 on the
charts, propelling the Joc brand to immediate platinum status.

The nation relished. There was a new face in Atlanta. Big
Block and his company were an instant fixture in the industry, Diddy was
praised for believing, and everyone was laughing their way to the bank.
Then . . . it all came crumbling down.

Like I said, I pride myself as a lover of hip hop. It is my generation. I feel like hip hop and I are family. So when things transpire within
it, I find that I become very concerned, wanting to know what's taking
place inside a world I have grown to love. As fans, when tragedy strikes
amongst the artists we've supported, we sometimes are treated like children in a household that becomes divided by two parents. We become
confused over split ups, and, in the end, we are left out in the cold, torn
and ignorant to what caused the problems in the first place.

This collaboration between Chino Dolla and me transpired
when my partner, Kevin "K Money" McGee, introduced us. Being from
California, I couldn't resist asking Chino all the questions I had relating
to Hotlanta, his road to success, the truth about Joc's hiatus, and the issues of beef between the city's artists. I felt like if anyone was credible
enough to speak on these issues, Chino was because I'd heard his name
mentioned in a few ATL rappers' songs.

I heard Young Jeezy shout him out on his song, "Don't Do It."
Yung Joc says in his song, "Patron," "Ask Chino Dolla about dat dopeboy magic." Then Shawty Lo has a line in his song, "Dun Dun," where

he says "Ask Chino, he know." And that's just what I did . . . ask Chino. After all my questions were asked, here's what Chino Dolla had to say.

Prologue

Flash Back

I can remember it like it was yesterday . . . .

It was two in the morning. While most were asleep, I, on the other hand, was wide awake, maneuvering through Atlanta's underworld with the nightlife. My Yukon Denali's cotton candy pearl paint job glistened from the fluorescent street lights. Speeding, I wheeled my 24-inch Elite rims in and out of traffic. I was a man on a mission, focused and in a zone. With my stereo system off, I fixed my mind quietly on the business at hand. I knew sleep wasn't an option until I'd done what I set out to do. This came with the territory. This was the life I had chosen to live.

My mental GPS had me bending corners out of memory. Eager to get to where I was going, I accelerated to the expressway, pushing 75/85 North until I reached my exit in downtown Atlanta. The lights of the city illuminated before me, spurring me to push on. The streets and intersections were a blur until I came to the side street I had been in search of. Once there, I made a right, slowing my vehicle to around 15

MPH. I was almost there.

The dark road was pitch black to the naked eye. Such a street would appear to an out-of-towner as a dangerous one. But for me there was no cause for concern. I held off my high beams for a more discreet approach. Blindly, I reached over to feel for my prized possession. Finding its square form on the seat next to me, I smiled and nodded, knowing I had exactly what the streets were craving for.

I crept forward, keeping my eyes open until I came to a few parked cars that were pulled to the side of the road. Inching past them I came to the black wrought iron fence that surrounded the property I was looking for. I knew that despite how gloomy and dark it appeared to be, once I arrived the whole atmosphere would change. Motivated by the vision I committed myself to, I wheeled onto the property, pulling past the fence. That's when the scene came into view.

Lamborghini, Rolls Royces, Bentleys, Cadillac trucks, Corvettes, Maserati and old school classics sitting on designer rims, were parked out front of an establishment that catered to anyone looking to have the time of their life. The neon pink sign shone brightly across the building, flashing a name the city had co-signed as one of the hottest clubs around: "BODY TAP." It was the place to be on that Wednesday night, and it seemed no one had plans on being left out.

Lines at the front and the side were both filled with Atlanta's finest hustlers and women. I steered my truck toward the valet parking out front, hoping that a space was available. By the looks of it, the place was filled up. Noticing a space, I pulled to an attendant while catching a lot of glances.

"Yo, Chino!" I heard someone say. I looked to my left and saw a familiar face I had no name for. I just gave back a nod and chunked da deuces.

A valet approached my driver's side. Moving fast, I snatched up my package and tucked it inside my lite leather jacket. "Park me out front," I told him as I hopped out into the cool morning air. Already knowing the cost was steeper to park where I requested, I quickly dished the young guy two twenties and kept it moving.

Being that I was making business rounds, I wasn't dressed for clubbing but my nondescript all-black outfit helped me to blend in just fine. The only thing that stood out as flashy was the gold and diamond chain I wore around my neck. My initials, C.S., dangled from it. The night, combined with my black shirt, set the diamonds at my neck and chest to sparkle like the moonlight does on ocean waves.

Now look, Atlanta's club scene is like no other place. Seven days a week you can find a club jumping like it was the weekend. ATLiens party hard and live life freely. That night was no different as they looked to relax and enjoy themselves until the sun came up. I, on the other hand, had my sights set on bigger and better things. Partying would come later.

I made my way to the front door, the entrance for the VIP section of the club. On my way I encountered a few hustlers I knew. Cats who on other occasions I had done business with.

"Dolla, what's hap'nin," one dude from Decatur asked.

"Same ol'", I replied, reaching out giving him and his crew some dap.

"Holla at me," he said. "I got that purp on file."

I thought to myself, that's a true Atlanta nigga for you. Always hustlin'. I told him I would, but some other time. Like I said, the partying would come later. As soon as I parted ways with them, I ran across a few more people, who I acknowledged before making it to the door.

I tripped on how all my grinding had me in the acquaintance of so many people on different levels. From street hustlers to business owners, I knew all those who I might need down this path I had chosen. So when I came through the entrance, the guy working the admission booth recognized me immediately, showing me some love for coming out.

"Yo Chino!" he said with a smile. Another larger guy was pat searching some dude who came in before me.

"What's up big dog," I replied. Then I gave him a quick head gesture toward the club. "Is X-Rated still in?"

He had a knowing look on his face. "Yeah, he's back there."

Perfect, I thought.

I had already removed the admission fee from my pocket and was about to hand it over when I heard a sweet voice call out from beyond the VIP's entrance.

"I got him."

Immediately I recognized who it was. Though I was on business, I couldn't help but spread a charismatic smile across my face as I turned and faced one of the baddest women in Atlanta. "What's up Tasha?" I asked.

Standing with one hand on a curvaceous hip, she said, "You."

I just shook my head and smiled even wider. You see, Tasha and I went back all the way to high school, where we had a short-lived fling.

At 5 feet 3 inches, 135 lbs., baring a 36-26-42-inch frame, Tasha's red-boned complexion set off features worthy of the title "Georgia Peach." I'm telling you, the women in Atlanta come in all shapes, colors and sizes. They pride themselves on keeping their appearance up and flaunting fat asses and thick thighs. Tasha was no different.

I told the cat working the booth to stay up and approached Tasha, who in turn led the way inside the club.

"How've you been?" I asked.

Dressed in a pair of form fitting shorts and a low-cut tee that showed off her belly button, Tasha looked from under her eyelashes at me and said, "Fine. How 'bout ya'self?"

I shrugged. "You know me, trying to get to da money."

Being that I rarely found occasions to relax and was always working, Body Tap to me was a good place to unwind. The atmosphere was festive and the women were turned up to the max. Although it was a spot that showcased fully exposed women, Tasha on the other hand, worked as a hostess and waitress, opting for a more discreet role.

As I watched her walk slightly ahead of me, I couldn't help but notice the fullness of her round ass cheeks. She turned her head catching me admiring her.

"So Chino, you drinking tonight?"

Busted, I looked away shyly. "My usual, Rosé and O.J. and a Henn and Coke for X-Rated, that's where I'll be."

She just laughed, continuing to stride with an extra twist in her hips, making her way to the bar.

In VIP, like always, it was full of girls with fat asses and titties everywhere. Some were dressed in sexy lingerie, thongs and other lace accessories. Others strolled around in nothing but high heels and garter belts stuffed with dollar bills. All of them smiling and catering to the clientele. Everybody was having a good time as the bass from Young Jeezy's hood anthem, "Trap or Die," vibrated throughout the club. Despite my urge to settle in, I knew I could not be detoured until my mission was complete.

Now this is how Body Tap is set up: as soon as you enter the VIP entrance, the bar is straight ahead, and halls are at your right and left. The hall to the left has independent VIP rooms overlooking the dance floor and common areas on the 1st floor. The right holds rooms and the place I was to meet my man X. So without hesitating, I made off in that direction with anticipation urging my steps.

Women whose naked jiggling assets bounced and swayed as they

brushed passed me barely got a glance as I followed the hallway to its
end. I knew X would be at his station doing exactly what he did night
in and out: keeping the spot crunk for all the partygoers. See, my boy
X-Rated is a well-known DJ in the "A," and for me and many others, he
was someone directly tied to the underground scene. For those in my
line of work, he was a "need to know" man, and I was glad that I knew
him first hand.

As I came to a door on the left hand side of the hallway, despite
the music, I gave two quick knocks.

"Come in," he yelled over the music.

As soon as I opened the door, X greeted me with a warm wel-
come. With his headphones on top of his head, he stepped away from
his perch at his turntables and embraced me in a half-hug. "Dolla! Damn
nigga, it took you long enough!"

"Dawg, I pushed straight here after I called," I replied.

He nodded. "So you got it?"

Wasting no time, I reached inside my jacket and removed the
package. "You know it. Hot off the press."

Right then we heard the door crack open only to see Tasha's
head peek in.

"Hey ya'll. I got ya'll drinks."

Both startled, X and I thanked her. Before she left, I made it a
point to tell her I'd holler at her after I was done. She assured me she'd
be waiting.

"Well," my good friend said to me, "ain't no need in fuckin'
'round. Let's see what 'chu workin' wit Shawty."

Without delay, I handed it over to him.

"You ready?" X could see I was a bit nervous.

I can't lie, I was anxious. I knew that the track on the CD was
fire, but like a proud parent, I only wished for it to succeed.

"It's now or never," I said, shaking my apprehension. "Let's do
it."

The man who had helped so many local artists in the city to
break their first single looked at me and said, "That's what I'm talking
about."

I stood and watched as he placed his headphones back over his
ears before returning to his turntables. Then, removing the CD I had
given him from its case, he placed my product into his system. Before
hitting the button to start my CD, he masterfully brought the song already playing to a cold mix. He performed his magic, hit a button and

then finally brought in the intro Nitti had finally settled on, a childlike voice that would later become his signature.

"This 'ah Nitti Beat!"

The opening came. No snare, no bass line. Just the simple melody Nitti had done on his keyboard. Its repetitive sound had X completely consumed. I stepped beside him, nerves jittery as I looked out of his booth and onto the scenery beneath us. People were bobbing their heads, which told me it had caught a few ears. Then, after eight smooth bars with Nitti talking, the beat dropped.

On cue, Joc's lyrical cadence came in as he began to rap about our everyday life in the A. With undeniable force, the bass line took control over everyone at the same time. In a flash, men and women began rushing the dance floor feeling the vibe. I looked and saw strippers getting into it, wiggling and working their respective poles to the intoxicating beat. The scene captivated me as I stood admiring the reaction. This went on as the rhythm and rhyme carried the party to another level. Then as the first verse ended, the intensity amplified just as Joc brought the hook in.

"...Meet me in the Traap, its going down...Meet me in the cluuub, it's going down...Meet me at the maaall, it's going down. Anywhere you meet me, guaranteed to go down!"

At this point, cats who had been playing the wall and huddled in their personal entourages, all of a sudden made way over to where one chick bounced up and down making her ass clap over the sound of the music. Big money ballers from the city, decked out in platinum and ice, bounced back and forth, making it rain to Joc's tale of poppin' tags and reppin' College Park

X Rated turned and looked at me as if to say he approved. Without saying a word, he proceeded to fire up a loud stick of Cush, filling the booth with an exotic fragrance.

"Ya'll got a hit Chino! I know one when I hear it Shawty. They feelin' it. I'm telling you, this the one."

After a couple hits of the good green, he passed it to me. I filled my lungs before exhaling a cloud of smoke while looking at the reaction the song was having on the crowd below us. My crew and I had put in a lot of hard work. And with all the steps backwards I'd taken up to this point, I knew I was now one step closer to something great. I was beginning to feel good about not giving up. I was headed in a direction I knew my grandmother would be proud of.

Present Day

When I finished telling my boy K-Money and his roommate, Don Twan, the quick version of what happened to me and Yung Joc, how I had come so far blowing him up and then ending up sitting right there with them, they looked at me like I was crazy as hell.

Silence passed between us as the uncommonly cold California winter breeze tore into our jackets. After a few seconds K-Money looked deeper into my eyes.

"After all your investments? After all you had gone through? Block did you like that?" K-Money asked like he couldn't believe what I had just told them.

I just nodded my head. I knew that K-Money could relate to the game that Block was running on me, because of the years he had in the music business himself.

"So is that why Joc hasn't been making any real noise? Because his real team ain't riding with him?" Don Twan asked me next.

"Basically," I explained. "You gotta remember that whatever formula got you to the top, you never change it unless it's broke."

"Or you find something better," K-Money offered. "But, which in his case, he didn't."

"Why you look'n like you're confused about something?" noticing that Don Twan was disturbed by something."

"Because I am, Chino," Don Twan said, his eyebrows drawn in

deep contemplation. "Dog, tell me why, after all you'd accomplished, did you still manage to end up living in one of the most dangerous places on da map?"

Just like I thought . . . .

At that moment I broke eye contact, turning my head in the direction of some dirt hills rolling off into the city of Adelanto. Don Twan's question was one I had asked myself a thousand times. And every time I sought a realistic answer, I always managed to come up with the same outlook.

"In order for you to understand," I began. "I gotta give you the whole story. Not only about when I started messing with Joc, but from the beginning. You gotta understand Atlanta and the streets. You gotta see my life through my eyes and understand why I was so determined to make it to that level in the game. You gotta see how one mistake can pull any person down, no matter how high they are."

"All right, you got me," Don Twan said, intrigued. "B'cause I wanna know."

"Yeah, me too," said K-Money in his signature cool tone, while making like he was checking a watch on his wrist. "Shit, we ain't got nothing but time."

Maybe this is what I needed, I thought to myself. Maybe I need to get all of it off my chest. To tell it how I saw my life. Maybe, just maybe, it would help me find some answers to questions lying hidden deep down inside of me. Something like . . . therapy.

And being that it was two full hours before we got off work and parted ways, I went ahead and took Don Twan and Money on a journey through my life.

Tour of Atlanta

Atlanta. It's not like other cities you've heard about in the world of hip hop. It's not a place where you can just walk inside some office, pass off a demo, and get a record deal. It's a place where the streets choose their stars. And because of this, you really gotta be about what you say. You've gotta put your work in, hustle and grind your way into the heart of the streets. This is the kind of dedication that enabled some of my favorite acts like MC Shy D, Kilo, DJ Keezy Rock, DJ Smurf, Raheem the Dream, Playa Poncho, Hitman Sammy Sam, Damage, and the A-Town Hardboys to become successful early in Atlanta's hip hop scene, laying the foundation.

Hustling from the ground up was all we had. I know right now it seems like all the major labels are focusing on us, but it wasn't always like that. Back in the day, we didn't have the big company record execs breaking their backs to get us national exposure. Yeah, Atlanta hosted the Jack the Rapper convention in the early 90's, where you could see the likes of 2Pac and many others. We also had Jermaine Dupree and his So So Def camp in College Park. JD was crushing the game with his group Kris Kross and their single, "Jump-Jump," and the first platinum selling female rapper, Da Brat, and her hit, "Funkda'fied." He was most definitely seeing success. But we in the streets didn't think it was possible to be a part of the industry. In JD's case, we didn't see his hustle coming from the ground up. We felt like he had been set up for success by his father, who had already been in the business.

For us street hustlers, all we had was an underground networking system people who may have known somebody who might be able to get our music heard in the streets. People like Atlanta's V-103 radio personality Ryan Cameron and pioneer DJ Greg Street. He helped to break a lot of hit records for our local artists. This is what we worked with for a long time. Grinding until one of us broke, changing the game in Atlanta's rap scene forever.

When a guy named Rico Wade, and his production company, Organized Noize, including Sleepy Brown and Ray Murray, took a local group called Outkast from the Dungeon to the world, he sparked hope in every young ATLien from Zone 1 to Zone 6, from College Park to Decatur. Every one of us, who had dreams of one day being an M.C. or owner of a label, was now burning inside. Even though Sleepy Brown's dad was a musician, we saw a group of guys straight out of the hood, like us, who made it.

In our minds, everything seemed that much more possible. The success we saw by cats like Outkast became our dream. Our goal became to grind and present good music to a city filled with millions of people, creating a buzz and hoping to get a major label's support. We knew that if the city backed us, we would have the promotion we needed to make it to the top. Atlanta's culture of supporting its own is historic, and its market for hip hop and R&B was like a reservoir of untapped oil. And we were like drillers looking to get rich.

    I provided this map to give you an overall view of the cities and counties that will be mentioned throughout this book. I feel it's important for you to have something to refer to in order to see the fullness of the journey I traveled in my city.

    Now, as you've seen in the map provided, Atlanta is not geographically designed like your average city. It is split up into different counties, each with its own cities, all combining to make Metro Atlanta.

For example:

Cobb County	Clayton County	Dekalb County	Fulton County	Gwinnett County
Austell	Forest Park	Chamblee	Atlanta	Buford
Marietta	Jonesboro	Decatur	Alpharetta	Lawrenceville
Lithia Springs	Riversdale	Dunwoody	Buckhead	Norcross
Powder Springs	Morrow	Lithonia	College Park	Snellville
Smyrna	Lovejoy	Stone Mountain	East Point	Suwanee
Kennesaw	Lake City	Tucker	Roswell	Dacula
Acworth		Avondale Estates	Sandy Springs	Duluth
		Doraville	Union City	Lllburn

   This is one of the reasons why you hear so many different artists reppin' different spots, yet still acknowledging Atlanta. Another thing rappers are likely to do is call out the "Zone" in which they live. The city of ATL is broken up by The Atlanta Police Department into zones numbered 1 thru 6. Here are the locations of those zones and a list of the most common hoods you hear artists reppin'.

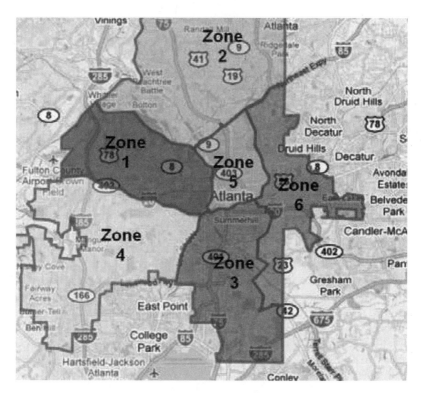

Zone 1: Bankhead, Bankhead Courts, Bowen Homes, Herndon Homes, M.L.K., The Bluff, 5th Ward, Simpson Rd., West End, Ashby and Cascade Road

Zone 3: Inglewood, Capital Homes, Summerhill, Mechanicsville, Boulevard, Cleveland Rd., Jonesboro South, Thomasville, Four Seasons, Grady Homes, Techwood, Carver Homes, Pittsburg Community, and Dill Avenue.

Zone 4: Adamsville, Ben Hill, Campbellton Road, East Point, Fulton Industrial Boulevard (F.I.B.), and SWATS.

Zone 6: (East Atlanta) Moreland Avenue, Sun Valley, Kirkwood, Edgewood, Flat Shoals, Eastlake, The Hamp, Gresham Road and Boulevard.

So, as you can see, there are a lot of areas in the city. This is how you might have one rapper in the "A" screaming "Zone 1 Bankhead" and another yelling the same thing, cases like in the Shawty Lo/T.I. situation where one of them lives in one hood and the other in another hood, yet they live in the same zone, causing one not to know the other. To the hip hop community it may look like one is an imposter when that's not the case. Both are from Bankhead "so it must be two sides!"

Ever since I can remember, Atlanta has been a party city. A place filled with an abundance of soul in our older folks and an extreme amount of energy in our youth. One way I can recall my generation exhibiting this is in my high school years with the dance crews. When I say the dance crews in Atlanta were and are a strong influence on the city's lifestyle, I mean it.

Fraternities and sororities of the historically black colleges of the AUC influenced Atlanta's high school dance through steppin'. Many college chapters existed in a junior form at many schools, and steppin' presented another platform for individuals to perform and compete.

On that note, you also might not know, but a lot of artists got their start loving hip hop because they were a part of one of these crews. These crews lived and breathed dance moves and routines. They would hang out at spots like skating rinks because that was the thing to do. Places like Jelly Beans, Skate Town, Screaming Wheels, Sparkles and Golden Glide were the hottest around. These crews would show up and break out with their newest moves, captivating the crowd or leaving horribly embarrassed. The Bankhead Bounce, The Ragtop, A-Town Stomp, The Muscle, all these dance moves were started by these types of crews.

You will also see instances where dance moves gained exposure through our rappers like in D4L's case (Laffy Taffy), Dem Franchise Boys (Lean Wit It, Rock Wit It), Yung Joc (Motorcycle), and Soulja Boy (Superman). All these are mirror images of the vibe our city has, a vibe that seemed to resonate with others all around the world.

Many had their first experience with Atlanta through the yearly festival FreakNik. Now only a memory, FreakNik would attract people from all over the U.S., and the world, who would come to partake in Atlanta's all-out partying, from the nation's small-time hustlers, to the mega-stars of that time. People of all races would come and rub elbows in one festive spirit. FreakNik will always be a keynote in Atlanta's history. The city has a large population that came during this time and to this day never left.

Another thing we've been known for is our strip clubs and regular clubs. You know (or heard of), Magic City and 112. But what some of you don't know about is the older clubs like Charles's, The Lamp Post, Silver Fox, Nightlife and Club Nikki's. These were prime spots that would set up platforms for our pioneer artists to become famous in the city.

The club scene also paved the way for our DJs. With our love for dancing, the DJs would provide high-energy tracks laced with gritty sounds for us to dance to. DJs like Edwards J and his mixed tapes inspired movements that brought about DJs like E-Z Rock and DJ Smurf (now known as Mr. ColliPark). Others such as Big Oomp and his Southern Style DJs (including two legendary DJs from Atlanta, DJ Jelly and DJ Montay) joined the ranks adding to the underground sound to be spread. The movement went on to create DJ coalitions like The Legion of Doom DJs, DJ Drama and The Affiliates, The Hitmen DJs, the Core DJs, the Super Friends and the So So Def DJs. All these are a result of how Atlanta evolved musically.

Back in the day, I would go out to some of our local clubs in my era like The Gate, Sharon's Showcase, 710, 321, The Gentlemen's Club, Atlanta Live, Illusions, The Bounce and 559. I would watch artists from other cities come in and perform. People like Uncle Luke, Master P, 8 Ball & MJG, Three 6 Mafia, and Cash Money would come, and I would realize how much of a major factor Atlanta was in blowing up their careers. I began thinking about how Atlanta's own needed to be on those stages, getting a piece of a pie others were eating off of. And I was on to something because no sooner than I noticed this, others in my city started making their own moves, transforming their games to be MCs.

Homegrown MCs and labels like T-Roc, A-Town Playas, The Corleone Family, The Diablos, Manish Man, A Dam Shame, Ghetto Mafia, D Money Records, Big Cat Records, and The City Boys though some of these are not names known to the world, these groups and MCs had a major impact on Atlanta. These are local legends who helped create lanes with some of the well-known labels and MCs such as Pastor Troy, So So Def, Grand Hustle, Ghetto Visions, Organized Noize, DJ Toomp, C.T.E., D.T.P., Attic Crew, Jim Crow, BME, Noon Time, Konvict Music, Bricksquad, Sho'nuff, Zone 4, Mr. ColliPark, OutKast, and Big Boi's Purple Ribbon label, Goodie Mob, Big Oomp, Rasheeda, Rocko, Duct Tape, Block Ent., MasterMind Music, and many others. With their work, now The ATL has become a place where hip hop lives and gives our youth a chance to achieve their musical dreams.

Most of these MCs and labels were built as products of our environment. They were molded by figures that influenced what we have today. Behind all the glitz and glamour and behind many of the artists' careers, there was always someone who helped to guide or finance them at their start, someone whose role might have been small but who was a big, key factor in their success, someone who had faith in the talent they saw and who wanted to assist in making these local acts' dreams come true. People who also helped guide the direction of the city, and who had a hand in sculpting Atlanta into the place it is now; in other words, the underworld. Some of these individuals you may never get a chance to hear about in no other place but in this story.

I am one of those individuals. I existed in this underworld, with the unknowns, pushing and promoting the artist Yung Joc, Gorilla Zoe as well as many others. And like the other unseen hands, I aided in the influence of Atlanta's rap culture. My goal was to better my personal situation along with those around me. And thanks to the Almighty, I had an opportunity to accomplish this. But not before I went through my own trials.

You see, life didn't decide to hand me my success on a silver platter. Matter of fact, it didn't come to any of my crew so easily. And if you plan on making it in the music industry, or any other field, then you need to be fully dedicated. As for me, blood, sweat and tears weren't enough to stop me from reaching my goals. And hopefully my experiences will help you endure the pain to reach yours.

This is my story...

The Beginning

Everything has its beginning. Even though it seems like, Joc, our crew, and I just popped up in videos, iced out with diamond bezels and platinum chains, the truth is our success didn't come overnight. It came with a lot of hard work, foolish mistakes, and learned lessons. Before I brought Joc to Big Block, before Block signed the deal with Diddy, and before the platinum record New Joc City was released, all of us were on separate paths. Everything has its beginning and this is the road I traveled, on that path to success . . . July 23, 1995

This was the day my granny, Ms. Willie Sue Stevens, said something to me that would stay with me until this very day. I was turning 18; I guess she felt it was time to open my eyes to life and its meaning.

"Chauncey," she began. "I wonder, what 'chu gonna do now?"

"What do you mean Granny?" not knowing what she was referring to.

"With your life son," she said, looking into my eyes. "What are you gonna do with it?"

Her question caught me off guard and I really didn't know how to respond. I knew she wasn't blind and that she knew I was into some things I had no business, so I didn't rush to answer. The last thing I wanted her to think was that I was playing her like a fool.

"Listen," she continued. "I have raised you to be a man, but now my job is done. The rest is up to you."

This small statement was so powerful that it made me look at myself and the life I had chosen. There was not much I could say I had going that my grandmother could be proud of. And for this, I began wondering what I was going to do.

You see, I grew up bouncing back and forth between East Atlanta and the city of Athens, and I would somehow find ways to fit into whatever environment I lived in. Athens was a small town 56 miles outside of Atlanta, and it didn't offer many opportunities. It was the home of my grandmother, and during this time she was who I stayed with on Spring Valley Road.

Athens was only known for two things: the University of Georgia Bulldogs and drugs. One was a top SEC school, the other an easy alternative for youngsters like me to make a living. Sadly enough, hustling the streets became the choice I made in this small town. And to me, it was the only option that made sense.

The side of town my granny stayed on was a rural area where public transportation was not available. Neither she nor my Aunt Blondeen, who helped raise me, owned a vehicle. That made maneuvering around the city kind of hard and even harder for a teen. I had family members with cars that stayed near, but they had their own list of problems going on. Adding driving me around to that list wasn't a priority.

The people in Athens referred to our area as "down by the way." One street in our hood was about a mile long, with about 11 houses on it. In between some of the houses were open fields filled with horses. This street went down a hill and into a dead end, making it a very private area. Everybody on this street was related through blood or marriage. Living in a predominantly black community, I watched most of the people do whatever they had to do to survive.

Even though most of my cousins around my age and I were raised in the church, some of my older cousins had made the dead end into a popular drug trap known as the Hubbard Hole. The name came from the last name of my family members that stayed in the dead end. I guess my cousins were tired of not having shit, or whatever their reason was for getting in the game, I don't really know, but they had a direct influence over me. I idolized them with their gold dookie rope chains, four-finger gold rings and nice cars.

My granny and aunt tried their best to keep me away from my cousins and their activities. They didn't want anything to do with drugs or drug money, just Jesus Christ. They always told me that through Jesus I would always have everything I needed. But I was more concerned with what I wanted, which was a car.

Aunt Blondeen always got me what I wanted growing up. But around the age of 12 or 13 things changed, and what I wanted, she couldn't afford along with trying to keep food on the table and the lights on.

The idea of getting into the mix to get some wheels so I could get back and forth to a job to help out around the house, ended with me being knee deep in the game. My cousins started me off by counting their re-up money, which would be a couple hundred thousand dollars. Seeing how diligently I handled that position, they moved me up and gave me the job of driving the cocaine to the spot where they cooked it into crack. For doing this, I wasn't paid any money, instead, I was given crack to sell. For every two and a quarter ounces of crack they cooked, I was given 3.5 grams (8 ball) out of the extra grams they had jumped the crack to. (Jump means stretching the cocaine to make more grams of crack. For example: making 28 grams of powder cocaine into 40 cooked grams of crack). At the end of the day, I would have an ounce or two to sell and by the age of 15, I'd bought myself a bucket, a Chevy Chevette, and I was on my way up.

Yeah, I had other things I was good at--football and making music-- but they weren't putting money in my pocket. Although I stayed with my grand-mother, I basically took care of myself. I had little knowledge of my father, only rumors of him, sisters, and brothers roaming somewhere in between Florida and Georgia.

I was my mother Norma's only child. And not knowing any of my siblings by my father caused me to form close bonds with my friends and cous-ins. Outside of hustling, I had dreams of me and my cousins Tellas, Jeremy, and Brantly becoming the next Jodeci. Together we formed a singing group called Extacy. We were really good, and while I couldn't sing a little bit, I could play several instruments, rap, and manage the group. I guess you can call orchestrat-ing us walking from door to door and having my mother drive us to local barber shops and hair salons singing for money to enter local talent shows managing. Our skills at the talent shows led us to finding new management from a guy named Z, making my managing career short lived. Then, due to me not being able to sing, I was quickly replaced in the group by a much better singer.

Besides singing with him, I was tight with my cousin Shane. He was my road dog. Shane, a few more friends, and I all jumped off the porch togeth-er.

One for all and all for one. We did everything together, from playing our first year of little league football at the age of 5 to running the streets until we were 17. At this age was when Shane was snatched out of my life, changing what I'd been accustomed to.

Shane had made a bad choice and went with some guys who decided they wanted to rob a convenience store. During the robbery, one of the guys killed the store clerk for no reason. With a murder involved, the police shook up the hood and they quickly found who they were looking for. The judge sentenced Shane to life plus some basketball numbers in prison, taking from me what they took from that clerk's family—a loved one.

Losing Shane fucked me up and led me to seek comfort in the one person I knew would be there, my granny. At this point, I kept close to her to make sure she was always straight. Even though other family members were nearby, I felt I owed her for taking me in after I was born. This came when my mother packed her bags and left me so that she could finish her last years of college. Besides my granny taking me in, I took life by the horns, feeling that I needed to make something out of what I had been given . . .which basically was nothing.

Well, one particular night I stayed out in the streets all night hustling. It seemed that twenties, fifties, and hundreds were raining from the sky, and I wanted to make sure I got my cut. I was posted down in the hole when my partner Marion came and found me early in the morning with some bad news.

"We gotta go to the hospital cuz," his words paralyzed me. "Granny had a heart attack."

When we got to Athens Regional Hospital, a receptionist helped us locate her room. Marion and I stepped inside, amongst other friends and family members who had arrived. The sight of her feeble body, with tubes coming out of her nose and mouth, lying on top of a hospital bed, took my breath away. This was exactly one week after she told me she'd raised me to be a man and asked "what I was going to do with my life?"

My granny passed away that day, and it haunted me how I hadn't been home with her that night. Instead, I chose the streets and the fast money. To not be with her that night caused me to place blame on myself. If only I'd been there! This blame ended up blinding me in many ways, and soon I lost complete focus on where I was going. After my granny passed, my aunt couldn't afford the house anymore and lost it. For me, this meant either back to Decatur with my Uncle Otis or making other plans. I chose to move to Lithonia with my mother's twin, Nancy, who also helped raise me, and to either finish high school or get my GED, then walk the stage with my class at Cedar Shoals. Following my granny's death, I made an oath to her that I would make something of myself. In 1996, I enrolled at the University of West Georgia. Initially, I did this because I believed it was what my granny would've liked to have seen me do. But in the end, it became something I completely misused, an opportunity I failed to capitalize on.

For me, college became a place good for three things: partying, fucking hoes, and selling weed. Because of this outlook, I found myself kicked out after only one year. I was just getting into too much trouble. I had been arrested for having a gun and was accused of shooting someone . . . all things I knew my granny would've been ashamed of. The only thing I can say is I left college with a name people would come to recognize heavily—Chino Dolla.

Following my expulsion, I stayed involved at West Georgia through parties I would throw. Me and some partners of mine would get two of Atlanta's hottest radio personalities to host for us, Chis Luva Luva (Ludacris) and Poon Daddy. Every time they hosted the parties, they were off the chain!

A real close friend of my cousins Nard and Deon ended up transfering to West Georgia from Georgia Southern College. His name was Lamont, and he grew up with my cousins in Winder, Georgia. Well, when he got to the school, he saw what me and my crew had going on with the parties. Mont (which we called him), would go on to suggest an idea for a major event we ended up putting into full effect: a grand scale party we called SlutFest.

SlutFest was centered around the ladies. We would have a "Shake-Ya-Ass" contest with the winner receiving $500. Also, we had artists come out to perform live. In a nutshell, we created an event that the city of Carrollton would surely never forget.

Besides that, my days and nights were filled with long hours of trapping (street hustling). My access to large amounts of drugs sent me on a mission to "be somebody." I contracted a tunnel vision aim to supply everyone I could find with whatever it was they desired. Ecstasy, cocaine, weed . . . you name it. This became my calling card to getting rich. But throughout all this, every now and then, I could hear my granny pleading with me. I knew deep down that I wasn't the man she intended for me to be.

Late '97 I found myself surrounded by a lot of friends and family members who were venturing into small businesses. My two partners, Lil-K and J-Jones, opened a music store in College Park on Old National Highway. They called it MADD Music and would soon transform it into an independent label. This motivated my cousin Nard to start his own music store in Athens. Entrepreneurship was in the air, and everyone I saw was looking to legitimize themselves within the business world.

By the time '98 rolled in I had found minor success in the streets, stacking up a nice amount of money. I was still impressed with the moves I saw others around me making: leasing buildings and starting businesses. So, motivated to take my hustle to another level, my cousin Q, my right-hand-man, and I opened up a wing stand called Wings on Wheels and literally started selling chickens. Throughout my whole adolescence, Q and I had been together in the streets making moves. We placed our restaurant on Candler Road in the city of Decatur. This was a good location, in between the Eastwick Projects and the Tony Valley subdivision. We were in the hood, and you know how much chicken sells in the ghetto. Hell, there was another wing stand close by and we still made a good profit. This proved to be a good idea and I began to feel like I was finally making some smart decisions.

Everything was looking up. Even though I was still hustling, I managed to juggle my time in the streets with running my business with Q. One individual who saw how serious I had become was my cousin Terry, aka Yak. Terry and our cousin Eric, aka Big E, started an independent recording label called Underground Sound, out in Athens. Like many, Yak saw how Atlanta had become a hot spot for other artists in the industry. He saw the talent around us and looked to build a foundation to launch the next platinum-selling artist.

When Yak told me about his venture, I thought it was cool. But when he asked me to manage his label, I thought he was crazy.

"I'm telling you cuz," he said seriously. "You live in the A, and you know a few cats already in the game. You'd be the best person for the job."

At the time, I had minor dealings with a few people who were either artists or mixed up in the music biz, one way or another. But all these were just cats I hung out with. Their music careers were something separate. As I listened to Yak, I began to realize that he really believed I could make his idea work. I thought on it. Yeah, I know a few people . . . Yeah, I could pull in a few favors . . . Yeah, we had talent all around us. That day I ended up agreeing to manage their label, embarking upon a new adventure. This would be the birth of me in the music industry.

Underground Sound was located at the back of an auto shop owned by both Yak and E. It was off of Winterville Rd. in Athens and would be where we began producing our music. Our first group went by the name Low Down and Duddy. They were two Athens rappers determined to succeed along with their manager called Slick. We began with the aspiration of being the new No Limit of Atlanta. The street money I was making enabled me to look like a successful hip hop entrepreneur. I already had the fly gear, blinging jewelry and hooked up whips. Along with my ambition, I set out to manage Underground Sound and its artists to overnight success. My goal: to make something meaningful out of my life.

I approached every person I met with the cocky aggression I felt everyone must have to make it in the industry: that "assured attitude." Whenever rappers or CEOs came to Atlanta, I would pull up on them, shoot them a card and a CD and tell them to get at me . . . that maybe we could hook up and do something. Even though they would look at me like "who in the hell is he?" I would keep my cool, like I was someone they needed to know.

I recall coming down on Lil Jon one day at a body shop called Neil's off of Columbia Drive in Decatur. The place was owned by the father of Sam, one of the Eastside Boys. Anyways, Lil Jon and his crew were making a lot of noise at the time, so when I saw him, I did my routine, telling him not to miss out on what I had going on. He was very receptive. I got him to take the CD, but beside that, he never called.

Another time, I gave the music we recorded to Wingo, from the group Jagged Edge. I felt confident about giving him the CD because I knew him personally. Out of all the people I had given out music to, I knew he could relate to true hunger. But my calculations were all wrong because he never got back at me either. This led me to question my whole approach to everything I was doing. Something about it wasn't right.

As a manager, I felt it was my duty to find the right lane and the right source that would provide the right exposure for our group. I was not the type to gas myself up to think something was good when it really wasn't. Low Down and Duddy had composed some good music. But good music wasn't good enough. They needed good effort on my part, the best I had to offer. Even if they had chosen a different manager than me, I was a part of the label.

One day a friend of mine named Corey, aka, C-Bone, gave me some advice. C-Bone was the right-hand-man of Big Boi from Outkast, and he saw firsthand the efforts needed to excel in the music biz.

"Chino," he said to me. "You gotta grind music like you grind a pack. In this game, these niggas ain't gonna give you a chance. You gotta take it!"

It was from that point on that I realized that the same effort I put into selling drugs, I had to put into pushing an artist. The grind would be the key that got my label mates and me to the top. And without that type of focus, we would continue to get what we were already getting. Absolutely nothing!

Bubba Sparxxx

Hustling in the music industry was interesting. I've gotta say, gaining experience as a manager and working on studio production made for a lot of life lessons. Though we had recorded some fire ass tracks, we still hadn't run into that perfect situation or person to propel us to the next level.

During the same year of '98, Duddy from the group introduced me to this white boy out of La Grange, Georgia he had been writing and producing for. I was not surprised because Duddy was always networking with other artists. Well, this white boy turned out to be none other than Bubba Sparxxx. But at the time Bubba was unknown, operating under a label called 11th Hour.

When I met Bubba we hit it off instantly. He introduced me to his partner, Fat Shan, owner of 11th Hour. Like me, Shan was ambitious and much the professional. Since he had been a producer for Jermaine Dupree at So So Def, Shan was looking to establish his own label amongst the ranks. Duddy, Bubba, Shan, and I listened to some of the music they were making, and I thought it was the truth. Duddy and Bubba made for a perfect match. I remember feeling like we were onto something big, like Underground Sound and 11th Hour could possibly make something happen.

Bubba's manager, Bobby, and I sat down and came up with a plan. Duddy would write and produce in-house for 11th Hour, while doing so as a hired hand under his home label, Underground Sound. To us this was a marvelous idea, one we felt would profit us all.

We wasted no time in getting to work. Duddy instantly went into the lab writing and producing; both he and Bubba were worth listening to. This process went on until they produced enough hits to package up and market. Then, like a running back looking to score a touchdown, Fat Shan took the ball.

With the go hard spirit C-Bone advised me of, I watched as Shan began grinding the material they'd produced like it was a pack of Columbia's finest. Major labels like Universal, Jive, Atlantic, and soon Interscope got the music fresh off the press. Shan wasted no time hitting up A&Rs and even CEOs like Jimmy Iovine. He was intent on finding a deal, praying that our dreams would come true.

Back home, we were doing our normal routine--recording and hustling--when we got word that Jimmy Iovine liked the product. I can remember being in complete awe because this is a man considered a legendary music mogul. The icing came when we were told that super producer Timbaland received the music and both he and Jimmy wanted to meet with the young white kid from Georgia named Bubba Sparxxx. Interscope was interested and we began feeling the first waves of success.

Bubba flew to New York to meet with the Interscope executives. When he came back home, he arrived with a wide grin on his face. He was a newly signed artist to a major label. Jimmy Iovine and his camp loved the music and Timbaland would sign on as a producer to ensure the music and credibility of this unknown white rapper. No other feeling in the world compared to knowing that all our business efforts, time, and energy had finally paid off. To us the sky was the limit.

So production began and soon the first single came out introducing the world to Bubba Sparxxx. It was entitled "Ugly" and had a bangin' ass track produced by Timbaland. When Interscope released a video depicting Bubba as a redneck-type country boy, sort of making light of backwoods living, everybody loved it. Bubba Sparxxx was an instant hit.

Meanwhile, our camp was feeling all the highs. We were all celebrating. But as soon as we began enjoying our movement, we got blindsided by a vicious blow. My cousins Yak and E got word that the paperwork wasn't right for the songs Duddy wrote and produced for Bubba. Then, to make it worse, Duddy found out that because he didn't have an ASCAP or BMI membership, he couldn't collect his writer's and publisher's share.

To say this was a wakeup call would be an understatement. There were things about the music biz, the legal aspects that we were ignorant to. Yak and E took it the hardest since they were the ones who were supposed to have all the paperwork and business in order. I took it hard because I had set everything up with Bubba's people at 11th Hour. I was disappointed and made a mental note to upgrade my knowledge of the game because mistakes like those were too damned costly.

Nevertheless, the spirit to keep it real called Bubba to do what he felt was right. With his newfound success, he sought to use every avenue he had to look out for Duddy, even with money out of his own pocket. Bubba knew Duddy had worked his ass off to help him succeed, so every time he got a paycheck, he set out a certain amount to shoot Duddy's way.

Continuing to take advantage of the situation, Bubba also used him as a hype man at shows. I guess he figured Duddy was the best for the job since he knew the material and they had worked side by side in the studio all those hours before the major deal. This move also put extra money in Duddy's pocket, so in the end fate shined on him, repaying him for contributing to Bubba's rise to fame.

From a business standpoint, Yak, Big E, and I were suffering from the realization that we weren't going to make a single dime off an album with platinum potential. From the start I began visualizing myself as being permanently in the business. I wanted to add the success of Bubba to my resume so bad that when it didn't happen I began questioning myself. *Was this music shit really for me?*

I felt like fate didn't agree with my dreams and I backed up from the music a little, focusing more on my wing stand with my cousin Q and my illegal dealings in the street. Like I said, the chicken gig was working. Also, the spot made available bits of clientele connected to the dope game, and that was a plus for me. Switching back and forth from the music biz to the food biz to the drug biz had become my livelihood. If one wasn't working the way I planned, I had other options to fall back on.

At the wing stand, I found out early on that we attracted customers who were mistaking us for the other wing stand across from us. This other was known for selling weed, and we soon began to worry that the police might get us confused. On any given day you could look in our lot and see gold Daytons on fly whips, chrome blades on Navigators and Benzes, and other exotic cars with candy paints. We felt the police might see this and think "drug dealers." But this is how our spot stayed because of the people Q and I associated with. Though the thought crossed our minds, we dismissed it, feeling that our having a legit business would protect us from any harm.

Working at the stand took my mind off the Bubba situation. Though I was genuinely happy for him, I knew I missed out on the opportunity of a lifetime. But all the grieving in the world wasn't going to put food on my table. I still needed to make money.

One day I was working at the stand, and it was during a drought. The streets were hungry for drugs, preferably cocaine. Well, as I worked, an older player from the Eastwick Projects came in and straight up asked me if I could get him an ounce of powder. Now I knew him pretty well so I saw this as an opportunity to check a quick $200 profit by selling it to him for $900, the cheapest price in town, since they were going for $1,100. I never sold dope at the restaurant, not wanting to mix the two, but I figured this one time wouldn't hurt. Or so I told myself.

"Yeah, ol' school, I can get that," I told him before stating the price.

"Cool," he replied. "But look, I gotta work and was trying to line it up for later on. Is it cool if I send my brother to pick it up? He'll have the money and everything."

I told him that would be fine and gave him my cousin's number, telling him to call it whenever he was ready. Even though I knew the old cat, I didn't know his brother. And I wasn't serving someone I didn't know. To make a long story short, when later came, I made plans to set the dope in a trash can out in the back of the stand. I would have this dope fiend I knew get it out once the dude's brother came and serve it for me. This was a good plan and a safeguard against getting caught up.

Well, on this particular day, one of my cousins named John John was working, and this fool got all in my business. He gets the trash can from out back and brings it inside without my knowing. When the time rolled around and the dude's brother came to cop, the addict couldn't find it. The whole time this is going down, I'm at the Amoco gas station next to my stand because I didn't want the dude to see me. So when I saw the addict looking for me, I thought he had already took care of business.

"Naw man," he said, "I can't find the dope."

Confused, I went back and looked before asking John John if he seen what happened to the trash can. Then he told me he put it in the closet.

"You did what?" I shook my head, mad and upset. Now that dude had seen me, I said fuck it. I went ahead and got the dope and served him.

As I served him, my street/spidey senses began going off at an all-time high. I began noticing small things that to me didn't look or feel right. After I gave him the dope, he asked me if I could get him four more ounces. This was odd because usually cats who asked to buy anything over an ounce would request anywhere from two and a quarter ounces, to four and a half and so on. Then my eyes caught the black, slick-bottom, pointed church shoes he had on: not typical dope boy attire to me, more like imposter wear. Finally, what topped it off were the crisp one hundred dollar bills he handed me. This set off alarms in my head loud as sirens. Something told me then that I had fucked up.

On January 26, 1999, my worst fear came true. Two weeks after I had served the guy at my restaurant, the establishment got raided by the Drug Task Force: the Black Cats. Even though nothing was found, the damage was already done. The realization of my being incarcerated became a harsh reality. All my ambitions had come crashing hard into a wall. My dealings in the streets had finally caught up with me.

Damn It!

I know you've gotta be asking yourself, how in the hell could someone in his position allow themselves to get caught up like that? Someone who has managed to establish a nice business for himself? Someone who has helped individuals like Bubba Sparxxx blow up into major artists?

Trust me when I say that these questions and more ran through my mind as I went through the humiliating process of getting cuffed and placed in the backseat of a police car. I watched as officers and agents ransacked my restaurant. With no regard, they spared no one; even going to the extent of pat searching the customers they hemmed up outside the place. Trust me, it was pathetic.

As I sat handcuffed, my cell phone kept blowing up; I mean one call after the other. The officer seated at the wheel made some slick comment about the calls probably coming from potential drug customers. Though I dismissed his accusations with a smart comment of my own, I silently prayed that they didn't confiscate my phone. The chance that the phone calls were coming from hustlers was good, and I didn't want to pull anyone into my mess.

Once they got me down to the DeKalb County Jail, I wasted no time requesting my first call. If I had learned anything from watching TV, it was that I had one free phone call coming. After they booked me in, fingerprints and all, they allowed me to contact whoever I wanted. I didn't want to notify the wrong person because I wanted to keep everything under wraps. I had a lot of unresolved business in the street, and the last thing I wanted was for people to think I was out of the picture. This might cause them to think they didn't have to pay me. I needed to call someone I could trust, yet outside the loop. Someone nobody really knew about.

I placed my call to a really close female friend of mine. She was pregnant with my child and very trustworthy. I knew that she wouldn't ask me any questions and see to whatever it was I needed done. But when I called, I ended up finding out something that added to my pressures. Come to find out the calls that were blowing up my cell phone were from her. Apparently, while I was getting caught up, she was going into labor.

So there I was, caught in a fucked up situation at the wrong time. I found out the next day that I had indeed become father to a lovely baby girl, Chanell. And despite my wishes to keep my arrest under wraps, the whole city knew. Like they say, bad news travels fast.

21 Days. That's how long I stayed in that hell hole. Orange jumpsuits, uncomfortable mats to sleep on, and unsanitary living conditions. When my lawyer got the court to issue me an $80,000 bond, I immediately called my Aunt Nancy to get me the hell out of there. It took every bit of three hours, but once I was free, it felt like I was resurrected from the dead.

"You're looking at four to five years," my lawyer, William McKenney, said when I went to meet with him.

"Four to . . . man, I've only been in trouble once for a little weed," I said. "Them charges at West Georgia were dismissed. How they gonna give me four to five years?" I couldn't believe my ears. Four to five sounded like fifty to life.

My life began flashing before my eyes.

The campus of West Georgia . . . flash . . . drug addicts running up and down Candler Rd. searching for their next high . . . flash . . . Yak's smile after I accepted his offer to manage Underground Sounds . . . flash . . . Bubba and Duddy's heads as they bobbed to a track in the studio . . . flash . . .

All of these images came to me as I sat in the parking lot of my lawyer's office. This is when my granny's voice came to me, I have raised you to be a man. The rest is up to you.

There was so much going on so fast that I couldn't think.

Later on that same day I found out that after the raid a health inspector stopped by the wing stand to do an evaluation. When he arrived, he saw all the broken glass from where the police knocked out the lights looking for drugs. That, combined with the rest of the damage, caused him to close us down until we got everything fixed.

I was in a fine mess. Not only had my actions hurt me, but they ended up placing others who depended on me in vulnerable positions. All I could think about was all the responsibilities I would be leaving behind going to jail. The newborn child alone would bring me enough stress. To leave this much responsibility on my female friend would be cruel, unjust, and unfitting actions for a real man.

And then there was Q. We stayed with my aunt in a four bedroom house in Lithonia, Georgia. The community we lived in was considered to be suburban, an area that blacks moved to once they got a little money. Well, with our wing stand closed down, my going away would place a burden on them. Since Q and I basically took care of all the bills, he would now have that much more on his plate. My aunt had just given birth to my cousin Keshon and wasn't in the position to handle any more financially. Realistically, they would all be set up for failure.

I'm telling you, it's hard enough dealing with the repercussions of an action and its direct effects on your own life. But when it also affects those close to you, it hurts even more. I had to do something, and I knew I had to do it fast. The baby's, Q's, my aunt's and my own survival in prison depended on it.

One day I was at a friend named Nicole's house. We were just chilling out, smoking some blunts. She'd heard what happened to me and wanted me to stop by her spot to kick it. I did just that, running down to her what took place. During our discussion, her sister's husband came home with a few of his Jamaican partners. Soon all of us were sitting around getting high, chopping it up. As we spoke, her brother in law twisted up some light green, lit it up and passed it to me.

"Damn," I said choking on the thick smoke. "this shit sum' fire."

"It's dat Cali Ganja," one of the Jamaicans said, smiling.

My mind snapped.

"Ya'll got some more of this shit?" I asked. Cali bud? Jamaicans? In Atlanta, that type of weed was in high demand. I began putting two and two together.

"Matters wha'cha try'na get," the other Jamaican, who wore a black, red and gold Rasta hat, said.

At the time, I was getting pounds of regular bush green for $550, but I knew those numbers were low compared to the prices of Cali bud. I went ahead and told them I'd only be interested if I could get a lot at a really good price.

"Ya know," the one in the Rasta hat began. "Ganja like dis' not cheap. But I'll tell ya what, since ya know my boy, half'ah ton at tree-fiftee a pound."

Three-fifty a pound! My mind began calculating. Half a ton

was 1,000 pounds. That would be $350,000. That was a hell of a deal since I could easily get $800 for each pound.

Without a moment's delay, I went ahead and told them it was possible, but to give me one week to line everything up. Quiet as it's kept, between my lawyer and other losses, I didn't have all the loot. But I knew I could get it up, even if I had to get one of my boys to go in half with me.

I left motivated, determined to get what I needed to cop what the Jamaicans offered. One way I managed to get most of the money was the deal Q and I worked out to sell the wing stand. We both agreed that there was just too much heat after the raid, and our putting more money into it wasn't a good idea. With me going to prison, we both could use the ends. This led us to settle with a buyer who paid us enough to be content with.

For the next few days, I ran around happy as hell. After a few more moves, I had the money and was looking to see if this was the come up I had been waiting for. With the Jamaican plug, I could stack up enough bread to hold my peeps and me down for a long time. Plus, weed didn't draw as much attention as cocaine so I could still get doe while staying under the radar.

$$$

It was bright and early, no later than 7 a.m. The only people moving were either going to school or on their way to work. For me, it was a good cover to disguise my illegal actions. I had a haf 'ah ton of Cali chronic on my mind that I was going to see about. And if everything went according to plan, I'd be plugged into a smooth come up.

I'd made preparations with Q to be my associate in this deal with the Jamaicans. With my half and his put together, we would be able to make everything happen. The day before, I'd called the Jamaicans and put everything in motion. I went ahead and contacted the Jamaicans that morning and told them I was ready. They told me I could stop by to check out the goods. This was all I needed to hear. I told them to expect me shortly. They assured me that they'd be waiting.

Q and I jumped in my Cutlass Supreme and set out to meet the Jamaicans at Nicole's house. I figured since I met them there, it would be a cool, neutral place to handle business. On this trip, we wouldn't be taking any money. The Jamaicans thought we should check it out first, and if we liked what we saw, we could take it to the next step. It sounded like good business to us.

The ride over didn't take long. I blindly navigated us to the house and parked on the curb, even though no cars were in the driveway. I cut off the engine.

"You ready," I asked Q.

"Yeah," he replied. "Let's go."

We got out and went to the door only to have it opened before we could knock. It was Nicole's brother in law.

"Hey, what's up y'all?" he said. "Come on in."

The three of us greeted each other. I introduced Q and we got straight down to business. He led us through the house, and I swear I could smell that chronic scent growing stronger with every step I took. We soon entered a small hallway before we came to a door. He opened it, inviting us inside.

"This way," he said.

Q stepped in first, then me.

There were two men inside the room. Immediately, I recognized both as being the ones I smoked with the week before. Of course I expected them, but you never know. One of them sat on a bed and the other stood by the window.

"Ayo," said the one with the Rasta hat. His eyes bloodshot red like the last time I saw him. "I'm glad'ju could make it."

I stepped toward him and shook his hand. Then I introduced Q.

"Well," he said. "How 'bout chu take a look at da Ganja?"

Quickly he nodded in the direction of his partner who had been standing there quiet all along. Taking the signal, he moved from the window and retrieved a large plastic bag from the opposite side of the bed.

"Of course," the Rasta began. "Half 'ah ton is a lot to move around. Here's a few pounds so you can see da' top grade."

The scent was already hanging thick in the air. But now that he pulled the bag out it multiplied times ten. There was no doubt what it was. But we still wanted to see it. Stepping close to me, Q and I watched as the quiet Jamaican opened the bag only to reveal thick, lime green buds covered with white fuzz. For a moment we just stood there in fascination. Then we looked at each other, giving each other that look: one hundred percent California chronic.

"I tol' you," Rasta said, smiling at our expressions. "Dat fire Ganja!"

We didn't need to see any more. After asking him how long it would take to get the half ton ready, he told us it already was. All he needed to know was when we were going to be ready. Long story short, we told him to give us thirty minutes to go get the money.

It was official. We were in!

Taking no time, Q and I shot back home, where we had the money tucked away inside two Louis Vuitton handbags. We also took the liberty of renting a U-Haul truck to transport the weed. Once we were ready, Q jumped in his Honda Accord, and I hopped in the U-Haul. The next thing you know, we were headed back.

While I was driving, I kept checking the side view mirrors. Every corner we turned and every car that passed, I kept whipping my neck side to side, thinking I saw the police. I guess us riding around with that much money made me paranoid. The last thing I needed was for my partner to get pulled over. But with all my worries, we managed to make it through the city without any disturbances. And before we knew it, we had returned safely.

I wheeled the big truck onto Nicole's street in Ellenwood like a NASCAR driver. As I pulled to the curb, I noticed a black Acura Legend as it pulled behind me. With Q parking in the driveway I watched in my side mirror as a female exited the vehicle. She moved quickly toward the house we were going to. I thought it was odd that she didn't pull in the driveway, since only Q's car was parked there. But my mind tossed aside all curiosity as I watched her thick ass cheeks shift side-to-side in a tight, form-fitting skirt. Moving fast, she didn't look in our direction as I took in her light-brown-skinned legs. I noticed a scar on her upper right thigh, like a gunshot wound that was being covered by a tattoo. And something about it made me realize a grave mistake made on our part. We forgot to bring the guns.

You see, it was understood that two pistols would be needed to ensure everything went straight. On our first visit, we took one handgun apiece but left them tucked away in my car. Why take them inside when they suggested no money? The problem came when we went to get the money. We rushed and left them in my car.

I rationalized with myself figuring we would be cool. Nicole's was a family residence and not some spot. Kids stayed there. As we got out of our vehicles, the girl shot inside the house only to return just as fast. I kept my eyes on her hoping she looked back. But she never took her eyes off the ground. When she passed I got a real good look at her fat ass, before I walked toward the house. I looked back again, a last time, only to see her sitting in her car patiently waiting.

I knocked at the door and the brother-in-law was on cue.

"Damn that was quick," he said. "Come on in."

This time, he didn't lead us to the bedroom. He took us through the kitchen and through a side door that led to the garage. Both Jamaicans stood casually amongst a lot of boxes and storage.

"Businessmen," Rasta said as soon as he saw us. "I like dat. Real businessmen."

"I like tho's tote bags," the quiet one said. "What design are dey?"

"Louis Vuitton," I told him. A weird feeling came over me as I got a good look at their eyes. They were crimson red, making them both look like black devils.

"Here's the money," Q said, as he dropped the bags and unzipped them both.

"All of it."

"Dat smell, what is it?" Rasta asked as he cringed his nose as the smell from the bags invaded the musky, stale odor of the garage.

"Moth balls," I replied. "I keep it on the old money to keep it fresh."

The Jamaicans laughed out loud.

Rasta looked inside both bags then broke a slight grin. In chopped up words he spat something that me and Q couldn't understand. I watched the quiet one go to this 6x5 foot cabinet, before bending and reaching inside. When he turned back to face us he had a semi-automatic machine gun in his hand.

"GET DE FUCK ON DE FLOOR!" Rasta's voice boomed in an authoritative command.

I was in complete shock. The whole time thinking damn, I've been set the fuck up.

The quiet Jamaican rushed toward us, causing Q and I to hit the floor.

"Please man, just don't shoot my cousin," I begged.
The only response I got was a knee in my back as Rasta quickly tied my wrists behind my back. My legs came next. Q soon got the same treatment, and we ended up lying there, side by side, on the garage floor. I felt Rasta's hand as it flew to my pockets, removing the U-Haul keys.
I heard the bags as they got lifted off the floor. The quiet Jamaican snatched them up, smiling at me the whole time.

"I've always wanted fancy bags like dees," he said before bouncing up the steps to the kitchen.

Rasta wasted no time either. Right behind his partner, he flashed his ass up out of there before we knew what hit us.
To this day, I don't know where the brother-in-law went after he led us through the house. All of them fled the scene, leaving my cousin and me by ourselves.

"Man," Q said. "I think I can get out."

His hands were pretty small, so he began to work them until he managed to slip one out.

"Come on," I said rushing. "Untie me."

Even though the coast seemed clear, I still had a fear of them coming back to finish us off.

"That's all the money we had," Q said as he untied me.

I didn't respond. There was nothing I could say.

After he got me loose, we noticed that everyone was indeed gone. Luckily, Q had left his car keys in the ignition, so when we ran out, we were able to jump in his car and go. Our intentions were to try to catch them.   But . . . it was too late. They were gone. It would be later that same night that we would go back to get the U-Haul.

The only thing different about this trip was . . . we brought THE GOONS!

$$$

Months passed and the day finally came for me to appear in court. I arrived with Mr. McKenney. I was numb from the idea of being sent away for so long. But just when I began to lose all hope, a blessing came.

Mr. McKenney worked a deal with the DA and the court: since I was a first time felon, I would be sent to a Boot Camp for four months. And if I completed the program, I could get the rest of my sentence suspended on parole/probation. I agreed to the terms happily and began feeling a little better about my situation. The Judge had given me some light.

I was given exactly one week before I had to turn myself in. This time I used for several things. I put up my vehicles, and I called all my important contacts to tell them the good news: I wouldn't be gone as long as expected.

For those initial weeks after I bonded out, I stayed shacked up with my child's mother before trying my hand with those Jamaicans. Since then, I hadn't spent much time with her, wanting to get things in order. But since my time had drawn near, she and my daughter stayed with me my last week as a free man, giving me some time to enjoy my baby girl.

Then, I did what I never thought I'd do in a million years.

On June 28, 1999, I went down to the DeKalb County Jail to turn myself in. Despite all my losses, I knew it was time to get everything done with.

Gucci Mane

I sat in the county jail for two months. I've gotta say that this time was probably the worst I had ever experienced. My brief stay before had already shown me how hard the living was. But the second time around hammered the nail in the coffin. I had to go hard.

I stayed connected to the world, seeing about everything important to me. Prior to me going in, I had spent a lot of time with my baby mama and our child. I wanted to continue to stay involved in their lives while I was down. I would be out soon and I needed her to know I would take care of my responsibility.

Also, during this time, my aunt would visit me. She came one time to tell me how things weren't going right at the house. Despite all the managing, she and Q weren't going to be able to hold down all the bills. They ended up agreeing that they should find a better situation for them both. She explained that Q was going to find a place of his own, while she moved to Athens. Even though I hated to see this happen, I knew deep inside it was for the best. I assured her that things would get back right once I got out.

Things in the world were already changing and fast. I didn't call too many people besides my baby momma, Q, and my aunt. But one day, I had the notion to call my cousin Carolyn, aka Nee-Nee, who was

Yak's sister. I wanted to see what had been going on with her.

"What's up," I asked as soon as she accepted the collect call.

That's when she hit me with a ton of bricks.

"I'm on my way to Carlos' funeral," she said, her voice filled with emotion.

"What?" I said as my heart dropped.

"Yeah, he killed himself last week," she said. "They didn't want to tell you while you were locked up, but I think you should know."

I was in complete shock. Then she hit me with another power punch.

"Chi . . . Chi . . . Chino," she began as she started crying. "Pete is dead too. He supposedly killed himself also."

I couldn't say anything as she went on into details. Pete and Carlos were family that I grew up with down by the way. Carlos stayed about five houses from my grandmother. At the age of five, during my first year of Little League football, he was my center. He made sure I got the ball every time at quarterback. At six, he was the first person I could remember getting into a fight with. When we were youngsters, he was one of the crew. All for one and one for all.

And Pete, he lived down in the hole. He was one of the two hustlers that started me off in the game. He was also one of the smartest and richest hustlers I had ever known. He was like 2Pac by his mind state, always encouraging. He would tell me to leave the game alone. That I could do more than what he was stuck doing. Pete had just stayed the weekend with me during FreakNik. That weekend he told me that I had a special gift, and I could be whatever I wanted to be. Along with telling me to just keep pushing, he guaranteed me I'd be somebody. This news fucked me up and made me realize I had to do something more with my life.

When the time came, I was transported to Alburess, which is in Middle Georgia. There was a prison there that housed the Boot Camp facility I had been sentenced to. For those who are not familiar with Boot Camp, it's a program that first-time offenders are sent to so that, hopefully, they would learn some type of discipline. It is based on a system similar to basic training in the Army and had drill instructors who dedicated their lives to breaking people down and rebuilding character.

That shit was crazy.

Cats from all over, age 16 to 25, were sent to do the program there. So many different attitudes and egos existed at that place, and many bucked the authority the drill sergeants exercised over them. Up at the crack of dawn and driven into the ground by evening, we did extensive workout routines every single day. Running, lifting, pushing, squatting, and crawling made obstacle course training look like a walk in the park. It was a real deal piece of work. One day I had come in from suffering an intense workout along with the rest of my group tired and sweaty as hell. The only thing that was on my mind was a hot shower. Heading straight to my bunk, I grabbed my towel and some clothes before rushing to get a shower head. That's when this light-skinned cat about my age, height and weight stopped me.

"What up Shawty, you Chauncey right?" he asked.

I looked at him not really knowing if I knew him or not. You know how you wonder if you've crossed the person's path on some drama shit? Well this is what I did, but I didn't get that vibe or remember anything negative.

"Yeah, I'm Chino," I said, throwing him a hint not to use my government name. What's up?"

"Man, you don't remember me, huh?" he said. "I'm Skinny's partna, Dee. We was at Skinny's studio together, remember? In Lithonia, but I'm from Decatur Shawty."

His face was coming back to me. Skinny had been my neighbor. Slowly I began nodding my head.

"Yeah, Dee. J.B.'s homeboy?" I asked.

He lit up even more.

"Yeah! You let us hear some tracks y'all had been working on," he said. "You said you was managing a label."

"Underground Sound," I said.

"That's it," he said. "Skinny told me you were going to boot camp. He said it was fucked up too because you had a few things major poppin' off."

"Yeah, we had a few things in the mix," I said.

"Aye, ain't that Cutlass and Navigator in Skinny's backyard yours?" he asked.

I had asked Skinny to let me park my cars at his place until I got out.

"Yeah," I said, my face showing concern. "Why, everything cool wit them?"

"Oh yeah, they straight," he said, easing my worries. "Yo look, imma let you shower. We ain't goin' nowhere so . . ."

"Yeah, we'll holla when I get out," I said.

"Cool."

Later on that night, I caught back up with Dee and continued our conversation from earlier. He had just arrived a couple of weeks prior and was trying to adjust. We talked about the A, and he asked me if I was going to mess with the music business when I got out. I told him about my thoughts of getting behind the mic myself.

"I've written a little," I said. "And I've also begun making beats."

"But why go from manager to rapper?" Dee asked. "Isn't that going backward?"

I sought to try and open his eyes to the way I saw the business, in that aspect.

"Not at all," I said. "Look, who better to market but yourself? Rapping is nothing new to me. I mean, I can do it, so I put together my own product then turn around and push and promote it. I can ensure every angle is covered without depending on anyone else. Think about it, that's how Master P started."

"It sounds like a lot of work," Dee thought out loud.

"But it's the only way to success – work hard, I agreed. "When my crew and I were working with Bubba on his stuff, it took a lot of grinding on every end. And they're still working, trying to finish the album. Believe me, it's not all peaches and cream."

Dee went on to tell me about my old neighbor Skinny and everything he had going on with the music. Like everyone else, Skinny was doing his thing, recording and trying to promote the camp he was with. But Dee went on to confess that Skinny hadn't had any success finding the right outlet for his songs.

"I got this homeboy," he continued. "He goes by the name Gucci Mane."

"Gucci Mane?" I asked.

I gave him a look. The name sounded crazy.

"Yeah, Gucci," he said. "He lives in Decatur. He's been trying to find somebody to network with, you know, help him get his shit on some tight beats and shit."

I had never heard the name before around the city, but as Dee went on about him, I began wondering how good he really was, especially since he was from East Atlanta. There was so much talent out there that it was impossible to catch it all. That's just how it was.

Over the next few weeks, Dee and I grew thick as thieves. Whenever we weren't being harassed by drill commanders, we were chopping up different ideas about music and the business. He also agreed that hustling the streets wasn't something he could depend on and sought to find something that he could get into that was less risky.

One day, he got a bright idea. He had been telling me about his partner Gucci so much that I wanted to hear him spit. He suggested that we—Dee, Gucci, and I—all hook up and do something after we got out, I told him it sounded like a plan and that I'd like to meet him.

By this time, I was weeks from getting out. My days, weeks and months had flown by so fast it made all my worries look like foolish memories. All I had on my mind was bringing to life all the things I had been dreaming about.

Conversations with Dee had only fueled my desires. They brought back that motivation I had almost lost during that mess with Bubba's first album. The only thing that troubled me was the fact that I didn't have the money I use to. It was going to be hard getting back out starting from the bottom, but I didn't have a choice. I had to make do with what I had.

When my 120 days were up, I had completed the program without one single incident. I cannot express the feeling that came with knowing it was finally over. Dee had mixed emotions about me leaving. He was sad about being left alone, but at the same time, he was glad for my release. I reminded him how he only had a month or so left himself and promised to roll out the red carpet when he came home. As for me?

I took the long Greyhound bus ride to downtown Atlanta jumping with anticipation. They had let the lion out of the cage, and I was
that much more focused than before. I didn't know what everybody had
going on, but once I hit the scene, I had made plans to take my hustle to
a whole higher level.

New Day

I got out December 19, 1999 to find everything I left in complete shambles. First off, my cars had been stolen. My aunt caught some guys riding off in my Cutlass. She notified the police, and for some reason, my ride ended up in the impound for so long that the cost equaled the price of my gold Ds, midnight blue candy paint, white guts and beats all added up together. Then my Navigator got hi-jacked from the club. I allowed one of my homeboys to get it from Skinny's house while I was in Alburess so he could keep it tuned up and shit. He took it out flossin' and, long story short, I had no wheels.

The next thing I was faced with was the surprise of my baby's mother having another child. My son named Christopher. Now I have no car, another child to support, and a messed up living situation to deal with. See, I found myself constantly bouncing back and forth between my uncle's place in East Atlanta and my aunt's spot in Athens. Both these places had little living space and because I was broke, I found it hard to adapt.

My Aunt Nancy showed me some love by letting me use her 1993 Chrysler LeBaron. It was a cold bucket with a two-tone, faded paint job. But I could never complain. Her letting me use it was from the heart, as she had never seen me so bad off.

My parole officer was on my ass about a job, another headache.

By me having the drug conviction, he was adamant on me proving to him I was willing to work.

Nard had opened a second music store in Athens and seeing an opportunity to get my PO off my back, I started working there. Nard was making good dealings with a cat named Big Oomp, selling DJ Jelly mixed CDs. Big Oomp was a street hot producer. Nard and he were a part of this music store coalition under a lady by the name of Orlinda Jarrison who'd been a part of Master P's movement. Being down with them, Nard was doing his thing.

Now, while this was transpiring, I decided to reunite with my old team over at Underground Sound. My boy Duddy made sure he got at me as soon as I touched down. Come to find out, he was still on the grind with Bubba and trying to push their Lo Down and Duddy CD. Duddy expressed his feeling on the direction Bubba was going with his CD. He felt some good would come from it.

Duddy told me how Bubba had come up with the name for his label: New South. They had formed a small crew out of Bubba, this cat named Scram and another dude I knew named Attitude. Their objective was to cut a mix tape called Bubba and the Mudcats. Timbaland would provide all the tracks.

On occasions, Duddy and I would shoot out to Bubba's new house out in Suwanee, GA. Interscope spent $300,000 for the place and gave it to him, setting him up in luxury. We would sit around and talk about our plans and how they wanted me to be a part of New South. This led to Bubba's inviting me to go with him on the road.

"The groupies," he said enthusiastically. "I'm tellin' ya, they go crazy for us dawg."

Although it sounded like a dream, I told them both to let me get right. Then they could count me in.

Low Down and Duddy had put together a project, but basically as a group, they hadn't progressed much. The same went for Yak and E. I guess they never found the motivation they had in the beginning. And despite all my attempts to revive that old spirit, the most we were able to accomplish was getting Low Down and Duddy an interview with Greg Street on his V-103 show. It was a good look, and I had managed to get along with Greg right off. But in the end, it wasn't enough to spark our old flame.

Underground Sound was sinking fast.

And so was I.

Even though my people were looking out for me, for the most part, I was doing bad. Yeah, they would buy me a little gear and take me out to Club 112 and The Gentlemen's Club and ball out. I would even get handed off a few hundred here and there to stay afloat.

But God blesses the child that has his own. And I needed my own.

Q was still struggling due to our loss with the Jamaicans. He was trying to make it by juggling a couple pounds of weed. He had shot me a couple pounds, but left only enough room for me to make tennis shoe money. This had me realizing how bad off I really was. Though I didn't want to get into any trouble, I had to do something.

And fast!

I tried posting down in the hole for some extra cash, but things just weren't the same without Pete and Carlos. I decided to play the top of the street where my cousins Bob and Bay Ray lived. Their neighbor Fred had a spot that was jumpin'. Fred welcomed me with open arms, allowing me to do what I do, as long as I got my dope from him. After a week, I quickly realized selling cocaine wasn't what I wanted. That put me back to square one, needing to do something else once again.

Well things took a turn when my cousin Stone got this plug on some fire weed from these African boys. He began ascending fast and would come through to holla at me from time to time. One day, he came through the store to check up on me.

I had become very frustrated with my situation. I was driving Ms. Daisy, staying with my aunt and uncle, and I wasn't able to provide for my children like I wanted. I had thought about it a million times and decided to get at my boy about some business.

"Chino," he called out as he entered the shop.

"Yo, what's up boi?" I answered. "Just the cat I've been waiting to see."

He stepped to the counter and asked how I was doing.

"Not good," I replied.

"You need to get some of these pounds of this new shit I got called mid-grade," he said.

"What's that?" I asked, puzzled.

"It's a higher quality than regular but not as good as dro," he explained. "Q told me he's been hitting you with one or two pounds of the regular he's been getting, but it hadn't been enough room for you and him to make something decent."

"Yeah, he's been taxing me a little, but I understand he gotta make something off of his money," I said.

Stone leaned in close to me, looking side to side as if to see if someone was around.

"Check this out," he began. "You know I've been serving Nard and Q. I also know you've been dumping a couple pounds for Nard on the low. This is what I'm going to do for you. Imm'ah front you a couple pounds of this mid for 9 hundred a pound. It sells for 11 to 12 hundred a pound and a hundred an ounce. What do you think about them numbers?"

For me, it wasn't much to think about.

"Yeah, I'm cool with it," I said.

"Cool. Just one more thing," he said. "We gonna be smart and make good decisions. All of that stuntin' and flossin' shit, we ain't doing that. We in this game to get money and keep a low profile. Fuck what people think. Let them other niggas draw all the bitches, robbers, and police to them. We gone ride low key, dress low key, and stack this paper up. You got me?"

I definitely understood where he was coming from because the last thing I wanted was to go back to jail. I made no hesitation asking for a starter of ten pounds. In a snap, my wish was granted and just like that, I jumped from the skillet into the fire.

We arranged for me to pick up the weed he had for me later that day. Everything from half ounces, ounces, and pounds I sold, trying to build a clientele for myself. I guess all that time being broke created a hunger inside of me because I was a mad man on the block. Day in and day out, I juggled my time between the music store and getting with old cats I knew, making money. I moved gradually forward, from struggling to bubbling, before everybody's eyes.

This was the beginning and everything started to look good for the kid. I was feeling like my old self. But I had that voice of caution in the back of my head, warning me to play it smart.

One of the first things I did when I got my money right was look out for my little ones' mother. Next, I helped my mother buy a vehicle so I could use it when I wasn't using my aunt's. I didn't want to cause any alarm from my PO so I got her a used 1994 Ford Explorer. It was the perfect ride because it was big and very useful whenever I needed to haul a lot of stuff--like large amounts of weed.

Around this time, Nard caught a case for trafficking weed, and it was looking like he might end up doing some prison time. So I did my best to help him keep his store and other businesses in order. That way, he wouldn't have to worry about anything while he was gone. I wanted to make sure he didn't lose all he had hustled for like I did. We had come too far for us to lose now.

By this time, Stone was letting Q, Nard, and me put our money in with his when he would re-up. He did this for a couple of reasons.

1. He couldn't supply us with what we were buying and supply his regular customers.

2. With our money, he could get more product, therefore making his price cheaper.

3. He could add 50 dollars to the price of each pound for his pockets, giving him a free profit.

Around three months after my release, I received a call from a person I had basically forgotten about., my man Dee from Boot Camp. He had apparently run into some people in the streets who knew me and got my number.

"Damn Chino," he said, sounding excited over the phone. "What's up wit ya?"

"Grinding nigga, you know what's up with me," I said with a laugh. "I'm out here in des streets making lanes like a city worker lil buddy. How long you been out?"

"Two weeks," he said. "And lovin' every minute."

After chopping it up, we made arrangements for him to come out to Athens to spend the weekend with me. I promised to show him a good time.

When Saturday rolled around, I found myself entertaining not only Dee, but also another homeboy of ours named Bugga. Chilling out at my aunt's, we caught up on what the other had going on. Bugga told us he was doing his best not to get caught up, and Dee was adamant about trying to find a hustle. Despite just getting out, Dee said he wasn't wasting no time trying to get his money right. How he put it was the streets were calling!

That night, I took Bugga and Dee out to the club. A place in Athens called The Blues Club. We drank, smoked, and got a few girls. While at the club, I told Dee what I had going on with the weed and how I had whatever it was anyone needed to cop.

"I got a partner out in East Atlanta," he began. "His name is Mario. It be jumpin' over his house. Everybody over there wants that mid-grade bud."

I asked him how often did he go over there, and he told me often. He went on to say how he had to go out there that next day and invited me to come.

"You might be able to move something," he said.

I figured it could turn into a good idea, so I accepted.

That night, we finished partying and when the following day came, we found ourselves in Atlanta. I had plans, and I also wanted to go over Dee's homeboy Mario's house. So after dropping Bugga off on Columbia Drive, my first stop was my house with my uncle on Gresham Road. As soon as we arrived, Dee looked around.

"Man, my boy Gucci stays right down the street from here," he said.

I hadn't heard Dee talk about his homeboy since Boot Camp.

"Oh yeah?" I asked. It was funny because my uncle had lived

there forever, and I knew almost everyone around.

While I went inside, Dee used his cell phone to hit Gucci up, and when I returned I learned he had made plans for us to meet up with him later. I really wanted to meet this cat Dee always talked about, to see how talented he really was.

After we left my crib, I took Dee and ten pounds of weed with me on a mission to serve a few dudes. I stopped in Bankhead Courts to see a few cats, and from there, I moved a pound to my man in Bowen Homes. Each spot took me at least forty-five minutes to an hour. Every time I went through the hoods, it was like that. And after about four more stops the day was over.

All the ripping and running through Atlanta ended up interfering with us meeting up with both Gucci and Mario. By the arrival of night, we found ourselves at Strokers, a well-known strip club in Atlanta. I called up my cousin Kenio, aka Babe, from Lithonia and told him to meet us there.

Babe and I had been tight, and getting money together ever since I moved to Lithonia. I needed to holler at him about this mid-grade and to see if he wanted to get down. I felt it was time for him to switch his game up and leave that white girl alone. But Babe, like most hustlers, felt it wasn't enough money in selling weed, and quickly dismissed the conversation.

Taking his comment for what it was, we took the initiative to party the night away. I told Dee not to trip; we'd make time to catch up with both his homeboys the next day. He was cool with it, and for the rest of the night, we celebrated being free from all that bullshit them drill sergeants put us through.

"Man, dats what's up." Dee said. "I had a helluva time."

"True dat." I said, waking up and getting ready for a new day. "That's what real niggas do."

I knew he was overdue for a good time, so what we just did just dusted the cobwebs off of him. The girls, the room at the Hyatt, and the money I put in his pocket was a show of my appreciation for him staying real while we were down.

It was a new day, and I knew we didn't have all the time in the world to kick it. I really wanted to see what was up with his homeboy Mario's spot, so I asked Dee if he was still down to go.

"Hell yeah," he said. "I told you, shit be rollin' over there. All the hustlers around there smoke."

That sounded like music to my ears. I grabbed the couple ounces and headed out to East Atlanta.

Mario stayed off of Flat Shoals in a neighborhood known for attracting fast money. He lived right in the middle of nothing but hustlers and gangsters, a prime area for me to get off a nice amount of green.

We got out my car and went to the house. An old man answered the door at our first knock.

"Mario in the back," he told us.

"Thanks," Dee said, leading the way.

Dee explained that the old man was Mario's grandfather; he was an old player from back in the day. As we weaved our way through the house, my partner led me to a room with the door standing wide open. When I stepped in behind him, I saw a cat around our age just hanging up the phone. He looked up at us.

"Dee, what's up Shawty," he said, welcoming us.

"Nothing much," Dee replied. "Brought my homeboy over to see if y'all try'na' get some of this fire ass mid-grade he got."

"What's up?" Mario said, looking up at me and nodding.

"Same ol'," I told him.

Dee introduced us and wasting no time, Mario asked to see what type of weed I was working with. Digging into my pocket, I pulled an ounce out and handed it to him. I watched as he opened the sack and inhaled deeply.

"Damn! That shit smell good," he said. "What you want for a whole pound?"

"I usually let whole ones go for $1,000 but you can get 'em for $950," I explained. "My boy Dee tells me y'all tight so anytime you need some you can get 'em for that."

"All right Chino," he said. "That's a bet." He seemed satisfied.

Mario was real cool. We posted up out in front of his spot and blew a couple blunts. Dee told him how we were in Boot Camp together and how hard we kicked it that weekend. We also told him I was into music.

"After we leave from here," Dee continued, "I'm gonna take him by Gucci's spot so he can meet him."

"Gucci?" Mario said. "That's who I was talkin' to when y'all came in. He's up on Moreland, on his way over here."

"Well, we're just in time then," Dee said.

No sooner than Mario told us this, a low key Chevy Lumina pulled to the curb.

"There he go right there," Dee announced.

I watched as a tall dark-skinned cat got out the vehicle. He looked like a typical Atlanta hustler to me: black tee shirt, jeans and some '95 Air Max's.

As soon as he walked up, Dee introduced us.

"Gucci, this is my partner Chino," he said. "Chino, this is Gucci Mane."

We shook hands.

While Dee explained to Gucci how my uncle stayed down the street from him on Gresham, Gucci and I were already realizing we knew each other. I had seen this cat on numerous occasions in the hood. I questioned him on it and we began shooting out names. Before I knew it, we found the link. My cousin Cedric and Gucci went to school together at McNair High. I was tripping because I remembered him and couldn't believe that Dee was talking about him the whole time.

That day, I posted up over Mario's and I made somewhere around $200. I chopped it up with Gucci about what he had going on with the music, and he gave me the usual. He was recording here and there, but mostly he was grinding, making ends meet. I told him I could relate and told him I planned to get back into it, after I got all my priorities in order.

These conversations with Gucci occurred often because I put Mario's spot on my route whenever I was in the city. During these times, I'd run into Gucci and get a clearer picture of the fact that he was serious about being successful in the music industry. Something told me he had it in him, and I promised him we'd hook up and do something together.

But at that time, it was understood that the first thing on our agenda was getting our money right. After that, we were looking to make our dreams come true.

Let's Get It

I rounded my first year out of jail with a bang. The connect with the Africans provided me with enough money to set myself straight. Hustling weed worked for me because I was able to make more than others did off of cocaine. They got dope money and I got their money. The fair exchange had me robbing the streets blind. We had the weed game on lock. The Africans were bringing us a ton (2,000 lbs.) to our front door. We controlled the market and still managed to keep a low profile. The game was being real good.

When 2001 came, I was determined not to get stuck in the same position I got stuck in before hustling the streets. I discussed this with Nard one night as we chilled out at the music store. He was still going to court for the weed case, and the time was drawing near for him to get sentenced. I felt like we needed to get our sights set on something concrete so that going to prison wouldn't always be in our future.

"All I'm saying Nard is that we could do it like everybody else in the A," I said. "Yak and E ain't motivated no more, but I'm still tryin' to do this music shit."

"I told you Mont finally graduated from West Georgia and he wanna do that STR8 Drop shit," he said in response, while shaking his head, his eyes drifting off, staring at nothing. "I probably got one last court date before I'll have to go in."

"What's your lawyer talkin' about?" I asked.

"I told him about that Boot Camp shit," he said. "He said he was gonna talk to the D.A. If I can get that then we could start something this year."

"That's what's up," I said, keeping my fingers crossed.

I knew nothing was for sure up in that court room, but I wanted to stay positive. I knew if we got one more chance, we could make it.

When the time rolled around, Nard received word from his lawyer that the DA approved a plea bargain consisting of him going to Boot Camp for 180 days. Although I told him about the harsh regimen, he didn't care. He was too happy to argue. Six months was nothing compared to the five years he would've been looking at.

April 26, 2001 would be the day that Nard set out to do his time. But before that, we sent him off with a party he'll never forget. Out at his mom's place in Winder, Georgia, we barbecued and showed him how much he'd be missed. There was nothing like going to jail, and after experiencing it firsthand, I made sure he knew that we were here for him. Because when it was all over, we had plans to turn our lives onto a whole new chapter.

$$$

While Nard was away at Boot Camp, I spent my time getting my money right. I had splurged a little and gotten a 600 Ninja street bike and a '72 Cutlass Convertible, which Q, Nard, and I bought to enjoy during the summer. The music store was suffering a little due to the sales of CD's decreasing, but I was hustling hard and stacking my money, so when it came time to back away, I could do so comfortably. I didn't want any issues with finances to cloud my vision. The only incident that occurred while Nard was gone worth mentioning, besides me having another son, had to be Bubba's album release party. This would be the first where I was part of the main attraction. I must admit that all the attention it caused just made my thirst for success increase even more. It was thrown in downtown Athens, and in that small town, this type of occasion pulled the locals and UGA students out of their residences by the carloads.

Everyone came out to see the red carpet rolled out in honor of the hometown artist. MTV showed up with cameras and microphones pointing in the faces of the "who's wvho". Duddy, Bubba, the crew, and I showed up at the scene in an all-black limousine. Timbaland showed up as well, pulling in right behind us. The news crews and paparazzi snapped pictures and crowded the red carpet into the small building. Inside waited three to four hundred special invites who had shown up to party.

That night definitely motivated me, rubbing elbows with producers and artists like Juvenile and others while sipping and casually discussing future label ventures. This is what I wanted to do, interact with those whose focus reflected mine; whose goals lay beyond the streets. The album release party left me with a refreshed vision of my goal.

When the time came for Nard to come home, he hit the ground running. Like we'd discussed, STR8 Drop Records was made official with Mont, Nard, and I as the heads of the label. I was comfortable with Mont because I knew of his determination from the SlutFest ventures we brought to life at West Georgia. I felt like all three of us combined for a good team. While down, Nard met a guy named Mongoose who rapped. My cousin liked his style, and once he got out he looked him up. The next thing you know, Mongoose became STR8 Drop's first artist.

The three of us got on our business. The first thing we did was hire a high powered entertainment attorney named Monica Ewing. After everything was legitimized, we began looking for beats. We had a homeboy named Polo who told us about this cat named Nitti from Decatur who made some hard ass tracks. Polo told us he was the one who made the track for the Memphis Legend 8 Ball's song called "Stop Playing Games." He also said Nitti was about to sign a production deal with JD at So So Def.

We heard this and knew immediately we needed to meet this cat. Mont asked Polo to hook it up so we could talk to him. If he was good enough for JD and So So Def, as well as pioneers like 8 Ball, we felt he was damn sure good enough for us at STR8 Drop.

It took Mont's partner a few days to hook it up, but he made it happen. After receiving directions, we all set out to meet this cat. Nitti had a place off of Candler Rd., right up the street from my old wing stand. I guess auto body shops were a popular place to have studios because Nitti operated out of one like Yak and E had. The scene reminded me of Underground Sound and of Yak and E's shop. This one was also slow on business. But fixing fender benders was not what my crew and I had gone there for. We needed tracks, the hardest in the city.

He met us out front, along with one of my childhood partners named Quan. I heard Quan was rapping and in a group called The Slick Boys. Come to find out, they were signed to Nitti's production company called Playmaker. Nitti greeted us with a real professional welcoming.

"Come on in, the studio's in the back," he said.

We followed Nitti inside until we came to where he made all his magic. Doing his best with what he had, Nitti operated out of a small office-like room. He had his MPC 2000 XL, Roland 1080 Sound Module, keyboard, Pro Tools/controller and speakers mounted up against a wide wall. A hole was cut into the wall and covered with Plexiglas that allowed him to see inside another room about the size of a small closet. This was where he had his microphone set up as a booth for recording lyrics.

As we began getting down to the business of prices, Nitti and I were looking and trying to figure out where we knew each other from. It finally came to us that we'd known each other from the church anniversary celebrations we use to go to each year. Both of us use to play the drums for our choirs. Years had passed, but basically he still looked the same.

We listened to a lot of his beats, deep bass, club-style bangers and hard-hitting gangsta tracks. He told us he was indeed working out a deal with JD. He also told us that he was trying to get a song by The Slick Boys on a sound track for a movie coming out called *The Biker Boys*. Nitti explained how he had done some beats for a hot group in Atlanta called A Damn Shame, and if we needed some features, he could hook it up with them, as well as 8 Ball from Memphis.

It was clear Nitti was a good plug, so we decided to drop a few dollars. At first he wanted $4,800 for a beat. But when we told him we wanted to buy a bunch, he cut us a deal: $2,600 if we got five or more. When it was all settled, we dropped twenty stacks, a clear show of faith in our artists.

If everything went right, Mongoose would have all he needed to do his thing: take STR8 Drop Records where we needed him to take it to the T-O-P!

$$$

At the top of '02, I made a decision to move into my own spot. Laying low at my aunt and uncle's was taking its toll, and being conservative had come to an end. I now had three kids by my babies' mother. The last one, Chauncey, was born two days before my B-Day last year. It was time to roll, plus my PO wouldn't trip because I had already shown him my grind the first year out, working at the music store. Me moving would only seem like a natural thing.

Now I had another cousin who grew up with Nard out in Winder, GA. His name is Deon and he was staying out in the city of Riverdale. Deon worked at the Ford Credit Center, where he would call and tell people that their car note was late. A lot of girls worked with him, and he became cool with them. They would come to his place often and for this I would always be over there. I mean I would be over there so much that Deon ended up suggesting that we get a place together. At the time it sounded like a good idea, so that's what we did.

Deon, his roommate Travis, and I moved into an apartment complex in Riverdale called Meadow View. The move had everything feeling right, and I celebrated by going out and buying myself a brand new 2002 Yukon Denali on 23s. I went and had it sprayed cotton candy pearl white to symbolize a clean slate and a new life.

My team and I were on to new, bigger and better things. And though the money we spent on beats was a bit excessive, I believed that we were going to make it work. We had that much faith in Mongoose. Opportunities for us to mess with some of the best producers in the city seemed right at our fingertips. And when you get a chance to deal with platinum-selling producers, you tend to throw budgeting out the window. All you begin to see are dollar signs.

Our next venture for getting Mongoose music came by way of another cousin of mine named Torrey. He is from College Park and went to a high school called Banneker High, where he met a lot of people who would become stars. One of those stars was a Grammy Award-winning producer known to the world as Mr. DJ. This music maker got his fame producing hit tracks for cats like Outkast and Goodie Mob. At the time, he was pushing his own production company called Camp David.

Mr. DJ was a part of a legendary crew called The Dungeon Family, a conglomerate of nothing but hit makers.

Torrey hooked it up so we could meet this dude. At the time, Mr. DJ stayed in Fayetteville, Georgia, way out in the woods. I remember we rolled out there deep, all looking like money. I was in my Denali on MJs, Nard was in a brand new Ford Dooley on chrome, and Mont was in his S Type Jaguar on 20s. We hit the road and soon arrived at a large fenced in property boasting a mini mansion. The music game had been good to this cat, and we were hoping that he could help it do the same for us.

When we got to the gate, we were buzzed in. After riding down a long winding driveway, we came to the house where we parked and waited.

A large Bull Mastiff sat ready to attack before a slim cat about our age came out to get him.

It was Mr. DJ.

"Come on in y'all," he called to us.

Everybody got out of his ride. As I jumped out the Denali, I was mesmerized by the man-made lake on the side of the house. To me, it took the property to another level. His spot would've made for a cool segment on MTV cribs.

We went inside, where everything was plushed out with color-coordinated furniture with wood and glass. He had a waiting area he led us to with a pool table and platinum plaques and Grammys all on the wall. Everything signified his prestigious accomplishments. Once we got comfortable, he introduced us to three of his partners. One was an artist of his named Sunny Valentine, the other was an old artist from the Dungeon Family named Lil Will, and the third was my partner Jimanice, who had been producing with Mr. DJ. We all dapped up before we went into the studio to hear what DJ had in store.

When I say this cat had his own style, I mean it. Mr. DJ had a sound to his beats I'll describe as "Think Tank Music." It was different, but it fit Mongoose's style perfectly. We all stood around bobbing our heads for about a full hour before we got down to business.

"Y'all can shoot me seventy five hundred a track," he said, answering our question. "I'll do that 'cause I know y'all just gettin' started."

Seventy Five! I thought silently. I knew success didn't come cheap, but it was getting more expensive by the minute. In the end, we made plans to meet back up with him. When we did, we bought two tracks for fifteen grand. I only prayed that the result would be something close to one of those plaques I had seen on his walls.

In another effort, we reached out for music from a local producer by the name of Carl Moe. He is better known for the track, "I Like The Way You Move," from Outkast's *Speaker Box . . . The Love Below* album. Carl Moe was a vet in the game. Torrey used his College Park connects once again and made it possible for us to hear some of Carl's music. When this meeting took place, we told him off the back that we wanted two tracks.

We didn't have a studio of our own so we used this white boy's named Brent in Douglasville, which is west of Atlanta. We scheduled Carl to meet us out there, about two weeks after our initial meeting. He came and brought the tracks we selected, and before the end of the night, Mongoose laid a song to one of them.

"Yeah," Carl said, nodding his head. "All da mutha'fucka needs now is a fresh ass intro. Man Chino, go inside that booth and lace that thang Shawty "

"A'ight," I said, jumping right on it.

And so I went in. I did my thang, and when I came out, we listened to what we had some more, over and over again. While bobbing his head, Carl Moe said, "You brought that thang to life Shawty. I'm telling you, you got flava Shawty."

"Yeah, but it's missing something," Mont said. "Like it needs a female on it."

"I can get Gangsta Boo if y'all want," Carl said.

At the time, Gangsta Boo was a huge success in the South, with her ties to Three Six Mafia and members (Hypnotized Minds CEO's) DJ Paul and Juicy J. We liked the idea, and the following week, Carl stayed true to his word. Gangsta Boo came through and did her thing and left $5,000 richer. As for Carl, we ended up spending $12,000 with him for the beats.

Even though we were getting some bomb ass beats, I somehow felt our approach to this music thing wasn't being managed right. We were spending money like we had an unlimited budget, when that wasn't the case. I believed we should've been investing low, while looking to profit big. That way if anything went wrong, all of our money wouldn't be at risk. When I tried to express this to Nard and Mont, I was brushed off.

Then the unthinkable happened.

After all our investments in Mongoose's future, this damn fool gets into an argument with his girlfriend. I mean an argument that he takes to a level that became detrimental to us all. Fueled by rage, Mongoose battered his girl so bad that she had to be hospitalized. The police ended up arresting him for a violent crime and sat his ass down in a 4x6 cell.

This would be a slap in the face to us all at STR8 Drop as we expected much more from him than that. With an order from the judge of no bond, Mongoose sat while we were left with an expensive amount of nothing! The only thing we walked away with from dealing with this dude was a good lesson learned.

Never invest in an artist who hasn't committed his actions to the overall goal of the team.

44

Pushing STR8 Drop

What a hell of a position to be in. We spent over $50,000 on beats and features for a rapper who was locked up in a jail cell. With no premiere artist for our label, I wondered what in the world we were going to do.

That's when Nard and Mont approached me.

"Yo, we got somebody to take Mongoose's spot," my cousin informed me.

"Oh yeah, who?"

"Well, do you remember that cat, Backwood Slick, the one who use to be with Mongoose all the time?" Mont explained.

"That's who y'all talkin' about?" I asked. I knew him . . . he used to be a part of Mongoose's side crew.

"Yeah," came Nard. "Me and Mont feel like he's our best bet."

"Ain't no need to rush," I said, cutting him off.

"You gotta listen Chino," he continued. "Look, Slick is cool. All we gotta do is erase Mongoose's lyrics off all those tracks and give 'em to Slick. After that, we go from there."

I looked at Mont, who had a confident look on his face. I saw that the decision had already been made. Though I didn't want to rush, I hated being stuck without a backup plan.

"All right," I said, not really in full agreement. "Let's see how it works."

We called up Slick and had him meet us at Nard's music store.

"Hell yeah," he said, excited at our offer. "Carl Moe, Nitti, Mr. DJ . . . man those tracks are fire!"

Although I was pleased to hear that he was willing, I still wanted to cover a few things with him. "Look Slick," I began. "as you see, we are dedicated to this shit . . . "

"Yeah, I know," Slick said, interrupting me.

"...And we just want you to know that we expect you to be as serious as us. That shit Mongoose did wasn't cool." I continued. "We're investing real money into this shit, and we can't have you on no stupid shit."

"Yeah man, if you need anything, holla at us. We don't need you catchin' no cases try'na hustle and shit," Nard jumped in. "We need you writin' and workin' on makin' hits. We try'na blow STR8 Drop up and we need you all the way turned up and focused."

Slick just stood and listened. By the time we were finished, I believe he got our point. After that, he went in full throttle.

Moving forward, we took all of the songs we'd already recorded to Brent's studio and erased Mongoose's lyrics. Then we put Slick in the booth to see what he had up his sleeves. With pure confidence, he put his best foot forward, popping off fresh bars and witty metaphors, showing lyrical dexterity. I listened and watched as Nard and Mont enjoyed his delivery. But the whole while, I was wondering if Slick's style fit that "Dirty South" flava. See, his delivery came off like a New York flow. Our market of Atlanta was fiending for that gutta' music.

That hardcore Trap Musik.

Things were starting to progress and for that much I was grateful. For a moment, that "Mongoose Catastrophe" threatened to set us back big time. But now we were back on track. And for this, STR8 Drop took some time to relax by going to Club 112. We popped a few bottles and enjoyed the girls while toasting to a new start. Though we had a lot of work to do, we celebrated overcoming the hurdles we had endured to that point.

As the night passed, we were all having a good time when Nard came back to the table from the bar.

"Aye y'all," he began. "I just got off the phone with Nitti. He got 8 Ball in the studio right now. He said if we shoot out there, Ball is willin' to do somethin' wit' Slick."

I looked at my watch and saw that it was 1:15 in the morning. Nard told us how he already had this lined up, talking to Nitti earlier that day. As for me, well I had mixed emotions about it. Yeah, Slick needed a song that the South would embrace, but I knew this meant more money for us to spend.

Mont, on the other hand, liked the idea, as did Slick who relished the thought of being able to record with a legend. So what ended up happening was, we left the club and went to a city called Conyers, far east of Atlanta, to a studio Nitti was working out of. As promised, Ball was more than willing, and we paid him $5,000 to record a song with Slick called "I Wish A Mutha Fucka Would." A song that, to me, fit the southern sound more than the others he'd made. For this, I felt a little bit better.

Now, being that Slick was going to be our bread and butter, I knew he needed us to promote him full blast. I got with my partners to see what they had in mind as to how we were going to make this happen.

"We have to get with cats in the city," Nard began. "Niggas like DJs and shit."

"Hit all the clubs," I agreed.

"How much you think they'll charge us?" Mont asked.

"Man, if we hit 'em with a couple big faces and buy some drinks and shit, they'll play it all night," Nard said, looking at me.

Mont liked the idea.

"Yeah, we gotta throw a few parties," Mont said. "Get the girls in the club involved. Maybe get some tee-shirts printed up with the logo and have them wear that shit."

Nard rubbed his chin while nodding his head.

"I like that," he said. "I think that might work."

The whole time they tossed ideas back and forth, it seemed that both of them forgot I was even there. But I knew they didn't want my opinion because I couldn't stop calculating all the money we'd have to spend going in the direction they were on. They'd just complain that I needed to loosen up. And for my choosing to remain silent, we ended up busting rubber bands, reaching out with our cash to kick off Slick's career.

Choosing "I Wish A Mutha Fucka Would" as our best song, we set out and hit up the club DJs.

Funky Darrell James was a So So Def DJ who worked at a strip club named Strokers. We went up in there and hit him off with "a few bills" just for him to play the song, for the girls to dance to. Funky Darrell kept it real though. He kept playing it as the people chilled out, so that was cool. The response we got was all right, but it seemed like people catered more to Ball's verse than Slick's. In the back of my mind, I couldn't help but think how it lacked that "It!" feel because of this.

Another well-known club was Magic City. We went there to see DJ Fernando. He ended up giving us some action and we took the place over for a whole night, throwing a party. Nard utilized Mont's idea to print up STR8 Drop shirts and panty bottoms to have the strippers dance in. At least $1,500 was spent on that shit alone.

This same approach we took to Platinum 21. Their DJ Foreplay had gotten word that we were spreading the wealth so he was more than willing to accommodate us. We hit him off with some cool pocket change and brought the tee-shirt and panty show out. I swear we spent at least $20,000 to $30,000 at each club we went to. Our message screamed "STR8 Drop – we're on the rise!" But my conscious was screaming, *"We're spending too much damn money!"*

I don't really know where we drew the line between partying and promoting the label, but I came to the conclusion that it was time to get down to business. We had previously met with Big Oomp at his office in Zone 1, off MLK. Our goal was to buy some beats from him. An Atlanta artist without a Big Oomp track on his CD seemed absurd, and when we told him this, he hit us off with a disc full of music. He told us to choose which of them we liked and to get back at him.

Well, one day I set out to one of his music stores off of Cascade Road. We had found a couple beats that we really thought were bangin.'

I felt like Slick might be able to pass his style off on Oomp's southern sound. As soon as I got to the store, I noticed DJ Jelly at the counter talking to someone whose back was to me. The customer turned around when I walked in. It was T.I.

"Yo Jelly," I called out, "Oomp told me to stop by and let 'chu know which of these tracks I'm try'na fuck wit."

"A'iight," he replied.

I stepped close enough to see that they had been going over some paperwork. Later I would find out that the papers were BDS reports, which shows how many spins a song(s) has been given on the radio.

"What's up Tip," I said casually; he just nodded.

In the city it was known that Tip was the hottest thing in the streets. But he had a lot of issues with the labels he was under. This caused his exposure to remain on a regional level. His first album "I'm Serious," came out through Ghetto Vision/Arista, and it seemed that they weren't really pushing him right. Word was that Tip gave the record execs an ultimatum: X amount of money or he's walking.

Tip and Jelly had returned to the papers.

"Yo Tip," I called out, having a bright idea.

"Yeah, what's up?" he asked, turning around.

"Let me holla at 'chu," I said.

"What's goin' on?" he asked, with a slight look of frustration on his face.

I just cut to the chase.

"Me and my boys over at STR8 Drop tryin' to put somethin' together with you, featuring an artist of ours named…"

"Nah Shawty, I'm try'na get my business straight," he said bluntly, before turning a cold shoulder to me.

I stood there frozen. His arrogance radiated strongly, showing me why he was always getting into fights in the clubs. But I brushed off the rejection and let it be fuel for motivation. I told DJ Jelly which tracks I liked and asked him to relay the message to Big Oomp. He assured me he would do just that. I left, eager to get back to business.

$$$

Though I was heavy on my grind with the label, I also kept my weed grind going. Because, honestly speaking, nothing else was paying the bills. And every time I turned around, STR8 Drop was acquiring new expenses.

One morning around 8 a.m., I got a call from Stone asking me to ride with him to meet the Africans. Without hesitation, I told him cool. When he arrived thirty minutes later, I was ready and waiting.

When I jumped in the car he looked at me and said, "these muthafuckas ain't been answering their phones. It's been two weeks and I need to see what's up with them."

I didn't know what the fuck he was talking about so I asked, "what's up boy, something wrong?"

"Hell yeah something's wrong," he said. "Them niggas got three hundred thousand dollars of my money."

This response caught me off guard because Stone had told us that the Africans weren't making any more moves for a while. I didn't say anything. I just peeped how trying to be slick caused him to fall into some shit.

During our ride to the SWATS (Southwest Atlanta), I started thinking how I needed to find a new plug. Luckily, I knew a few cats in the city I could buy a couple pounds from until I could put something together in Arizona.

Stone interrupted my train of thought.

"There is one of them niggas right there," he said.

I turned my head in the direction he was pointing and saw the main African dude we had been dealing with coming out of his braid shop, right where we were headed.

Stone pulled into the parking lot and jumped out of the car, catching dude just as he was getting into his truck.

I got out of the vehicle just as the African began telling Stone they had some real bad problems. At the sound of his words, I knew my thoughts were correct. Time to find a plug.

$$$

Still on the hunt I stopped by Mario's house one day to see what he had going on. His spot had become a lucrative place for me, as I would either make money off of him or someone else. Mario was a true hustler and exactly the type I liked to be around. Well, when I arrived, I just so happened to run into Gucci Mane chillin' out front with Mario, shootin' the breeze. I had one of our STR8 Drop shirts on, trying to market the label 24/7, not only in the clubs but in the trap as well.

"What up Chino," Mario called out.

"Nuttin' much," I replied. "What's up wit'y'all?"

"Plottin' a come up," Gucci answered. With bloodshot eyes he pointed at my shirt.

"I fuck wit' some cats who got a label and music store called STR8 Drop, on Gresham," he said. "You be fuckin' wit them too?"

"Nah, this is my label," I explained. "Me, my cousin and my homeboy Mont pushin' this young nigga called Backwoods Slick."

What he said struck me in a curious way because I had seen that same music store he was talking about. And little did he know, so had my whole crew.

"Who owns that spot?" I asked.

"Well," he began. "My homeboy Black. We be recording up there too. You should come up there and check me out."

Although I wanted to hear Gucci's music, I felt he should've known something.

"Man, our lawyer is supposed to be contacting them cats, about using our name," I said. "We got that shit trademarked."

"Oh yeah?" he said, surprised. "Well that gives you a good reason to come up there yourself. My man Black is cool as shit. If you holla at him both of y'all might get it worked out ya 'selves."

"All right then, when?" I asked after thinking about it.

"How about tomorrow?" he asked with a smile.

Well, to get straight to the chase, I agreed. He told me to meet him up there at 12 o'clock so I made sure I cleared my schedule. I pulled up, I spotted him standing in front of the store, parked and hopped out.

"Okay," he said, nodding his head. "I see you made it."

"Yeah," I replied. "You know I fucks wit yu Shawty."

Before we went in, Gucci explained to me how he had already spoken to Black about me coming and that I wanted to speak to him about some business. He went on to tell me how he hadn't told him about the issue, leaving that up to me.

"Imm'ah go get him so y'all can holla first," he said.

Gucci ran inside and soon returned with this dark-skinned cat who he introduced as Black. Then he stepped to the side while we talk-ed.

"So Chino," he began, "What's up?"

Matching Black's cool demeanor, I explained to the brother how he was using a name for his label that was already under ownership. When I got done he simply nodded, being very understanding.

"Yeah, someone got at me earlier today . . . some lawyer," he said.

"She works for us," I told him. "We didn't know if you knew about us or not, so we wanted you to understand the push we got goin' with the name."

Black just laughed to himself.

"That's crazy b'cuz I didn't know," he said. "That shit is a mutha fuckin' coincidence."

After we discussed more about what we were doing with the music individually, we concluded and went off inside the store to hear Gucci lay a few verses. I was glad to clear the air about the name STR8 Drop and the fact that we didn't have to get lawyers involved. The rest of the time I enjoyed getting introduced to Gucci Mane the artist. As he rapped over the tracks Black had provided, I realized that he had his own style, style that separated him from the rest.

Gucci Mane was a real southern rapper.

That night, before I left, Gucci pulled me to the side and confided in me how he felt that Black and his crew weren't going anywhere. He told me he saw my grind and said he wanted to be down with my crew. I told him I'd get back at him. I loved the idea and wanted to make it work. So, the next day, I discussed it with Nard and Mont while we rode to see about some beats.

"Chino man, we already got our hands full wit' Slick," Nard told me.

"Yeah Chino," came Mont. "Let's take it one step at a time."

At that moment, I began wondering if I had a voice in this partnership. It seemed like I always got outvoted.

"Look," Nard said to me. "We need to focus on what we got now. Let's just go up here to see what Shit Talk and Travis got for us. After we put Slick out, we'll look to put others on. Until then, let's just focus on him."

And once again, I just let it go. But as we rode toward Bankhead, I was entertaining thoughts on how to get Gucci involved.

Shit Talk and Travis were two up-and-coming producers who worked out of a music store on Bankhead called Toe Jam. We found out about these two from a homeboy of ours named Jemelle, who went to West Georgia with Mont and me. They had a studio in the back and some beats they wanted us to listen to. When we arrived, we went in, and heard about ten tracks before I decided to step outside for some fresh air. As soon as I exited the store, I saw this dude about my height, weight and complexion, casually dressed in some blue pants, a light blue button down, and Polo boots. He was carrying a CD in his hand.

"Yo," he said to me. "Is Shit Talk in there?"

"Yeah, he's in the back.," I said.

"You look familiar," he said, looking at me closely. "What's your name?"

"Chauncey, what's yours?" I answered without thinking.

"Jasiel, but they call me Joc," he said.

For a moment we just stood there trying to figure it out.

"You make beats?" I asked, thinking it must've been music related.

"Nah, I be rappin'" he said, holding up the CD. "You know, try'na get somethin' goin'."

"Oh, you be rappin'?" I said as thoughts ran through my mind.

"Yeah," he said.

"Well let me hear what you workin' wit Shawty," I said.

"I ain't trippin' but this is old material," Joc said with a shrug. "I haven't been in the studio in a while. Plus, we need a good system. My ride ain't got the right sound equipment in it."

"Man, don't trip," I said, nodding toward my Denali. "Let's go to my truck."

We set off to my truck and got in. He handed me his CD and sat back while I placed it in my factory-installed Bose CD player. With that done, I waited patiently before the first track began to play.

The beat was mediocre but that's not what I listened for. I wanted to hear his delivery. It didn't take long for me to hear that he had a feel-good swagger to his flow, kind of reminding me of Nelly. I bobbed my head to the mid-tempo, really liking his style. In the end, I told him so.

"Man Joc, that's nice," I said.

"Yeah, you think so?" he asked.

"Yeah," I said and nodded.

I told him what we had going on at STR8 Drop and about our artist Backwoods Slick. By the time we separated, me and Joc exchanged numbers and I made a mental note: *I'd keep all my ideas and suggestions from Nard and Mont until we were finished with Slick. That way I could save myself a whole lot of rejection.*

One day, while I was making moves, I received a call from Bubba. He wanted me to stop by his house because he said he needed my opinion on something important. Even though I had a lot on my plate—I hadn't reported for my probation because I'd been so busy and could have a warrant any day now—I dropped everything I was doing for a friend in need. Forty-five minutes later, I was sitting in his living room—me, him and Duddy.

"Man," he explained. "Interscope wants me to change my music for the second album."

"Change your music?" I asked. "I don't understand."

He went on to explain how the people at the label felt that the backwoods/country boy image depicted in the video "Ugly" set him apart from other white rappers. They believed that this would propel him to platinum status and they wanted to capitalize off of it. They wanted him to rap more about country stuff. To paint a musical image of the pigs and shit like that.

"Man, Bubba, you ain't gotta do that," I said, upset because I felt they were setting him up to look like a damn fool. "You don't need to prove nothing. You already got street cred from that Archey song, as well as a following from your skills. That country redneck shit was good for a video concept. I mean it was funny, but trust me, it's not a good overall sound for who you are. Hell, we know you are country, look at your name, but it's more to you than that."

"That's the same thing I said," Duddy chimed in.

Bubba listened, although I could tell he was indecisive.

"They also told me if my second album did good they'd give me a million dollar label deal," he said.

We all fell silent. Taking in what that meant.

"All I'm saying Bubba is that it could backfire," I said. "If it works then fine, but if it doesn't then you'll lose a lot of fan base and you still won't get the label deal." I let that sink in.

"But no matter what, I'm with you," I said.

With a distant look on his face, Bubba nodded his head.

"I appreciate that, and I know you got a lot goin' on with your probation," Bubba said. "But I want you to know that I'ma put something together so when you get out it'll be on, somethin' where we'll all get paid."

That day I left confident that something good was going to come from all that was going on. Not from the ideas of Interscope taking Bubba's music further into country rap; that was suicide to me.

Instead it would come from the people I had come to know. I hated the thought of me going to jail, but I was sure glad I had made good contacts for when I got out.

Polo and Petey Pablo

In February, Atlanta hosted the N.B.A. All Star Game, and that weekend was off the hook. A few of my homeboys and I took the time out and partied from that Thursday all the way to Sunday when the game took place. Before the game, my crew and I set out to Lenox Mall in Buckhead to pick up some gear so we could be super swaggin' for the event.

That Sunday, the mall was dumb packed. People from all over came out to see the game, and the fire department came out and ordered the mall closed due to overcapacity. There were that many people! There were so many good-looking women that I caught a slight strain in my neck. One little honey walked past me, and after locking eyes for a long moment, I couldn't help but think, *damn, she pretty as hell.* She was light bright, damn near white, rocking her hair long and flowing. She wore a nice little BeBe outfit boasting a low cut shirt, showing just enough cleavage, and some form-fitting white jeans snugging her hips just right. She set the outfit off by wearing some designer heels. After a few steps, I turned around only to catch her doing the same.

"Excuse me," I said casually. "May I speak to you for a minute?" And without hesitation, I proceeded to pour on the charm. This little beauty was from Nashville, Tennessee, and after getting her number and finding out she had come to see the game, I told her I'd make it my business to catch back up with her. She said she'd love that and would be looking forward to it.

After that weekend and a few phone calls, I would shoot to Nashville to relax with her, in between grinding. She had a nice crib, her own job, and a car. She was very independent, with a 6-month-old son and maintaining a successful single life. With her, I had my own little duck off spot, where I could think and not be distracted by all the things at the crib.

One day, Mont came by my apartment needing a favor. He was taking his family on a trip and wanted me to swap cars with him. Though I loved my truck, I knew his Jaguar would surely keep me entertained while he was gone. So I told him it was cool, knowing he'd only be gone a week.

While Mont was out of town, I moved through the city incognito. Everyone was used to me being in my Denali, not the S-type. I was shining on dudes too hard and I could smell the hate. I was beginning to hate hustling the streets. It was starting to seem not worth all the risks that I was taking. Friends were turning out to be snitches and everyone was going to prison. The streets were dripping blood as cats were getting murdered left and right. And the more money it seemed you made, the more you had to spend to duck those lying to rob you. Plus, I aspired to gain much more than what a brown paper bag or a backpack could carry. I wanted real success, the kind that came without the hassles of police investigations.

"So how was the trip?" I asked after Mont returned my truck early in the morning.

He looked nervous and concerned, like something was bothering him.

"Chino, my neighbor told me that the Feds asked him if they could use his house to camp out and watch me," he said.

"Dog, you need to lay low," I said, not knowing what to say, but stating the obvious.

"I am. That's why I'm going to leave the Jag with you," he said. "I'll roll one of my low key whips until shit dies down."

Mont stayed awhile and I did my best to keep him relaxed. But when he left I realized how stressed I'd become. To hear the Feds were on him only intensified my concerns about my own wellbeing. I mean, I had been driving his car! That meant there was a damn good chance that they were mistaking me for him and followed me around.

That shit had me spooked as a muthafucka!

Trying to keep my cool, I went about my days keeping a low profile myself. One day Deon came back to our apartment upset.

"Let's buy a house," he said.

I was lying on the couch in the living room watching the news (probably waiting to see whose face was going to pop up first, mine or Mont's).

"A house?" I asked. "Why, what's up?"

He exhaled a long breath.

"Man, that nigga Travis can't pay his share of the rent this month, again," he said. "And I'm tired of carrying his ass. Plus all the money we spend on bills and shit . . . I just think we'd come out better buying a house."

I could tell he had been thinking seriously about this. But little did he know, so had I. Sitting up, I began to put on my shoes.

"You know, yesterday I jumped out of my truck and that old lady who lives two doors down pulled in next to me," I said. "She gave me this peculiar look and I started thinking about how I got all these expensive cars at this apartment complex. I just be feeling uncomfortable, like people be all in our business."

"So what do you think we should do?" Deon asked, rubbing his chin.

"I think we should go house shopping," I said.

It seemed like my stress level went up a notch with all that was going on. Duddy called me up to see how I was doing and I confided in him about all the things that were bothering me. From the money we were putting into STR8 Drop to the Feds on Mont to my being uncomfortable living in my own apartment.

"I'm telling you Chino," he began, after I vented. "All you do is hustle. You need to take a break. When was the last time you just chilled out, ya know, got away from it all?"

"Last night at Pinups," I replied.

"Man, not at no strip club," he replied with a laugh. "Seriously, you know what I mean."

Honestly, I couldn't remember. And I guess my silence spoke for me.

"Dog, what you need is a getaway," he said.

"And go where?" I asked.

"How 'bout with me and Bubba on tour?" he said. "I'm tellin' you, the hoes, and the parties and…did I mention the hoes?"

"Man, I ain't got no time to go on tour right now," I said with a laugh. "I got the label and lord knows it's always somethin' with that."

"But that's the problem," he said. "All work and no play. Listen Chino, you need to let it go. Feds watchin' niggas, the streets is hot . . . just say 'fuck it' and come wit' us. I promise it'll do some good."

Duddy pleaded with me. I could tell he wanted me to go more out of concern than for fun. And he was right. I needed to unwind and get away from the heat for a minute. I concluded our conversation by telling him I'd think about it and he said cool.

Deon's decision to move seemed like a good one. We got with our cousin Nikkia about the issue. Nikkia was a real estate agent, and we needed her to help us find somewhere nice, quiet and discreet. It took about a week but she found us a three bedroom in Riverdale. It was a nice subdivision in a family oriented neighborhood off of Highway 85. We paid $120,000 and looked at it as the same amount of money we'd end up spending on renting our old apartment rather than owning our own house. Now all the vehicles and hustlers coming to see us wouldn't be subjected to suspicion.

Trying to keep my mind free of worry I decided to hit a cook out with my homeboy from the hood, Mario W. After getting my truck shined up on Covington Hwy. I shot to Evans Mill Rd. and picked him up. With us both clean as new nickels and the truck looking spit shined, we headed to I-20 West on a mission. But before we could get on the highway, we were pulled over by a hating ass DeKalb County police officer. He said he'd stopped us for loud music, which was a cold lie because I had factory sounds and my windows up to keep people like him out.

Being a dick, he called back up and once they arrived a full fledged harassment process took place. They so disrespectfully put that nasty ass K-9 all in my truck only to find nothing illegal. The only thing they found was 9 stacks I had in my middle console. When they found it you would have thought they hit the GA Lotto only to be left high and dry when they realized they had to return it. My whole hood was on the scene including my God mother Chris who blasted them every second of their harassment. Unfortunately I was taken to DeKalb County for a probation violation where I was kept for a while.

One day in the county jail, I was standing out in the common area looking at videos with the others. I hadn't been interested in music, or hearing it for that matter, but something caused me to stop and look. I guess my interest had been for a reason because no sooner than I stopped, I saw that Bubba had a new video. It was set in the country; dirt roads and wide fields. Timbaland popped on the screen playing a guitar and singing a chorus about a bottle of "shine".

I shook my head as I realized what I was witnessing. This was the single for Bubba's 2nd album.

I'm not going to lie…when I saw that video I really began to wonder about Bubba's future. I mean, I liked the song but to me it wasn't a good look. During the rest of my stay there at the county, I would think about that video and Bubba's decision. Along with everything else, it seemed that things with Bubba had changed as well.

All I could do was hope for the best.

While in the county I'd associated with my homie Rasheed from East Point. When I got there he hadn't seen me in a while and said he heard I was messing around with the music thing.

I really didn't go into it too much. Basically, I told him how it was a learning experience. I also explained how Bubba had asked my opinion on Interscope's request that his music portray his image on his second album and the idea behind his recent video.

"I saw that video," he said. "Timbaland playin' the guitar?"

"Yea, that's it."

"Keepin' it real, I didn't like it."

I wasn't surprised..

"He let them convince him to do that and he didn't need to," I said. "I think he felt pressured because he wanted to keep them happy. They told him if it did good they'd give him a million dollar label deal for his own company."

"Damn, that would be sweet."

"It would, but it has to do good first."

After about two weeks, of being free I was burnt out so I shot out to Bubba's spot to see what he had going on. When I got there, I just so happened to catch him and Duddy on their way out of town.

"So what's up," Duddy asked. "You down or what?"

"I don't know," I said. "It's just so much…"

"Exactly," he said, cutting me off. "You need to unwind. What's a few days?"

I started to think. Then out of nowhere I heard myself say, "fuck it. When y'all leavin'?"

"Right now," he said with a smile.

It was a spur of the moment decision.

Bubba told me going with them would be a good learning experience, giving me an upfront view of how the business worked when it came down to the touring side of things. Also, he told me that since I thought I was a big playa, he wanted to see how I handled all the women.

It was at this point when I realized that my work life interfered drastically with my personal life. Despite a few female friends, and a baby mama who I'd been distant with for some time, I really had no interest in chasing pussy. I was all business and this was dull. Yeah, I needed to unwind and maybe some good, hot groupie pussy would do just that.

At this time I was still dealing with my PO, and leaving meant I had to go through him. I told him about my dealings with the music way before this and he knew about my relationship with Bubba. Matter of fact, I was getting autographed pictures from Bubba for his son. So, when I asked him for a few days to go on the tour, he didn't hesitate to give me the thumbs up. He just told me to make sure I reported when I got back.

Bubba had three shows lined up, all of them in the Carolinas. He told me how he had to fly out to Miami with his manager, Bobby, to meet Timbaland. Me and Duddy would ride in my Denali since we were so close to the first show in North Carolina.

After getting all the directions and information I needed, me and Duddy hit the mall and grabbed a few outfits. By the time the sun started setting, we were riding comfortably on the highway. We took this time to chop it up. Before long the topic turned to STR8 Drop and how things were going there.

"What happened with Mongoose should've made y'all a little more cautious with money," he expressed. "But y'all have to expect that buying beats from cats like Mr. DJ and Carl Moe ain't comin' cheap."

"Yeah. I realized that," I told him. "But we gotta pay off them DJs to play our songs."

"And buying lingerie for the dancers to strip in was a good move," he chipped in. "It sounds like y'all are on point, just going over-board on the beats."

Duddy's input really helped. As we rode, I thought seriously about everything going on with the business I was in. There was so much happening not only financially, but also with the situation with Mont and the Feds. Duddy reminded me how conspiracies worked and the last thing I wanted was to get caught up in Mont's business. With the cars, houses and the label, we could all end up with tax evasion, money laundering charges and some more stuff.

It took about five hours, but we finally arrived in the city of Charlotte. North Carolina was a hell of a place, and if you've never been there, I encourage you to go. Bobby had already made reservations for us at the Marriott Hotel. As soon as we arrived, me and Duddy went in and got the key. After that, we unloaded our stuff into the room, grabbed a quick shower, and ordered us some food.

It must've been three hours or so before Bubba arrived with Bobby and Scram. Bobby informed us that the first show would take place in less than two hours. This caught me off guard. When I voiced this, Bobby reminded me how no time was wasted in the music business. Everything from flights to shows to meetings was all scheduled. The trick was that you had to stay ready because those times were liable to change at any moment. And this happened often.

Bubba, Scram and Bobby all got ready, and before we knew it, we were all ready and shooting back out the door. Scram told me how they finished the mix tape: Bubba and the Mudcats. They had brought a few thousand copies to give away for promotion. I couldn't wait to hear it myself, knowing Timbaland had done the production on it. Scram then asked if I was going to get on stage.

"Nah," I said. "I'm just gonna sit back and watch."

He just shrugged.

"All right, but ain't no feeling like being up in front of the crowd," he said. "It's a rush!"

We arrived at the venue and people were everywhere. Bobby had already instructed us on when Bubba was supposed to go on and everything. So when we got there, the event had already begun with another act ripping the stage. Bobby stressed the point of Bubba getting in and getting the job done. So when the time came, that's just what he did.

I stood backstage and watched as Bubba went into his zone. With Scram and Duddy as hype men, Bubba rocked the crowd, which sang along with the lyrics of his first smash hit "Ugly." Bubba also had this white DJ who mixed and cut the records, keeping the jams coming. The bass vibrated in the auditorium as girls of all shapes, shades, and sizes, bounced and screamed at the trio on stage. I was mesmerized how in between every song, Bubba and the crew screamed out New South and passed out the mix tape. The electricity was alive in the building and I was taking it all in.

As an extra treat, Bubba's DJ put on a solo act that shut the place down. I mean this white boy acted a fool on the turntables. With the use of hip hop favorites, old and new, this cat mixed and scratched songs, blending them together while performing unbelievable acts at the same time. He took off his shirt, shoes, hat, and other articles of clothing before putting them back on—all without missing a beat. Doing a handstand and scratching with his feet, he continued to put on a show. The crowd went bananas, and by the end of the night, there was no doubt . . . Bubba Sparxxx and his crew had rocked the house in North Carolina.

Back at the hotel, we celebrated.

"Man, y'all killed that shit," I said to everybody as we sat around.

"I told you," said Bubba. "Did you see all the women in the crowd?"

"Yeah," I told him. "But we came and went so quick, I didn't get a chance to holla at any."

"Don't worry," came Scram. "We've got two more shows left and I assure you, we'll have our share before it's over."

Bubba had this partner who was recording us on a digital camera. He was in there catching every moment live. That's when Bubba turned to the camera and said, "New South is official! And I'd like to announce that my man, Chino Dolla right here, is our new Vice President."

Everyone started making noise and lighting blunts. The cat with the camera took some time to catch what he felt was the beginning of something special. As for me, Bubba's announcement caught me by surprise, but I'd be lying to say that I wasn't excited. The thought of being attached to his movement could've turned out to be the best thing that happened to me.

The following afternoon, Bubba rented a van. Now two vehicles deep, we drove down to South Carolina to do a show at Columbia College, an all girls' school. Bubba was slotted to perform on a ticket that also included Ludacris. Luda was blazing the nation with his DTP movement, and it was sure to be a live event. Our crew was joined by another Atlanta native who was networking in the industry, who went by the name Polo Da Don. Polo had been part of a group called Jim Crow and signed to a major label. Jim Crow had a hit single called "Holla At A Playa" but they didn't receive the success they intended, so Polo continued his career as a producer. Him and Bubba became cool because of their ties to Timbaland. Polo was sort of under Timbaland's wing, getting mentored on the ins and outs of production and the industry.

The all girls' school was a blast. Spurred by the sight of all those ladies, I decided that this was one show that I wasn't going to stay in the dark for. As soon as Bubba's set came up, I found myself bouncing on stage with him, Scram and Duddy as hype men. With the pounding of Timbaland's track to fuel my adrenaline, I entertained the heated crowd with bottled water in hand. As I tossed water all over the girls, they enjoyed every minute of it. Scram was right, it was a rush. I had a blast and even hollered at a few girls after the show. But that's as far as it went because we had to get right back on the highway for the next show.

"We got one more show, the best one yet," Bubba assured me. "Down in Myrtle Beach."

And with only one stop to eat, we all jumped in our rides and headed out. Me, Duddy and Scram in my Denali, and Bubba, Bobby and Polo Da Don in the rental van. This would be our last show and this time I was looking forward to getting up with some of the fine ladies in South Carolina.

Freaky Teaky's. That's the name of the club we were to perform at. Once we got there I knew the night would be off the hook. Freaky Teaky's had this small kiddie pool on stage for the women to pour milk on themselves, and other shit. They also had swings throughout the club. The place was packed and a Carolina favorite by the name of Petey Pablo was on the schedule to perform with Bubba. Petey was on a high after releasing the hit song "Raise Up," a song highly favored by radio DJs in the area.

As far as the women . . . it was unbelievable! If you haven't guessed by the name of the club, admission age was 18 and up. The event brought women out in their tightest, most flyest clothes, which made me feel like a kid in a candy store. Me and Polo had been kickin' it real hard, stalking possible ladies to take back to the room Bobby had reserved for us. Polo was a true snow bunny slayer. Me on the other hand, didn't discriminate.

So while the show was going on, we began pulling young women aside. By the time it was over, we managed to gather up about seven sexy honeys.

"Aye Chino," Polo said, pulling me aside at the hotel, "man, we need to get our own suite."

I thought about it. Bubba had invited Petey to come back with us. That made seven men in two rooms.

"I don't know about you," he continued, "but I plan on hittin' somethin' tonight."

And so did I.

"All right, let's go," I said.

Me and Polo separated from the group just as they went up to Bubba's room. Quickly, we went to the lobby and got the receptionist to book us another suite. When we were finished, we headed up to the room.

Inside, me and Polo joined the rest who had already been drinking and smoking. Polo chose to remain sober while I went ahead and got me a few drinks. Bubba, Duddy, and Petey Pablo had been dipping in and out of the bathroom inconspicuously treating their noses with cocaine. But despite how they tried to remain low key, I could tell by their actions that they had been getting fucked up. As the alcohol kicked in, I started looking around at the white meat, red bones, and dark-skinned beauties sitting around, all of them giggling and flirting freely."

"YO, CHECK THIS SHIT OUT!"

Everybody froze at the loud announcement and looked up to see a drunk Petey Pablo standing by the bathroom. His jaws were clenching and unclenching as he spoke.

"It's as simple as this," he continued. "If y'all hoes ain't fuckin', y'all need to get the fuck out!"

Instantly my high disappeared. I couldn't believe this geekin' ass nigga. We had all these bad ass bitches up in here and he was on some run-the-pussy-off shit.

Girls started getting up, so I looked at Polo, who knew we had to do something quick. Two fine ass Italian looking girls got up and walked out and I saw Polo give me the look. He headed for the door and I was right on his heels.

"Hey baby girl," Polo called out to one, "where y'all going?"

"We gone," said the one on the left. "Ya boy up in there on some bullshit."

"Well look, me and my boy Polo here got a suite upstairs," I said. "We was about to leave anyway. Y'all can come up there and kick it with us if y'all want."

Both girls looked at each other. The end result . . . party of four.

Polo and I matched up. Inside the room we separated, with him going to one room and me another. He had this slim girl with long hair. I had a short, thick girl who sported her hair long and curly. I had intentions on releasing all my pent up frustration, and all my long hours on the grind, out on her. I was just rubbing my hands together in anticipation.

As time passed, I made my girl comfortable while we were relaxing in the room. We talked and I did everything I felt was right, but when I finally got straight to the point, she just froze up on me.

"I just came to kick it," she said. "I don't wanna have sex, because then you won't respect me Chino."

"You know what? I understand," I said after exhaling a long breath and showing no sign of being upset. I got up from the bed.

"Excuse me, I'll be right back," I said.

I left the room madder than a muthafucka. I'm not gonna lie, I wanted to see if Polo was having the same problem. I was determined to fuck something.

I came to the room Polo was in and tapped two times before opening the door. And what I saw stopped me short. Polo was standing with his pants caught up around his ankles. He had his girl positioned naked on all fours across the top of the bed. He had his hands on her cream colored hips, fucking the shit out of her. As soon as I entered, he looked back without missing a stroke. Baby was too into it to notice me as she arched her back, moaning out in pleasure.

I stepped in and closed the door. Polo continued his thang as I rounded the bed to face her on the other side. The girl looked up and as she realized I was there, she showed no panic. Her eyes were glazed over in extreme pleasure, staring back at me. Then with eagle eyes, she focused in on the crotch of my pants. Taking the cue, I unbuckled my belt, unzipped my pants, and pulled my dick out, only to have her reach out and grab it with a warm hand. With her body rocking with Polo's thrusts, she then closed her eyes and opened a hungry mouth, swallowing me whole. Her warm wet lips and tongue almost sent me over the top.

"Oh my gosh! Girl, what are you doing?"

The intrusion caused me and Polo to look up. It was her friend.

"I'm sorry, I'm sorry," she said as she jumped up, gathered her clothes, and ran over to stand next to her friend. "They made me do it."

What the fuck! My mind couldn't process the words I had heard. Here was this girl, who needed no coercion to do what she was doing. I stood there fixing my clothes, watching as she began crying like an innocent nun.

"Hold up," Polo said suddenly, "we didn't make her do nothing."

The friend held the girl who began balling her eyes out.

"All you rapper niggas do is try take advantage of pretty girls like us," she said. "If my friend said you made her, then I believe her. Y'all were raping her and I saw you."

I wanted to kill both them bitches.

"Hey, hey," I said calmly, "nobody got raped, O.K.? We was all just chillin' remember?"

Still holding her friend, who by now was almost completely dressed, the girl said, "I don't remember shit. But if y'all don't want us to call the police, then it's gonna cost ya."

And just like that, these hoes laid down their cards. We had been played. From that point forward, I learned that if a female didn't openly consent in front of others, then she couldn't go with me. I never thought that a shot of pussy could ever be the ruin of a well-needed time off.

Never again, I told myself. Never again.

Usher, T.I., Joc

The ride back from South Carolina was cool. Polo and Bubba rode with me and we got to discuss what we each had planned for the future. Bubba expressed that his wish for me to be V.P. over New South was genuine. He told me that he needed someone to push it that would do it some justice. To him it was more than a label. New South stood for the unity blacks and whites shared by way of the Civil Rights Movement. It would resemble the new south we lived in, a reality check for all those racist whites who didn't want integration. Bubba said he felt he owed it to me because of what happened when he got signed and Interscope axed us out of the picture. And despite how much I told him not to trip, he insisted. So I wasn't going to say no.

Polo explained to us that he was doing production. His hope was to get a production deal with Interscope. He had been studying the game from the sidelines, waiting for his time to blow. A time that he knew would come if only he stayed persistent.

During the course of our drive, I elaborated on what I had going on at STR8 Drop. I had some of our material and played them everything from instrumentals to the songs Slick had recorded. Soon, me and Polo began sharing concepts. I told him I was looking for tracks like the "Dope Man, Dope Man" beat by N.W.A. Old school, gangsta beats. Polo nodded and told me he had exactly what I was looking for.

When we reached the city of Atlanta, we dropped Polo off downtown at his apartment. We agreed that we should go out the following night to have a little fun.

The tour was cool but it still felt like work. With this, we could all go out and just simply relax.

It was around 9 p.m.

Bubba pulled out his forest green Escalade on 24-inch blades and me and Duddy was in my Denali. It seemed like a good night to step out and see what The ATL had in store. We called up Polo and told him we were coming so when we got there he was already dressed and ready to go. The electricity in the city was strong. And while most places viewed a Monday night as preparation for another day of work, Atlanta kept something poppin' for the 24/7 partygoers.

One spot in particular that everybody went to was Puffy's restaurant on Peachtree called Justin's. We cruised through the parking lot to see what the scene looked like. The place had begun gathering a nice crowd of customers. Making plans to return later, we then drove across the street to a B.P. gas station. People were pulling in by the car loads. Some were fueling up and some were hopping out of their rides to holler at girls. I pulled my Denali to a pump, jumped out, and went to the driver's side of Bubba's Escalade.

"Y'all want anything?" I asked him and Polo.

Bubba reached in his pocket and peeled off a fifty dollar bill. "Yeah, I'll go ahead and fill up. Polo do you. . . "

He stopped mid-sentence, his eyes fixed on a car that had pulled to a pump. Waiting a second, I found out it was none other than Usher, T.I. and a couple of their partners.

"Now here goes this dude," Bubba said suddenly. "I need to see what's up with this shit right now."

Now let me explain why he would say this…

Bubba had this bone with T.I. concerning a song he had done with Killa Mike and Bone Crusher called "New-New." In it, Tip constructed his concept around it being a "New South," with him as the front-runner. And with Bubba pushing New South as his label, promoting it at all of his shows, he felt like Tip was taking his idea and running with it. Thus, the beef . . .

I stood watching as Tip and Usher got out of their car. Bubba had expressed to me how he felt about all of this months earlier. And with the way Tip brushed me off some time prior, I ain't gonna lie . . .I was for the drama.

"So what," I asked. "You wanna holla at him?"

Bubba's eyes narrowed to slits. "Fuckin' right."

But Polo cut in.

"Look," he said to Bubba, "that issue you told me about, let me holla at him. We cool. I'm tellin' you, it might all just be a misunderstanding."

At first Bubba gave a look like he was against it, but ended up agreeing anyway. Me, I was down for whatever he was, but in the end, I'm glad Polo got involved.

As it turned out, it was all a misunderstanding. Polo got both of them together and smoothed everything out. When everything was said and done, we all ended up going out and kicking it in Buckhead. During this time I found out that Tip was going through label problems and this in turn adversely affected him working with other artists. So when he told me at Big Oomp's store that he was "trying to get his business straight," he meant it literally. If he had done a song with Slick, his label might not have cleared it and the money I would've given him would've gone down the drain.

This became another lesson I learned in the music biz, about understanding the contractual situations that other artists were in before getting them involved in projects, a lesson that would save me a lot of time and money down the road.

After that night, I returned to my regular life of the music business and hustling a little disgruntled. I dreaded coming back. Even though the tour brought about the messed up situation with that girl, I found it to be very motivational and educating. Meeting Polo also proved to be a valuable asset and we lined it up so I could check out some of his music. But I told him I needed to get an update on what Nard and Mont were doing with Slick. After that, we could get together.

Going from hotel room to hotel room, I can't explain how good it felt when I finally went home and slept in my king sized bed. Unlike the apartment, the new house provided a peace and quiet that was priceless. No nosey neighbors, no cluttered parking spaces. It was everything I dreamed of and more. When I came back, I filled Deon in on all that had happened. He just laughed at how those hoes got me and Polo. And when I told him how I thought it wasn't funny, he just laughed even more.

I caught up with Nard and Mont at the music store. I had come in early, only to catch them already on the grind.

"Well if it ain't Mr. Tour Bus himself," Nard called out as soon as he saw me. "How was it?"

"Ahh, it was cool," I said, downplaying it. "You know, Bubba did a few shows. One in North Carolina, two in South."

"Anything exciting happen?" Mont looked up from the stack of papers he was mulling over.

"Yeah," came Nard, "I know y'all fucked some hoes."

"Nah, no hoes, just work," I said. They weren't getting a free laugh off of me.

Both of them looked as if they were searching for signs of a lie. I felt like I was being interrogated. Then they shrugged it off.

"Well, it's good you're back," Nard said finally. "You can help us get ready for next week."

Totally confused I asked, "What up next week?"

Both of them looked at me like I lost my mind.

"SlutFest," Mont said as if it were a no brainer.

I just shook my head. Damn, I thought. I had only been gone less than a week and already I forgot about the event. Spring had come so fast that it caught me off guard. Seeing my absentmindedness, both of them updated me on what they already had in place.

Flyers had been passed out at West Georgia by this cat, Botche and his crew, so the students were already informed. Although they knew it was going down every Spring, we always liked to promote to let them know there was indeed a Spring Break party coming. This would be our third SlutFest, but our first as STR8 Drop Records. Mont predicted it would be as big as our last, so he got it lined up so we could throw it at the fairgrounds in Carrollton, right by the college.

"I've been getting calls from everybody," Mont said. "Niggas wanna perform. No matter what happens, Slick has to do his thing."

"True dat," I said seriously. "This will give him some experience on stage as well as allow us to see the crowds' reaction to the music."

"Yeah, the more we promote him, the more exposure for the label, Nard agreed. "SlutFest will be the perfect stage for that. What do y'all think, should we get a thousand STR8 Drop shirts printed up?"

I just slapped my forehead. Here we go again . . .

Mont lined up one act outside of our circle to perform at the event. He got the Pimp Squad Click (PSC), who had been bubbling real hard under the momentum of the squad's frontrunner, T.I. They did their thing for free, knowing of the exposure they'd get. Low Down and Duddy did a few cuts and then we presented to the attendees, Backwoods Slick. As I suspected, "I Wish A Nigga Would" got the best response from the crowd and I was glad we scheduled that one for his last performance.

As customary, we had our traditional "Shake-Ya-Ass" contest and other prize-winning events that got the girls involved. About 2,000 people showed up, making it our biggest SlutFest ever. It was off the chain.

For some reason, while we were doing the show, I couldn't help but think about the kid I had met at Toe Jam music store, Joc. Something about him made me curious, like I felt some sort of connection to him, like I felt there was something there I should explore. To me, his music wasn't outstanding. He could use better production. Maybe some harder Gutta sounding tracks, but his flow was cool. I told myself after everything was finished, I was going to look him up.

The show went well. Overall, Slick did pretty good. I still felt we needed to find him a better song for a single, one that depended on his talents and not those of others. Low Down and Duddy did their thing, as usual, but they had more experience so I expected that. PSC rocked the house with Kountry Kaine, A.K., and Mack Boney, keeping the crowd hyped. That, along with all the fine ass girls made for another landmark event. West Georgia would lie in wait for the next one. I knew this for sure.

About two days later, I tried to see if I could catch up with this cat Joc, so I found the number he had given me and called him up.

"Hello," came a voice over the phone.

"Yeah," I'm lookin' for Joc," I said.

"This him, who's this?" he responded.

"Chin. . . Chauncey," I said. "We met at Toe Jams a couple weeks ago."

"Yeah," he said, "I remember, what's going on?"

I really didn't know what I had in mind so I said, "Aww man, I just finished up a few things and I had some free time. I was hoping to catch back up with you, when you get a chance. Get a little more info about what you got goin' on."

"All right," he said, "well I ain't doin' nothing now. If you want, you can come out to my spot."

I told him I could. Come to find out, he stayed very close to me, in Riverdale as well. He lived off a street called Garden Walk, and when he told me this, I let him know it wouldn't take me long to get there. We ended our conversation with me telling him I'd be there in less than 15 minutes.

Joc stayed in a two-bedroom apartment with his wife and their 2-month-old baby girl. When I got there, he introduced me, telling his wife I was into the music thing. She was very nice and me and Joc sat in their living room discussing some of the things he had going on.

He told me how he was working by passing out flyers and other minor things. He was also writing lyrics for this dude named Roc, who was trying to put out his girlfriend Tocha. She had been a part of a well-known group back in the day called Xscape. They had songs like "Just Kickin' It" and "Who Do I Run To?" Songs that gave them some real national spotlight. For Joc, writing material for Tasha was his greatest accomplishment. Besides that, all he had was the old material he let me hear, songs that he recorded with a homeboy of his named Joe, the producer of the tracks.

As he talked, I found myself assessing his character. Things like him being an at home father stood out to me. He seemed passionate about being in the music industry, and he appeared not to mind working hard to get there. He was mild mannered and very attentive whenever I spoke about what we had going on over at STR8 Drop. He asked a lot of questions when I told him about my experience with Bubba on tour. He was like a sponge looking to soak up all that I had to offer.

I had one of the mix tapes of Bubba and The MudCats in my truck, so I asked him if he wanted to hear it.

"Yeah, just let me tell my wife imm'ah step out for a sec, All right?" he said.

I understood that. "All right, I'll be outside."

When he came out, we sat in the parking lot breaking down each song. I let him check out Duddy and Attitudes' flow and went into distinct points on the production. Attitude had a song he loved and I felt it was a hit as well. This let me know we had common taste. We must've sat there for hours, and by the time we were finished, the sun had begun to set.

"Man, it's getting late," he announced. "I need to get back in before my wife kills me. I know she has something she needs me to do."

I just laughed. Then shaking his hand I said, "Man, I respect that. Listen Joc, im'mah be in contact with you some more. I stay right down the road, and to be honest, I feel like all you need is someone to help you put what you're trying to do together. And I'm willing to help you, whenever you got the time."

He just nodded. "Chauncey, I'm free all the time. All you gotta do is call." Hearing him call me Chauncey reminded me to ask him to call me Chino like everybody else that knows me.

And with that, me and Joc forged a bond, the beginning of better things to come.

Game

For the next two to three weeks, I spent a lot of time getting more acquainted with Joc. Between my time spent with Nard and Mont, I would stop by his apartment and pick him up. Something inside of me identified with him. Maybe it was his willingness to listen to my advice in regards to his career. Maybe it was my need to be heard. Whatever it was, I had found someone really cool to kick it with, someone who shared a desire to make something happen with himself.

Now, I had also been going over to Nitti's studio at the auto shop on Candler Rd. on a regular basis. During all those times we were buying beats, I would find myself chopping it up with him about production. Like I said, we had a history back to when we were kids. I wanted to know more about the production side of the business because I still had a love for the craft of making beats. So taking advantage of his knowledge, I'd ask questions from time to time. We had just recorded a song called "Cooking Contest" with Slick and a crew from Scottsdale called A DAMN SHAME. The song was about cooking up dope. A DAMN SHAME were some of the hardest street cats out. They were Atlanta's rawest Trap Musik rappers and we felt they would add a raw edge to Slick's music. After recording this song, me and Nitti found ourselves becoming good friends outside of the music world.

I took Joc by Nitti's studio, wanting him to meet Nitti and show him the kind of work cats were doing in the city. By this time, I had grown to respect Nitti and his style of music. I also felt like he had the sound that Joc needed to compliment his flow. We all grouped up in that small space with the hole and Plexiglas in the wall, listening to Nitti run through a catalog of tracks.

"So what do y'all think?" he asked when it was all over.

"For real, your shit is hard," Joc responded.

I hadn't heard a track I didn't like. "I can see why JD wants you Nitti. Honestly, you got a sound that's not like everybody else's. It's hard, it's street. . . "

"Yeah," Joc interrupted, "that boy got that hard-hard."

I really had no ulterior motives by hanging with Joc. I wasn't trying to convince him to be down with STR8 Drop and I wasn't trying to manage him. I just enjoyed chillin' and bouncing ideas off of him. Taking him by Nitti's was something I hoped would give him a broader outlook on who was available to network with. I was in no better position than him, as we both were still looking for success. It had gotten to the point where my intentions were to share with him some of the contacts I had.

That's what I'm all about. Each one, teach one.

One day Joc called me up and told me he had someone he wanted me to meet.

"She's like my sister, Chino," he explained. "She be rappin' too. I was tellin' her about you and that I wanted her to meet you."

I had been listening over the music we had of Slick and was getting more interested in other artists with each song I played.

"What you doin' in about an hour?" I asked.

"Nothin', I'll be at the crib," he answered.

"All right, I'll slide through."

That night we went to Bankhead, to a spot called the Mexican Bar, which is now called Club Crucial. A spot owned by Derrick and T.I. This is where he set it up for us to meet this girl whose name was Brandy.

Brandy was waiting for us when we arrived. She was very polite and as we began to talk, I could see she had that same determination as

Joc. Like he said, they were very close, like homie, lover, friends. I found out that she was messing with this lady from Memphis named Carolyn Miller, who had a label called In Control. Joc had also been involved with this woman, along with other artists and producers. She had them all under the banner of the "In Control Click." Brandy felt confident in Ms. Miller's ability to take her career to the next level.

"So what do you call yourself?" I asked.

She smiled. "Ms. Behavin'."

I liked it. Even though Brandy looked feminine enough, being pretty and petite, she also gave off a tough vibe—like she'd cut a bitch if she had to.

The atmosphere inside the pool hall was relaxing as we continued our discussion. I told them about Slick and the SlutFest gig we threw out in West Georgia. Joc told her about Nitti and the tracks we listened to. By the end of the night I knew just about all of their dreams and aspirations. It became apparent that they believed Carolyn Miller would be the one to take them to the top. When I dropped them off, I found myself wondering more about this woman. The way Joc and Brandy looked whenever they said her name, made me feel like I needed to meet her for myself.

The opportunity to do so came the following night. I was in traffic, just coming from my aunt's, when I received a call on my cell phone. It was Joc.

"Yo Chino. Me and sis is up at Spondivits Seafood Restaurant on Virginia Avenue, and we got Ms. Miller with us," he said. "She just got back from Memphis and we were tellin' her about you. You should slide through."

The restaurant they were at was close. "Yeah, I'll be there in a sec'."

Although I had a few other things on my agenda, I wanted to meet this woman. Who knew, maybe she would turn out to be a good contact in the future. And being that the business was about "who you knew," it was always best to meet as many people as I could. Because where I was at, it was a long way to the top.

I arrived at the restaurant maybe 20 minutes after I talked to Joc. Entering the restaurant, I passed my main man playing his guitar number as usual. I found Joc and Brandy sitting at a table with a dark-skinned woman who looked to be in her early forties.

"What up Chino," Joc said, getting up.

I gave him some dap and a half-ah-hug. "Ah, you know, makin' moves." I looked to Brandy and the woman. "Ladies."

"Hey Chino," came Brandy. "This is Ms. Carolyn Miller. Ms. Miller, this is Chino. The one me and Joc were tellin' you about."

At this point, the woman stood up. Immediately I noticed that she was about the size of two of me. She was taller, at 5 feet 10 inches in height and weighing about 270 lbs. But I could tell by how she moved, she felt every bit of herself, bouncing and moving with the grace of a bonafide diva.

Giving her best smile she said, "Hello Chino, nice to meet you."

I shook her hand. "Likewise Ms. Miller. I've heard a lot about you."

She gave a small laugh. "All good things I hope."

"Yeah, interesting as well."

"Good, I'm glad," she said. "Oh yes, please call me Carolyn."

"Of course," I said with a nod.

We all sat down at the table and got comfortable. I saw that they had already eaten which was good because I had just got through punishing a #3 from McDonald's.

"I was just giving Carolyn some background on you," Joc explained to me.

"Yeah," she said admirably, "you've seemed to be busy in the city."

"A little," I told her. "I got a few things going on."

"Like what?" she asked.

I ran through my usual spill about STR8 Drop, Slick, the contacts I had with all the producers we bought music from and my relationship with Bubba. She seemed impressed when I told her about my involvement with Bubba's first album and how he wanted me to be the Vice President of New South.

"But enough about me," I said to her. "Joc and Brandy told me you're doing big things, not only in Memphis, but in Atlanta as well."

She looked modest. "Well, I've got a few things goin'. First, I'm trying to get Brandy and Joc into more shows. We've done several but the more we do the more exposure."

I agreed.

"Next up is for Ms. Behavin' here to get in that studio," she said. "I plan on starting production on her next single as soon as next week. I'm lookin' for the right producer and I can't figure out if I want to go with one of my in-house producers or Jazze Pha."

I was impressed. "Oh, you know Jazze Pha?"

She smiled. "Yeah, we go way back."

"She's the one who brought Jazze Pha to Atlanta," Brandy announced.

It seemed to me that this Carolyn Miller had her shit together. She was lining up shows, pushing her artists, and networking with big named producers. All the things needed to succeed in the music biz.

I found out during this meeting that Carolyn was well-connected in the city as well, knowing a few choice people who could aid her in getting her artists showcased. During this hour or so get together, we shared with each other insight and intentions relating to our respective labels. By the time it was over, we agreed that keeping in contact could prove to be useful in the future. I told Joc I'd be calling him soon and told Brandy I'd see her as well. I was always up to networking with new labels, artists and producers. There was a hunger there that many lost after they came up. And by my assessment, Carolyn Miller had that hunger, wanting to see her In Control Click being just that—In Control.

After I left the restaurant, I went downtown to check on a few things not concerning the music business. It was around 11 p.m. as I was about to get on the highway and go back home when something made me think of Polo Da Don. I hadn't seen him since the night me, him, Bubba, Duddy, Ken, T.I, and Usher all went out and kicked it after clearing up that misunderstanding. I figured I should give him a call to see what was up. So I did.

"Yo Chino," he said, surprised over the line, "I was wondering when you was gonna get at me."

"Yeah man I know," I responded as I maneuvered through traffic. "Shit's been busy this way. I was downtown and figured I'd call to see what you were up to."

"You know me," he said. "I'm in the studio. If you want, you can stop by."

Polo told me he was at a studio called Hit Co. It was a company owned by L.A. Reid, a publishing company with offices and studios inside its building. Many major artists were associated with the company and I saw that Polo was doing his best to steer himself into a major position. It was also located downtown so it took me no time to make it there. When I did, I found Polo in the studio, putting his finishing touches on a track. I waited patiently until he finished.

"Man," he said, "it's been a long day."

"You ain't lyin'," I responded.

Getting up from behind the mixing board, Polo told an engineer that he was done. Then turning to me he gave a nod. "What's up Chino, what you got goin' tonight?"

I shook my head. "Nothing really."

"Come on then," he said. "I got some bad little chicks on deck. Wanna roll?"

"'You already know me, let's go!" I said.

And just like that, I found myself on a whole new mission, fuckin' with Da Don.

We left my Denali in the parking lot of Hit Co. and took his Land Rover instead. Polo told me he had two mixed girls who were supposed to meet him at this club in Buckhead called The Living Room. When we got there, we found the girls eagerly waiting for him to arrive. And when they found out he brought a friend, they didn't even trip. They just rolled with the punches—just the type I like.

We must've spent all of 20 minutes in The Living Room before we jetted out of there. Polo got at me about getting a room and I told him I was down. We jumped in his truck, with him driving and me in the back sitting between both girls.

"So your name is Chino?" the one to my left asked.

"Yeah baby, Chino Dolla," I said.

"Umph, big dolla," the one to my right said, while rubbing my chest, her voice soft and seductive. "When we get to the room will you show me why they call you dolla?"

"Oh fa'sho," I told her. But of course, I wasn't talking about giving her money, but instead how I'd have her giving me money.

Polo came to a stop light on Piedmont Road and the girl to my left leaned up front toward him. "Hey baby, do you think you could stop at a store and get us somethin' to drink?" she asked.

"Yeah, we can do that," he responded.

When the light turned green, Polo crossed the intersection as the girl spotted a store and said, "Hey, there's a store right there, stop at that one."

Polo just looked in his rearview mirror without saying a word. Meanwhile the girl at my right was busy seducing me.

"So, you a rapper or something?" she asked while playing with my diamond encrusted C.S. pendant.

"Nah baby, I don't rap. I own the label," I said. With my hand sliding up her smooth thighs I could feel the heat between her ever parting legs. I couldn't wait until we got to the room.

Polo made it about three blocks down and the girl to my left saw another store. "Hey baby, there's another store right there," she said leaning up front again and pointing. "You see it don't you?"

But Polo kept driving past it.

The girl asking said, "Why didn't you stop? Didn't you see the store? What's wrong wit . . ."

Out of nowhere, Polo hit the brakes. Scccrrreeech!

Caught unprepared, everybody was thrown forward.

Baby girl who was asking the questions flipped head first, landing in between the front seat. The girl on my right fell forward and sideways, getting stuck between the passenger door and seat. I, on the other hand, planted my feet and only suffered a small jerk forward. In the end, the girls were tossed around like small rag dolls as we sat in the middle of the street.

"What the fuck!" one of them yelled.

But Polo's voice came even louder. "You dumb ass hoes! Get the fuck outta my truck! Right-the-fuck-now!"

And with that, stunned and confused, the girls gathered their things and got out, only to be left standing in the middle of Piedmont Rd. in a complete daze. This would be the second time I fucked with Polo on a mission to get some pussy and it ended up in a mess. I was really beginning to see that Polo was a wild dude.

The following day, Carolyn Miller gave me a call.

"Chino, how would you like to come on board with me and my label?" she asked.

Her invitation caught me off guard. "Come on like, as a partner?"

"Yeah," she said.

I didn't know what to say.

"Chino I've got things going on that can benefit us both," she said. "All I need is someone who's as dedicated as you to help me put it all together. Of course I could do it by myself, but I feel you're just the right person."

I was flattered. "Listen," I began, "how about I give it some thought? I gotta see how things are goin' on my end. When I do that, I'll let you know."

She seemed pleased with my response. "All right then, but don't take too long deciding because this plane is about to take off and I assure you, you don't wanna miss it."

Over the next few days, Carolyn's offer stayed on my mind. The reason being was that the things she had going were more up my alley. Nard and Mont seemed to be so blinded in their attempts that they couldn't see that we weren't making any progress. Even the Bubba situation wasn't going anywhere. I had called him to get an update and he was basically under ridicule from Interscope because his single wasn't doing so good, which meant there might not be any label money for New South.

He had begun messing with Mr. DJ over at Camp David, recording songs. This came by way of his affiliation with Rico Wade and the Second Generation of Dungeon Family. Throughout 2001, you could easily find us over there at the Dungeon, as Low Down, Duddy and Bubba would lace some of their music with that Organized Noize sound. I guess his alliance with Timbaland's Beat Club and Interscope had run its course. So really, he was back to square one.

That's when I got an idea.

I didn't want to abandon my cousin and Mont because I felt like we could still get somewhere. I was just waiting for them to listen and see my vision. Until then, I figured that I'd help out Low Down and Duddy by taking them over to Carolyn, that way they could be involved with something moving. I would have my hand in it through them, while still running my label at STR8 Drop.

I called Carolyn and told her my plans to join her and to bring over an experienced group looking to attach themselves to a team. She loved it, and from there we set things into motion.

From the start, Carolyn told me that she had already begun moving forward with Brandy's project and she wanted to complete that before we got into Low Down and Duddy's. I agreed since Duddy was already experienced in production; he got on board to help Brandy by making her some beats and Joc supported by helping her with song concepts. Brandy already had a song that Carolyn's in-house producer had made called "Bottle Action," which she felt was a good lead single. In it, Brandy rapped, "I don't fight, I don't argue . . . I just hit that bitch wit a bottle." It was raw and edgy—two elements that fit her personality.

About three weeks into recording Brandy's CD, Carolyn came to me with a business contract. "Here you go Chino, I had this drawn up yesterday."

I took it and read it carefully. She had it constructed where she would receive 70 percent of all proceeds, and I would receive 30 percent. At the same time, I was to put in all the finances for the projects to be done.

"Carolyn," I began, "I can't agree to these numbers."

Putting one hand on her hip she said, "Did you think this was going to be done by a hope and a prayer? Look, we can work the numbers later. Right now I need $5,000 so I can catch up with my car note and mortgage."

I couldn't believe what I just heard.

"What does your mortgage and car note gotta do with the business?" I asked.

I heard none of her response that followed. I was too busy thinking how I had gotten into a bad situation..

Carolyn was on some bullshit.

Regroup

I couldn't believe that Carolyn Miller would try me like she did. I called Joc and told him what she pulled and he couldn't believe it either. He really believed that our joining forces would be a good thing, and so did I. But in the end, I let him know that I was cool on the idea. It seemed to me that Ms. Miller was simply trying to capitalize off of me instead of rightfully sharing the duties it took to make our venture successful.

I guess she thought she her one (A Sucker).

It was 2003 and to be honest, I felt that my success was being delayed. Why? Well, I felt I was making some bad decisions on who I dealt with. Not to say that everybody was like Carolyn Miller. It was just that my vision wasn't coming to fruition and I was really beginning to wonder if I would've been better off on my own.

$$$

One night, on my way home from Athens, after finding out that Big E had caught a Federal indictment for distribution of cocaine, I bumped into Joc at a liquor store on Riverdale Rd.

"Damn Chino," he said. "Where've you been?"

"I've been busy as shit," I explained. "What's been up?"

Our attention was drawn out to the parking lot where some white cat was blowing his car horn. "Yo Joc, come on!"

"Look, I got my number changed," Joc looked at me and said. "You got a pen?"

"Naw, put it in my cell phone," I said.

He dialed it in and told me to hit him up the next day because he had something to tell me. I told him that I would and we parted ways with him shooting out the door.

I went the whole night wondering what he had to tell me. I was hoping it was some good news. I really wanted to see the best happen for him. When the next day came, I gave him a ring around noon to see what was up.

"Man, it's like you fell off the map," he told me.

I laughed. "Nah man, I said I was gonna stop by your apartment when I got some free time."

"Yeah, because I was beginning to think you might've been holding what Carolyn did against me and B," he said.

"I would never do that," I said quickly. "No matter how I felt about that shit she tried to pull, I would've never put y'all in the middle of that. It had nothing to do with y'all."

I could tell he was glad to hear that.

"Good, I was glad to see you last night dawg, because I needed to run somethin' by you," he said. "It's about Carolyn."

I was curious. "Well, don't leave me in suspense. What's up?"

Joc told me how she had put together a meeting with this A&R person and while they were in his building they bumped into Nitti. They talked for a few seconds while Carolyn went into some offices. At this time, Joc slid Nitti a copy of Brandy's song, "Bottle Action." They exchanged numbers, and a few days later, Nitti called Joc to tell him he liked the song. He also wanted to know if they were still fuckin' with me. Joc told him that I had fallen back because of the issue with Carolyn.

"Chino, he called me and told me to bring Brandy by his studio," he said. "I did and he let us hear something outta this world."

He had my attention.

"Nitti took Brandy's song and put a new beat to it," he said in surprise. "I couldn't believe it. It's like he took her shit to a whole 'nother level. I'm tellin' you, it's a hit!"

"Did Brandy like it?" I asked.

"Like it? She loved it!" he said.

Joc told me that Nitti explained how he might be able to get her a deal with So So Def, but she would have to sign on to his production company, PlayMaker. I, on the other hand, saw how Nitti recognized that I was out of the way and was putting his move down. And even though I was wondering why Nitti hadn't said anything to me, I wanted to know something else.

"So what did Carolyn say?" I asked.

Joc started laughing. "That's what I wanted to tell you. We told her about Nitti and how we knew him because of you. When she heard this she said we didn't need him or his deal, even though we told her she'd still be involved."

I couldn't believe that she was being that emotional. "Man, if he can get y'all a deal then that's cool."

"Yeah, but she says we're gonna get our own deal," he said. "To keep it real, she's acting like she's in her feelings."

"Well, this business ain't got no room for feelings." I told him. "It's all about getting the job done."

He agreed. By the end of our conversation, I had an even clearer picture of this Carolyn Miller woman. And I was much happier that I saw her true colors before I got too deep in the business with her. The way she was handling things, neither Brandy nor Joc would see any success. Like they say, "God don't like ugly."

As time passed, it seemed like I had begun getting caught up in the mundane, unsatisfying routine of dealing with Nard and Mont. It just wasn't as exciting as I wanted it to be. Of course, it was a business, dealing with building a label, but I felt more suffocated in my role than I ever did. I could see that they began to notice it too but because they were so focused on their own individual objectives, they couldn't really see that I had a problem with how things were being handled.

When my birthday came in July of that year, I made plans to host an event that would help to relieve my stress. I was turning 25 and I wanted to celebrate it with a bang.

One night, I went out to Magic City to relax with a few of my homeboys. With my birthday nearing, I set out to have a good time. As we began enjoying ourselves, I saw an entourage come in and I immediately noticed who it was. Heading the pack were three underground kingpins--Big Meech, J-Bo, and Ill Will, aka Illz--leading their crew and calling themselves BMF (Black Mafia Family).

Since Meech's birthday was at the end of June and Illz's a few days after mine in July, both partners celebrated the whole month long. Will and I were acquainted, but Meech, I didn't know personally. I knew he had seen me around, back in the day, at a strip club my God-uncle Sam Carroll had managed called The Gentleman's Club. The three of them and their crew all came to where we were at the stage, and by the end of the night, we all began kicking it together.

Meech called out to a waitress and before I knew it, she was coming back with some guys who were carrying big cardboard boxes. Meech and Will began tearing into the boxes and withdrawing what were none other than shrink-wrapped bricks of $1 bills. It was at least $100,000 worth! Then both of them began passing out the bricks to their crew and to us, to throw at the girls on stage. Now we had already spent about $15,000 of our own money, splurging in the club. This was definitely going to be a good night for the girls and the establishment. It got so crazy this night that it was ridiculous. I ended up telling Will about my plans to throw a fire ass birthday party for myself at this lake out past Gwinnett County called Lake Lanier. I invited him and his whole crew to come check me out, which he told me he would. By the time I left the club that night, I was no doubt feeling a whole lot better.

Lake Lanier is a camping area located outside of Gwinnett County about 45 minutes from Atlanta. The park provided all types of attractions like a huge lake for boating, fishing and water skiing, a water park with slides for adults and children, horseback trails and the wonderful scenery of Georgia's vast greenwoods held cabins you could rent to enjoy the wildlife. I went ahead and lined it up to kick it there for my birthday. And everyone I fucked with was invited. I had about 200 hundred invitations made for all of my family members and closest friends. Deon, who was just as excited as me, handled all the invitations for the event, which was to take place that following weekend. He treated it like a concert. My cousin Nikkia handled renting the hotel rooms, which were located on a man-made beach, for the guests. She also rented cabins for me and my crew. When everything was lined up, and that Saturday finally arrived, we were all set to go.

It was gonna be the shit!

Mont brought his boat out and me and Q brought the jet skis. Nard's dad, Uncle Kenny, brought out his whole motorcycle club. My man C-Bone showed up. Joc and his wife were there. I had food and drinks galore. Joc turned me onto a guy who owned a meat truck and I had a guy who drove a beer truck so I dropped a couple of stacks and got a shit load of both. For the liquor, we hit the army base and stocked up.

When everything was set up, my cousin Buster cranked up the grill around noon, getting things right.

People were showing up by the car load!

Some of our crew tried to bring their personal horses, but in order to get into the park they had to pass by the guard shack. The guard working the booth wouldn't lift the guardrail for them because he said the park already provided horses at the trail. So they turned back. Nevertheless, by the time 4 o'clock rolled around there was at least—I swear—every bit of 1,000 people who had showed up. That was 10 times the number of people we expected!

People were partying everywhere. We had music bumpin', girls were walking around in two-piece bikini thongs, and the cabins equipped with Jacuzzi's added an extra asset to the atmosphere. My cousin Demetrius sat in the hot tub surrounded by about six lovely ladies so long that by the time he got out, he was as wrinkled as a California raisin. I just looked around at all the people, all my closest homeboys and family and I felt good.

I didn't have a care in the world. But then came the drama . . .

"Yo Chino . . ."

At the mentioning of my name, I turned around and saw about twenty Hall County Police Officers making their way through the cabin.

Immediately I froze up. I had set out bowls of weed on the tables and counter tops, for anyone wanting to twist up. (To keep it real, it wasn't that mid-grade or that chronic. Hell, I was already feedin' they asses). One officer, who led the pack, walked right up to me.

"Who's 'n charge here?" he asked.

I stepped up. "I am sir."

He looked around, chewing on a big wad of tobacco. Then in his deep southern drawl said, "Wut 'ur ya, sum type 'uh rappa?"

"Nah, it's my birthday and . . ." I stopped short when he spotted a bowl of weed sitting on a table next to him. My worst fear came to life when he reached over and grabbed a handful, putting it to his nose.

"Dammit boy! I got bettur shit grow'n in my frunt yar 'den dis," he said.

His deputies started laughing.

"Ya got da park ova' capacity," he announced. "People still try'na get in and we's turnin' em round at da gate, fuckin' wit'chew."

Just when I was about to speak, he held up a hand.

"Now, it's ya burf'day, I unda'stand, but'cha gotta cut down ya camping. A'iight?"

I nodded. "I got'cha."

"A'ight then." Turning to his officers he said, "Let's go boys." And he walked off, still holding the handful of weed he gathered out of my bowl.

By this time, everyone was aware of the police's presence. I had to get with my crew so they could get the word out to everyone except our family and closest friends that we appreciated them for showing up but we have to shut it down. At the time, I had been ducking a few females because I'd invited the girl from Tennessee and her friends to kick it with me. So needing a little time to kick it to a few chicks, I hit a few of my boys off with a couple of dollars to take Tennessee and them to Club 112, to show them a good time and bring them back later. As for the rest of the guests, they understood and slowly but surely began leaving.

When Sunday morning came, the ones who remained were packing up to leave. By the time 11 a.m. rolled around, the only ones left were Nikkia, me, my crew and the girl of our choice. Q came and asked me if I wanted to go to the water park. Joc and his wife had already expressed an interest in going. My girl from Tennessee seemed to like the idea, so I said what the hell.

The water park was live that afternoon. Kids and adults were everywhere having fun. The girls were out getting acquainted which left me, Q and Joc to ourselves, giving us some "man time."

"Man, it was off the chain last night," Q said.

"Off the chain ain't the word," Joc agreed. "Did you see all those people?"

"Yeah, it was cool," I said. "I just hate the police made everybody leave."

"Yeah," said Q. "But we still did our thing. Happy Birthday cuz."

"Yeah Chino, happy birthday."

As we sat there talking about the party, Q brought my attention to something. He informed me that the speedboats and crowd across the lake were Big Meech and his crew.

I just nodded my head, seeing that Will and Meech took me up on my invitation.

As my mind drifted off dreaming about all the things I wanted to come true in my life, I was brought back to reality by Joc's voice. "Chino, we can still do this music shit. You know that right?"

He caught me by surprise.

"What makes you think I'm thinking about stopping?" I asked.

He shrugged. "I just don't see the spark in you like I saw when we met. It's like that Carolyn Miller shit knocked the wind out of you."

Damn, I thought. Was it that obvious?

Q spoke up. "You know what cousin? I gotta say though, you have been lookin' stressed lately, but not yesterday. To me you looked like you were havin' a good time and I'm glad man. For real."

As both of them made their observations known, something

hit me. Something I hadn't realized since I had been doing STR8 Drop, since I had been trying my hand at music, since my release from boot camp—I had been stressed. A stress that weighed on me every day except for two times I could remember. One was during the tour with Bubba; the other was right then.

I inhaled a deep breath of fresh air through my nose and exhaled through my mouth. It felt good. The sun hung high in the sky, with no clouds to block it. The laughter of kids filled my ears as water splashed and cries of excitement rang loud and clear. I felt no stress and right then I realized that I only experienced this feeling whenever I was far away from The ATL.

No, correction, it wasn't the city—it was the responsibilities I had to the people in it, the things I had obligated myself to.

The rest of the afternoon went and we had a ball. Later that night, everybody left, leaving me and Joc by ourselves. We ended up staying until that next day, still having fun riding the jet skis and drinking as much as we could of the beer that was left over. Whenever we were alone, he would make it a point to encourage me to not give up on the music. But little did he know, I would never walk away from my dream, although I was planning a different route to get there. For that moment, my main goal was to invest in something. Maybe I could open up a movie theater, then buy my own house, relax for a minute and leave all that scandalous drama of the rap game to those willing to stomach it.

Carolyn Miller . . . STR8 Drop . . . Bubba and Underground Sound . . .

Misguided, unwarranted expenses . . . wasted money . . . artists going to jail . . . all work, no pay . . .

All of these things and more had me feeling like all of my dreams, my visions and my goals would take a lot more work than expected.

Stand Up

After my birthday bash, I found it hard getting back into the rhythm of things. Even with all of its bright lights, Atlanta just couldn't seem to cheer me up. I knew it was more about the things transpiring in my life and the direction I was going in. Even years after my oath to make something of myself, I was still stuck in the same cycle, hustling the streets day in and day out. Regardless of the business ventures and investments I explored, I still ended up selling something illegal to stay afloat.

"I raised you to be a man...the rest is up to you."

These words began echoing in my mind more and more as I realized how much I had steered myself away from what was expected of me. I needed to get myself back on a meaningful path by making a firm decision. Was I gonna be a hustler all my life, selling drugs? Or was I gonna take my business skills and turn legit? I settled on going legit and told myself right then that whatever it was I was trying to get, I had to get it now. Because when I was done, that was it. I would never look back.

I gave myself a one year time limit to do my thing. And to be honest, I felt a little resolved. It's like my take-charge attitude toward my own life gave me the confidence I needed to make it through the bullshit that was stressing me out. I had finally settled on the fact that if something was going to work, if my dreams were to come true, it was going to be because I willed them to. I had to make concrete decisions.

My first plan of action was to catch up with some guys I knew who were bringing the mid-grade from Arizona. I arranged it where I could get 100 to 200 pounds from them every trip. From doing prior business with them, they knew I had family that was buying 20 to 50 kilos of coke. My guys would try to get me back in the coke business by offering me a price where I could make a large profit brokering deals for my family. But I had made a promise to myself that I would stay away from the coke.

That white girl was nothing but the devil.

See, every time I fucked with coke, something bad happened. First, my grandmother died. Then I went to boot camp. So I figured it was best for me to decline their offer. I told them I had somebody else who could handle the job for them: my cousin Nard. I felt it was no need in letting all that money go by, without somebody I fuck with making it.

Getting everything out my system, I took to the streets hard. I hit old spots, new spots, made offers others couldn't match, sold small bags to large packs, everything I could to get my cake up. I cut out middlemen and dealt with people myself. I was like a mad man, setting a goal to stack up a million dollars. Although this amount was setting the bar high, I had seen cats in the hood that had done it 10 times over. I needed to make sure I had enough to live comfortably and to do what I needed to business wise.

Nard and Mont saw my tenacity. As long as I provided my share to STR8 Drop, they were cool.

They had us falling victim to one of the many tricks in the music business. The music exec's trick to eradicate the competition. It's one of their number one Jedi mind tricks. The music industry is just like the streets and is run by sharks and magicians with smoky mirrors. I can recall one time while in the studio with Bubba, I overheard one of Interscope's execs saying, "every rapper in the game is in competition with every other, so what better way to beat the competition than to get rid of the competition." In my mind at the time, I was like *what the fuck is this nigga crazy talking about killing muthafuckas in here?* Is this what happened to Big and Pac? Then he went on to explain himself. Since we were in the studio with a few chicks and bottles of liquor, it kinda looked like a video shoot. He said the reason this was a popular thing in rap music was because labels sent a subliminal message out through videos saying this is what you have to do and should look like if you want to be a rapper. When you look at a rap video you see the artist surrounded by fine women dressed in brand name clothes, draped in expensive jewelry, drinking expensive champagne, and driving luxury cars. This does two things: 1. Get rid of other rappers already in the game by sending them into bankruptcy if they can't sell enough to recoup all the money the label spent to make them look like a star. 2. Keep up and coming rappers spending all their money on looking the part instead of investing in producing a decent project and promoting their music. And number two was what I didn't want to knock us off. True, we had cash but a fool and his money will soon part, which was not a part of my plan.

While all of this was going on, I received a call one day from Dee. We had only been in contact with each other whenever I needed to cop a few pounds from his Jamaican chick. Our different lifestyles had led us in opposite directions, so a call from him was odd. The days of us just hanging out and kicking it was rare. So when the call came through, it kind of caught me by surprise. Nevertheless, I was glad to hear from him.

"I just called to see what was up wit'cha," he told me. "And also to tell you about ya boy Gucci."

At the mentioning of his homeboy, I grew alert. "Gucci? What's up with him?"

"Man, you ain't gonna believe it."

Dee explained to me how Gucci had done a song called "Black Tee" with a local group that was getting a lot of radio play. JD had a group called Dem Franchise Boys who had a song called "White Tee," and I guess Gucci and this local crew came with their own twist. The thing was, the song didn't belong to Gucci, as he was only a featured artist. It belonged to this local crew who had him to do a verse. Well, apparently Gucci felt that the crew wasn't pushing the single right so he took it upon himself to market it, going to the extent of telling people it was his song. "Word in the streets is those young cats he recorded it with are mad as hell," Dee said. "They feel like he stole their single and is looking to get all the credit."

I was a little upset myself because I felt like if I would've convinced Nard and Mont, he wouldn't have had to do that. "Where's he at now? Have you seen him?" I asked.

Dee exhaled a long breath into the phone. "Well, I haven't seen him. But we've talked. Chino, the niggas in a mental hospital, or in a rehab, out in Alabama."

I couldn't believe my ears. "For what?"

"He said he been going too hard on those X-pills," he explained. "But I think he's layin' low. You know he hit a lick on some niggas from Savannah."

Now it was getting worse. Dee told me how he had heard in the streets that Gucci set some niggas up to think they were gonna get some work, only to leave them high, dry and penniless. Now, according to Dee, those same cats wanted him dead. Not really sure how to feel or what to do, I told Dee that when he talked to Gucci again, tell him to hit me up. Then after our conversation switched to me and my plan of getting out the game, I told Dee we needed to hook up some time soon. We set it up to meet over Mario's the following day, before I hung up.

Weeks passed and one day me and Deon were out in Athens taking care of a few things. By late afternoon, we were finished and headed back to Riverdale. This was a day that would become pivotal in my decision-making in moving forward with my life. Before we reached our house Deon was talking on his cell phone to someone while insisting we stop at Blockbuster's to rent a few movies. But something inside of me told me *naw and to make it to the crib*. So following my instincts, I made it to our driveway. I pressed the remote to the garage, pulled in and parked.

We got out of the car and I went to the door that led to the kitchen. I placed my key in and unlocked it. Now the first thing I noticed was that the alarm didn't give its usual "beep-beep" sound, which notified me that I only had several seconds to punch in my code. This made me look around and that's when I saw the back door to the kitchen kicked in.

"What the fuck!" I screamed.

To my surprise, it looked like someone had trashed the place. My eyes caught our alarm system on the inside door panel torn from the wall, with wires hanging everywhere. The siren to the alarm was on the ceiling and that was torn down. It was apparent that someone had broken in.

I looked down and all sorts of stuff was strewn all about. Splintered wood and pieces of dry wall lay on my carpeted floor. The whole while my eyes were darting side-to-side, conscious of my surroundings.

Deon was still behind me. I was thinking, *Was it the Feds? Or robbers?* I didn't hear any sounds and by the looks of things, whoever it was had come in and rushed out. When I got into the hallway I immediately noticed silver coins: quarters, dimes and nickels spilled onto the ground, like a bag busted. This made a long trail until I came to the stairs where I was met by another eyesore. Clothes that I recognized as mine were everywhere.

"Ah shit, my room," I heard myself say. Gripping my .40 caliber, I took the stairs two at a time, praying that the police hadn't been in there. Rushing into my bedroom I saw what I dreaded. Everything inside was tossed up, my mattress, my dresser drawers, everything was flipped and snatched out as someone searched it from top to bottom. I looked in my closet only to find half of my clothes were snatched off the hangers. I had an expensive collection of exclusive Air Force Ones and gator shoe collection I had bought from Canada, and they were all gone. But the coldest was when I noticed that my small personal safe, which had around ten stacks in it, was missing. It also held both of my big-faced Jacob and Company watches.

But to make matters worse, whoever it was, they took my underwear. *What kind of muthafucka steals a playa's Polo drawls??*

"Damn," I heard Deon say at the sight of my room. "Somebody tore yo shit up."

Without looking at him I asked, "You check the rest of the house?"

"Yeah, everything else is cool," he said.

That's when I looked up. "Whoever did this only came in my room?"

He shrugged. "Yeah, it looks like it. Look Chino, the insurance company ain't gone cover this shit without a police report. You straight?"

I was still trying to process somebody only targeting me. Nobody knew where I stayed.

"Chino," he said, getting my attention, "you straight?"

"Huh, oh yeah. I mean, nah. Hold up." I realized what he had said. I had a stash in the guest bedroom, two fifty-pound bales of mid-grade put up in the closet. Moving fast, I snatched them up and placed them in the trunk of this low key bucket I was pushin' and got them away from there.

For the rest of the night, my time was spent giving police reports and cleaning up a mess I had no idea who caused. Too many variables puzzled me.

For one: our alarm should've notified the police but it didn't because our phone was off. The phone was only off because I was hustling so much I found no time to pay the bill. It's not like we used our house phone anyway. But usually, if Deon knew I failed to pay a bill, he would do it himself. Why not this time? For two: like I said, nobody in the streets knew where I lived. Only family. Deon, on the other hand had all sorts of friends he would bring by and I had told him numerous times about bringing them over. That was just playing it too close, and when it came to the streets, and so called friends, you couldn't trust anyone. And three: Why was my room the only one targeted? They couldn't have known me or they would have known what happened to the last nigga that tried to carjack me in the West End. So many questions and not enough answers. What did I think, that Deon had something to do with it? Honestly, no I didn't believe that. But I did feel like it was an inside job and that one of his "friends" was the culprit. In the end I came to a solid conclusion—it was time I looked into getting my own spot. The thought of somebody invading my privacy bothered me big time. The fact of the matter was niggas didn't have what it took mentally to make something happen for themselves, so they looked to get it off those who did. The last thing I needed to worry about was whether or not I'd be comfortable in my own home.

Maybe that was it. I'd become too relaxed, which is a no-no in the game. So to stay sharp so I could stay on point, I withdrew to myself even more. I hustled even harder, wanting to see my goals accomplished. Now that I saw my own place in the near future, my quota of 1 million dollars seemed that much more important. It's like I needed it now more than ever. And although I wanted to move ASAP, the truth was that I couldn't until my money was right. Another house meant at least another $100,000, because in order to spend money, you gotta make money.

I wasn't the only one having living problems. Joc called me one day and told me he lost his apartment in Riverdale and had to move in with his pops in College Park. He was having problems financially and with a wife, son, and daughter, he felt even more pressure to make something happen for himself.

You know, when people I care about struggle, I feel it's my duty to help them. And at this time, I became troubled because in order to help others I needed first to help myself.

I went to my cousin Nikkia and told her about my concerns.

"Well Chino," she said. "What you need to do is invest."

"Invest in what?" I asked bewildered.

"Invest in property," she explained. "You need to take some of the money you making and reinvest it, so that your money makes money. That way, whenever you want to buy a house or a car, you'll have the legal finances at your disposal."

Liking the idea I said, "Well I got money. How much do I need?"

Nikkia looked at me skeptically. "Chino, I'll help you but I will not help you invest any illegal money. You need legit money."

I shook my head thinking.

My cousin looked upset. "Boy, you mean to tell me you ain't got no legit money? With all that shit you be doin' . . . all those shows y'all be . . ."

"That's it!" Nikkia had made me realize something I had forgotten. I explained to her how me, Nard and Mont had made off good with our last SlutFest. I took in about $15,000 for my share. Money I had saved in a bank account.

"Perfect," she said with a smile. "That will do just fine."

And with that I put my first investment in the real estate business in my cousin's hands. According to her, it would help to generate the kind of money I need to establish my own foundation. She knew I wanted my own place and promised that I would be able to put down on some property real soon. The only thing I needed to do was be patient.

Meanwhile, I assessed my personal life, looking at the women I was dealing with. I was still involved with my little chick from Tennessee. Plus, I had this other little chic I was messing with as well in Atlanta, and we were getting pretty close. She was fine as fuck, a girl I'd met through Travis. He was messing with her cousin, and we got to know each other one day when I was chilling out over at his apartment. Baby was light-brown-skinned with long hair past her shoulders.

She had a little waist and a fat ass that was rounder than my chick from Tennessee. This girl was no taller than 5'5" and had light freckles on her face. She was from St. Petersburg, Florida and had a child by a rapper by the name of Pastor Troy. You may know him from his underground hit, "No More Play in GA" and other songs he had during his career. But dealing with her brought about a few problems with him because he was intent on running her life, despite the fact that he was a married man.

An incident had taken place between Pastor Troy and his baby mama one night while we were eating at a restaurant in downtown Atlanta called Houston's. He saw us enjoying ourselves and called her cell to confront her.

"Now he wants to call me," she said.

I told her to answer the phone.

"Hello," she said calmly, but with an attitude.

"Who's that nigga?" he asked in a loud outburst.

Now by this time, me and the girl had gotten really cool. So much that I was not only looking out for her, but also the child he had so outwardly neglected to support.

"None of your business," she spat back.

"If he wanna know who I am, tell him to ask me, not you," I told her (staying real playa about the situation).

She was about to say something before I cut her off.

"Tell 'em for his info, I'm the nigga buying clothes for his little boy and right now I'm trying to have a meal wit' my girl," I said. "So I'd appreciate it if he got himself in check and respected our privacy."

She just looked at me, unable to speak. It was like she froze up. I don't know if he could hear me through the phone but she put the phone down and said, "He hung up."

I was glad I handled it the way I did because I wasn't into getting all aggressive behind women. It just wasn't my style. But sometimes dudes needed to be put in their place, especially when they weren't being man enough to handle their own responsibilities.

Both were cool but I needed to make a decision about who better fit my situation. In a calculated move, I made up my mind to make Tennessee my main girl because she had more going for herself. And knowing I planned on moving forward, I felt she could assist me more as she had her own career going. And I could do without the baby daddy drama.

Wasting no time, I called her to see what she thought about taking our relationship to another level. "I want you to move out here with me."

"To Atlanta?" she asked surprised. "With you and your cousin?"

"Yeah, but it will only be temporarily." I explained. "I plan on buying a house, so we'll be moving in there shortly after."

She loved the idea. Only thing she needed was a few months before she graduated from college. After that, it was all good.

With everything in motion, I still kept a low profile. Slowly but surely, I found myself more interested in moving and keeping up with my investments with Nikkia than the music. But every now and then I would slide by Nitti's studio to see what he had going on—which was always a lot.

Once when I went by, Nitti told me about this dude from Zone 6-Kirkwood, named Block. I knew of Block from the hood but not personally. He came through Nitti's studio a couple of times while we were working on Slick's material. One time he had one of my big homies with him named Darryl who used to look out for me. He was good friends with Block and told me he had invested over 300,000 grand with this dude Block in a label called Block Entertainment and he hadn't made shit happen yet. Well long story short, this dude Block approached Nitti about buying some beats for this group he was putting out called Boyz 'N Da Hood. The members originally consisted of Big Duke from Zone 6, Big Gee from Zone 3, Jody Breeze from Griffin, GA, a dude from South Georgia named Young Jeezy and Trick Daddy from Miami.

Later, I heard that Trick ended up dropping out of the group because when Young Jeezy went into the booth to drop a verse, Trick felt like he sounded too much like him. He ended up causing a scene by telling Block, 'What the fuck is this? This nigga got my whole style. He sounds just like me! Man, you need to work that shit out. You know what, fuck this, I'm gone!' And just like that, Trick Daddy quit the group. Nitti told me this caused Young Jeezy to switch his whole flow up and find himself on the mic.

I had heard of Young Jeezy through Mr. DJ. He was just networking in Atlanta and had recorded some songs with Mr. DJs artist, Sunny Valentine.

Making his moves, Block had sought out Nitti because he had landed a deal with none other than Sean "Puffy" Combs. As fate would have it, Puffy's baby mama, Kim Porter, was from Columbus, GA and Block knew her. This in turn got him an opportunity to approach Puffy with his idea for a joint venture. Puffy liked the idea to venture into Atlanta because it was hot. He had already formed Bad Boy South and was seeking talent.

I thought it was a hell of a move, just the right situation for Nitti to be in. Providing beats for a group under Puffy's guidance could turn out to be beneficial for him. So taking the opportunity, Nitti hit him off with a couple of beats and Block used one to record a song which was put on a Boyz 'N Da Hood/DJ Drama mix tape called "Dem Boys."

"This is the type of shit we're capable of Chino," he told me. "I'm tellin' you, it won't be long now."

I loved the fact that I was seeing more success around me and it motivated me that much more. I would round out 2003 eager and focused. I had everything lined up and was prepared to take the new year by storm.

Though I made the decision to move Shawty from Tennessee out to Atlanta with me, I still reached out to my other chick I'd been kicking it with for the holidays. She was a really good person and her son deserved better than what Pastor Troy was providing. For Christmas, I shopped for my children and for him as well.

It was the season for giving and I planned to give to all those around me the opportunity to have a better life. This game was full of high-class fakers and selfish people. With me in it, there would be at least one more muthafucka that others could count on.

That's for sure!

New Day

It was the top of '04. When baby girl from Tennessee moved down to stay with me, I was already beginning to see my plan unfold. Nikkia had invested the money I'd given her into a couple of properties, and by her reports, things were going well. She was serious about me not using illegal money. A few years prior, she'd convinced me and Nard to attend Barney Fletcher real estate school, and there we learned techniques in investing that we'd know how to apply when we gave up the game. I made sure I'd paid attention in class because I knew hustling the streets was going to end for me one day. But up to that point, me and Nard had neglected to use what we had learned.

Now Nard, he didn't care how the money came, as long as it came. I believe if he made a million a month in legit money, he would still try and make 50 stacks a year flipping dope. It was just him being addicted to the hustle.

Staying on top of my personal business, I finally put together how I was going to keep my cash flow growing. One day I got a call from my dude from San Bernardino, California named Maurice, aka Reece. He asked me to meet him at his condo in Buckhead ASAP. He and some of his people had moved down to the A fucking with me on some money and muscle shit. They were Crips and found Atlanta a nice spot to get away from all the gang activity and to get money.

Reece told me he had just gotten back from a trip home where he ran into a Mexican friend of his who he hadn't seen in years named Hector. He told Reece that he was living in Phoenix, Arizona and working with his family. Reece went on to say that Hector's family was a part of a well-known drug cartel out west. And once he told Hector that he was living in Atlanta, Hector informed him he had family in Atlanta doing business. But he was looking to start his own operation in Atlanta because of how lucrative the market was. Wasting no time, Reece arranged for Hector to fly back to the A with him so we could meet.

Soon as I arrived at the condo, we got straight down to business. Hector was around 25, and after talking to him, I saw he was very ambitious. He wanted to start doing business immediately. All we had to do was work out all the details.

What we needed to work out was how we were going to get him the money from Atlanta to Arizona. He wanted to mail the mid-grade weed from Arizona to Atlanta, 20 pounds per box. He told me 20 pounds was a safe weight and didn't draw attention.

But see, I was skeptical because me and Nard had gotten packages caught up like that in the late nineties, sending that bush weed in from Texas. So we sat and worked out our differences, coming up with a plan we felt comfortable with.

He immediately addressed my concerns about mailing the pounds in, telling me how he had an inside connect who worked at U.P.S. Ironically, I had a partner who delivered packages for U.P.S. and instantly I saw how this could work. Hector went on to explain how his people already moved large amounts of money so we arranged it where as soon as I received the product, I'd take the money to them. The only catch was that I had to give them an extra $50 on each pound I got in.

I loved the idea and was ready to get the ball rolling. The only thing left for me to do after that was get with my partner who drove for U.P.S. For the right price, he was willing to be down. He explained to me how he had to pay somebody who worked at the warehouse to pull the boxes when they came in. From there, they'd make sure our stuff made it to his route.

After that, I went and rented two houses in the area where he delivered to so the packages could be sent there. When the time finally came for everything to go down, it couldn't have been any sweeter. Hector did his part shipping them out; my boy's people at U.P.S. got the boxes, got them to his truck and he delivered them on a wonderful weekday afternoon.

$$$

Deon had become a little disappointed about me wanting to move, but in the end, he was cool with it. He understood that getting my own place was one of my goals anyway.

As for my girl, her job transfer to Atlanta went successful and she settled in with us nicely. I made sure I set her down and explained my vision. She already knew that I was in the music biz but I wanted her to know I had serious plans on becoming the next Russell Simmons, P. Diddy, Baby, Master P, or Jay-Z. And this would call for a lot of time, hard work, and dedication from me. I went on to tell her I had her and her son's back and I was going to make this happen for us. All I needed was her support, and for her to believe in my dreams. After listening to this she looked me in the eyes and told me how she was with me 100 percent and would do whatever I needed of her to make my dreams come true. Also, more than anything, she wanted me all the way out of the game and didn't want to lose me like her son's father. Hearing this, I was ready to take off.

One day, I was chilling at Nitti's studio when Big Block stopped by to drop off a few copies of a mix tape he had put together for his group. He had taken a chance and jumped out there and paid DJ Drama $25,000 to make a Boyz 'N Da Hood Gangsta Grills CD. Nitti had produced about three songs on the CD, so I took a couple to pass out, to support the movement. Since that we three were all East Side representers, I figured it might just benefit me in the future.

That night, Deon came home while I was relaxing on the sofa and said, "A Chino, guess who I bumped into, and told me to give you his new number?"

"Who?" I asked.

"Joc."

I had been wondering what he had been up to. I had been so busy trying to get myself established that I hadn't had much time for anything else. Wasting no time, I dialed the number and let the phone ring. Right when I thought nobody would answer, somebody did. It was a lady.

"Hello."

"Uh, yeah," I said quickly. "May I speak to Joc, I mean Jasiel?"

I heard the phone being sat down as the woman called his name. "Jasiel, telephone!"

Moments later he picked up. "Yo, this is Joc. Who dis?"

"It's Chino," I responded. "What's up man? Where you at?"

"I'm staying with my aunt out in Douglasville," he said.

"Oh yeah," I said to him. "What's been going on with you?"

He explained how he had moved from his dad's place in College Park. Joc was tripping because I never made it out to his dad's to see him. We chopped it up and I told him how I was looking for a new house for me and my girl to move into. I also told him about the break-in and how I took that as a sign.

"I feel you Shawty," he said. "You gotta make sure you take care of you."

I told him I was making it a must to shoot out there, to scoop him up. It had been a while since we kicked it and I wanted to know how he'd been keeping up. Come to find out, times had been hard for him. Moving from their apartment to his dad's then having to pack up and move to his aunt's had been a humbling experience for him. But I promised him times would get better and that he was doing the right thing, sticking in there with his wife and daughter.

It wasn't but a few days after I called that I began shooting out to his aunt's and kicking it with him. It was good to see that despite his financial strains, his spirit hadn't been broken. I wanted to lend my advice and motivate him because I knew that if he stayed focused he could make it to see a brighter day.

One afternoon while my girl was at work, I decided to go pick Joc up. By me not hustling as much I had more free time on my hands. After sliding through his aunt's, me and him went and scooped up

Brandy. She was still in somewhat dealings with Carolyn Miller. I took them both to Greenbriar Mall, where we shopped a bit. That day I let them hear the Boys 'N Da Hood mixtape and told them that Nitti had done a couple of the beats, along with the hottest song on there. I also gave them a little history on Jeezy, how I came across him at Mr. D'Js spot recording a song with Sunny Valentine and how he was the next in the A to blow. My purpose was to motivate them by showing them how cats were making major moves. I wanted them to believe that despite all our past drama, everything we wanted to happen was going to happen. They just needed to stay at it.

I must say, everything was going according to plan.

A few days later, Nikkia called to tell me that she had sold another investment property. "What do you want me to do with your percentage?" she asked.

"Well," I began, "you already know I wanna get my own place. Can't we just use what I've accumulated on a down payment?"

"Yeah, we can do that but you haven't made enough yet for a down payment on a house the size you want with your credit score," she said. "Chauncey, I can't guarantee you your money will flip that fast. Sometimes it takes a while before property sells."

I thought for a minute then an idea came to me. "Well, what if I put some with it."

"Boy I told you, I ain't messin' wit no illegal money!" I could hear anger in her voice.

I just laughed. "I know, I know, I know. I wasn't talkin' bout that."

She was a bit confused so I explained spring had arrived once again and that meant one thing: SlutFest. Mont had called that morning to tell me everything was a go and that we were set up for the first week of April. I just told Nikkia that I'd use my cut from the show, like we did originally, to do whatever was needed. But this time I would go extra hard in the paint, making sure I made the most of the opportunity. I'd sell shirts, hats, set up my own stands . . . whatever needed to be done to make an extra dollar.

"Now you're using your head. You're a salesman; you've only been selling the wrong product. Sell anything else and you'll be rich."

Little did she know I was already hood rich. But to keep a low profile, I played along with her.

With Nard and Mont, we threw a SlutFest that was bigger and better than even our last. Taking our usual approach, we enlisted some of the hottest MCs and groups out of Atlanta. One of those groups was out of Zone 1-Bowen Homes, going by the name D4L or Down 4 Life. Me and one of the guys, named Shawty Lo, had been cool for some years. He was a real hustler and we'd crossed paths and kicked it from time to time. Lo and his boys Fabo, Stuntman and Mook B had been riding the waves of their success in the music business. They had been associated with Atlanta's elite underground forces like Raheem the Dream and D-Money. So when the time came to showcase their song, they took the stage and performed a single of theirs growing popular in the A called "Bet'cha Can't Do It Like Me," hyping up and exciting the crowd.

Rounding things off, we got Slick to do his thing and put on all of our usual events. I did just what I planned to do and hustled everything from shirts and hats, promoting STR8 Drop and other fly shit that the girls liked. When it was all said and done, I racked up an additional $17,000 dollars to put toward my investment with Nikkia. As soon as I called her and told her of my accomplishment, she expressed how proud of me she was.

"See, I knew you could do it!" she said.

I just laughed. "Yeah, funny what you can do when you really want to. I'm tellin' you, I gotta get my own place soon Nikkia. It just ain't gonna be right until I do. You know I got this girl out here with me."

She had met my girl at my birthday party, but that was it. When she asked if my girl had made the full transition yet, I explained how she had transferred her job and was still getting to know the city better. Nikkia asked me a few more questions about her and at first I began to wonder where she was going. But then she told me.

"Chauncey, ask her about her credit."

I was confused. "Her credit?"

"Yeah," she said before explaining, "She has a good job, and if her credit is good I might be able to get you both into a house without any money down. This way you can use everything you've made to spend on furniture and decorating."

It sounded like a good idea to me so when I got home I hollered at my girl.

My girl went on to tell me that her credit was indeed excellent and when I asked how she felt about buying a house in her name, she was all for it. I told her she wouldn't have to worry about any of the expenses associated with getting the house. And how this would leave me free to spend what I had on hooking the crib up. She loved the idea so I called Nikkia and told her the good news.

"Great," she said, "I'll start looking for y'all immediately."

It took about a week or two but Nikkia found us a nice ass spot out in Riverdale. It was a mini mansion that sat on one and a half acres of land. It had 6 bedrooms, 3 ½ baths, 2 stories high, and a full basement that had enough room to build a studio and whatever else I dreamed of. A family had just moved out and the carpet had a lot of traffic because of the kids. I saw a lot of other things that needed work but it was cool. I'd just spend my money on fixing it up. Nikkia informed me that they wanted $220,000 but with my girl's good credit, I wouldn't have to put up a down payment.

This was a blessing from God.

I proceeded to give Nikkia the green light to cash me out on my investments. I had a lot of work to do and having my own home was just one more small step toward me accomplishing my personal goal of unlimited freedom.

I kept in touch with Duddy and Bubba, who were constantly on the road. Bubba's second album wasn't doing well at all. The sales were low, and it was beginning to look like a failed effort. Whenever they would come back home, we would discuss how important it was to use the shows out of town to continue promoting the New South brand. Bubba told me New South was popping off even if Interscope didn't finance him with the label deal; with the exposure he already had, it could still work. We figured all he had to do was to keep doing shows. The rest would take care of itself.

I couldn't count on that so as me and my girl began to settle in, I spent my time also handling my responsibilities at the label. One morning I was lying in bed talking on a conference call with Nard and Torrey, talking about what all had been going on with STR8 Drop. I wasn't satisfied with our progress. The song Nitti produced for Slick, "I Wish a Muthafucka Would", featuring 8 Ball, just wouldn't catch. And although Jermaine Dupree placed it on his So So Def's compilation CD, it seemed like nothing was working. So I gave them my opinion.

"I think we should find a new song to push," I said. "It's no need in pushing a song that's not catching."

"Nah Chino," came Nard. "We just need to keep working this song until it pops."

"Yeah," came Torrey, "we done put a lot of money into this song."

"Spending more money won't fix anything," I said. "Sometimes you gotta accept your losses."

As we went back and forth I became frustrated. Then both Nard and Torrey said something that drew the line for me.

"Well if you got all the answers," came Nard, "why don't you show us how to do it then?"

"Yeah Chino," Torrey chimed in, "I wanna see what you can do."

"All right," I said confidently, taking it as a challenge. "I will."

And with that, I disconnected the call thinking to myself how the day had brought about a change of events I never saw coming.

MasterMind Music

After I hung up with Nard and Torrey I went into a trance. I was determined to prove them that I was indeed focused and that my vision could come to life. Too much had transpired in my life to quit. From losing Shane to the death of my grandmother, all that had made me a warrior and I was going to live up to the oath I made to be somebody. But while sitting there in bed, I realized that before I could get anyone to believe in my dream, I had to be honest with myself first. I had to believe.

I began thinking of how I could've found success in music long ago, but I had been faking. From my dealings with Bubba, to Big E and Yak, and now with Nard and Mont; I had been content with looking the part while settling for selling drugs. And while looking at things and all the people I knew, I could have made it happen from the jump. All that stood in my way was me. All I had to do was get up off my ass and put the same effort into the music game as I did into hustling the streets.

Sitting there thinking helped me to realize I could've been on top and this woke me up. That morning I jumped out of bed with a take-charge attitude and went straight to work. It was time for me to do what I should've been done. . . BLOW THE FUCK UP!!

Wasting no time, I went to a music store called Pro Audio in Decatur off Memorial Drive, in search of everything I needed. I was already musically inclined and from my dealings with Duddy and Nitti, I was up on all of the name brand equipment needed to create a quality sound. With money I had left over from my investments and savings from the SlutFest, I bought all kinds of stuff. I got a Tritan touchscreen keyboard, Roland 1080 sound module, MPC 2000xl and MoPhat. I bought the newest Pro Tool controller, the M Box1, which turned out to be the cheapest on the market. Also I got a 16 track Mackie board, a G4 Mac computer, a 12 inch sub-woofer and two mid-range speakers. And to top it off I bought a high-quality microphone. When I was finished I paid for everything and began loading the equipment in my Denali.

"Shawty, what's up," a voice called out to me.

Quickly I turned around and saw one of my partners from Decatur. Ironically, his name was Chino as well. "Yo, what's up?" I responded.

He was on his way into the store. "Nuttin' much, Shawty. I see you puttin' one together."

"Yeah," I replied. "I just bought a house and I've got a big ol' empty basement to do something with. So I figured I'd start my own label."

"You know that's what I do Shawty, build studios," he said. "And I got a fire producer for you, if you need an in-house."

"Damn bra', you about five minutes too late," I said. "I just paid the guy in the store to come and hook everything up for me. But if I ever need an upgrade I'll let you know. But what's up with the producer?"

Chino told me about this guy named Elvis who had come to Atlanta from Memphis to work with Jazze Pha, but things hadn't worked out for him.

"Dude is nice too," Chino explained, "the only thing is, he doesn't have nowhere to work out of."

I loaded the last box in my truck and closed the back hatch. "Yeah man, I'd like to check him out. Maybe we can do something."

Me and Chino exchanged numbers and he told me he'd give me a call and hook me up with this Elvis cat. From there, I left feeling good, ready to get to work on my studio.

On the way home, I called Torrey and told him to meet me at the crib. I didn't want to tell him what I'd bought, so I tricked him into thinking I had two girls that were ready to get down. If I knew anything, it was that dudes moved faster for some pussy, than for some food or money. Even though we had our words this morning, I knew he was still down with his cuz. As soon as I bent the corner to pull up to my house, I saw Torrey sitting on the trunk of his car, in my driveway talking on his cell phone. Before I could park and get out of the truck, he was on me.

"Aye boy-boy, where dem hoes at?" he asked.

"Here they go," I replied as I popped the rear hatch of my truck.

At first he was confused but then he said, "Ah shit," at the sight of all the equipment. "You ain't playing. You got everything we need to make our own beats."

"That's the point," I told him. "This way we'd save a lot of money. Instead of spending thousands, this will be a lot cheaper."

For the next twenty minutes, we unloaded all the equipment. Then we went out to Best Buy and bought a big wrap around glass desk to sit all of the equipment on. We also bought ourselves two big black leather office rolling chairs to lounge in. When we were on our way back, the installer from Pro Audio called me and said he would be at my place within the hour. I was glad because I wanted to get everything hooked up before it got too late.

We were putting the desk and the executive-style chairs together when we heard the doorbell ring.

"That's probably the installer," Torrey said.

I shot up the stairs and it was him indeed. Dude introduced himself as Robbie. He was around his mid-20's and light skinned. I showed him to the room where I wanted to make the studio and he hooked everything up as well as showed us how to run the Pro Tools. I had never run Pro Tools. At Underground Sound, we recorded off an A-Dat machine. Nitti had Pro Tools but I never really paid any attention to how it operated. After that, we put a mic jack in the closet right outside of the room to make a vocal booth.

Robbie left and both me and Torrey just stood looking at what we'd accomplished.

"I'm gonna call Joc," I told him.

"All right," he said, messing around with the equipment.

I hit Joc up and told him what I did, telling him he should come over. I gave him directions and he said he was on his way. In less than an hour, he was at my door with his wife accompanying him. By this time, my girl had gotten off of work, so she entertained Joc's wife while we did our thing in the basement.

"I brought this track," Joc said, holding up a CD.

He explained that the dude Joe, who produced all the songs he let me listen to when we met, made the beat. We popped it in and that night Torrey used as much as he could remember, from what Robbie taught him, to record Joc's first song entitled "1-2 Wayback."

The song was WACK AS A MUTHAFUCKER!!!

It was right then that I realized how much we needed beats. I mean, I could play some drum patterns but I couldn't play any keys.

The next day Chino called me.

"Yo Shawty," he said, "I holla'd at my man Elvis. We try'na slide through."

I told him he was right on time and gave him directions.

I was alone when they arrived. Chino introduced me to Elvis. He was in his early 20's, about 5'5," brown-skinned with green eyes. I wasted no time, taking them straight to the basement.

"This is it," I said, showing them the place.

"You got a nice setup," Elvis expressed, looking around.

"Thanks," I replied. I asked him if he knew how to work everything and he said yes. He walked up to the Triton keyboard and, without hesitation, began playing a five second arrangement. I knew skills when I heard them and he had skills.

Meanwhile, Chino checked out what I had done. "Man," he began, after his final inspection, "I can freak this spot Shawty." I said, "I need to put some Plexiglas in the booth, so we can see in the studio."

Chino agreed by nodding his head.

By this time, Elvis had walked away from the keyboard. I was sitting in my business chair and welcomed him to sit next to me, in Torrey's seat. I got straight to the business, telling him what I had going on. He gave me his story about Jazze Pha and it amazed me that Jazze let him get away like he did. Nevertheless, I opened my studio to him telling him how I could use his talent. In the end, me and Elvis came up with a handshake agreement where I would pay him $1,500 to just crank out beats for me. And in return, I would let him work in the studio whenever he needed. Our meeting lasted about 30 minutes before him and Chino left. He'd take a few days to make preparations and then we'd get started.

Meanwhile, Chino and I got back together the next day. My mentioning the Plexiglas in the booth had given him an idea, so we lined it up to go out to Home Depot. There he got me some wood, casting and Plexiglas, everything I needed to build what I wanted. When we got back to my place, he took his time and, for a good price, put together the booth I envisioned.

After a couple of days, Elvis returned as promised and my studio became his second home. Come to find out, he stayed all the way out in Acworth, which was forty minutes north of Atlanta, with his wife and son. Because I stayed 20 minutes south of The ATL, the long drive caused him to spend many nights at my place. This was cool because it gave him time to acquaint himself with the whole crew. Joc loved what he could do and they ended up having good chemistry. And wasting no time, we began to bang out songs. From that point forward, Elvis became MasterMind Music's personal in-house producer.

Things were looking up!

After about two weeks of recording, some drama kicked off. Just as I was beginning to see everything come together, I got a call from the least-expected person—Ms. Carolyn Miller.

I was chilling at my spot waiting on all my boys to arrive when she hit me up on my cell.

"So this is how you gon' play me?" she said right off the back.

And I was confused as ever. "Man, what in the hell are you talking about?"

"You know exactly what I'm talking about, slick ass nigga."

I didn't play all those slick talk games. Especially when I had no idea what she was talking about. "Look, I ain't wit' all the games. Explain yourself or get off my line."

"I know you had somethin' to do with Brandy leaving me, and

signing wit' that nigga Nitti," she said in a frustrated voice. "That's all y'all wanted anyway, to push me outta the way."

Oh shit! I thought; see . . . I knew Brandy was upset at Carolyn. She felt the woman was holding her back and that she was thinking about leaving Carolyn for Nitti and So So Def. But I had been so caught up in what I was doing that it slipped my mind. But this was solely on Brandy, her decision alone.

I laughed. "Carolyn," I said calmly, "nobody pushed you outta the way. You pushed yourself. You was so caught up in your own bullshit that you couldn't see what was best for your artist. And now, it seems Brandy has her faith in someone else."

"What!" she screamed. "Who you think you . . ."

But I cut her off. "Stay up." Then I hung the phone up in her face.

To be honest, I was glad for Brandy. She did what she felt was best for her. When I spoke to her, I got all the details about how JD had given her a single deal for her song "Bottle Action" and Nitti signed her to his production company, PlayMaker. For her, Nitti was a better person to deal with. He had been making moves with the other group he was pushing called the "Slick Boys," and for her, he seemed more business minded. I congratulated and reassured her that I had her back.

In the meantime, I got back to work. I called up Lo Down, whose real name is Carlos, and asked him to jump on board with me. Carlos hadn't really been pushing hard since his days with Duddy and us at Underground Sounds. Carlos was not only a good rapper; he also had a sense for the business. Something I admired about him. I wanted him to get back involved in the music, as well as surround myself with people I knew. I had come up with a name for my label and it was time to get everything legitimized.

"MasterMind Music." he played with the name to see how it sounded. "I like it and it fits you Chino."

I looked at Carlos and said, "This is my first time doing it on my own and I want it done right. I want MasterMind to be more than a label; I want it to be a real company. Man, it's time to blow!"

Carlos saw how serious I was and he was ready to rock and roll, just as everyone else was.

With him at my side, I went and made sure I was 100 percent legit, all the way around the board. I got my business license, incorporation, tax ID number, bank accounts and all. After spending filing fees and filling out pages of paperwork, it was official. I then reached out to those closest to me, appointing certain positions aimed at their strengths. I made Joc the President, Torrey the V.P., Deon the Head of Promotion, and Nikkia my Secretary. I also had a talk with Q, telling him how we were going corporate and that we didn't have to duck the police anymore, and that I needed him to use his real name because he was going to be the Chief Financial Officer of the company. And from that point on, he began presenting himself as Marquet. MasterMind music was in full E-F-F-E-C-T. And I stayed focused on my vision, doing just what everyone wanted me to do.

Show 'em how it was done!

After I got myself official on a business level, I put the word out on the streets, to get their support. To do this, I took the old fashioned route and called almost everyone I knew.

First, I called up my cousin Kenio, aka Babe, from Lithonia. He had a lot of cats riding with him and I told him I was trying to get a movement going. He said he would call our homeboys in the hood like Turk, Big Ralph (R.I.P.), Dread, Danny Man, Mario, Dorrie, Twon and Torey, to let them know what was up. Kenio sounded more excited than I was about the label. All he kept saying was, "Let's get this money cuz! Let's get this money!"

After that, I reached out to my Decatur and East Atlanta partners and put them on game. J.B., Dee James, P.D., Darius, Paul, Eric, Shawn, Rico and Tony were all with it.

Next, I made a call out to my homie Big Wu from Mechanicsville, in Atlanta. He was a big time street hustler, who was respected by everyone. He had influence with local movers and shakers like Big Oomp and Bone Crusher. Big Wu was game and loved the fact that I was finally doing something on my own.

I had Joc call up our partners and his cousins in ColliPark and his Wildwood crew, and tell them what was up. Vick, Fresh, Stacks, A.K., Rock, Redman, Vincent aka Dog, Jabba, Body Bag, Blue, Montez and Mike. All of them said they were down and told us whatever we needed of them, they could be counted on.

Making sure I reached out to everyone, I made a call out to California to Reece and O. At the time, they were visiting home but I wanted to let them know the deal and to tell them that they were going to be the heads of the Goon Squad, with Ju-Ju and Travis. Then I hit Ju-Ju and Travis to put them up on game.

Now it was time to reach out to my people down by the way. With Big E gone to serve a five year Fed bid, Underground Sound had run its course. So, I hit Duddy and told him my plans, and once things jumped off, we had to do a Lo Down and Duddy album. He was all game and I told him to let Yak and my two younger cousins, Leon, aka King, and Hanif know what was up with the movement. After calling my cousins Dimitious and Mopreme, putting them on game, I made my last call.

The last call I made was to my little cousin Tony, out in Athens. I saved this call for last because it meant a lot to me. You see, Tony had been under my wing ever since his big brother Shane got sentenced to life in prison. As the years passed, I never let Tony go without me keeping him straight. When I was copping half tons and tons of weed, I put him on. Tony was a true hustler and had a strong crew in his hood, Spring Valley. He had Big Herk, Marty, Carlos, my other cousin, Kendrick, Reco, Eric Ollie, Dreeko, Jeff, Wesley and many more. Well now that I had this music thing poppin' I wanted to turn him on to that as well.

I wanted everyone I knew to be on board. Because when shit jumped off, I wanted to take them with me. I also wanted the world to see the support a real street cat got when the streets was behind him. I was plotting ahead of time for the shows and other events to come. Having my boys present, draped up and already getting money, would just prove that MasterMind Music wasn't a commercial label. It was from the streets, for the streets. No ifs ands or buts about it.

"Young Joc?" Joc asked.

"Yeah," I said looking at Joc. "It's catchy."

"You don't think it's too much like Young Jeezy?" he asked.

I shook my head. "Naw, because you are young and your name is Joc."

He thought about it for a minute, saying it over and over again.

Then looking as if in deep thought he said, "Yeah, I like it. Young Joc."

This would be the day he adopted "Young" onto his name. The only difference to come would be how he'd spell it. Y-U-N-G, as if it were Chinese, plus to set himself apart from the other "Youngs."

Sticking to the script, MasterMind Music was moving full throttle. Every day, sometimes for days on end, me, Elvis, Carlos, who changed his rap name from Lo Down to Shawty Slick, Joc and Torrey, would be camped up in my basement recording song after song. Nobody questioned my mission to find that perfect record that we could go ahead and push 100 percent.

Around this time, a lot of things were happening in Atlanta. The music scene was getting really crazy. One of the artists doing big things was someone I had already predicted to blow--Young Jeezy. His association with Big Meech and his crew had him front running a full fledge B.M.F. movement, real street hustlers going mainstream. Jeezy had a single with Bun B from U.G.K. and Bleu DaVinci called "Gettin' Money Over Here." The song was turning into a hit in the clubs and everyone in Atlanta was feeling it.

The success of Atlanta's own just inspired us even more. Motivated, we focused on making an even harder hit. We knew we needed to make something that would be hot in the clubs. With this frame of mind, me and my crew got together to construct a song that mirrored the type of night we experienced all the time in the clubs—out twenty deep with the likes of Big Meech, his mob and Atlanta's underground street elite partying the night away, a track that would be so hard it would be no denying it as a hit.

Well, one night such a song had finally come to us. Me, Joc and Elvis were in the basement and came up with the beat. It was influenced by Master P's "No Limit Soldiers" hit song, with the same piano melody and an up and down 808 bass arrangement. After Elvis put the finishing touches on it, we just let it bang, bouncing around in the studio like it was the club. Me and Joc were feeling it so much that we began popping off bars for a hook that was motivated off of what we had been doing in the clubs, and off how Jeezy's movement had been going with the types of songs he'd been making.

Joc took over rapping, "Thousand ones, Grey Goose / Turn around let me see you get loose / I'm in the club, in da back / In clear ice dressed in all black . . . "

I directed him into the booth where he not only laid the hook, but ended up knocking out "Thousand Ones."

The vibe of the song was feel-good and we felt like it fit not only us but all of Atlanta's partygoers to the tee. The beat was banging so hard, and after listening to it, actually partying to it, right there in my basement, we all concluded that the song we were looking for was finally here.

I knew Joc had it in him and I knew my crew had it in them. I was beginning to see a bright future. The only thing left for me to do was get the songs mixed and get it out into the right hands--something I was eager to do.

Can't Stop The Hustle

Elvis had this white dude that worked at Doppler Studios, an engineer named Ralph, who he said could mix our song for us. Doppler Studios was a big time studio off of Piedmont Rd. in Buckhead. This cat Ralph recorded and mixed songs for major artists like T.L.C., Prince, Trey Songz, Outkast and a lot of pop stuff. Elvis said his mixes went for around $1,200 to $1,800, but he could get them done for $150. The catch was, we had to drop our music off and he would do it in his spare time. That meant there would be no guarantee of how long it would take to get the mix back. But for the price, I was cool with it.

So Elvis hooked it up for me to meet Ralph and drop the song off. Ralph ended up transferring the Pro Tools session from my external drive into his, and about a week later, he called me up.

"Hey Chino," he said, "stop by Doppler around nine and hang out. I got that mix complete."

Me and Joc went out there and we listened to "Thousand Ones" in the "A" room, with the million dollar sound board. Now, like a lot of white boys that I had come across, Ralph hadn't put that deep bass mix that we love in the south so, I told him to give it that feel. He made the changes and I couldn't help but feel good because this was all me making moves with the artist I believed in, working on our stuff and not being in a big studio with other niggas doing their music. When it was all said and done, Ralph put the finishing touches on the mix we desired. And although I knew another mixer named Niko who worked with a lot of other rappers at Patchwork Studios, Ralph became my own personal mixer. He became that extra piece I would add to my arsenal, making MasterMind Music that much more complete.

Then another piece fell in my lap. My homeboy Chino came through again. He knew a guy named Kenny Mix, who was a professional at mastering songs. He worked for big artists just like Ralph and he only wanted $125 per song. Kenny ended up putting a warm master on it and it came out great. A lot of artists in the city used Glenn or Rodney Mills, who both did great work, but to me Kenny was better. He just didn't turn all your levels up and have the sounds distorting, like a lot of other masters I knew of.

It was crazy how everything was coming together for me, as if my grandmother's rested soul was moving the pieces I needed to finally get my life in order. Ralph and Kenny gave us that perfect sound we needed to make "Thousand Ones" radio ready.

With the song finished, we took it to a couple of clubs and let a few DJs see what they thought. When I was younger, I used to hang out a lot with my partner named Darius Carroll. His father, Sam Carroll, used to manage almost every strip club in Atlanta and I got a chance to see how songs got their first shot at making it. By seeing this, we hit all the strip clubs. First we hit two in Decatur, one called Pinups where DJ Outlaw worked and Strokers, where my man funky Darrel James worked the ones and twos. We hit Magic City, Pleasures, Platinum 21's (now Kamal 21) and Blazing Saddles (now club Blaze), all in The ATL. My dude DJ Cloud worked at Blue Flame. He played it and liked it. Body Tap had my guy Playa Poncho D-Jayin' and he showed us love. I'd go hang with him there and when he worked at Magic City. Our mission was to get an overall response from the club and our song was getting the response we were looking for.

One day Joc came into the studio early, ready to get down.

"Man," he began. "I went out to Platinum 21's last night and got the song played. This cat I know heard it and approached me about doing somethin'."

"What's his name?" I asked, curious.

"Eric Miller. Him and Big Mason put out Drama back in the day," he said. "He told me he just got out of the Feds, from doing seven years."

Eric Miller. . . Eric Miller...The name didn't sound familiar to me. But I knew Big Mason. "So what did you tell him?"

"After I told him about you, I just shot him my number," he explained. "Then I gave him some dap and went about doin' my thang."

I nodded my head. Up to this point, I saw the significance of believing in omens. Maybe this Eric Miller will be another piece in the puzzle, I thought.

Everything was unfolding at a rapid pace.

Elvis was banging out that heat and Joc was killin 'em. One day I walked in the studio and heard what I knew would be Joc's second single. It had a slow vibe to it. Joc had put a smooth flow to it and all he needed was someone to sing the hook. I got my man Lil' Will to sing on it for Joc. Lil' Will was a member of the Dungeon Family and had a hit back in the day called "Looking For Nikki." He had sung on rapper Slim Calhoun's single "All These Lonely Girls Wanna Cut," but since then he'd been down and out, trying to make a comeback. Being that he was my homeboy I hooked him up, shooting him $750 to do the job. It was more than he was expecting but I knew he needed it. When we got finished, the track was hot. Its laid back vibe was a definite winner when it came to catering to the ladies. A must on any CD.

By this time, Jermaine Dupree had taken off with Brandy's single, printing it up to get the promo rolling. With Nitti's production behind it, the song was getting a lot of response in the clubs. The only obstacle she faced throughout the whole ordeal came by way of the name she went by. Apparently, another girl already had dibs on the alias Ms. Behavin, which prevented her from using it. But she found a clever way around all of that, settling for a shorter version of Ms. B. Brandy continued her stride, doing shows and promoting her single full throttle.

Brandy's success was picking up fast. Nitti being the CEO and producer, meant he had to dedicate more time to her project. And being that he had his other group, "The Slick Boys," eager to get their thing going, this wasn't a good thing in their eyes. Nitti had managed to get a song of theirs on the soundtrack to the movie "Biker Boys," but that was about it. The word was, they felt he was beating them for the royalties.

This, combined with being put in the shadow of Brandy, resulted in Nitti returning to his studio one day to find all of his equipment gone. His suspicion was confirmed when he received a phone call from them stating that he could have his "shit back" when they "got their money."

I hated to see my main man going through these problems but I knew it came with the territory. Sometimes artists were just not patient or trusting enough, and in his case, both caused the Slick Boys to turn against him. I didn't say much about what happened to him because I had street-like mentality, and I didn't want to give him any advice that might get him or us, in trouble. I just didn't need anything to deter me from my mission. I had a banger on my hands with Joc's "Thousand Ones," and I was determined to work it into the right hands. I wasn't going to wait until we had a whole CD; I knew all we needed was a hit. And Joc's song was that.

Getting things on the roll, I made up copies of the single and started handing them out to all the DJs in the clubs. I used a black Sharpie marker to write on the CD Joc's name, the song title and MasterMind Music. I did this so they'd know who the artist was and the company it came from. Well, somewhere in the process of all this, Elvis ended up bumping into Jazze Pha. He gave Jazze a copy, telling him what he had been doing. Elvis wanted to show his old music partner that he was indeed on his grind, while also trying to get someone to help with a distribution deal. Jazze ended up giving him the ol' "Let me see what I can do," but in the end, he actually did a lot more than we expected.

"Bottle Action" was gaining momentum and Joc found himself at Brandy's side, playing as her hype man during shows. At one in particular, Joc bumped into this young kid he knew who called himself Chris Flame. Joc knew him because Chris had helped out in a studio for a producer Joc knew back in the day. As they talked, he told Joc he was doing his own production now, before giving him a couple of CDs full of beats—one for him and one for Brandy. They parted ways with Joc getting his hook up. A few days later, he brought me the CD.

"He told me he's interning at Hot 107.9," he said.

"Oh yeah," I said, taking the CD and placing it in the computer as he explained the encounter.

"Yeah," he continued, "at first he gave me one CD for Brandy, but when I told him I rapped too, he gave me this other one. He's been makin' beats and trying to get 'em in the right hands. I also told him about "Thousand Ones" and he told me he could get it played on Dig It or Ditch It."

Dig It or Ditch It was a segment that Hot 107.9 ran during their 6 to 10 p.m. show with the Duddy Boys. In it, new artists would have a chance to have their song played. After the song finished, 13 callers would call in and comment whether they "dig" the song or if the station should "ditch it." With my business mind, I immediately began seeing how a connection with this young kid, Chris Flame, could be beneficial.

I pushed 'play' in the iTunes program, starting the CD, and sat back while the tracks came in. The first was HEAT...and so was the second, third and fourth beat we listened to. Me and Joc found ourselves catching whip lash from bobbing our heads so much.

"Damn," I said in total shock. "Where's this kid from?"

"East Point," he said.

I think Joc knew what was coming next.

"We've gotta catch up with him," I said in all seriousness. "I like his style."

Joc told me he was on it and that he would give Chris a call and hook up some sort of meeting. I saw this young dude as being an asset. All I needed to do was get at him. The rest would be history.

Brandy was on her biz and had gotten a booking manager from New York whose name was Troy, but went by Fats. One day me, Fats, Joc, Brandy and the crew were on our way to one of Brandy's shows. We were all piled up in a van when I popped in the CD with "Thousand Ones." Instantly, the vehicle was filled with the vibrant rhythm we'd grown to love.

Fats looked at me in surprise. "That's Joc?"

I forgot he hadn't heard the song. "Yeah, what you think?"

With his face scrunched up like a foul odor was in the air, rockin' his head side to side he responded, "That shit is bangin'."

"You think so?" Joc asked from the rear seat.

"Hell yeah," came Fats. "It's perfect for the club. Matter of fact, Chino you need to let me work this."

"Work it like how?" I asked.

Fats proceeded to give me a small spill of what all he could do for us. Then Brandy jumped in: "Well for starters, I think it's hot enough for Joc to open up my shows with it. That way he can get 'em crunk before I hit the stage."

To me it sounded like a good idea. I ran it across Nitti one day and he loved the idea as well. And being that Brandy was scheduled to do a bunch of shows, this would give Joc some extra exposure.

Brandy began performing all over the Southeast, so we stayed on the road constantly. Nitti had another artist by the name of Young Capone. He had a single deal under So So Def for his song "I'm Hot." So he went out with us on occasions, trying to get a buzz going as well. During our time out on the road, Brandy kept it realer than some cats I knew. She made sure she got extra rooms and extra travel money for us. She did everything in her power to keep us comfortable, accommodating all of our needs. Our camps, Playmakers and MasterMind Music, were like one family. And just like B wanted, Joc opened up with "Thousand Ones," giving us an opportunity to showcase in front of crowds eager to hear that hard-hitting club banger sound promised from a label like So So Def.

While we were home, in between traveling, Joc got at me about that young kid Chris Flame. "He wants us to meet him."

"All right, where does he stay?" I asked.

"Not at his house," he corrected, "he wants us to come to his job."

I looked confused. "Up at the station?"

"Yeah," he said.

"All right, when?" I asked.

Joc looked at his watch. "In about 30 minutes."

This was just how I liked things. "Well, what are we waiting for?"

And with that, I grabbed my keys.

Hot 107.9 is an Atlanta-based radio station with legendary ties. Where people like Ludacris, his manager and half-CEO of their label,

Disturbing the Peace, Shaka Zulu, got their starts. Ludacris and on-air co-host Poon Daddy, became the A&R for D.T.P. Carmelo Anthony's wife LaLa also worked at the station, adding yet another success story to Hot 107.9's legacy. And being that so many notables came from there, I was sure by listening to this kid Chris Flame's beats that he would be nothing less than its next up and coming.

Me and Joc found the station after calling to tell Chris we were on our way. When we arrived, we went into the building, caught the elevator to the floor we were instructed to get off on and met Chris in the lobby, waiting for us.

"Yo Joc, what's up," he said with all smiles.

Joc gave him some dap and introduced us. Chris was around 21 years old, about 5'8", light-skinned and, though young, he carried himself with an air of professionalism. After I shook his hand, he led us into a backroom where he worked.

"So you listened to the tracks I gave you?" he asked Joc.

"Yeah, we both did."

I cut in: "What 'chu try'na get for some of them?"

"Well," he began, "a lot of them are old and some of 'em was already used by a few niggas. But I could make you some new shit for a good price."

I nodded, "So you got a studio?"

He looked grim, "Nah, but. . . "

"Don't trip, I got one for you," I said. "I just built one at my house, and if you cool with it, you can use my equipment to make shit for other people. In return, you just knock the price down for the beats you make for us."

He thought about it. "It doesn't sound bad. How about I come check y'all out and let you know then?"

Sounded good to me.

"Hey Joc," he said. "You bring a copy of your song?"

Joc pulled out the CD we had brought. "I got it right here."

Chris took the copy of "Thousand Ones" and we listened to it right there. When it finished, he immediately expressed how much he liked it. He told us he could get it on the show, but to give him some time.

I was glad we went to check this kid out. We stayed and talked to Chris a bit longer, but because he had to get back to his thing at the station, our time was cut short.

Chris promised us that he'd give it a hell of a shot to get the single played and we made plans to hook up at a later date. Both me and Joc left feeling like we got something accomplished.

And a week later, our efforts were confirmed.

We were leaving the basement to go and get some beer and wings from this restaurant called MoJo's. When we got in my truck, I just so happened to turn on the radio when the announcement was being made that the song was coming on. Me and Joc immediately began calling people to tell them we were about to be on the radio. People were also calling us and we had to tell them instead of us calling each other, we needed to be calling the station to vote. I must say, it felt pretty good hearing our work going out to over a million listeners.

When "Thousand Ones" finished, the callers started calling in. From the opinions of Atlanta's very own, the song was a banger, perfect for the club and we received love like never imagined. Joc got all 13 "Dig Its!" The only downside was the Duddy Boys were calling the artist of the song Young Joe, which later we found out, was because they couldn't read my handwriting.

Joc got back at Chris the following day, inviting him to come out to my house. He accepted the offer and soon I had him, Elvis, Joc and Shawty Slick all in the basement getting acquainted. Chris loved our vibe and when he heard Shawty Slick rap, he felt we had something good going. I just stood back watching everybody chilling out and couldn't help but feel as though something good was in the making. Our time together seemed to have no end and Chris soon forgot about the money he could make. He just wanted to be down.

Young Chris Flame never left my house after that day, giving MasterMind Music another player on its production side.

My basement was the place to be. Me and my crew would be up in there for days. Like I said, Elvis stayed all the way in Acworth, so he would stay at my house five nights a week. Shawty Slick stayed in Athens, so he stayed nights at a time as well. Joc was still staying in Douglasville, which was 40 minutes away, so him, his wife and daughter would stay over nights cause he was always in the studio. Plus, his beat up, white, short-body Cadillac was always breaking down.

Joc recorded a song with Shawty Slick called "Nan Nudda Pimp Like Me," produced by Chris Flame. The song was jammin' so I took it to Ralph and Kenny so they could do their thing. Ralph was beginning to love the music we were making. Another big named songwriter and producer named Brian Michael Cox had a studio he worked out of in Doppler and word that we were making some heat spread through the industry heads real quick. That's how a lot of news spread in the A. Who was working with who, and on what? This occurred due to people being at certain studios such as Zack's, Patchwork, Doppler , Stankonia, etc. Some people just hung out at these spots hoping to get put on somebody's song because a lot of big name producers and artists went there.

One of those who did this is my partner, Lil' Will, who I got to sing on Joc's slow song. One day we were up at Patchwork; I had stopped by real quick to holler at him. He was up there doing some new music for Young Jeezy. We chopped it up and the next day he hit me with some news about my boy Gucci.

"Yeah Chino," he said, "yesterday when you left, Gucci came up there and played a track made by this producer he be messin' with, that moved to the A from San Francisco, named Zaytoven."

"Oh yeah?" I was glad to hear my boy was back on his thing.

"Yeah Shawty," he said, I ended up singin' a hook on that thang. Then Jeezy and Boo from Boo and Gotti jumped on it. That muthafucka's jamming! It's called "So Icy."

Me and Will chopped it up some more. He wanted to make sure that if needed him to do anything, he had me. I told him I'd holla when I had something.

Not wanting to be lazy, me and Joc were hitting up clubs in the city that had open mic contests. We did The Ritz on Old National on Monday, J-Paul's on Tara Blvd. on Tuesday, Akini the Black Mack from Hot 107.9 showcased at Peacock on Auburn Ave. on Wednesdays and we did that also. We hit up 20 Grand East on Thursday, and we hit

whatever club was jamming during the weekend. All of this just to get
the song heard. Whenever Joc wasn't on the road with Brandy, we did
this knowing that from the shows out of town, to the clubs in town, we
would soon catch a buzz.

We were on our grind!

Though neither was tripping off money, I still hit Chris and
Elvis off with a few dollars to keep them comfortable. For me, shit was
getting serious and I didn't want any problems like money to slow us up,
or cause problems in our camp. I needed everything to go smoothly so
I could focus and keep my eyes on the ball.

One day, I was in my office looking over some possible avenues
and ideas I could experiment with to showcase what we had, when Joc
busted in the room. He was obviously upset.

"Yo Chino, dem niggas stole our shit!"

Even though I didn't know what in the world he was talking
about, I found myself getting mad because he was. "Who you talking
about?"

"That nigga Jazze Pha," he said. "That nigga T.I. got a song all
over the radio called "Get Loose." It's produced by Jazze. I'm tellin' you,
that nigga stole our shit!"

I listened as Joc ranted on and on about how he thought Jazze
took his song from Elvis and gave it to Tip. Personally, I hadn't heard the
song but I went ahead and put up with his huffing and puffing the whole
time I was browsing the web.

"Look," I told him, "how 'bout I take you to lunch and we try to
figure out what's going on?"

Still upset, he calmed down enough to concede. Exhaling a
deep breath he said, "All right man, but I'm tellin' you…"

He broke off in mid-sentence shaking his head.

Though Joc was disturbed, I was adamant about figuring out
my best approach to marketing what we had. My mind was distracted as
we jumped in my Denali. As Joc adjusted his seat, I turned the ignition,
starting the truck.

That's when I was blindsided. Because I didn't have a CD in my disc player, the radio came on Hot 107.9 and lo and behold, the song Joc was talking about was on.

Tip was talking about, "…girl get loose", just like Joc had been doing on "Thousand Ones." The tempo was the same, as well as the sounds. On Joc's song he had elected to use the line "drop down and get your eagle on, girl", to begin the second verse. At the time, Nelly had this for a song and it was hot. Well, as we sat listening to Tip's song, and Nelly comes in on the second verse rapping, "…drop down and get your eagle on, girl."

I couldn't believe my ears. I turned my head to look at Joc, who was just sitting there.

"I told you," he said with confidence. "They stole our shit!"

It was right then and there that I realized just how vicious the music game really was. To describe the emotion that I felt at that moment could only be summed up in one word.

HEATED!

Jermaine Dupri's Birthday Bash

After Jazze Pha took our concept, we just kept on pushing. Joc made contact with the guy Eric Miller, the one he bumped into at Platinum 21. Me and him both thought it would be a good idea to reach out to him and see what he had going on. Joc called and found out that he had a studio and got the location so we could shoot over there and let him hear some more of our music.

Eric had a rented space in an office building off of Cheshire Bridge Road, where a few other people rented studio space. One dude who had a spot there went by the name of Tom Cat. He was the engineer who'd help develop the artist Big Gee from Boys 'N Da Hood. Me, Joc and Shawty Slick all went over there together. We let Eric hear some of Joc and Slick's songs, and he liked what we had and was really feeling Slick's hardcore street lyrics. He told us that we could use his studio anytime we wanted and asked me if I had an entertainment lawyer.

I thought about what Jazze Pha had done. "Na, but that's somethin' I need to look into."

"You really need one in this game," he told me. "I got this cat I'd like to introduce you to named John Christmas. He's a young black dude who really knows the biz."

I told him I was down with it and after a little more of choppin' it up, we left to get back to work.

I hadn't been out just to party in a while. Every time I did hit the clubs, it was to promote one of our songs. I had been hearing on the radio that Jermaine Dupree was celebrating his B-Day at various clubs and strip clubs all week. It was on that Thursday that I decided to call Nitti and see where they were hitting that night and he told me a place called Jazzy T's off of Columbia Drive. I told him to expect me to be in the building. That night, I got dressed and went out. When I got there, the girls who worked at the club catered to JD and all of us who came to party with him.

The next day I called up Nitti. "Man, I'm on my way to Miami," he explained. "You need to fly down here; it's goin' down! JD's keeping it going, partying tonight and Saturday."

I'd heard Jermaine was taking his bash to Miami. "Damn Nitti, I wanna come but I gotta see…"

He cut me off: "Boy, you ain't gon' do shit. Man it's red carpet VIP only, and I can get you on the list. Ain't shit to do in the city anyway. Plus, we could do some networking."

I listened and soon agreed. I'd already done my share of partying and I didn't want to get too caught up in that. But his reference to networking would make the trip worth it. It was a no brainer that A-list celebrities would be down in South Beach for the event.

I hollered at my girl, who was off that day, and told her I needed her to go online and get me a plane ticket, for the next flight out to Miami. She was upset, saying I was always partying and she never got to do nothing. I blew it off because I needed to rub elbows with the people who were where I was headed to. But despite her concerns, she did what I asked and when the time came, she dropped me off at the airport with me not putting too much thought into her worries. She'd just have to learn to understand that this was what it was going to take for us to become successful.

I arrived in Miami late that Friday evening and caught a cab to the Lowes Hotel, where Nitti was staying. I got a suite, changed my clothes and got up with Nitti. He was with a promoter at So So Def named Kadefay and some more of the label's employees. JD had a niece named Tearis, who was with them as well. She's a pretty, young chick with a caramel complexion who also worked for the label. We were all together, riding comfortably in this So So Def wrapped van bending corners up and down Ocean Drive, Collins, and Washington Ave., kicking it.

We bent a couple more blocks and soon we pulled up to Bow Wow and his peeps. When we stopped to pick him up, I was sitting in the seat next to the sliding side door. I snatched it open and saw a startled look on his face.

"Who are you?" he said arrogantly trying to hide his fear.

Gritting my gold teeth I said, "Im'a gangsta!"

Kadefay laughed. "Get in nigga! That's Ms. B's folks, Chauncey."

We started laughing as Bow Wow and his crew jumped in. We kicked it until it was late, riding around and having a good time while listening to the numerous hits So So Def had released that I'd forgotten about. At about 9 p.m. we all hit our hotels to get dressed for the VIP party. Kadefay came back and picked me and Nitti up from Lowe's, and we went to the club. When we arrived, JD's mother, Ms. Tina, was out at the front entrance. I had met her a couple of times at the So So Def office in Atlanta. Ms. Tina was on the long red carpet that led up the sidewalk and into the club. Photographers lined the red carpet snapping pictures. We made our way to the desk at the door, where a woman asked for our names while referring to a guest list. Several big-named basketball and football players were unable to get in, along with a couple of well-known rappers as well. Money couldn't buy admittance to this event, but I didn't have to worry about it. I got my VIP wristband with the others, which gave us access into JD's private VIP section, next to the dance floor.

By the looks of things, it was going to be live. And like Nitti said, a lot of well-known top executives were in the house. I found myself glad that I did fly out.

Now, JD's section wasn't really that big. It was in the upper-left-hand corner of the club. The DJ booth was by us as well. A big wrap around sofa covered the whole section. Me and Nitti stood up on the end of the right side of the sofa, next to the dance floor.

"This shit is live ain't it," Nitti said to me as we sipped on Patron.

My eyes were on Janet Jackson, who was standing in the middle of the sofa. She was standing behind JD as he spoke to some of the people who had walked up to him. "Yeah, it's poppin'," I replied. Something about Janet intrigued me.

"Ayo," came Nitti. "Is it me or does Janet Jackson keep looking over here at us?"

I realized then that that's what was bothering me. I thought I saw the same thing. "Man, I'm not sure but it seems like it."

Or maybe it was the Patron...

Da Brat, Bow Wow, Shaquille O'Neal and his wife at the time, Shaunie, Paris Hilton and the great Quincy Jones were some of the many celebrities present. During the day, a few things happened to spice up the night. Paris Hilton seemed to upset Janet when she hugged on JD a little too long. I got a chance to speak with Quincy Jones, which was a privilege. Then to our surprise, JD jumped on the turntables and told everybody to get to the dance floor. He put on some old Michael Jackson as he shouted out dedications and jokes to people in the audience. He told Quincy Jones he had to be crazy to produce the shit Michael was singing because it was so good. He also hollered at me, saying he was watching me because I was on the floor grooving with his niece Tearis.

During the night, I got a chance to meet some executives and producers I might need to know later on. All in all, I had a good time, but I wish I could have gotten to Paris before Janet ran her off.

The next morning, Nitti showed up at my door. "Get dressed. Let's hit the city."

I ordered room service and got some breakfast. After we ate, we hit Ocean Drive and had some drinks at Wet Willie's before getting with Kadefay and Tearis. All four of us went to the horse track and did some betting. None of our horses won but at least we had some fun.

"Tonight is the last party," Nitti said to me as we went back to the hotel to get ready. "Ain't you glad you came?"

I couldn't deny it. "Yeah, man."

I mean, everything is going smooth with my team, and soon this will be all day, every day.

But right now I had to remind myself that this trip wasn't just a social one, but for business also. Yes, I was there to kick it for JD's birthday, but I was also trying to acquaint myself with others in the business.

That night me and Nitti got fresh from head to toe and set out to the next club where JD's party would be held. This event was open to the public and when we got there, everything was in full effect. Everyone and more from the last party showed up. This time, those same athletes and stars that weren't on the guest list the night before, were there. The club was filled with big-named entertainers and everywhere you looked, you could see the sparkle of diamonds twinkling off of earlobes and platinum encrusted necklaces.

Nitti leaned over to me at our table. "Check out'cha boy Bow Wow."

I looked and saw the young star heading toward us, flossing with three chicks about my age on his arms. All of them were bad as hell! Smiling I said, "Fa sho, that lil' nigga gonna have a ball tonight."

Nitti agreed.

A few females that we had met coming into the club, found their way to our table. Nitti was his usual self as he accommodated them. This cute Puerto Rican-looking girl found a seat next to me. We began conversating and she told me she was a radio DJ. Then she began asking me all types of questions. I kept it cordial, watching as her eyes kept shifting from my platinum chain to my platinum bracelet.

"So, what do you do?" she asked.

"Ah, nothing special," I began, "I'm working at Wal-Mart right now. But that's only temporary."

The smile on her face immediately faded.

"Hey y'all! What's up?"

Quickly me and Nitti turned around to see who it was calling out to us. When we looked, we saw it was none other than Da Brat and Trina, the 'Baddest Bitch' in the M.I.A. with another one of her friends. "Yo, what's up," we responded.

The girls who had been sitting with us instantly got up from the table. The way Trina and Brat walked up was like we already had previous plans. Their demeanor said, "Y'all bitches need to leave!"

"Have a seat," Nitti said to them.

Da Brat looked at me and said, "Chino, what you up to?"

I winked. "You already know." You see, Da Brat had been in the A so long that we all looked at her like our own . . . which she was. We were a little acquainted and it was always good to see her. And though many know how beautiful she is from seeing her on television, seeing her in person is like a trillion times better. Da Brat is superfine. Thick, flawless skin and an angelic face obviously getting better over the years.

I turned and looked at Trina as Brat introduced us. In my greeting, I informed her it was good to see her out.

"You know I couldn't miss out," she said smiling. "A party in Miami ain't a party 'less I'm in it."

I had met Trina once before, at a show we promoted in Athens when I was at Underground Sound. I knew she didn't remember so I went along with their introduction. She was cool as hell and very down to earth. All of us ended up chilling out together, enjoying the party. I had some weed I'd gotten from a friend of mine earlier, so me, Brat and Trina lit up and smoked even though neither of us really smoked. It was funny because the green wasn't shit but we weren't tripping. We were all just having a good time.

The party was live; JD showed up and thanked everybody for coming out. The DJ kept it crunk all night and there was never a dull moment. Nitti had caught back up with the chicks that were at our table earlier and told me they wanted to kick it. Then Da Brat approached me about chilling out with her and Trina afterwards. I told Nitti I was cool and that I was going to chill with Brat and Trina and that I would catch back up with him in the morning. And for the rest of the night, I kicked it with two of the finest ladies in the game, feeling like a king. We got drunk and sometime around 4 a.m., I parted ways with them even though they invited me to their hotel. I kept telling myself to stay focused on why I came...

But not going with them was probably the hardest decision I'd ever had to make in my life.

The next morning I woke up with a hangover. I grabbed my cell phone and hit Nitti.

"Man Chino, I'm already on the road back to Atlanta," he told me.

"Damn already." I looked at my watch on the dresser: 1:23 p.m.

"I tried to call you," he said. "I had to go and meet JD early this morning at Michael Jackson's house. That's where him and Janet stayed all weekend. When I left I just jumped right on the expressway."

I rubbed my eyes and sat up to clear my head. "All right, well my flight is scheduled to leave around 4 o'clock so I'll see you in the A."

"Cool," he responded. Then he asked. "Yo, what happened with Brat and Trina? Did you…"

"Man, you trippin'," I said cutting him off. He just laughed as I told him I needed to get myself together and that I would rap with him later.

After I showered and packed my things, I called my girl and told her to pick me up at the airport around 5, giving an hour for the flight. But it was just my luck that one of the biggest hurricanes ever was planned to hit Miami that evening, cancelling all flights. After doing like the rest of the people in the airport, sleeping on the floor for a couple of hours waiting to see if flights would resume, I went and rented a room for the next two days before I could get another flight. But when the weather finally cleared, I got my things and headed home.

"Hmmph, bet'cha had a good time," my girl said upon my arrival at the airport.

As soon as I got in the car I could sense her attitude. "It was cool," I said, tired and ready to go home and sleep in my bed.

She smacked her teeth, "Cool, hmmph. I bet."

I did my best to pay her no attention as she went into all sorts of allegations. She even went to the extent of charging me with "fuckin' wit' groupie bitches." Now here I was, trying to make shit pop; a little ol' dope boy from Atlanta rubbing elbows with Janet Jackson, Quincy Jones, and Paris Hilton, trying to put my hustle down in the music business. Thoughts of Da Brat and Trina, and my decision to spend the rest of that night alone, came to me. And here she was accusing me! Didn't I explain my dream to her?

I just shook my head. I'll be on top in no time, I told myself as she kept on fussing. I thought about all those people I got a chance to meet. Once I have a valid reason to deal with them, I'll call and holla, I thought. But right now, I'm not ready.

And as I rode home, I let my imagination take me to a place where accusations and constant nagging were obsolete. I was too busy being thankful than to let my girl's insecurities bring me down.

Keep On Pushing

When we got back from Miami, Brandy was scheduled to have a photo shoot at this salon out in Buckhead. I was determined to consume myself in work, in order to bring my vision to life. My girl was beginning to irritate me with all of her interrogating questions. Working seemed to be my only refuge. So when Nitti told me about the shoot I took some time to go and support B.

It was late when I arrived. Brandy and Nitti were already there, along with three others. Brandy was almost finished with her poses as a professional cameraman snapped off shots of her at different angles. After about an hour or so, Nitti's manager, Ian Burke, showed up with a stack of vinyl records in white sleeved jackets with the Bad Boy logo in blue all over them.

Giving Nitti the stack he said, "They finally got the single for 'Dem Boy's' printed up. Here's a few."

As Nitti handed me one he asked Ian, "Did they put my stamp on the intro?"

Ian shook his head. "Nah."

Immediately Nitti's whole demeanor changed to being upset. You see, Nitti had created his own signature for the beats he made. At the beginning of each of his tracks, he inserted an innocent sounding childlike voice which would say, "This 'ah Nitti beat", letting everyone know he was the creator. Having the song blowing up was great promotion for him. But to have it as a single, backed by a powerhouse like Bad Boy and to not have his stamp on it would rob him of having the world know he made it.

Upset, he asked, "What can we do about it?"

"Nothing," Ian told him. "You see, we didn't have it stipulated in the producer agreement. So technically, they've done nothing wrong."

When the photo shoot was finished, we left and Nitti parked his white 4-door Dodge sedan at Ian's office so he could ride with me. We went out to kick it for the night so he could get his mind off of what had occurred. Nitti told me it was fucked up that they pulled that shit and Ian should have been on top of it. Then he asked what I thought.

"I think you and Ian got blindsided. Who would've expected you would have to put specifics about a tag in a contract? But I know Ian knows his shit," I explained. "If there was something he could do he'd tell you."

Ian was old school. He'd formed the group TLC and managed Organized Noize and OutKast, so it was no doubt he was on point. Now he ran ASCAP administration in Atlanta for the members in the Southeast Region and by him being Nitti's manager, I knew he wasn't going to let my boy get misused.

Nitti knew it too. "Damn man. From now on I gotta make sure I have that shit in my agreements."

I agreed and knew he had learned a valuable lesson. Nitti was doing the best he knew how to do as far as running his company and dealing with his artists. He would attend most of Brandy's shows and functions. One particular night Brandy had a show lined up at The Eastside Bounce, out in Decatur. Me, Joc, Nitti and our crew caravanned out there. And it was there that Nitti ran into some more drama.

The door people had us all lined up at the VIP entrance. We were being pat searched and Nitti was up next. That's when Ziggi, from Nitti's old group, The Slick Boys, came from out the club and onto the foyer.

"Yeah nigga," he said, with his face twisted up in a mean mug. "You betta not come into the club. If you do it's gonna be problems!"

Nitti immediately stepped back and I stepped out of line with him.

"What's up?" I asked.

I could see he was wrestling with himself. "Man I ain't goin' inside."

I was looking into his eyes trying to see if I saw any fear.

"Chino, I ain't try'na kill that nigga," he said. "Ya feel me?"

I had to think. Nitti stayed strapped with his 9mm, all the time. Even in the club. I concluded that he was both scared and serious. And you know what they say, "a scary nigga will kill you." He said he didn't want to ruin Brandy's show with all this drama. I understood and told him not to trip.

So Nitti left and I went inside. As soon as I got in, Ziggi pulled me to the side.

"Yo Chino, I ain't got no problems wit'cha Shawty. You's a real nigga," he said. "But Nitti on some BS and he knows it. That nigga owe me and my boys."

I've always been the type to stay out of other people's business. I had heard Nitti's side and I understood how Ziggi and his crew felt. But it wasn't my place to get involved.

"Y'all just need to work things out," I said casually. "But for right now, let's just chill out."

He just nodded. "A'ight Shawty."

I gave him a few parting words and found my way to where Joc and our crew was. I didn't mention my conversation with Ziggi. There was no need in bringing all that negative energy into our circle. We just didn't need it.

$$\$\$\$$$

Time was flying and I was trying not to let a day go by wasted. Both Joc and I were still grinding, doing open mic shows on and off. Some Wednesdays, him and Shawty Slick would do "Nan Nudda Pimp" at The Peacock. We had really been hitting spots but didn't have much going on. And Joc hadn't won a contest up to that point. But I had to stay positive because I knew success only came after much struggling.

During this time, Nitti didn't have a place to work out of. I mean, he had worked it out with Ian where he could put a studio in the back of his office, at the ASCAP building, but that was under construction. And being that he himself stayed all the way out in Stone Mountain, Nitti began to chill out at my place a lot, working on shit when no one was there. The basement was a perfect hangout for him, with its full bathroom, living room set and TV. It was almost like a bachelor's pad.

Well one morning, after we had been out all night, Nitti woke up early and was knocking out a couple of tracks. I woke up and went down there and he began asking me how to dump the tracks he had made into the Pro Tools as stereo tracks, by using the M Box. He wasn't used to the cheap ass M Box and it only offered 2 inputs, one for equipment and one for a mic. He was used to the Digi 002 Pro Tools controllers. So I rigged up the cables and ran a left and right from the equipment into the Mac keyboard and then into both channels of the M Box and tracked the beats in stereo. Elvis and Flame had taught me how to work my way around everything so it was coming in handy.

When I was done tracking the beats, I started an 808 drum pattern.

"I like that," he said all of a sudden. "Let me see something."

Nitti got up and started messing with it. But after two more sounds, we got stuck. That's when I started to track it in.

"You like that shit?" he asked.

"Yeah," I said.

"Well go ahead and put everything in my external drive and I'll see what I can do with it later," he said rubbing his chin. "It needs something. It's too plain."

By this time it was after lunch. Nitti told me how Boys 'N Da Hood were doing their photo shoot that day and asked if I wanted to go down there.

"I wanna holla at Block about some business," he explained.

I was down so I told him let's roll. We wrapped everything up we were doing, jumped in my truck, and called Block to get the location.

Big Block told Nitti that they had indeed already started and were at the corner off Boulevard and Memorial Drive. So we shot down there, making it just in time to see Jody Breez, Duke, Jeezy and Big Gee posing for the flick that ended up being their album cover. As soon as we jumped out, we started greeting everyone. That's when me, Nitti and Block started talking.

Nitti told Block, "Look, we need to join up, and I'll be the production company for the group. And we do some splits on the credits."

Block busted back saying: "Nah, nah. We gon' do it like we been doing it! You gon' make the beats and I'm gon' come wit' the money and buy 'em. And that's it. Ain't nothin' else to talk about."

I looked at Nitti who had this crazy, perplexed expression on his face. He tried to reason for a moment with Block but when he saw it wasn't going anywhere he just cut it short. We left that day with him making no progress. On the ride back I analyzed both sides. I knew Block was looking at it as business, just like Nitti saw an opportunity and tried to get in.

But hey . . . that's just how it goes sometimes in the game.

The nightlife in Atlanta was getting out of control. One incident hit close to home when my partner Larry, aka Bodybag, and three others got shot at club Atrium. Larry was in our goon squad and also produced tracks. Anyway, on October 12, 2004 when he was working as security at the Atrium, an incident occurred where two members of the B.M.F. allegedly shot up the club, leaving Larry injured. Afterwards, he said that some cats from the crew came up to the hospital and offered him $10,000 not to say anything to the police. He assured them that either way, he had no intentions on doing any talking.

And like Bodybag, I had my own problems. Despite staying focused and showing my girl how serious I was, it still wasn't enough to stop her from tripping. Here I was, juggling trying to blow up my label and be a provider and father. On the weekends, I would have my three kids and sometimes during the week. Then I'd have her son who had come home from his grandparent's in San Antonio, Texas. I made sure I spent time with her on her days off, taking her on shopping sprees in New York, nights out on the town in Atlanta.

See, I didn't believe in taking my girl around the game or the music biz. As far as the game, what she didn't see she couldn't tell and the body snatchers couldn't kidnap who they didn't see. I didn't take her all out to the club with me while I was promoting or to the studio when we went to record. Plus I knew she'd be like, 'Let's go…I'm tired.' I knew she didn't understand. To me that wasn't her place. It was mine, as being aspects of my job description. How couldn't she see this? Elvis, Chris and Joc all had girls who never hounded them when they stayed at my spot working all night. But every time I stayed out, my girl would blow my phone up. And this was beginning to bother me. Why?

Because out of all the time I could've FUCKED not one, not two, but three to four bitches at a time, I didn't. Why? Because I had her.

Shit was getting out of control. It was getting to the point where a girl could say "hi" to me in the grocery store, someone I knew from elementary school, and she'd accuse me of fucking her.

The shit was crazy and I was doing my best to find a reasonable solution for it. The holidays were coming so I told myself I'd set some time out for her and the family, to show her that I loved her and use that time to explain my vision again. Maybe she needed reassurance, I told myself. I was looking to fix what I had before it got too bad.

Staying on our grind, I had lined up a show for Joc in Athens and the time had come for him to perform. One of my partners named Blackout, who was in this group called DSGB (Down South Georgia Boys) with Pastor Troy, had fallen out with Troy and he asked if he could roll with us. He also needed a place to record. Blackout had his own style. He was 5'8", medium build, dark-skinned with dreadlocks and wore black finger nail polish and shit. He looked like a real live devil worshiper. A native of College Park, Blackout was really unorthodox, but I knew the industry had love for him.

That night we all rolled out to Athens. We also had a new song. Joc recorded one of Chris' beats called "Come and See It For Yo Self". It wasn't mixed or mastered but it had a clear enough sound to perform. So we hit Athens; everyone dressed in all black. Slick did some songs, him and Joc did "Nan Nudda" and then Joc did "Come See It For Yo Self". We rocked the spot and were leaving on cloud nine when one of my partners Wayne tried some super goofy shit with Joc's wife.

Now it's one thing to have a cat holla at your girl and he didn't know she was taken but it's another to have him do it and after being told she got a man he insists on being disrespectful. Well this is what ol' boy did and in the end, it caused a small commotion. Me being a true boss, I had to quickly resolve the situation before things got out of control. So I told Wayne to chill and control his guys because we'd gotten too much money together for shit to jump off over some dumb shit. Niggas not involved got to screaming at me.

"Chino, man, don't bring dem niggas down here no mo!"

I quickly told them sideline niggas: "I do what I want when I want to." As soon as I said this I just got my crew together and we dipped. I didn't want nothing major poppin' off.

I knew Athens could get real crazy for out-of-towners. A few years prior, one of my big homeboys Suge had made MTV News for stabbing a white rapper from Tennessee named Hay Stack who had come to do a show with Bubba. I had to break that shit up before blood was shed. I didn't need this happening to anyone in my camp. But it was a good lesson for Joc. Now he'd understand why I didn't like bringing my girl with me when I was working.

Outside of doing shows, we were still going hard in the studio and had recorded a good number of songs. But I didn't feel we had that right song yet. That's when Joc and Elvis dropped this banger called "Heart Attack".

Elvis had the beat sounding like the Neptunes produced it and we did our usual routine, jamming to it right there in the basement. We started playing with the hook and we came up with the Heart Attack concept saying "Ooh, ooh, she's havin' a heart attack" and some more shit about how a playa be so fresh that when a chick see him she be about to have a heart attack. After playing with it for a while Elvis jumped on the mic and sung the hook on some Pharrell-type shit. Afterwards, we listened to it, jamming, and came up with a dance where we put one hand over our heart like Fred Sanford did when he said, 'It's the big one, I'm coming to join ya honey.'

And that was that. We had done it again. Some crazy shit that was bangin' like a muthafucka!

Somewhere along the way me and Joc got into a conversation about Carolyn Miller and how she almost had a heart attack when she saw this rat crawling on the floor when they camped at her mother's house in Memphis.

Elvis lit up. "Carolyn? Man I know her."

Joc began to explain how he had been messing with her and during the process both him and Elvis realized that they had met before, when Elvis rode back from Memphis to Atlanta with them. It was crazy how we all had crossed her path and were now together ourselves.

So the song "Heart Attack" came out good and of course I went through my same routine. By now my man Ralph at Doppler Studios was waiting until late for us to bring in our work, as we did piece-by-piece enjoying working with us. I then took it to Kenny for finishing touches.

To test out our new recording, me and Joc went up to a strip club called Babes, where my man DJ Cloud worked. He loved Joc's stuff. It was close to Thanksgiving so the club had a pretty good crowd. Cloud put "Heart Attack" on and the crowd started nodding to it.

"Yeah," he told us, "I'm feelin' this."

Me and Joc smiled at each other as we did the little two step Fred Sanford on the low. I could see a video concept clearly in my mind.

When it was finished, Cloud announced to the crowd: "I got some more new shit fa y'all."

That was our only song so I watched curiously as he inserted another CD into the CD player. When the track came on, it sounded kind of weird so I asked him, "Who is this?"

"Dem Boys D4L. Ya know, Fabo and them from Bowen Homes. It's called Laffy Taffy."

I ain't gonna lie, by the time the hook came in I thought it was a joke. But then I looked out at the crowd and saw everybody bobbing their heads.

"It seems I got two bangers tonight," Cloud said.

And by the looks of it, he was right. From an executive's standpoint, I knew the people made a hit a "Hit."

Damn, I thought, looking at how they responded to D4L's song. You never know what could blow. You just never know.

One night out, I bumped into my man Lil Will and Sunny

Valentine. Will told me how he was bringing Sunny by my spot to check out some beats. Although they knew I was on my hustle, word was getting around that I had something good going on over at my studio. They had heard I had a production crew making that heat. For them to seek me out, while knowing Mr. DJ and all the others in the city who were certified platinum producers, told me something.

By late '04 the song Will did with Gucci, "So Icy," was blowing up Atlanta's radio stations. Will had been in negotiations with C.T.E. to sign as an artist. And being that Jeezy featured on "So Icy," he would have

It's Business

The new year started off good. It was the top of '05 and we had big plans. Me and Joc were still hitting open mics, just trying to do what we felt would help our grind. In between working in the studio we kept it as part of our routine for two reasons: (1) So Joc could work on his showmanship and (2) So we could get some exposure for his music.

One particular night me and him hit up J-Paul's. DJ Ace was doing open mic night and the contest was supposed to be fierce. Like I said, up to this point, Joc hadn't won any so me and him both kinda had chips on our shoulders. We arrived at the club and Joc partook in the normal routines of adding himself to the group of MCs before finally it was his time to perform.

Even though Jazze Pha did what he did, Joc still would do "Thousand Ones" from time to time, which was what he did. Every time he did it he got better with it, adding more stage presence than the last time. Taking the stage tonight, he flowed through his verses, bobbing to the music. When it was over, he received a hefty applause from the audience. My boy rocked the house.

After Joc, a few more artists hit the stage and did their thing. But it was one in particular who stood above the rest, getting an identical response from the crowd as Joc. In the end it was determined that both

Joc and this cat had been a tie and so the host of the event ordered them to a rap off right there on the spot.

Ol' boy went first. He clutched his mic and, flowing to a track provided by the DJ, spit slick rap bars not only aimed at Joc, but at the judges for considering them a tie. He got "ooh's and ahs" from the crowd and, to be honest, I didn't know how my boy was going to hold up.

When the dude was finished, the DJ put another track on, signaling Joc's turn. Joc looked at the DJ and signaled for him to kill the beat. Then with a cool, calm demeanor he found a stool that had been sitting unnoticed on the stage and pulled it up in front of his competitor. Taking a seat before him, Joc lifted the mic close to his mouth, so that the crowd could hear every word he spoke. From his clothes, to his fake jewels and to his almost missed busted shoes, Joc pointed out all the things wrong with his opponent. The cat said he was ballin', Joc crushed that. He said he was in the trap, Joc questioned his money based upon his appearance. And as far as them being a tie . . . Joc's lyrical flow and content clearly excelled. And when he was done, the crowd made it official.

Joc had murdered the man.

After it was over, me and Joc sat in the club celebrating and getting fucked up.

"You did your thing," I told him. "I never heard you bust that one before."

He smiled, "I freestyled it. Just went in."

I had heard him come off the head a few times but for him to do it without a flaw to win a contest was impressive. The boy had skills. I was glad he won and for me it was confirmation that we were on to something great.

It was around 2 a.m. when we finally made it back to my house. To my surprise, my girl hadn't been up waiting to curse me out. I was so glad, because I was drunk and didn't feel like arguing. I climbed the stairs stumbling, taking my clothes off along the way. I was so tired that as soon as I hit the bed I was out. Then . . .

The sun hung high in the sky on a wonderful afternoon. A flock of birds flew together in the distance as I looked around, taking in the outdoor scenery. I was nervous, confused and trying to figure out what was going on. My surroundings were familiar to me, but yet I couldn't figure out how I'd gotten there. Somehow, through space and time, I found myself standing out on Spring Valley Road, in Athens. The street I grew up on as a child.

"Chauncey . . . Chauncey!"

The voice calling sounded familiar as well, causing me to turn toward it. As I did my eyes fell on the home I was raised in with my granny. A home I had grown to love, which held so many memories.

"Chauncey, boy, come inside," the voice called again. It was my granny calling from behind the screen door.

"Here I come granny," I heard myself holler back as I made my way to the house.

The sound of laughter came from my right. I turned and looked only to see two faces I had not seen in years. My two childhood friends Peter Hubbard and Carlos Long. Both restored at an age between ten and fifteen.

"Boy, yo' grandma gon' whoop yo ass!" Peter called out.

Carlos just laughed. "Yeah, wit' a big ol stick!"

I could feel the excitement and fear at the same time. The thought of their suicides somehow invaded the reality I was in. I took in the smiles on their faces while saying nothing in return. They just kept laughing before turning and walking off down the street.

I'll see y'all later, I thought to myself. Not knowing when, but knowing I would.

As quick as I could, I made it across the street and on to the house. I opened the screen door with an eerie feeling overcoming me. With my eyes locked forward, I took in the scenery of my grandmother's home as I stepped inside.

"Chauncey baby, come here." As soon as I heard her voice, I looked and saw her seated comfortably in her rocking chair. A floodgate of emotions opened up inside of me as I watched her face smile upon me. "Come sit next to your granny."

Without saying a word, I let the door close behind me before I made my way next to her. For some reason I couldn't find my voice as I wanted badly to tell her how much I loved her. But instead, all I could do was sit with my hands folded in my lap.

"Baby," she said with care and concern, looking me directly in my eyes, "you know I love you and I would never tell you anything wrong."

I nodded my head.

"Chauncey," she continued, "I didn't raise you to be running 'round in the streets like you've been doing. You ain't no man, selling them drugs and destroying your people . . ."

Her face turned soft and compassionate before me. I knew that she was not pleased.

". . . I didn't raise you to be like that. I raised you to be a real man! How do you expect me to rest in peace knowing you're still in dem' streets?" she asked.

My eyes shot open with my heart pounding in my chest. I looked around expecting my granny to be standing somewhere near me. My temperature was high as sweat covered my body. Visual images of Joc rapping against dude, Peter and Carlos, and the home of my grandmother flashed through my mind's eye. Then, realizing I was in bed, I quickly turned my head and looked at my clock which illuminated its red digital numbers in my dark room.

5:02 a.m.

It was just a dream.

I sat up, with my girl next to me still fast asleep. My mind was racing over the meaning of the dream and my grandmother's words to me. Questions then began shooting through my head as I began to question myself and my intentions, in regards to my life. Why was I still hustling? Was I afraid to let go of the game? And if so, did this mean I didn't fully trust in my vision for the music? My thoughts went back to boot camp and how terrible a time that was. Peter and Carlos came to mind, then Shane. I sat in bed thinking of the comfort I lived in, but how also it could easily be snatched from me at any given moment.

These thoughts consumed me for the rest of the morning, causing me not to return to sleep. I was so moved by my dream, and how real it felt, that I challenged myself to make a definite decision between the streets and the music business.

In the end, I chose the music.

To solidify my decision I called the two people I was dealing with and told them to meet me at my partna Reece's spot in Buckhead. I'd been supplying only these two for some time. Once I got them together I told them I was out of the game. Of course they didn't take me seriously. But when I fronted them the 200 pounds of mid-grade weed I had left, they knew I was serious.

"So you out? Just like that cuz?" Reece asked after they left. I knew he couldn't believe I was giving up the sweet move we were bustin' with the Arizona connect. "Yeah, I'm done. From now on it's strictly the music."

I explained all the hustling was over. I told him that I threw the chirp phone away that Hector used to hit us on. Because he was fam, I broke down how I'd been tripping and had accomplished what I'd set out to do streetwise. I was straight. But I confessed to be addicted to the game like a user was, getting high off of the racks of money I was stacking as a dealer. When it was over, Reece understood. I knew he was still skeptical about my real reason for quitting but I made up my mind to keep that a secret. I knew that if I wanted God to bless me, I had to be living my life right. All the way right.

$$$

The guy Joc introduced to me named Eric Miller turned out to be a good connect. From the day we went to his studio and talked, I couldn't stop thinking about how he said I needed an entertainment lawyer. I'd been making plans to get back at him about the dude he'd mentioned. And when I finally called, Eric was more than willing to introduce me to his inside man, John Christmas.

I met John up at this new Phat Burger off Piedmont. It was the first ever in the city of Atlanta. One of his clients who played professional football opened it as a side business venture. When I arrived, I saw the SUV he told me to look for parked in the lot. I parked my truck and jumped in with him.

"John Christmas," he said, flashing a smile and extending his hand.

"Chauncey Stevens", I said, accepting his hand. Something about seeing this relatively young brother up on his business, helped to confirm I was doing the right thing with my own life.

"So, let's get straight to it Chauncey. Eric says you got some good music. Let me hear something."

I wasted no time pulling out our material. He sat there listening and by the time the CD finished he loved it. John then went on to tell me how he was about to retire from his line occupation, but that he liked what we had. He asked me a few questions about what I wanted out of life and I answered them truthfully. I explained how I wanted to make something of not only my life but of those around me as well.

He nodded, agreeing to my response. "You know what, I wanna teach you the biz . . . are you all registered with ASCAP or BMI yet?"

I was familiar with both ASCAP and BMI but I didn't know exactly what they were. I told him how we weren't members yet but that I had printed off the applications online.

"Do you know why you need to register with them?" he asked next.

"Well," I began, "I know the basics: if you're an artist, writer or producer you need to set up a publishing company with one of them, so you can get paid when your song is played on the radio."

He nodded. "Yes. And also anywhere else that your music is heard, including performances. If you plan on rapping or writing, you need a writer's membership and publishing company. Now my retainer fee for you is $2,500; only because of Eric. With that I'll help not only your knowledge of this game, but also your contracts for your artist and producers."

I contemplated his price.

"Listen Chauncey," he continued, "I've worked with a lot of artists. Some local, whom you may know such as Big Block."

"And as big as this entertainment world is, it's really small. There's only a few important players. The rest change all the time. Your longevity depends not only on the quality of music you give to the world, but more so your knowledge of the game. And for some reason, I have a strong compulsion to give you this knowledge. But in the end, it will be up to you. What do you say?"

Sitting across from him, I examined the whole situation and came to my conclusion.

"How do you want that?" I asked. "Cash or check?"

On My Hustle

It had gotten to the point where Joc was staying with me on the regular. One morning I went to my office and found him there, printing out some stick-on labels from this CD designer program we had on the computer. This youngster in my hood named Gabe had drawn a young version of Joc on a tricycle, with shades and jewelry on. He'd given us this picture because he was a fan of Joc's music. We kept it figuring we could use it for something.

"I like that," I said over the sound of the printer spitting out CD covers.

"Yeah," he said consumed in his work. "I figured I'd use it to promote the youngster's talent."

I was admiring the image on the covers while sort of laughing inside. I knew he was doing this because of how bad my handwriting was on the other CDs we had given out to the DJs. As soon as I sat a stack of the covers down, Joc turned away from the printer with the look like something was weighing heavy on his mind.

"Man Chino," he began, "I don't know what I'mah do."

I didn't know what he was talking about so I asked. "What's up?"

He exhaled a long breath. "Shit just fucked up for me right now. I mean, to be honest, I've been crashing over here with my wife and daughter because my aunt told me we had to go. She's complaining saying I ain't never there, neither me or my wife have a job, and how we aren't helping with the bills."

I didn't know what to say.

"Then my 'Lac done broke down again, and I ain't got the money to get it fixed. I would've taken my wife and kid to my father's but the garage I'd turned into a room got flooded so we can't stay there."

I knew he had been bouncing back and forth, between his aunt's and father's spot, until his situation got better but by the sound of things, they were only getting worse.

Joc explained how he was trying to get Brandy to give him a few dollars. He said she had been paying him something like ten percent off her shows, for being her hype man. But he spent that as soon as he got it. He explained how in the beginning she was getting $1,000 to do a show and as time passed she was getting $3,000. He felt she had made a lot by now and should shoot him something for helping to write on her hooks. He told me how he hadn't received anything off her single deal, because it was only for $5,000. And how the lawyer got a piece, Nitti got some even though So So Def paid him separate for his beats, which left only a small piece for her.

"Look dog, y'all stayin' here for a minute ain't nothing," I said when he finished. "So don't let it get to you just stay focused. In the meantime, how much money do you need?"

He shook his head, "Nah Shawty I..."

But I wouldn't hear of it. "Fuck all that how much?"

"About $1,000," Joc said.

And like that, I went in my pocket and peeled off a rack, giving it to him with no hesitation. "Here you go," I told him.

"Chino, I appreciate it."

I just smiled. "I know. It ain't nothing."

Helping Joc in that hard time really boosted his self-esteem and made him that much more hungry for success. We kept recording and hitting up open mics, to keep putting our sound out there. At a few clubs, we bumped into Gucci, and on one of these occasions, I introduced Joc to him. They had met each other in passing but nothing formal. They spoke and before we all parted I told Gucci we needed to get together to do something. We'd been saying we would since we first met over at Mario's house. He agreed, saying it was long overdue.

While everyone was doing their thing, I got with Nitti on various occasions to go up to PatchWork Studios. There we would kick it with Jeezy, his manager coach K and his A&R Shikar Stewart (R.I.P.) from Def Jam. Me and Nitti would go to give them some of our tracks to listen to. Jeezy's first album was highly anticipated at this point and if we could get a few tracks on it then it would help us move forward.

When the top of '05 rolled in Joc, his wife and daughter "officially" moved in with me and my small family. His living situation just got even worse so they took over the guest room in my home. Of course, I wasn't tripping. I knew times were hard for them. And at the time I didn't mind.

My focus was on my team and the music. Between me, Ms. B, Nitti, Elvis, Joc, Flame, and Shawty Slick, we had been doing our best to keep our eyes on the ball. Sunny Valentine had become a regular at the studio. He said he was done messing with Mr. DJ and soon him, Joc, and Slick found themselves coming together in the booth from time to time. As a visionary I saw they had good chemistry and although they were solo artists, I started a group and called them The Wiseguys. I was just trying to approach the game from all different angles.

In February I was still in need of getting all of my business in order. So when John Christmas stopped by my studio to bring the contracts I requested he was right on time.

"So this is where y'all make the magic," he said admiring my set up. "Looks professional."

"Thanks," I replied.

John then got right down to business. Pulling out a manila folder from the briefcase he carried he then removed several sheets of paper and handed them to me. "I've drawn up the artist agreements for Joc and Slick and producer agreements for Elvis and Chris."

"You also mentioned a contract for the group," he continued. "That one is at the back."

I had given him a call a few days prior, telling him about Sunny, Slick, and Joc and their group The Wise Guys. "Yeah, that's good."

John took a seat. "Listen Chauncey," he said in all seriousness, "I'm a member of this black radio coalition and I think you should join in. It will put you in the company and contact of the people who will help you get where you're trying to go."

I was all ears. John spoke more about this coalition. He gave me all the benefits it presented and before he left he gave me the contact information to a lady named Terry, who he said would help me register as a member. John thoroughly convinced me and a couple of days later I called up Terry, got with her to pay the membership fee and joined. To me this was money spent wisely. Instead of splurging 20 racks in the club promoting a song like I'd done the past, I was now investing in ways that benefit my company in the long run. Something I felt comfortable about.

MasterMind music was in full gear. Shawty Slick recorded a song with Chris Flame called "Hey Ma" that he wanted to be a single. Joc was feeling "Heart Attack" so I started looking for someone that duplicated CDs. Nitti told me he had a dude named Terrance who duplicated and made flyers. I went ahead and pressed play for these to be the first two singles I pressed up. And meanwhile get some color flyers done as well.

We got with this guy Terrance and did a small photo shoot for the flyers. Joc wore a casual sky blue button-down dress shirt, some dark blue slacks with dark suspenders. We rented the top floor hotel room in downtown Atlanta because we had this idea to put a skyline behind Joc, and we wanted a live one. Joc posed out on the balcony, with the skyline behind him and got his sessions out of the way. Then along with some of the goon squad we all took a couple flicks all over the hotel.

For Shawty Slick he got his crew of Lil' Derek, Mack, Reid Johnny and some more guys to flick up with him. He went on to take his shots in front of a white 73 Chevy old school donk. He was dressed in all black: black hoodie, black jeans, black leather jacket, black A-town fitted cap with his diamond jewels on. For the design of the flyers we put "Hey Ma" written in yellow along with his name. On Joc's we had "Heart Attack" and his name done in red. After that we topped both off with the MasterMind logo, which I got designed by a guy who did graphics and sprayed T-shirts in the Southlake Mall. I put my contact information on them as well, just in case anyone wanted to get at us.

Networking hard, me and Joc had a homeboy named DJ Dre who was a member of the Legion of Doom DJs. He called up Joc and told him they were having a big showcase and we should sign up. He advised Joc that we go to their office off Old National and meet up with the president of L.O.D., Mr. Ray Hamilton.

We sat in Ray's office as he listened to some of Joc's songs. He really liked what we had. Then he gave us sponsorship packages. For different prices we could do a different number of songs. By MasterMind having two artists I needed the most time possible. So I ended up giving LO.D $1,000, locking in enough time for my crew to do their thing.

When the night of the showcase came, MasterMind music hit the spot deep. All my homeboys and The Goon Squad showed up full-fledged. I hired three girls as backup dancers from this chick I knew who had a dance studio. When the time came Joc performed "Thousand Ones" then him and Shawty Slick did "Nan Nudda Pimp". After that, Slick did "Hey Ma" and Joc closed it out with "Heart Attack", while Elvis took the liberty to sing the hook.

Their performance was a blast. Tables were set around the club with all the artist's music and flyers on them. When we got off the stage, all the DJs came up to us if we had any more copies of the singles, because they were all gone off the tables. So we gave them the rest of the CDs we had of Joc and Slick's music which was about 1,000 copies. After the L.O.D. showcase all the DJs in the crew knew exactly who MasterMind Music was.

With the rest of the CDs and flyers we didn't give away at the showcase we flooded every open mic in the city. One night at the Ritz on Old National Joc hit the stage and killed everybody. He had took the time to make his own show CD so on this night he came out and performed "Thousand Ones" in some jeans, a hoodie and a fitted cap. He had the crowd rocking after the first hook. Then a "Boom" sounded off like an explosion. Then you heard a sound like a door slamming. Then sounds of clothes stripping off came. The whole time Joc acted in sequence with the sounds, taking the liberty to remove his pants, hoodie, and hat, leaving him standing before the crowd in some slacks, a dress shirt, and tie. Then "Heart Attack" came on, causing the crowd to go crazy!

I knew he was a star before, but after that performance I was for sure we were on to something.

Nitti and I were working hard on making something happen on our own ends. I called him one day and explained that I wanted to buy some beats. So he came through the studio and played some tracks for me. Ironically one of the tracks so happened to be the beat me and him started the morning we went out to speak to Block, at the Boyz 'N Da Hood photo shoot. Nitti hadn't really done much more to the track, other than add a sound or two. Neither here nor there I told him I wanted it. I needed four tracks: two for Joc and two for Slick. He told me to give him five grand for them then he made me a copy on a CD.

With the beats I bought I gave a copy to Joc and Slick. Joc ended up picking the track I helped make while Slick picked another. I got with Nitti and let him know which ones we liked, but also told him we wanted to hear more. I didn't say anything about me doing half of the track for Joc because I wanted to see how he planned on playing it. Nitti was my boy so I knew he knew what time it was.

So, Joc went on and wrote to the beat. He made a song for him and a girl. Just messing around and having fun we involved our girls to help us record part of the hook until Brandy could come and do it herself.

The hook went something like: "Left my girl at the house/ tonight I'mma ball out. . . " Then the girls came in: "Left my man at the house/tonight I'mma ball out. . . " and so on.

This was basically the concept: You left your significant other and stepped out to have yourself a really good time. It had a catchy melody and sounded like it was going to turn into something. When Nitti finally came back through, we let him hear it and I ended up giving him a copy. Although it was a rough draft, he could hear what we were working with: Another possible single for Joc.

Me and all of my crew: Joc, Slick, Sunny, Elvis, Chris, and Ms. B, stayed grinding hard in the studio. During those times we would fantasize about how it was going to be when we made it. How we would hit the award shows, what we would wear, the fame, fun and benefits of finally getting to the top. It was a vision we had all come to want badly. One we all believed in.

Because me and Joc stayed together, and were always hitting up clubs to get our music played we would have these talks as well, just one on one.

One day he told me, "I'mma make sure we all get rich one day Chino. And no matter what, you ain't gonna have to worry about shit."

His words told me that he really appreciated all I had done for him. And whether or not we did make it, his appreciation made it all worth it.

Back In The Game

Being involved in the underground scene kept me up on all of the moves that other people were making in the city. Like John Christmas told me, players in the game change all the time. And for some, trying to stay in the game and keep the hustle going was just as important for them now, as it was when they got started.

One player who was trying to reestablish himself was my boy Bubba. When I heard he had cut his ties with Mr. DJ over at Camp David and signed with Big Boi's label, Purple Ribbon, I was glad to see him still in the mix. But I hated the fact that he dipped out on Mr. DJ after all the hard work he put into trying to bring Bubba back. Bubba had it in him and I knew as long as he stayed focused and left the dope alone he could get back some of his original status.

Now while I was doing my thing on the music end, I found myself thinking about all the bills I had to pay. Car notes, insurance, day care, child support on my children and not to mention the mortgage and the living expenses for everyone who was living with me. My girl had a job but that money only went so far. I mean, I had money saved up but because I wasn't hustling anymore, I didn't want to blow what I had before we made things pop off with the music.

My girl had started to really get into her feelings. "I mean, what are they gonna do?" She asked about Joc and his wife. "They ain't try'na get no job?"

My girl would start complaining to me about them staying with us and it was really getting on my nerves. She was saying how she didn't have any privacy any more. How she couldn't walk around naked after I wore that ass out and how they were eating up all of the food she was buying. She also complained about how they made her part of the bills more than she could afford. She was even tripping that she couldn't sleep in because not only would I wake her with my sinuses when I woke up but Joc also did. She acted like she didn't see that they were having problems. But to satisfy her concerns I promised I'd talk to Joc, to see what their plans were. It quieted her for the moment, which was good for me.

One day my cousin Reece came by my spot and told me how he was having some problems. Since I had backed up from the game he had continued on doing his thing, moving shipments of mid-grade from Arizona.

"So what happened?" I asked.

"Man," he began, shaking his head as he sat with a long, drawn look on his face. "One of the shipments got jammed up and now I'm short on what I need to make another move."

"Damn, it's that bad?"

"Yeah," he confirmed, "and it's crazy too because I just got this new plug on that exotic shit. That Purp and that Kush. That shit that be bringing in that real paper."

I had heard about how Purp and Kush took over as the main choice in the streets. The market for it had grown to the point where if you wasn't selling it then you really wasn't making any money.

"So look 'cuz," he said, rubbing his hands together. "I came because I need you, for real. Now I know you done wit' the game but I gotta proposition for you."

"You put up the money and I'll do all the work. You don't have to do shit and you'll bring back a few hundred grand if you fuck wit' me."

He had my attention. "Run the numbers to me!"

Reece broke it down like this: $3,200 for a pound including shipping. In Atlanta he'd get $6,000 which was $2,800 profit. The catch was in order to get it at $3,200 a pound he needed to buy at least 100 pounds which is why he needed me. He only had enough money to buy 30 pounds because of the loss he took.

"So you need me to cover the other seventy?" I asked.

He read my mind. "Yeah 'cuz. And I know that's a lot of paper but I'm telling you. . . straight up, it's worth it."

That was $224,000! Even though I had it, the amount was a lot for me to be gambling with at that point in time. I thought about it and saw how I really wasn't reneging on my vow to leave the game alone. It wouldn't be me, but Reece who was doing the hustling.

I sat there thinking while my dude waited patiently. Then, convinced that it was the right thing to do, I agreed. "All right," I told him. "I'll give you a call in the morning. Then you can come by to get the money."

Reece was happy. "Good lookin' cuzzo," Reece said. "I'm tellin' you, Imm'ah make it happen for us."

He better, if not, Imm'ah be really fucked up.

The next day Reece came after I called and I hit him off with $224,000 in cold hard cash. He explained that after he paid the cost, the shipment would make it the following week. Then as soon as he got it he'd dump it and have my paper plus profit off the top. I knew he was on his business so I let him leave to do his thing.

Meanwhile, I sat on pins and needles.

To say I wasn't worried would be a lie. I didn't need any losses. But I knew Reece was trying to get back on his feet so I kept reminding myself that he would do everything he needed to make it work, so he'd come back up.

By the time the following week came, all my worries were taken care of when Reece came through to settle his end of the agreement. He returned with the $224,000 I initially gave him, along with $196,000 profit. In total, he gave me $420,000. Not bad for a week and a half investment.

"I told you 'cuz," he said with all smiles, "like taking candy from a baby."

"Yeah," I said, looking over the stacks of money he'd brought in backpacks. "That exotic moves fast."

"Fast? Shit, that shit be gone in no time," he explained. "But hey, I gotta bounce. But before I go I wanted to tell you Imm'ah put another shipment together in about a month. So if you try'nah blast off again we can do it."

"A month?" I asked. "Why so long?"

"Certain times of the month it's an easier trip . . . just try'na be smart."

I told Reece that there was a good chance I'd do it again . . . $196,000 profit that fast wasn't something to turn down. With all my expenses the money would be well needed. Especially until me and my boys finally made that breakthrough we were so desperately grinding for.

Gucci Mane had been recording his new album up at PatchWork so me and Nitti made our way up there to let him hear some beats. With Gucci having a good buzz going on in the streets, getting a song on his project would be a good placement.

"Yeah, I'm feeling these," he told Nitti.

"I got some more." Nitti said.

"Well what 'chall doing tomorrow?" he asked us. "Imm'ah be up here all week."

"I got a few things to take care of," I explained.

"I don't really have shit poppin' tomorrow I'll come back through if you want me to," Nitti told him. "I'll just bring my drive with me."

Gucci liked that idea.

"All right. Well I'll be here."

And for the next couple of days that followed, Nitti made it his business to be up there with Gucci going over tracks. He was doing everything he could to get something on the album.

It was around four in the evening when my girl came in from work, tired and frustrated.

"What's up baby?" I asked, sensing something was wrong.

"I quit," she announced flatly. "I'm just having too many problems at that place."

My girl went on to explain to me what had been going on but to be honest I wasn't paying any attention. In my mind I was laughing, thinking she must have felt like Joc and his family was getting a free ride so she deserved one too. And to think, how much she complained about the bills, to let something like "too many problems" cause her to just quit like that. But I didn't trip because she was my lady. And I would ride with whatever choice she made.

My real concern was for Joc and his family. I guess God heard my prayers because soon after my girl quit her job, Joc came back with some good news.

"Me and my girl landed a gig at Ruby Tuesday," he told me. "Now all we gotta do is work and save up."

That sounded good to me. "Well look, don't worry about nothing. Food, bills. . . I got all that. Y'all just focus on saving like you said, so y'all can get back right."

"Yeah," he said. "It won't take long to get enough up for another apartment."

"It's nothing," I told him. I didn't want anything in return, from him or his girl. I just didn't want him to be in the streets. I just wanted him to have a chance, so we could make it.

Joc just smiled knowing I truly believed in him.

Deon had rented the house me and him bought, to a lady not long after I'd moved out. Having trouble paying the mortgage, he moved in with his girl and refinanced the place, pulled out all the equity and opened up an auto shop. I took Joc up there with me one day to see Deon because although we put the house in his name, we went half on buying it and he hadn't given me any share of the rent he was receiving from the woman living there.

As soon as we pulled up, we saw Sam. Joc looked at me and said, "I know that old nigga right there, that's Sam."

"Oh yeah, you know old Sam?" I said. "Jump out and see if Deon's here."

Sam was in the box fucking with a motor he had pulled outta an old bucket when we pulled up.

Joc jumped out and went over to Sam. "Is Deon here?"

Sam wiped his hands on a towel and said, "Nah, tell ya brotha he ain't come in yet."

Joc replied, "That's my homeboy Chino in the truck."

I sat listening to them with my window cracked.

"Oh, well as soon as he comes in I'll tell him y'all stopped by."

Joc said all right and got back in the truck.

The issue between Gucci Mane and Young Jeezy had the streets talking beef. The song "So Icy" had brought about some bad blood between the two as it gained momentum at a fast pace. The word was that Jeezy wanted $50,000 for his feature. Or, for him and Gucci to work something out where they could both license the song for their solo albums. I guess Gucci wasn't with giving him his song or 50 racks. So Jeezy retaliated with threats to hit him with a "Cease and Desist" on the song so it wouldn't get played on the radio or get released.

Now at this time Jeezy had a song banging hard in the streets call "Trap or Die". And that Spring I hit the video shoot to fuck with my nigga. They were filming at a place called Jean and Son, a car interior shop located off Gresham Road. Everyone got their car interior done there. I'd gotten the guts and top done on my '72 Cutlass convertible. I guess Jeezy chose this spot to shoot because it was a well known place in East Atlanta. If Jean and Son's did your whip, guaranteed your shit was on point.

While at the shoot I met this white lady in her mid-30s named Christina. She was from Alabama and was into marketing. She had observed me earlier talking to everybody, chilling with Jeezy, and wanted to know what I did for a living. I told her about MasterMind and we talked about branding my company and so forth. When we were done talking we exchanged info then I returned to where I had been chilling with a group of guys when Big Meech arrived and walked straight up to us, rocking his big BMF chain blinding everybody the way the sun was shining on it. Meech's crew had now grown big in the city and Jeezy was reppin' them hard. We were all kicking it when I noticed a white guy across the street standing out in plain view. The man, I realized, was taking pictures of us with a camera with a big dumb ass lens attached to it.

"Man, that's the Feds," I said directly to Meech.

He just waved it off. "Man, fuck them folks! We used to 'em any way. Dem punks always be around."

His nonchalant attitude made me recall a few times at the clubs when we had been partying. You see, BMF did it so big that everyone took notice. Pulling up in luxury cars, making it rain on the strippers until the money was up to their knees. I remember how the hoes at Magic City and Platinum 21 would carry trash bags full of ones afterwards. And how the clubs would run out of ones, asking the dancers to recycle them. The private parties Meech would throw after closing hours for his crew and cats he fucked with. How they would be doing doughnuts in Ferraris in the middle of the street leaving Magic City and the billboard they had downtown.

Oh BMF wasn't just rumors, these niggas were bigger than life!

But it was how I had seen one of Meech's crew members run up to one agent's car, after a late-night at magic city that got me to thinking. On this occasion the agent had apparently fallen asleep in his car and this cat scared him awake by knocking on his driver-side window. "Wake up dude." He called out. "We about to go." And just like that the cat ran back to the BMF group who were now getting into their whips and leaving.

This thought, along with seeing the cat taking pictures, brought me to reality. These cats were carrying it like they were untouchable.

After I'd mentioned the Fed's presence and seeing how nobody basically gave a damn, I made the decision to slide off. I didn't want anybody else's heat to get on my hands. I already had my own issues to deal with. If there was one thing that I knew was true it was this: Once the Feds got on your bumper then 9 times out of 10 it would end one way: Prison.

Changes

It was April 05. "So Icy" had taken over most of the southern states. That's when Lil Will hit me up, telling me how they were shooting the video at Club Atrium.

"Why don't you come on out." He asked.

"All right," I said. "I'll be there."

The Atrium is located off of Memorial drive, in Decatur. I shot out there and met him and Gucci on the set. The first thing I noticed was Gucci's jewelry. This mutha fuçkin' nigga had come up! And was looking like the brickman. Like he was supplying the whole city with dope. He had this big dumb ass "So Icy" chain around his neck. I don't know what clarity of diamonds he had in it, but the piece was big! I wondered if this was the chain Jeezy said H.B. had bought for Gucci that came from the middle of the mall, in his diss song.

I pulled up on him. "What's up? I see you lookin' good. You ready to do your thang?"

"You already know," he replied.

The Atrium had a swimming pool inside, and that's where they were to shoot Will's scene singing the hook. Many questioned whether Jeezy was going to show up or not. I was hearing that he wasn't but I guess they worked something out because he did do his part. His "Trap or Die" CD had moved over 250,000 copies and the issues between him and Gucci was really causing tension.

But I knew Gucci wasn't even expecting Jeezy. He was doing his thing regardless and while I was there I noticed a change in the song I didn't before. Originally Boo rapped the 3rd verse. Now that verse was gone leaving Gucci to rap an extra verse. One thing I had to say about Gucci that I really admired was how he wasn't letting anything get in the way of him making what he wanted happen. By the night's end, he shot his scenes and made sure he got himself that much closer to bringing "So Icy" to the world.

Time was flying, Slutfest has rolled around once again. By now I had so much going on that I only took part in getting the talent. I did this only to make sure Joc and Slick performed. As usual it was a packed event. Joc and Slick rocked the spot preforming "Nan Nudda Pimp Like Me." By this time, the song "Dem Boys" had taken off. Me, Nard and Mont knew it was a no brainer to get the group to perform, but when we were informed that Jeezy wouldn't be joining them, we were able to get them for half the price. Young Jeezy had been the chosen golden boy, nicknaming himself Jeezy "The Snowman." The group was designed to springboard careers and that's just what Jeezy was doing. He and his partner Kinky B had their own label called C.T.E. (Corporate Thugs Entertainment) and he had attached himself to Big Meech and B.M.F. His manager, Coach K, was getting him $15,000 a show, the same amount as the group. So how could you expect him to show up for our show, to only split the same earnings with three other people? In the end, Jody Breeze, Big Duke and Big Gee still did a good job. But it was evident that the people still wanted to see Jeezy the Snowman.

$$$

Reece had planned to make another move, so he called to see if I was trying to get down again. I told him I had been waiting on him. After much thought, I went ahead and took a chance, investing the whole $420,000 I had made back on the last deal. He also sent what he made off of the last time. I figured I'd go all out for one: To get all I could get while the getting was good, Two: I could use the money and say fuck a deal and put out our own shit without touching my stash, and Three:

To help Reece get all the way up on his feet. I wanted to accomplish all this as fast as I could, and put my savings back up. I looked at it like: the more product, the more profit, the quicker I could be done with it.

A week passed as usual, and on the day of the big drop, I got a chirp from Reece to drive by the drop spot. This was not according to our previous plan, but because I had so much invested, I didn't hesitate to get involved. He asked me to look and see if it looked like strange people were around. He explained how him and his boys were in the lookout house and didn't want to leave out and draw any unwanted attention. Plus, our boy was saying only one of the boxes made it to his route.

Quickly I jumped in one of my low key whips and rode through the area and sure enough, I saw a couple white guys sitting in unmarked cars, on the side of the street. Reece had described a few cars for me to look out for, cars that had rode by. And everyone fit the description of the vehicles these white guys were sitting in. If you had any type of street dealings, then you knew immediately that these guys were cops. Reece said that only one package made it, and he had never had one hit and the rest miss.

Now this package that made it, it is what Reece and his boys were trying to get. It was also what the white guys were sitting there waiting for someone to pick up. This waiting game went on for three whole days. Finally, after giving up, the officers took the liberty to go and get the box off the front porch Reece used as the drop off spot.

Now with our packages lost and one confiscated by the police, we found ourselves out of $600,000 worth of product. And a $420,000 loss on my part was enough to make my head spin.

I was trying to recover mentally from my loss by grinding harder on the music. Joc came into the studio and sat next to me one morning. "Have you heard Gucci's new song?"

I looked at him. "Nah."

"Well, Nitti done gave him my beat. The one I wrote to when we had the girls helping with the hook."

He was talking about the track I helped make. "What?!"

"Yes," he continued. "Gucci got the same melody and everything. He just changed the words."

I couldn't believe my ears. Just the thought of Nitti doing something like that to me was out of this world. But I kept my cool. "Don't trip," I told him. "As soon as I get up wit' Nitti Imm'ah holla at him."

It wasn't but a few days after that that I'd finally gotten a chance to address the issue with Nitti face to face. By this time I had heard Gucci's song.

Gucci rapped over the track: "Shorty gotta ass on her (on her)/ Imm'ah put my hands on her (on her)/ Imm'ah spend'ah couple grand on her (on her)/ Imm'ah pop'ah rubber band on her (on her). . ."

It was bumpin'. But when I hollered at Nitti I was all business.

Nitti laughed. "Nah fam, it ain't like that. I was just at Patchwork wit' Gucci and he heard it. He liked it so much and told me how he really wanted it. So I let 'em get it."

I knew he saw Gucci's growing buzz as a potential wave to the top but for him to take what I had going on to make that happen, without getting with me to see if I was cool with it, was crazy.

"But don't trip," he continued. "Imm'ah give Joc some fire. Real talk, I got 'chall. Promise."

I nodded. "All right, Imm'ah hold you to that."

The whole time I was thinking, Damn. It was just like the dope game. Even the person next to you will cross you out, to make a dollar.

You know, it's easy to get down and discouraged when things aren't going right. No matter what I did, nothing could take my mind off of the money I'd lost. It's like my mind wouldn't rest a second and I knew I had to do something fast.

I called Reece, who I knew was in an even more messed up position than I was. "Dog fuck that," I said after much contemplation. "We gotta go again."

I heard a long breath exhale over the line. "Chino that shit wiped me out. I'm fucked up."

But I didn't care. "I'll put up the whole three hundred-twenty grand. All you gotta do is line it up and let me know when you ready."

"You sure?"

"Damn right," I said with no hesitation. "I done came too far to lose that much and not try to get it back. I ain't got no choice."

"All right," he said. "Let me do my thang."

And that was that. One thing any hustler dislikes in the game is a loss. In the streets we're taught to bounce back up when we fall. And that's what I intended to do.

Bounce back.

Now while I was preparing to invest into the move, my partner Travis came to me about a possible plug with our music. He knew this girl who knew a guy out in L.A. who wanted to set up a meeting to see us. This coming to me at this time was like music to my soul. Just when I was beginning to feel discouraged, heaven sent me some hope.

I told Joc what Travis hooked us up with. "This might be it," he said, excited.

"Might be," I said to him. "But we won't know until we fly on out there."

Being on top of it, I told Travis to hook it up and went ahead and booked me and Joc two tickets, a couple weeks in advance. They weren't as cheap as I would've liked but I had no choice. Travis also got a ticket to accompany us on the trip. Our plan was to fly out to L.A. and then drive out to Vegas to chill and have us a good time.

When the time rolled around, Reece had everything lined up. He did something with our plug to where he was to head out West also. So he told me he'd catch up with us in L.A. and shoot out to Vegas with us. It was on a Thursday night that me, Joc and Travis made the trip. We landed in L.A. with two rooms booked at The Radisson at the Kodak Center. We also rented an Expedition to move around the city in.

The meeting was not until that Tuesday so we planned on having a little fun first. That whole weekend we kicked it real hard. Marlon Wayans threw a party that Saturday at some club and we had a hell of a time there. Me and Travis had a home girl who lived out there, who had attended Spelman College in Atlanta. We called her up and she took us to some big Japanese restaurant to eat. All together there was seven of us, four girls and three dudes. The bill came out to be $2,200 including wine and drinks. A bill that ended up falling all on me.

When Sunday came, we headed out to Vegas. Reece had come

that morning to ride with us to San Bernardino, where we dropped him off. He let me know we were going to be good that following week and that he was going to drive out to Vegas later that night and catch up with us, after he got with O and his cousin C-Nell.

Joc had worked on the railroad in San Bernardino when he was around 18 and he knew this chick out there. So he called her up and to our surprise, we ended up taking her and a friend of hers out to Vegas with us. We used them to pass out CDs we had printed. And, we gambled.

Me and Travis' home girl and her friend from L.A. drove down to kick it. But they left Monday morning. We also had to take Joc's home girl back to San Bernardino that Monday, which at the time was an inconvenience for me. See, I was down at the crap table about ten grand and I wanted some get back. So we took them back and did a turn around, shooting right back to Vegas.

We spent all day Monday gambling. Reece and O were bouncing around but I was stuck at every casino's crap table. Finally, around 2 a.m. Tuesday morning, I got hot and won about half my money back. That's when I took a break. Joc and Travis were tired and ready to leave but I couldn't. Although I took a break, I fully intended to win back ALL my money. Taking another loss was not in my plans. I guess Joc and Travis saw this so they went and got the SUV from the valet, got in it and went to sleep. I ended up staying in the casino until 8 that morning before I won back all my money, plus $400. Satisfied, I was ready to head back to L.A. to meet with dude from Universal. So I found the SUV and we got back on the road.

The meeting was at 2 p.m. I was so excited to see where this might take us but when we finally met and spoke to the dude, I was immediately disappointed. This guy had an independent distribution deal with Universal for a couple of projects. And he was trying to sell distribution through his own company for $30,000, leaving us to be responsible for our own production and promotions. That shit he was talking about went in one ear and right out the other. The meeting only lasted 30 minutes.

I was a little upset. I really wanted. . . needed a breakthrough. And I was hoping that was it. Our flight left that evening was at six so that left us enough time to turn in the rental and eat before our plane left. The whole trip was a waste of time.

Back at home my palms were itching and I was waiting on the shipment to hit that Reece had put together. We had made a few adjustments to ensure everything went right this time. We changed what business the packages came from, where it would be dropped and we tracked it's whereabouts the whole step of the way. Finally, it made it to the U.P.S. in Atlanta and my anticipation grew drastically.

That's until something happened. Some way, form, or fashion, we had been busted and the packages never made it out of U.P.S. I couldn't believe my luck. This brought my entire loss to $740,000.

Damn near a mill ticket.

A Twist I Never Seen Coming

After the loss, I went into a daze. Nobody but Reece knew how much of a hit I'd taken. Every time my girl complained now, it fueled my fire. It was hell keeping my composure but I had no other choice. Too many people were banking on me to bring things to life for them: Elvis, Chris Flame, Joc, Slick and now Sunny.

I wasn't the only one going through trials. Though Gucci now had his video out, drama had escalated between him and Young Jeezy to a vicious point. It all began with a dis song Jeezy made offering a ten grand reward to anyone who brought him that big ass So Icy chain Gucci was sporting at the video shoot. The word was that this stripper from the club Blaze got Gucci to her apartment and five cats busted in, trying to cash in on Jeezy's offer. Some say the stripper chick was in on it. This little fiasco turned bad for the would be robbers, as well as Gucci. During the robbery, gunfire erupted leaving a dude named Henry Lee Carl III dead. So on May 24, 2005 my boy found himself sitting in the county jail fighting a murder charge.

An unthinkable turn of events.

The music scene continued on. Block's group Boyz 'N Da Hood, dropped their album June 4th, causing an uproar in the streets. As for Gucci, he ended up bonding out of jail the day his album dropped, holding a real gangsta persona from the street's perspective.

Meanwhile, I was trying to get back on track.

The Essence Festival in New Orleans had come and Brandy had a show lined up at a car show B.M.F. was doing. Neither I nor Joc had planned on going but that Friday I went ahead and rented a car. I needed a getaway and felt nothing was better than a work related one. The Essence Festival was always on and poppin' and you never knew who you might run into.

Hitting the road, both me and Joc shot to New Orleans to see if we could do some promotion. We didn't have a room reserved so we banked on getting one when we got there. That turned out to be a bad idea because as soon as we arrived we found that everything was booked up: from the big name hotels to the motels in the hood. But we lucked up finally staying at the hotel Fats, B and crew were staying at. Now, with that settled we spent the rest of that Friday night relaxing and going down on Canal Street to kick it.

That Saturday came around and we hit the park for Brandy's show. B.M.F. had the place on lock! They had Bentleys, Phantoms, Ferraris, Lamborghinis . . . you name it, they were out for the car show. Me and Joc had some CDs and flyers on deck so we started moving through the crowd, passing them out, while the performers did their thing. By the time Brandy got finished with her set, the show was over. Seeing everybody leaving, we packed our stuff up and headed out also.

"Damn dog, look at them niggas," Joc said at the sight of how the B.M.F. boys were rolling.

I looked and saw how they had a swarm of police following them, like how they escort diplomatic officials from Zamunda. When I was passing out CDs, a partner of mine from the crew invited me to a yacht party they were throwing. But at the sight of all those police, I figured I'd pass. Like I said, I didn't need any one else's heat on me, so I hit the city of New Orleans.

That evening me and Joc hit up Canal Street and bumped into three fine ass chicks I knew from Cali that lived in the A; we all kicked it, ate and hit a few clubs. If you know about New Orleans during The Essence Festival and Mardi Gras, the clubs be jumpin' from the day to the night. We even hit up some parties thrown at hotels and one hosted by Lil Wayne and a few more artists.

After running around all night, me and Joc left my home girls to go back to the hotel and change. Brandy and Fats told us that they were all heading back to Atlanta. We told them we'd catch up with them, changed and headed back out. We told my home girls that we'd meet them up at the Harrah's Casino. Even though my back was up against the ropes, I still couldn't seem to resist the urge to be greedy and gamble. Maybe that's why as soon as I got to Harrah's, I got hit upside my head real quick--$3,500 at the crap table.

During this time, my home girls kept calling for me and Joc to come party with them.

Joc was right at my side. "Man you can't catch a point," he said.

Blowing on the dice in my hands I said frustrated, "Shit, I better. 'Cause I ain't' leavin' til I do."

It was getting late and my home girls were getting restless. Being that we didn't have a room anymore, me and Joc had plans to stay at their hotel for the rest of that weekend. Well, around 5 a.m. I finally got back on top. Buy by then, the girls had left us and weren't answering their phones. So me and Joc decided to sleep in the rental car, in the parking lot of their hotel. Sunday, we spent the whole day passing out the rest of the flyers and CDs we had made.

When I got back in Atlanta, I couldn't help but to think of how I sent my money off like I did on that move with Reece. My bed was hard and I was the only one who had to lie in it. Nevertheless, my mind continued to race to figure out what it was I could do to generate some cash. And I soon came up with a reasonable decision I felt was safe for me.

I called my cousin Nikkia.

"So what 'chu try'na do now?" she asked me after hearing my problems.

"Same thing we did before," I explained. "Jump on some property. I just need something coming in, to pay the bills."

"All right," she said, always willing to assist me.

And just like that, my money would soon be at work. What I had left in my savings is what my life depended on. And I really needed to see some profit fast. But like everything else I had gotten in to, this also didn't go well. It would end up taking three to six months for me to see any type of return on my money. By that time, I had spent up a shit load of cash, with the rest tied up in real estate. The need for money was getting worse. My only option left was to pray for the music to pop off—sooner rather than later.

Joc and his girl having jobs at Ruby Tuesday was really helping out their situation. But how come it seems like every time you make it halfway up the hill, something pulls you back down? We were having complications when I would be out looking for property and my girl would be out looking for a job when they got off work. That would cause them to be locked out of the house.

Then Joc's Cadillac broke down again. Me and Brandy would pitch in and pick him and his wife up from work. His car sat in front of my house until he got paid. Once they got back rolling more timing problems occurred. This led to Joc and his wife posting up over his wife's friend's house or going to his dad's after work.

One day Joc called me and asked me to pick him up over at his dad's house off of Creel Road in College Park. I had been over there several times as of late. I would pick him and his wife up there when they would crash over there. During those times, I had met his little sister Chelsey, his little brother Daloreum and his stepmother. But I never met his pops. I mean, I would see him come to the door from time to time. From a distance I'd toss up a hand and wave at the man, get one in return, but we never really "seen" each other up close.

Well on this day I pulled up and Joc and his dad was out front looking under the hood of this old black Chevy Impala with another man. I parked my Denali and got out, and walked up to the three men. "What's up y'all?"

They all turned around and who I saw standing there shocked me. The man who I'd seen all those times, when I dropped off Joc, his dad was none other than Stan!

"What's up Chino?" Joc said.

I was still looking at Stan who said to me, "Hey boy!! I ain't seen you 'n lord knows how long. How ya mama and 'nem doing? I told ya uncle to tell you to call me sometimes."

"You know Chino?" Joc asked Stan.

Stan smiled. "Boy, that's Cha! That's my boy right there."

With a look on his face more confusing than mine, Joc said, "My brother Cha? The one who you used to talk about all the time?"

"Yeah," Stan explained. "That's him."

While we all stood there processing what was happening my mind began racing.

You see, the way it went was two men were speculated to be my father. Stan was one and the other was a man named Dewayne. When I was younger, Stan would always come around when I had lived with my uncle, out in Decatur. He would always give me a couple of dollars and tell me to be a good son. But as far as I knew, my pops was a man named Dewayne Lewis. And the only brothers and sisters I knew of were Tina, Tron and Marcus, three who I'd met only two or three years prior. Up to that point I hadn't seen Stan or Dewayne in forever. The last time I saw Dewayne I was around ten. He came by my grandmother's house and gave me a baseball bat. He had me run around the house to see how fast I was then told me my brother might be faster.

The last time I heard from him was when I was around 17. At that time, my mom had given me the phone with him on the other end talking about, "Boy you ain't out there hustlin' the streets are you?"

I asked him, "Who the fuck you think you are asking me what I was doin'? You ain't made sure one piece of food ever reached my mouth."

Then I hung up on his ass!

By the time I was 20, I went down to Albany, Georgia where he was living, to pick up his son Marcus. I had just met him over the phone and asked him to come stay the summer with me in Atlanta. Dewayne knew I was coming, and when I got there he didn't even have the nerve to be around to see me. That really hurt me to my heart. And that day I concluded that Dewayne couldn't have been my dad.

I mean, who would do their own child like that?

Wiping his hands on a towel, Stan looked at Joc and said, "Boy you been sayin' Chino…that boy name ain't no Chino. If you would've been sayin' Cha or Chauncey I would've been known who you were talkin' 'bout."

See Cha is a nickname my family gave me. I got it because when I was young none of my young cousins could say Chauncey; they'd say

Cha. Joc had heard Deon, Torrey, Quet, Nikkia and Shawty Slick call me Cha but he chose to call me Chino. For real, he just never put it together.

So now Stan was standing there claiming me with a proud look on his face. That was when something clicked and filled in all the questions of if he was really my dad or not. And for accepting me like he did, for me he was. Me, him and Joc talked that day and me and Joc left feeling a lot more closer.

As we rode back to my place, Joc just kept saying how he had heard rumors of me but that I was out of town somewhere. And all I kept saying in response was, "Damn, all this time. . . "

I had already taken him in like a brother. But now that it was official, it just all seemed surreal.

Can't Believe It

Up to this point I had done good keeping the overhead down on promoting our music. I'd spend a couple hundred with club DJs to get our songs played but as far as spending a lot on excess promo, I was cool. I knew it was a waste trying to be famous without any product to back it. I knew plenty of dopeboy labels that had notoriety for wasting money. These were those who had their artist's faces all over the city, but nobody could name a song from them.

Doing my best to stay focused, I worked hard at pushing MasterMind closer to its goal. Finding out that Joc and me were brothers seemed to give me a newfound motivation, which was something that I needed. Never in a million years did I imagine us having a connection like this. But I wasn't the only one who couldn't imagine it. As soon as my girl found out, she began bitching at an all-time high.

"Your brother!" she said. Her voice was loud and vibrating off of our bedroom walls the night I found out.

"Yep. That's crazy huh? I said. "We might have the same pops."

I had explained to her before about Stan and DeWayne, and how I had already felt about the situation. But instead of being happy for me, my girl got even more fed up.

"So this means they're going to stay here longer? I just can't take it." she fumed.

I assured her that Joc and his wife would be on their feet soon, and then they would be in their own place. I couldn't find it in my heart to kick them out, even if Joc was or wasn't family. So to deal with my girl's nagging mouth, I just found more things to consume myself in.

One thing occurred that stemmed from the hook up John Christmas gave me. The Black Radio Coalition I'd joined was throwing a showcase at a membership mansion just north of downtown Atlanta. They invited me and my crew to the pool party and I figured it would cheer my girl up if I took her along. I hoped that her coming and seeing what we had going for herself would give her some faith in all of us. Joc went ahead and invited his wife as well, turning it into a small intimate affair, with family along.

At the show, Joc did his thing. He performed "Heart Attack" and everybody loved it. When he got done, people were approaching us smiling and wanting to know more about what we had going on. Some of these people were professional women who had ties to the industry. Between these ladies and the other girls who spoke to us because they liked our music, this infuriated my girl who started tripping out of nowhere.

"I'm ready to go Chauncey, I'm tired, " she said while I was in the middle of talking to a guy about marketing our music.

I realized why she was really tripping but I tried to be patient with her. Honestly, she had me upset that I had even brought her along. "All right, just give me a few more minutes."

I guess she couldn't wait because she started acting up even more. "I'm tired. Let's go now!"

The guy I was talking to looked at me and said, "Uh, Chino, I'll talk to you later, all right?"

I smiled. "Cool man, and thanks for the input."

He returned the smile and returned to his mingling. Meanwhile I sought to address the issue with my girl. "What's the problem? Don't you see we try'na meet some people?"

She smacked her teeth. "Who, all dem hoes, all up in y'all face?"

Now here I was trying to involve her in the important things, to show her our progress. Doing this so she could be at ease. So when I'm gone at night she'll know what I'm doing. But all she could manage to see was negativity.

That afternoon, me and her ended up getting into it. I obliged her by leaving. Not because of her asking, but because I didn't want to present myself as unprofessional by arguing with her in front of people. When we got into the car our arguing continued and she winded up telling me to pull over so she could get out of the car. At this point I lost all care for her attitude and pulled over to let her out. After that, I rode around in silence with my top down on my cut dog, wondering how long I could put up with having her being insecure. I was shocked to find her car was gone by the time I got home. I figured it was best for her to be out for a while, so we didn't argue anymore.

A few weeks following this incident, some stress was relieved in my home when my girl finally found a job. And Joc and his wife skillfully saved up enough money and found themselves an apartment off of Garden Walk, in Riverdale. I'd dealt with this chick in the past that worked in the rental office so Joc got the hook up, avoiding all the red tape and began moving in immediately. He hit up Rent-A-Center and got furnished up with a big screen T.V., entertainment system, and all the furniture he needed. I was glad to see him and his girl making progress, and I prayed it would finally bring peace between my girl and me.

But that was only wishful thinking.

No sooner than Joc and his wife moved out does my girl invite her female cousin from Nashville to move in. She tells me that her cousin is going to school, or some shit, in Atlanta and needed a place to stay until she got a job and her own place. Now here she went, after all that nagging about bills and not having peace, to moving another mouth to feed into our home. I told her it was on her, but I wasn't paying nothing extra. By this time, my tolerance level was really low. My financial problems had me stressing out and my girl's bitching continued on and on about the time I was putting into my music dreams.

One Sunday while me and Joc was in the studio, my girl came home from work later than usual. The night before I had been out at Doppler Studios and I had my phone off became Nextel would send signal into the session, whenever the phone would ring. I guess she had called a couple of times and I didn't answer after I'd told her my phone would be off and I'd call her later on my way home. When I was done I kept my promise and called but by that time she had fallen fast asleep. Well that morning she was on her way to work and I told her I had something to do that evening so as soon as she got off she needed to make it back to get her son. I usually kept him on Sundays but I had a really important appointment I needed to keep.

Well that night when she walked in I said irritated, "I told you I had a meeting today, what happened? I tried to call but you never answered."

In a smart ass tone she responded, "I was on a date like you was last night," referring to when I was at Doppler Studios.

I couldn't believe what came out of her mouth. Then to my surprise she just turned and marched up the stairs, still talking shit. I was in no mood for all her drama so I went upstairs to see what was the matter with her. When I got to our room she was sitting on the bed, so I sat next to her. And as soon as I did she turned, violently pushing and hitting me.

"Get away from me! Get away Chauncey!"

I grabbed her and held her to stop her blows. The commotion called the attention of Joc and her cousin who had arrived home just before she had. Both came storming into the room to see what was going on.

My girl yelled to her cousin, "Call the police! Call the police!"

Her cousin wouldn't budge, despite her request. She could easily see what was going on.

I ended up letting her go as soon as I felt she wouldn't continue hitting me. Upset, I told Joc, "Man, let's go," and we headed out and jumped in my truck.

As I pulled out of my driveway, I could see my girl in my rearview running behind my truck yelling and making a scene. I knew the neighbors must've thought I was beating her ass out there because from what she told me later, they called the police. But I think she did.

I ended up staying at Sunny's house for a few days, sleeping on his sofa. My girl didn't want me at the house, and Sunny would laugh when I would be on the phone begging to come home. It was crazy how she had the locks changed where I paid the bills.

When I finally did make it home, I was greeted by a welcoming sight. My clothes were piled up in front of the door, bleached white, and some more shit. I was so mad that I went straight to her closet to return the favor but then I had to stop and think. I bought this shit, I said to myself. So instead I bit the bullet thinking how dirty this bitch was.

But this was only the beginning.

A few days later, around 9 a.m., me and my homeboy Brian were sitting in my studio. I was cooking up some heat for him. Nobody was home and I was all the way in my zone. Brian was working on a project and my dude Chase was managing him, and had booked the session. Being that my cash was low, I would sometimes sell beats or studio time as a small time hustle.

Well, in the middle of vibing, we heard someone banging on the basement door hard as a mother fucker. Brian had just gotten done smoking a blunt and I had my .40 cal pistol in my lap.

Something told me to hide it so I got up and placed it in the kick drum of my drum set. Then I went and checked the door.

I looked out the window. "Who is it?"

"Clayton County police! Open the door!"

In reality I was doing nothing wrong but at the mention of "police" my heart stopped. "Go to the front door," I replied. "I don't have the key to this door."

As soon as I turned around I saw Brian's high was wiped clean from his face. "Damn nigga, what they want?"

"I don't know, just chill down here."

I ran upstairs and as soon as I made it to the front door, I opened it up. There two officers stood.

"Are you Chauncey Stevens?" one asked.

"Yeah," I replied.

The other said, "We've got a warrant for your arrest."

In shock I asked, "For what?"

"Sir, please turn around and put your hands behind your back."

Then they asked if anyone else was in the house.

"Yeah, my partner is downstairs."

"Are there any drugs or weapons?" One asked. "I smell marijuana. Do you mind if we look around?"

"Sure. But not in my private areas." Immediately my mind went to my kick drum.

The officer assured me that he wasn't going upstairs, or in any of my cabinets or closets. They led me while they looked around my living room and kitchen, before going downstairs in the studio. My eyes went straight to Brian who by that time was trying to play it off like he was totally consumed in the beat I was making.

"Excuse me sir," the officer called out to him.

"Oh yeah, yeah. Hey what's going. . . "

"Do you have any identification on you?"

"Yeah, here you go."

The officer ran his name while the other one checked him to see if he had any weed. When asked, Brian told them he had smoked it all up. Once he was cleared they then escorted me out of the house. I assured Brian that all of this would get cleaned up and we'd continue where we left off. Then I turned to the officers to get some answers.

"What's the warrant for?" I asked.

"A domestic dispute."

As soon as we were leaving my property, my girl pulled into the driveway with her cousin. I couldn't help but feel major resentment toward her. The police were cool enough to let me holler at her and I told her to come bond me out. She said she would, the whole time not looking surprised or anything. That's why I doubt the neighbors called in the first place.

On my way to jail I thought about how I didn't need this kind of shit in my life. Me locked up for fighting a woman! I could've really gotten in trouble if they found my pistol. And it would've been all over a lying ass broad. Once I got out, I said that was done trying to please her. From that point it would be all about me. I would try to make it work, but I couldn't help but to think she was out to bring me down after all I'd done for her and her son.

MasterMind Coming Into Its Own

Elvis had been going up to Eric Miller's spot recording music with different artists and he'd convinced me, Slick, Sunny and Joc to do the same. Being that Eric's spot was in the city, it was closer for other artists to come to. Really recording with other artists wasn't at the top of my list. I'd been focusing on my production for my own crew. I'd made a few hot tracks. One was a beat using the melody that played at the end of the movie Scarface, adding a jamming 808 bass line arrangement to it. I had written a hook that I had Joc record called "Fuck You Pay Me."

Two lines to the hook went: "I don't front work nigga, fuck you pay me. I don't fuck for free bitch, fuck you pay me…" and so on.

After Joc finished, he laid a verse and when Sunny and Slick heard it, they jumped on it. The next thing I knew "Fuck U Pay Me" became a Wiseguy song. Just fucking around, Nitti would go with me up to Eric's studio sometimes. I'd let him hear what we'd recorded new. I played the "Fuck You Pay Me" record for him which made him believe the Wise Guys might just work.

I really must say that my production crew was beginning to spread its wings. Elvis's dealing up at Eric's spot brought me into the acquaintance of this little chick we will call Ms. S. She was an R&B singer. One day, Elvis called her while we were there.

When she arrived, I couldn't help but notice how attractive she was—a major plus for a female artist. But when she finally got on the mic I was blown away.

Joc thought the same thing as he nudged me. "Yo bra', she got it."

I nodded. "Yeah, she sounds good."

When the session was over, I had already made plans to approach her about being on the team. So I stepped to her and we made some plans to do some more work together soon after.

Nitti had finally gotten his studio up and running at the ASCAP building. He was working on Ms. B and Capone's music and was trying to get placements on other people's projects as well. It had been a while since we had picked out those four beats from him. I'd already paid him the five grand he wanted, all we had to do now was the work. We didn't do any paperwork or anything for the beats. I was just to get a receipt from his manager, Ian, just in case any problems were to arise.

Meanwhile, Nitti was on his grind. He had been in the studio working with this kid named Goldie from Indianapolis, Indiana. Goldie was under a guy named Rodney and a guy named J.B. Goldie had a cool flow and kind of sounded like Lil' Wayne to me. Rodney was funding his project and had beats from Manny Fresh and a few others. I met Rodney when I went to Nitti's studio to hangout and to see when Nitti would be free to work with Joc. That night we all ended up going out to the bar to kick it.

Rodney had this black 645 BMW drop top, with some 22-inch rims on it. Nitti rode with me and on the ride over he gave me the rundown on Rodney.

"I don't know where dude is gettin' his paper, but he's loaded up," he explained. "I'm tellin' you Chino, he's puttin' major cake in this kid Goldie. And as long as the money's right, I'm in."

Before we hit the bar we stopped at Rodney's place so he could change. Dude had the top floor condo at a building in Buckhead with a panoramic view. This dude's spot was player. It had valet parking, upstairs/downstairs, marble floors, and a bar on the roof outside the door to his spot. For entertainment, he had a pool table and flat screen TVs everywhere. This dude was doin' his thing.

That night we all kicked it hard. Even though I didn't agree with dumping big money into a project, I still admired Rodney's ambition. He believed in Goldie like I did my crew. That night I enjoyed being with those who shared a vision of success similar to mine. We toasted to the good life and talked about how life would only get better before it was all over if things went as planned.

When July came, my girl looked to soothe me by taking me to New York for my birthday. With all the things that had transpired between us, this didn't make up for it but I was willing to play along. I'd see if our relationship would work out while staying strictly true to what mattered most—me and my vision. But to keep it real, I did need a break.

So, me and my girl went to the Big Apple and we stayed at The Renaissance Hotel in Manhattan. During our time there we rode the red double decker buses through all the boroughs, rode the ferry boat out to see the Statue of Liberty, and went to see Ground Zero where I read the wall of names of all the victims who died in the 9/11 attack. I also hired a limo driver for all day that Saturday and my girl tricked me into treating her to a shopping spree on 5th Avenue.

Now while I was enjoying myself I noticed something that I considered extremely major. While in Brooklyn (actually all over New York) I continued to see advertisements of Jeezy's solo debut: *Thug Motivation 101*. Jeezy had SnowMan posters all in New York! This was big for a southern rapper to have going on in a place known for the birth of hip-hop. It was almost unheard of at the time. His album was to drop July 26th, 3 days after my birthday.

But like all things positive, Jeezy had a lot of drama surrounding his movement. Word on the streets and in the industry was that the Feds had pulled up on Jay-Z and Def Jam to see who Jeezy was signed with, C.T.E. or BMF The Feds wanted to get Meech and his crew on money laundering and some more shit. Def Jam had told Jeezy to quit reppin' BMF on his songs and shouting out Big Meech. The Feds had also sent a bulletin out to radio stations, telling them not to play any BMF music. My inside radio program dude put me up on it. The Feds wanted to try and stop Jeezy's spins, or spins where he referenced BMF Shit was crazy!! Nevertheless, his presence was still strong.

For the rest of my time in the Big Apple me and my girl partied all weekend. Before I left I bumped into this young kid named Benzino on Fulton Street in Brooklyn who made shirts like the Miskeen shirts. We exchanged numbers after he ensured me that he could make some promotional shirts for MasterMind Music.

When I made it back from New York, I received a call from a lady by the name of Christina. She reminded me we'd met at Jeezy's video shoot and that she was the young lady from Alabama who did promotions. She told me she was in Atlanta, and wanted to meet me so she could tell me what all she could do for my company. She sounded real professional and confident, so I agreed to meet her at this bar in Buckhead. I arrived and soon was approached by this jazzy little white woman, with blonde hair and blue eyes.

"Hello Chauncey, how have you been?" she asked offering her hand.

"I've been doing okay," I said cordially. Not wanting to rush but having a few things planned that I had to do, I told her, "I don't have much time so let's get right down to business if you don't mind."

"I understand so let me just get straight to it," she said.

"I've got a lot of connects in Alabama with state politicians and club promoters," she explained. "So throwing concerts and different functions are some of the things we can do for starters," she continued.

Sitting across from her I could tell she was feeling me. But I wasn't going to be distracted. I didn't want to fuck up what could turn out to be a good connection.

"Listen," I began, "how about I send you some music on my two artists, Joc and Slick, so you can get 'em to the clubs in Montgomery and Mobile and after we get a response we go from there."

"Sounds good," she agreed.

"And yeah, I think we can do some things." I smiled, concluding our meeting.

"Well, it was nice seeing you again," she replied, returning the smile.

"Same here," I said as I walked her out. "The next time you're in the city call me. I'll introduce you to a few artists you can make a few dollars off of, getting their music out there in Alabama."

After my meeting with Christina, Nikkia called me to tell me about some property she'd found.

"They need some work done," she explained.

"All right. How about we get together tomorrow and go take a look at 'em?"

"Sounds good."

The next day we got together and went to Simpson Road to view a few houses. She explained what it was going to take to get the properties. I estimated that fixing them back up was going to be a lot more than I planned on tying up. But I had to do something.

"Let's do it," I told her.

"Are you sure? You don't look certain."

"Yeah," I assured her. "I'm just gonna have to budget what I got left until it sells."

And with that, she made it happen.

While I was dumping more money into property, everybody else was still heavy on their grind. Nitti was trying to get Young Capone an album deal at So So Def. His "I'm Hot" single didn't do that good. So Nitti was cooking up another single by him called "Lights, Camera, Action" and had me in the studio checking it out.

"So what do you think?" he asked when it finished.

"Yeah," I said nodding my approval, "I think it's better than the "I'm Hot" single."

That was what Nitti wanted to hear. "I'm tellin' you Chino, Young Capone is a star. Out of everybody I bet he'll be the next blow."

His statement caught me off guard. "Out of everybody like who?"

"Everybody. Shit, Joc…" he said with a shrug.

"Hold up! You think Capone is hotter than Joc?" Nitti almost had me ready to crack up. Capone was a good hard rapper but he didn't have what Joc had.

"Are you serious?" Nitti asked. "Capone is a star."

"And Joc ain't?"

"Honestly, naw bra'. Joc is cool but he ain't got no style."

"No style?" I asked.

"Yeah, and his rhymes are corny."

I just looked at Nitti dumbfounded. So this is how he really felt? So much made sense to me at that point, and I began to realize a lot of things. That was why he never recorded Joc on any verse or song. That's why he never worked with him when he called Brandy and signed her. Then he brought up another issue about Joc that was unrelated to talent.

"Joc be runnin' around in them Nike football cleats every day," he said humorously. "He even be performing in them. What's that all about?"

My cousin Torrey used to clown about the same thing about Joc. But Nitti didn't know why I didn't dress Joc up or give him money like so many do their artists. I wanted to build a hunger inside of him so he could have something to talk about, something to give him motivation to change his situation. I knew hunger grew hustle. What need was there feeding him to get full before his success actually came? No, I wanted him hungry!

In the end, I told Nitti how I felt about Joc and that despite him not believing, one day he would. Joc had what it took and I promised him he'd see and bear witness like everyone else would.

Nitti's doubt spurred a fire inside of me and caused me and Joc to be inseparable. Joc's 'Lac had broken down again so I was taking him and his wife to work and picking them up whenever Brandy wasn't. Little League football had started and my oldest son Christopher was 5-years-old and starting his first year. I decided to help coach his team at Glenwood Park, in Decatur. When Joc would be off, we would record all day at the crib, then he would go to practice with me and then we'd shoot to this studio Elvis was using off of Church Street in Decatur and record.

Elvis had one of his homeboys from Memphis, who called himself Real, in town trying to do his music thing and would be in the lab with us recording also. This guy named X from New York who'd invested in Elvis, had a house that he let artists live in not far from Elvis' house. So Real was staying there. He had been to my crib a few times with Elvis. He was a cool dude and him, Joc and Elvis started doing some crazy ass songs together, calling themselves some crazy ass shit like A.D.D. But Elvis was still building relations with beneficial people.

Young Chris Flame on the other hand, had been over at this studio on the backside of Peters Street in downtown Atlanta. It was run by my partner Rick, who owned the Funk Shop Music Store, which was downtown also. Flame had been down there recording with this kid him and Joc grew up with that used to dance in East Point named Alonzo. We called him Zoe for short. Zoe made beats and rapped. He was a talented kid.

I started falling through the spot when him and Flame would be getting down from time to time to hang out. Also, I liked to get a look at all the up and coming talents. I was glad to see Flame getting out and involving himself in the underground stream of things. Like Elvis, he was also building his brand in the heart of Atlanta.

We had finally gotten into the studio with Nitti, and Joc recorded to the other beat he picked, from the two I'd paid for. He did a song called "You Can Have That Bitch." It was a jamming ass street cut, but it wasn't that hit we needed.

Around this time, Joc had gotten behind on his rent and needed $1,000 to catch up. It had only been a short time and he was already behind from paying Rent A Center, daycare, and rent. It was obvious that Ruby Tuesday wasn't cutting it. Plus, I saw that he was a little careless with money, by some of the things he bought. And at the time, I had budgeted myself down to my last dime. But I went ahead and gave it to him and by the next week, he needed another stack. I just didn't know what to tell him.

"Bra', shit's rough for me too." I explained. "All my money is tied up in renovating those three properties. This is just bad timing. You know if I had it. . . "

"I know," he assured me despite his pride being hurt at the thought of not knowing what else to do.

Sad to say, Joc and his wife ended up losing that apartment. They ended up moving into this "pay by the week" motel off of Hwy 85 in Riverdale. I would help them out from week to week, when he needed it, to pay the rent. This didn't hurt me as much and it kept him and his family nice and warm in the meantime.

There were so many factors that stressed the importance of us making it that I began praying more and more for it to happen soon— not only for me, but also for Joc and his family, Elvis, Flame, Slick, and

Sunny. I wanted to see everybody that fucked with me to be able to properly provide for themselves and their family. Ms. B was the only one so far that had a foot in the door.

I continued staying focused, working hard at my label. The Wise Guys had a few good songs but Slick had fallen back some, spending time in Athens trying to juggle and stay on top financially. Sunny was running around working a lot. He told me how he got with some dudes named Dame and Big Rick, who wanted to get behind him on a solo project. He also said that these same cats wanted to meet me and that they thought The Wise Guys had good material.

Starting from needing money, I began working on beats more and more, which turned into a good stress reliever. Ironically, this led to a project of my own. Of course, I had everybody else's stuff to do first, but when I was done with theirs I was seriously entertaining thoughts of pushing my own shit. The only thing was that I had never jumped behind the mic before. Yeah, I'd written a lot of hooks and helped everybody with their verses. Oh yeah, once I jumped on a song back in the day with Duddy at Underground Sound. And what's funny is everybody who heard it liked my verse, telling me I snapped on it.

But rapping wasn't something I really wanted to do; although, I wasn't completely against the idea.

Dope Boy Magic! It's Goin' Down!

One night we were all in the basement hella deep. Me, Joc, my boy Vick was over with his homie Nick, and a couple more dudes. We were drinking, smoking weed and whatever else you could imagine. Everybody was chillin' out as I began to flip through some tracks.

"Whoa! Hold up Chino," Vick said at a track I'd switched to. "What's that? Who did that one?"

I said, "Me."

Everyone in the room gave each other twisted expressions as they began rockin' to the beat.

"Nigga, that's fire," Vick said, amped up.

The track just so happen to be one of the ones I called myself setting aside for my own project. And although I'd heard it a zillion times it seemed to jam harder with everyone enjoying it. "Yeah," I said to Vick. "That's that 'Dope Boy Magic.'"

Vick looked at Joc and Nick. "Dope Boy Magic," he said, nodding his head. "That's hot."

"Yeah," came Joc, "Dope Boy Magic."

The name struck a chord in us, sounding like a good name for the track. Soon me and Nick began putting together something to go with it, a few lyrics to give it some direction. When we got through Joc had something already laid out so we went ahead and constructed a hook. With that finished, I then wasted no time and set up the tracks for vocals and sent Joc in the booth to lay his part. Then I had Nick go in to do what he came up with.

Now this is where shit got complicated. This fool Nick was so geeked up from sniffing cocaine that his mouth was twisted to one side and every time he spit I couldn't get a good read out in the system. Then finally we figured out a solution: We had Nick turn his whole body so he faced sideways, leaving the twisted side of his mouth to be lined up directly with the mic. Voila! That nigga's shit came out crystal clear.

As he spit: "I gett'ah nine in the morning, by the night it's just plastic/How you do that? I call it Dope Boy Magic/Fresh to death every day, like I jumped up outta casket/How you do that? I call it Dope Boy Magic.

I spent time getting it right, stacking the hook so it sounded perfect, and by the time we got done, it was late. Joc went in the booth and did a few more vocals and then the session was over.

After everybody left, I pulled the track back up and had Joc fix a few more things on his verse. Right then he took the liberty to rewrite a few things as I put the music back on. While he was doing this, I grabbed a piece of paper and jotted down a verse myself. When we got finished, Joc went back in the booth and laid a new verse and when he finished, we moved on to some more things we had to do.

A week or so later me and Torrey was sitting in the studio fucking around and I pulled the song back up.

"I want you to record this verse for me," I told him, picking up the paper I had scribbled a verse on.

"Yeah right," Torrey said with a laugh.

But when I hit the booth, he saw I was serious. I placed the headphones over my ears and when I knew he was ready, I closed my eyes and went all in. When I finished, I stepped out and returned to see how it sounded.

Torrey looked surprised. "Man, I liked that shit."

"I need somebody else on it that's really been in the streets," I explained to him. "Somebody like Jeezy."

After I sat with Torrey and listened to it and was satisfied with what I had, I gave serious thought to getting Young Jeezy on the song for real.

Well, it just so happened that same day I had to go up to Zack's studio, where Elvis was working on some shit. When I made it, I saw some of Jeezy's guys outside, so I took the liberty to holler at one of his partners named Clem.

"Tell Jeezy I got this song I want him to get on," I said.

"A'ight," Clem said in a cool manner.

I told him I'd call him later in the week to see what was good.

In between getting back at Clem, my partner C-Bone had finally made his way by my studios to lay something down. Early on his advice for me to hustle the music I managed "like a pack" never left my mind and I really wanted him to see the progress I was making.

"I see you Chino, you've added a little more shit in here," he said at my hookup. "You got everything you need now."

C-Bone had seen major studios fucking with Big Boi and Andre 3000. But I wasn't looking to compete. "Man, I'm just gettin' started."

I went on to let him hear some of our music but when he heard "Dope Boy Magic" he said, "That's it! I need to jump on that."

I didn't disagree. I looped the track for him and let him do his thing. Bone went in the booth with a verse and I recorded what he had. That now made three of us and it sounded so fire I decided to scrap the immediate urge to get Jeezy on it and save a few dollars by keeping C-Bones' verse.

Meanwhile, my girl's cousin from Nashville finally came to her end of staying with us. During this time the girl never got a job, barely helped babysit like she originally said would be no problem, ran a phone bill up in my girl's name and never put a red penny toward a bill. I can't even recall being told thank you!

As for Joc, it had been a while since we had recorded with Nitti. And since I paid him, I told him we needed to get back in the lab. He agreed and put it together for us to join up in the studio that Friday.

When we finally made it happen, me and Joc arrived to find Nitti chilling out with Rodney and J.B. The two cats that were pushing the kid Goldie. This young kid Greg, a new producer calling himself G-Phonic, tracked out a beat while everybody exchanged greetings. When G-Phonic was done, Nitti started up a drum pattern. It couldn't have been no more than 15 minutes before he was finished. It was simple but it had a nice vibe to it.

Immediately, Joc began writing to it. Him and Nitti came up with a melody and we began giving Joc little words to change. When I saw him and Nitti had it, I went outside and kicked it with Rod and J.B.

Well after some time of conversing, I went back inside to see how much progress Nitti and Joc had made. Joc had finished writing his verses and was on his way in the booth. When he finished all three parts, he came out satisfied.

"I got this hook I've been holding on to," he told us. "I think I should put it on there."

He then told us how it went, but me and Nitti both disagreed.

"You need a big hook for this," Nitti explained to him.

"Yeah," I told him, "something like a slogan."

Nitti came up with a bright idea. "Chino, why don't you do an intro."

I shook my head. "Nah, I'll let you handle that."

Hearing my opinion Nitti shrugged and then got up to go into the booth. He got on the mic and played around with some things, saying his name and then Joc's. Finally he came out.

"That'll do for now," he said. "Let's chill and pick back up tomorrow. I got a few other things to take care of."

Me and Joc agreed. Nitti made me a copy and then told Joc to think about what we told him about the hook.

"All right, I'm on it," Joc said.

As soon as both of us got in my truck, I popped the disc in and played the track while we rode. Being by ourselves helped me and Joc to vibe a little better. The song put us in the mindset of one of Juvenile's songs. The next thing I knew, Joc started mumbling something to the beat.

"... goin' down. . . "

Something about the phrase caught my ear. "What did you say? Say it again."

Still bobbin' his head, Joc looked at me and said, "It's goin' down".

"That's it," I said. "It's goin' down!"

The very next morning me and Joc hit Nitti's spot amped up. When we arrived, Ms. B was already in the booth putting in work.

"Y'all all geeked," Nitti said as we stormed in wide-eyed. "I know that look. Y'all got somethin'."

"You better believe it," I said.

We wasted no time explaining to Nitti the concept and he agreed that it fit our vision to make this one a statement song. Something that would help build Yung Joc as a brand.

"Yeah," Nitti said, "It's goin' down", "I like that."

Now at the time, that's all we had so we filled in the rest of the words right then, coming up with the first four bars to the hook. Then we got stuck.

"Ain't no rush," I told Joc. "We just need to let it come naturally."

He agreed. "Yeah, just keep playin' the track. Let me hear it some more."

Nitti kept the track on loop so Joc could continue vibing. With nothing for me to do, I figured I could handle a little business. I needed to shoot to Lenox Mall because I wanted to pick me up something to wear out that night. When I told Nitti he said he wanted to roll with me.

"Y'all just chill out," he told Joc and Ms. B. "We'll be back in a minute."

When we got back, Joc and Ms. B were in the studio deep into their work. They had come up with an idea and recorded extra vocals onto the hook. After the four bars, they added "Do it do it do it do it" like a chant to crank up the song.

Both me and Nitti looked at each other immediately, shaking our heads in disagreement.

"Nah Joc," I said. "We think we should just loop the four, and that's it."

He looked unsure. "What, y'all don't like. . . "

"Nope!" Nitti and me said in unison.

Nitti went ahead and took the liberty to erase what they'd recorded, before looping the original lines so we could hear how it sounded. After the crunked up version, the original's simplicity seemed to stand out even more, carrying Joc's flamboyant bars through the speakers, sounding melodic and superb.

Joc rapped: "Meet me in the traaap…it's goin' down/meet me in the cluuub. . . its goin' down/meet me in the maaall…it's goin' down/ anywhere you meet me guaranteed to go down!"

As I sat rocking to the beat, my mind kept telling me that something was missing. Then it hit me. Throughout the whole song, Nitti hadn't placed a high hat on the track, making it sound too plain. When I expressed this to him, he looked at me from behind the mixing board, listening for himself. Then he came to a conclusion.

"How 'bout I meet 'chu halfway," he said.

Curious I asked, "What do you have in mind?"

Nitti proceeded to do his work.

When he finished, he listened and then turned to me. "What'chu think?"

I nodded. "Yeah, that's it. Now all it needs is to be polished up."

"It's Goin' Down" sounded like a sure fire hit if I ever heard one. And "Dope Boy Magic" was right on its heels, on some street shit. So while Nitti still did his thing getting "It's Goin' Down" cleaned up, I sought to get "Dope Boy Magic" mixed since it was ready.

I called my boy Ralph at Doppler and told him I had some work for him. Of course, he told me he had my back and that he was free that night. So me, Joc, Ms. B, Elvis and a few chicks shot out to Doppler to chill out while Ralph mixed the cut. Nitti ended up hitting me during the session and I told him to fall through.

As soon as Nitti heard "Dope Boy Magic," he immediately wrote some bars, saying he had to get on it. I didn't trip and Ralph said he had

no problem recording his verse. So now I had me, Joc, C-Bone, Playboy
Nick on the hook, and Nitti on the song. It was turning into a collabo-
street anthem. By the night's end, it came out hard as hell, leaving for me
to only have to give it to Kenny for the mastering.

"Drop it off anytime," Kenny told me. "Give me two-three
weeks tops, and it'll be done."

Kenny's words were music to my ears and I knew I could count
on him to come through as promised. When I got the first chance, I did
as he instructed and dropped it off and he got it back in no time. When
I finally got it back and popped it in my system, "Dope Boy Magic"
sounded like a certified hit.

My anticipation was building.

$$$

Joc couldn't afford to stay at the motel anymore so he and his
family had to move all the way out to Acworth, in X's artists crib. X had
heard some of the stuff that Elvis, Joc and Real had recorded and liked
that crazy ass shit. He wanted to do something with them as a group. X
had been trying to meet with me about the idea, but I was caught up in
trying to get the songs Joc had recorded finished up. Plus, I didn't think
it was a good look for Joc's solo career, because of the style of music he
was making with Elvis and Real. But I really appreciated X for helping
him with the place to stay.

When I got with Nitti he told me "It's Goin' Down" was finally
polished and ready. He changed the intro and adlibbed throughout the
song and added his signature tag "It's a Nitti beat." He put a light mix
on it which wasn't hard because of the lack of sounds in it. I decided to
go ahead and hit Kenny back, who told me to bring it through. But as
soon as Kenny put it in his system, he found the bass too strong, so I had
to take it back to Nitti to bring the levels down.

"That's much better," Kenny said of the change when I made
it back to him after a week of me going back and forth with the mix.
"Now let's see what we got."

I had already foreseen "Dope Boy Magic" being a song I could target the streets with, while "It's Goin' Down" was clean and fly enough for both the streets and commercial radio. Call me crazy, but I thought it was that good. But despite my growing anxiety, with our product finally finished, I knew one way to find out how good this new solo from Joc really was. And despite the time of night, I decided to make one last stop—Body Tap.

One Step At A Time

"I think we got one!" My voice boomed. It was hard to hold my excitement the next morning as I called Joc to inform him about what happened at Body Tap.

"Bra', last night after Kenny mastered "It's Goin' Down," I jumped in my truck and went downtown to Body Tap to let X-Rated play it. Playboy, they was on it. I felt so good that I smoked a blunt of Kush with X-Rated and got so high I missed out on hooking up with fine ass Tasha I went to school with."

"They went crazy like that?" Joc asked.

"Did they?" I said. "Joc, I'm telling you, the muthafuckas was actin' like it was a song they heard before. The dancers worked the stage, niggas made it rain dollar bills. Man, X-Rated ran it back a couple times and the crowd couldn't get enough."

He laughed. "So they feelin' it huh?"

"Feelin' it ain't the word." I went on to tell him about my plan.

" What we need to do, until we get some copies pressed up, is hit all the clubs and get the DJs to play it. You know this has always been the routine, but this song is special. Wait 'til you see the response it gets."

"All right."

"Also, we need to hit some open mics," I said.

Joc was in compliance like always. And he was down for whatever. I also hit Nitti and told him and he told me he had also begun letting people hear it in his studio.

"Niggas love it," he exclaimed. "They say it's a hit."

"I'm tellin' you Nitti," I said, "this one might be it."

So going with my feeling I set everything in motion. Me and Joc showed up to clubs and open mics to see if we would find the same response I found at Body Tap. I called up my partners who Deejayed and of course they gave me my shot. I swear, as soon as they put the record on, it was like the whole club went into a trance and Joc found himself stuck as well. Seeing that same response everywhere we went, had to be the greatest feeling in the world for me. And to know that Joc, my brother, was a part of it made it that much more special.

We hit the Ritz, Peacock and 20 Grand and 20 Grand East, doing open mics. At 20 Grand East we ran into this cat named B-Rich who had been out in the streets grinding like we were. He had an artist he was trying to blow up calling himself B.O.B. We would all bump heads at different venues so we showed each other some love and like us, B-Rich and B.O.B. really didn't have much going on, let alone a song at the time in major circulation. B-Rich felt we had a winner also and agreed to help get the song around to a few DJs like funk Darrol James and a few others, which was a good look because B-Rich was on his grind. The only difference between us and them, if you ask me was, at the time, we were going a little bit harder.

I mean, we were everywhere!

"Hello Shawnda?" I said into my cellphone.

"Yeah, this her."

"This Chino I need your help."

Shawnda was a homegirl of mine who I found out duplicated CDs for only .50 each. I told her how I needed one thousand done up ASAP and she didn't disappoint.

"When can you drop 'em off?" she asked.

"Today," I said.

I dropped her off three songs: "It's Goin' Down," "Dope Boy Magic" and a song Elvis produced for Joc called "Tic-Tac." The faster I got the copies, the faster I could pass out our material to all the DJs in the city. It was really time to get this music shit on and poppin'!

$$$

When Christina made her way back to the city, she hit me up. I had just gotten the copies back from Shawnda so I told her to meet me over my homeboy Travis' spot. I spent a lot of time at Travis' house. It was one of my duck off spots and it was close to the city, being in Buckhead. I told her about me having some music for her so she told me she would meet me in no time.

Travis wasn't home and I had been chilling out, channel surfing and drinking Patron and Coronas on the sofa when she rang the doorbell.

"What's up?" she said when I answered the door.

"Ahh, nothing much," I said with a smile. "Come on in."

When Christina walked past me, I noticed that she was all dressed up. She had on a blue business suit that matched her eyes, high heels and her hair was curly and cascading down her back.

"I got a meeting downtown in about three hours," she explained. "Do you mind if I chill out here until then?"

I shrugged. "Nah. I ain't doin' shit."

She smiled. "Cool."

Inside I helped her get comfortable, giving her a drink and playing the music I'd just gotten back.

"I like that," she said about "It's Goin' Down." "That's your artist?"

"Yeah, my brother Joc."

We began conversating, discussing a variety of topics. Not long into our discussion, she asked for directions to the bathroom. I showed her the way, like it was no problem. She then returned about 10 minutes later and we continued where we left off. But it was after her fourth or fifth time to the bathroom that I began to realize that this ho was playin' with' her nose. All the signs were there as she would come back to the sofa with her eyes all bucked out like Tracee Ellis Ross.

At this point the Patron had me leaning. I can't really explain how it all went down but all I know is one minute we were talking about booking shows in Alabama and open mics and the next thing I knew Christina was on her knees in front of me, rocking my mic! Shit, I just went with the flow. And I felt no guilt. I was like "fuck my girl" at this point and it was time to do me.

Christina was no stranger to a dick. After she manipulated big dog out of my drawls she kept me relaxed with a nice slow paced deep throat. She slid her lips and tongue from the base to the tip of my pipe, while looking me in the eyes the whole time.

"Mmm! You taste good."

I just looked back into her ocean blue eyes. After about fifteen good minutes of this I came to the point where I couldn't take anymore. "Get up," I instructed.

She wasted no time and she knew what I wanted. Right there on the sofa she hiked up her skirt only to expose her soft milky thighs and a pantiless, hairless pussy.

No lie, I must've fucked this girl in about 50 different positions. From the sofa to the floor, to the window to the wall! The alcohol had my dick rock solid but when I was finally about to cum she hit me with some of that ol' Monica Lewinsky type porno shit.

"I want you to cum in my mouth."

That was it! I couldn't take no more. She swung around from the doggy style position I had her in, grabbed my dick at its base and hummed her way up and down its length. Meanwhile I placed both hands in her blonde hair pushing her farther down, as far as she could--nd then I busted.

When we were done, I found myself exhausted as hell. Christina had taken one last trip afterwards to the bathroom, this time I think to freshen up. When she came back, she stood over me with a smile.

"I gotta leave sweetie," she said. "And for the record, that's all you gotta do. Just give me that good dick baby and I'll do whatever you want."

I just nodded and told her I'd call. After all the bullshit my girl had taken me through, some new pussy with no drama felt good as hell. I knew I'd be hitting her back real soon.

$$$

It had gotten to the point where we had hit all of the DJs we had come across. Every one of them we gave copies of the songs we were pushing. Our mission was to get "Dope Boy Magic" and "It's Goin' Down" or any of the others on V-103's station with host Greg Street or on 107.9 with the Duddy Boys. We also wanted to get them on a couple of mix tapes.

It was Labor Day weekend and I was cruising downtown by myself. While I was driving Nitti called me.

"Yo Chino, you got a copy of the song wit' you?" he asked.

I knew he was referring to "It's Goin' Down." "Yeah," I said.

"Look," he explained. "Do you think you can shoot a copy up to 107.9? I just talked to DJ Montay and he said he could get it on for us."

That's what I needed to hear.

"Just text him," Nitti continued. "As soon as you get to the station he'll come out and meet you at the door and get it."

This proved to be the exact thing we needed because my dude DJ Smooth, who worked at a station in Macon, GA had time slotted to DJ at 107.9 that coming Monday and was going to play the song also. He was to do the Labor Day Mix, where other DJs got their time to shine on a bigger station.

"I'm on my way there now," I told Nitti.

Shit was feeling right. All I needed to do was continue to grind, keep believing and being patient.

The Closer We Get The Farther It Seems

After hearing Joc's music, Christina called me and said she wanted to meet him. I had already told him about her, and how she was working to get us some exposure out in Alabama. I also told him that all she wanted me to do was give her some dick from time to time, and she'd be straight.

Well, one day when me and Joc were bending corners, Christina hit me. "I'm in town," she explained. "I wanna see you."

"All right," I told her. "Meet me over my partner's place, where we were at last time. And Joc's with me too, so you can finally meet him."

"Cool." She sounded excited. "I'll be there in about ten minutes."

As I made my way to Travis' spot, I told Joc how she wanted to meet him. He knew it was good to keep all those willing to work on our behalf in our corner—especially the ones who believed in our music.

Well we ended up beating Christina to Travis' but not by much. No sooner as I began putting the key in the door did she arrive, pulling up behind my truck. Then she made her way to the porch where we had just stepped in.

"Christina, this is Joc," I said, introducing them.

"Joc, Christina."

They shook hands and we went inside.

As we made our way into the living room, Christina let Joc know how much she liked his music, and he thanked her for the compliment. It was getting pretty dark outside as we talked on the sofa about what she had going on in Atlanta. After about 20 minutes that's when she turned to me.

"Chino, can I holla at you in the back room?"

The only room in the back was the bedroom, I thought. "Yeah."

I got up after her, taking a glance back at Joc who just smiled. "I'll be right back."

Following Christina, I went into the bedroom, leaving the door open. She went and sat on the bed as I stood up against the dresser.

"Come here," she said in a seductive voice. She had on a jogging suit that she began unzipping the jacket to, revealing that she had no bra underneath.

"Take your clothes off," she instructed. "I wanna give you a massage."

I did as she asked. Meanwhile she continued to undress. Then when I finished I laid across the bed on my stomach, relaxing as she began to massage the muscles in my back. After she had done this a while she then told me to flip over.

Taking up a new position, Christina started by kissing me from ear to ear, then on down to my dick. After a few minutes of slowly sucking me, I was ready to fuck the shit out of her. After rolling on a condom, I turned her over quickly, slamming my dick into her tight ass pussy.

I couldn't control myself. I was plunging into her with extreme force, like I was trying to knock a hole through her spine. She was making all sorts of funny ass noises, like farm animals and shit. I was fucking the goat shit out of her! Then she started hollering for me to slap her on her ass. This bitch was a real deal freak. I guess all of the commotion caused Joc to get curious because no sooner than I began smacking her round ass did I see him standing in the doorway. Me and Christina just turned, looking right in his direction.

"Damn dog, this pussy is good," I said, not missing a stroke.

Christina just moaned in agreement while continuing to look Joc eye to eye.

"Come on, get you some of this," I told him while taking another swat at her pink cheeks.

Joc snapped immediately out of his trance. Then in a flash, he began stripping out of his clothes.

That night, me and Joc put so much dick in that woman, I think we hit every hole on her body. She swallowed every nut we could muster up. We had to go for at least 6 hours straight! After we finished, I knew that this was the life I was supposed to be living. Not all that bullshit arguing I was getting at home with a woman who I'd only done right by.

Now as for Joc. . .

His wife stuck with him even when he couldn't put food on the table. I had been ballin' and had gone through a lot of gold diggin' bitches who cared less about who I was besides knowing my money. He, on the other hand, wasn't so seasoned. He had his share of pussy before his girl but he'd gotten married young. I knew this music shit was going to bring countless females like Christina. I just felt that as long as he could tell the difference between his real love, and these fly-by-night groupie hoes, he'd be all right.

I was really making shit move with the CDs I had. I was hitting up club DJs and having them add the song to their playlist. Once I established this at a few choice spots, I figured it was finally time to call the Goon Squad out, all my boys who I enlisted to support the movement. It was time to show the streets of Atlanta how serious we were over at MasterMind Music.

Now, at this time there was a club on the Southside called 20 Grand. It was off of Old National. It used to jump like a muthafucka on Sunday nights. The place was super big, with two different sides to party on. One side had a big ass stage, and on these Sunday nights, they'd have certain artists perform. With a little networking, I managed to get to the DJ and hooked up where Joc could do his thing. And with this in effect, and the whole squad in the house, we looked to turn 20 Grand out.

When the time came, Joc fell into his element. The countless open mics and other performances I had him doing was really paying off because all he kept doing was getting better. And when he performed "It's Goin' Down," he had a line where he said "…they say Joc where you stay? Tell 'em College Park . . ." and being that's where we were it seemed the whole club erupted, vibing to the song even harder. The whole scene was surreal and with the squad in the house I knew from that point we had to roll like this every time we performed.

Keeping the ball rolling, Jermaine Dupree had a So So Def pool party going on at a big hotel in downtown Atlanta, and Nitti had it hooked up for MasterMind Music to get the VIP treatment. I had some Yung Joc tee shirts made in black, with the picture of the little boy on the tricycle on the front. The whole Goon Squad showed up wearing a shirt, 30 to 50 deep!

It was this event that caught the eye of everybody at So So Def. Nitti told me getting them to jump on board wouldn't be a problem.

Next, me and Nitti went personally up to V-103 and had "It's Goin' Down" played on JD's So So Def radio segment. JD had this show every Saturday night around 8 p.m. At this time, he'd bump all the hard hitting underground shit. A lot of people who didn't really listen to the radio listened to this show because it was all new hits. And having the opportunity to get our song played on V-103 before a million listeners was big. While up at the station, we ended up running into L.L. Cool J doing his thing with Greg Street and the legend gave his opinion that we had a hit.

"So So Def wants to fuck wit' us," Nitti told me later that night in his studio.

"Oh yeah? What are they talkin' about?"

Rubbing his palms together, Nitti let the suspense build before giving me the details. "They want to give us a single deal with five grand up front. We'll have to do the splits, but remember, it's only an advance. And I'll go in fifty-fifty with you on everything."

Hearing this I looked at Nitti like he had lost his everlasting mind.

"Five stacks?" I went in my pocket and pulled out a little over that amount. "Man, I keep that for spending money."

And although I was hurting financially and needed the

opportunity, I couldn't see this sort of deal happening.

"Look," I continued, when I saw he had a look of disappointment, "have them holla' at John Christmas. All right?"

He agreed.

Somewhere along the way, Nitti and his manager Ian had come up with a way where he could get a part of Joc, as a possible agreement. They were even willing to go less than the 50/50 he suggested before. When Nitti got back with me about it, I told him I wanted to wait and see what John worked out. Meanwhile, I got Joc a lawyer named Phaedra Parks, someone to go over his MasterMind contract with him. She was to get with John about making some revisions to it.

"I need the new contract without merchandising included," I explained to John when I finally talked to him. "When can you handle it? Because shit's brewing fast." At the time, he was out of the country taking care of his other business.

"I'll be back soon," he told me. "I'll get the contracts revised as soon as possible. In the meantime, I talked to So So Def. I gotta get back at them as well. When I do I'll tell 'em we're still deciding."

"All right, thanks."

I knew Nitti's persistence was because things were picking up. And even though JD was interested, we still needed to be patient. I didn't want to jump out there and commit myself, Joc and the rest of the team to a deal that didn't complement our work ethic and accomplishments in the street. Shit, we had been struggling all this time. What was it to us to struggle a little longer?

Two DJs contacted us about putting "It's Goin' Down" on their mix tapes, for a little sponsorship. One had called Nitti and DJ GoldFinger, who I talked to at J-Paul's where we had been getting the song played. I'd gotten more copies pressed and gave them out to all the Goon Squad. I mailed copies to a home girl of mine who bartended at a club in Gainesville, FL so she could give them to the DJ down there.

I'd accumulated a ton of DJ contact info that I'd reach out to later. But for the time being I reached out to DJ KoolAid, DJ Infamous, DJ Aries, DJ Buu, DJ Holiday, DJ Don Juan, DJ Black Bill Gates. And once things picked up I'd check with two people I knew who worked records. Jerry Clark who was cool with 107.9 program director, Jerry

Smokin' B and Orlind Garrison, maybe she could get at V-103's Program Director Reggie.

During all of this, I finally got my ASCAP membership cards back in the mail. After talking to John, I had begun the process by printing out applications, filling them out and putting them in the mail box. ASCAP stands for American Society of Composers, Authors and Publishers. ASCAP, BMI (Broadcast Music Incorporated) and SESAC (Society of European Stage Authors and Composers) are the major performing rights societies in the U.S. But ASCAP and BMI, by far, are the largest. SESAC has only 1 percent of all performing rights.

Anyway, I'd done my research and saw I definitely needed to be a member of one of them. I chose ASCAP because Nitti was a member and at the time, it was free. I had signed up to be a writer and started my own publishing company as well. (For details about how these rights societies work, how to set up your own publishing company, and other benefits, check out my book: 10 Rap Commandments).

As for Joc, he had filled out papers for BMI but he hadn't received them back yet. The tripped out thing was he'd done his years prior. So Nitti got this chick to register Joc's song in both his and my catalog. I would just give Joc his share once things started moving. We gave Nitti 60 percent: 50 percent for doing the track and 10 percent for his help in writing the song. The rest we kept.

After this was done, I continued to ship copies to other places in the U.S. I sent copies to my partner DJ Tiz down in San Antonio, Texas. I'd met him in a strip club down there when me and my girl went out there to visit her parents. While there, I used some time to do a little networking.

My cousin Reece had gotten a shipment out to Cali. Travis and JoJo hit up Mississippi. We were reaching all the places we could because we knew, when heard, that the song would catch like wildfire. In Atlanta we were getting good responses, and after much thought, I settled on having John see about hooking up a meeting with me and Big Block over at Block Ent., seeing how he represented us both.

"I'll see about it," he assured me.

But every time I'd bring it up he'd just brush off the suggestion.

I also sought out a guy in the city who had been doing music for a while, named K.P. or Keven Prather. K.P. did T.I.'s shit when he was under Ghetto Vision. He was the V.P. of A&R at Sony. I bumped into him one night, told him what was up and he told me to get at him when I was ready. I went ahead and sent him the song, both in the mail and by e-mail. But when we talked afterwards I could tell that he wasn't interested.

Oh well.

A DJ who showed us a lot of love was DJ Hersey from Hot 107.9. Hersey worked at Blue Flame and the club was feeling "It's Goin' Down" so he put it on his 5 p.m. mix show, at the station. He was the first to do this. Because Hersey's son played Little League football for Ben Hill, where Big Oomp's son played, I had a chance to build with them both. Every year at this tournament at Grady Stadium, when Adamsville, Gresham Park and my son's team, Glenwood, and others would meet, we'd all be sitting around betting on the games and talking shit. So remembering me from those times, Hersey immediately jumped on board with the movement and spread the word to those who might be able to help, like his good friend Carl Moe.

I was moving at 100 M.P.H. around Atlanta trying to make things pop. One day while me and Joc were out and about, I stopped in at Zack's studio to see what was up with Elvis. He had been busy working on some shit up there. I'd hit him and he told me to slide through; so I did, finding him in the big recording room.

As soon as I entered, I saw Elvis get up from a chair and motion to someone at his left. "Ayo, this my man Chino Dolla right here. And that's Joc."

I looked to see who he was referring to and was surprised as hell when I saw my main man Polo Da Don.

"Chino," Polo said just as surprised to Elvis. "This who you've been talkin' about?" He jumped up excited. "This nigga damn near got me a rape case, fuckin' wit' some hoes, touring wit' Bubba."

I laughed. "Damn Polo! What's up?" I approached him and we dapped each other up and embraced in a half-hug.

He said, "Boy, I ain't seen you since we went and fucked wit' Dallas Austin and Jazze Pha that night in the studio."

"Yeah man, I've been busy tryin' to get my label off the ground,"

I explained. "I've been pushin' Joc's shit real hard."

Elvis had told me he had bumped into another producer up at Zack's, but I didn't know it was Polo. Polo had heard Elvis do some stuff on the keys, liked it and had him working on a few things. At this time, Polo's career was idling, about to take off like a G-4 jet.

"Man Elvis," Polo said shaking his head. "This who you've been working with huh?"

"Yep."

Laughing, Polo continued, "This nigga wouldn't even give me thirty two hundred for a beat, when he was giving Nitti all that money for tracks, back in the day. Back then he was fucking wit' Bubba. Shit Chino, you even brought Joc by my spot."

"Yeah I did," I said, remembering the time. "But I was done payin' for beats by then. Have you heard Joc's new song?"

"What new song?"

Elvis said, "That's who was on that CD I let you hear. The one Nitti produced. The one you said you had heard somewhere before."

Looking at me Polo said, "Yeah, yeah. I heard it."

I gave him a look back like my team was really onto something. "Polo I'm tellin' you, you need to jump on this. Muthafuckas is feelin' it."

He just nodded and said, "Yeah man, we'll see. You remember my artist Rich Boy? I'm still trying to get him off the ground."

But this was all I got from him. From So So Def's offer of five grand to John brushing off my requests to meeting with Block and now Polo, it seemed no one was taking us seriously. Even my boy C-Bone downplayed me when I asked him to hook something up, for me to holler at Big Boi over at Purple Ribbon. Everybody just kept saying the same ol' thing.

Yeah, we'll see.

Gotta Make It Happen

My girl flew down to San Antonio to bring my stepson back home before school started so I finally found some peace and quiet for a change.

I'd been noticing a change in Joc around this time and it seemed that piece of new pussy he'd gotten from Christina put an extra bounce in his step. I was feeling a little guilty because I felt llike the one to blame for his new behavior. See one night he got a number from this thick ass chick at J-Paul's after a performance—a cold hood rat with a fat ass.

The next night he came and found me in the studio. "A bra' can I use the truck to pick up baby girl I met last night at the club?"

I gave him a look. "Where she stay?"

"In Morrow."

This wasn't too far from my crib in Riverdale. "All right, go ahead."

Joc bounced off feeling himself and soon he was back with ol' girl.

Lil' mama came boppin' in behind Joc dressed in some cheap ass cut off shorts, Reeboks and a tank top. She was looking like some bonafide action with her ass cheeks poking out the back. But when

I looked at Joc he had this crazy look on his face like something was wrong.

"Yo Chino," he began after tossing me my keys. You ain't gonna believe what happened."

He went on to tell me a detailed story about how when he was waiting in the parking lot for baby girl to come out, just chilling and playing some beats in my truck, he noticed a dude in the rearview crouched down low, slowly creeping up the driver side.

"Man, I thought something was fishy when this car rode by, like a few minutes before," he continued. "Next thing I know here comes this cat with a long ass screwdriver in his hand . . . like he was about to try and peel your ride."

I couldn't believe my ears. "For real?"

"Yeah. I had the seat all the way back so I know he didn't see me. But when I peeped him I immediately fired up the engine and that nigga hauled ass like a tailback."

I just shook my head. It was a shame that now even the outskirts were infested with car thieves like Southwest Atlanta and Decatur. And I wasn't upset with Joc. That shit could've happened to me as well. Only difference would've been that fat pistol I kept just for anyone trying to make me and mines their next meal on the table.

So after he ran it all down, I smiled at his little friend, and I could tell how she smiled back that she was possibly game for anything. Shit, she probably had never set foot in the presence of a true playa living in his own crib as big as mine.

"How you doin' tonight lil lady?" I asked.

"Fine," she replied.

That's when Joc stepped in. "All right bra' we gone."

I watched as they left up the stairs, knowing he was taking her to one of my rooms. So being the "perfect host" that I am, I waited some time before I went up to see if they wanted some drinks and found them just chilling out.

Baby was all with it and so me and Joc ended up chilling and shit with her, drinking and watching a little TV. I could see he wasn't used to working with hoes like this so I started to commend her, asking her to stand up and show us how fine she was. Oh, this got her going. She stood up with both hands on her hips proudly displaying what her mama gave her. Joc's eyes lit up as she bounced before us. We both started smacking her on the ass causing her to blush.

"Boy stop," she said to me after looking to see what Joc was going to say.

"Girl, he ain't trippin'," I told her. And instead of saying so, Joc just sat there. I figured he was afraid by doing so it would fuck up his chances at getting some action.

All right, I said to myself. I know what Imm'ah do.

I left the room telling them both to have a good time. But after about 20 minutes I slid back to the room only to find the lights were off. I could hear light moans telling me that Joc was up in that pussy. First I peeked my head in and then finally I stepped into the room.

Instantly I saw baby girl's eyes glittering in the dark as she realized I was in there. She didn't stop gyrating her hips as Joc stroked her in the missionary position. This was the first sign that she was game. But why as soon as I approached the bed did this fool look back at me, stop fucking and lay down beside her? This threw everything off, making her grab the cover on the bed to cover her breasts. Then helping her, Joc finished up by pulling the cover over the rest of her body.

Without saying a word, I just backed out—but not for long.

I was determined to get me some of that juicy booty.

After about 10 minutes, I slid back into the room, this time more quietly. Joc now had her bent over, hitting it from the back. I walked up behind him in the dark and tapped him on the shoulder, causing him to jump a little. When he turned to face me, I gave him a look and he finally got the drift.

Without using any words, me and Joc worked in sync to pull off one of the world's best switch-a-roos. We started by him taking his hands from her waist and putting them in the air, while he continued to slow stroke her from the back. With his hands missing we sought to make her think my hands were actually his. So I slid my left hand on her ass cheek Honestly, I tensed, anticipating her to instantly flip over like "no y'all didn't" but she looked back at me, licked her lips and continued to enjoy the ride.

That was my cue.

Immediately I removed my hand, stepped to the side and stripped completely naked. Then, I came back to the bed where Joc was still hitting her in the same position. I could smell her pussy's light musk in the air and it only made me wanna hit that more. So with our plan in tack, me and Joc performed our hand trick but this time this fool put his hand back down, after I placed mine on her ass. So we had his left hand on one side, mine on the right and now his next to mine. That made three hands.

Baby fell flat on her stomach and looked back over her shoulder. "Na-uhhhm" What y'all doing?"

By this time, I had taken flight for the door. Stopping at the sound of her voice, I didn't know if she was fronting for Joc because I know she looked at me, but I didn't care, I was gone. I knew it was dark as hell so I immediately came to a halt and stood like a statue. You should've seen me standing there, stuck in mid-stride with one foot off the ground and my arms frozen in a swinging motion. I swear, I stood there stuck for what seemed to be 10 minutes before she finally said, "I see you."

Joc busted out laughing and I fell to the floor busting up too. Shit was crazy. From there, I just crawled out of the room. I guess the moonlight from the window was shining on me, just when I thought I was doing something.

It was this incident that showed me that Joc was going to need some work and time, seeing how not all women were the wifey type and how the bigger we got in the music game the farther from the wifey type these women actually got.

Yeah, he needed a lot of work

One day DJ Dre called me and Joc and said that the Legion of Doom were having a cookout at their office on Old National.

"Y'all need to come out," he said.

So me and Joc got dressed to go because we knew a lot of DJs would be there.

When we arrived, we found out some business was having its grand opening and the L.O.D. were catering the event for them. There were models and the works. This one model had all the dudes trying to holla at her and she was constantly turning them down. She caught my eye as soon as I arrived with her light skinned china doll look. I had already come up with my game plan by the time she made her way around me. I figured with a face like hers, I could use her for a photo shoot or something.

Sliding up next to her I said, "What's good?"

Turning to me she responded, "Hey."

"Listen, soon I'm having a photo shoot for my label and it's just not gonna come out right if you're not a part of it. So give me your number and I'll be in touch." I gave her no room for rejection.

She laughed. "I like that one. What's your name?"

"Chino Dolla. I'm the CEO of MasterMind Music. What's yours?

"They call me China," she said.

I went into more about what we had going on and soon we exchanged numbers. I assured her that I was all business and told her how I had an ol' lady at home. But it was when I told her how I thought she was a little young for me anyway that she lit up.

"I'm grown," she said with a smile. "I'm 18."

Smiling I said, "All right, cool."

$$$

My partner Fresh Stacks had gotten a copy of Joc's song and let Carl Moe hear it. Carl Moe wanted to meet Joc, so they got together and Joc let him hear some more music. Joc told him in the process that he was messing with me and he shot word that he wanted to meet up.

"Y'all got some heat," Carl told me in a real serious tone.

I could tell he was surprised. "Thanks man."

"Who did that "Dope Boy Magic?" he asked.

I smiled. "I did."

Carl started laughing. "Man, I love that shit! Boy you makin' beats now?"

"Yeah, and that's me rappin' on the second verse."

It was too much for him. "Boy, I knew you had it in you. Remember what I told you when you did that intro on Backwood Slick's song? The one I produced? I told you to keep fuckin' wit' that mic. Now look at 'chu."

It was his look of genuine happiness that made me feel proud of myself . . . like I had accomplished a lot. Carl Moe didn't know he'd poured fuel on a fire.

He went on to ask me what I was doing with our music and I gave him our basic routines. Doing shows, getting shit in DJs hands, etc.... Somehow I went on to explain how I had a few connects but nothing seemed to bite back. I also told him how Nitti wanted to go in 50/50 with me and that he thinks he can get us a single deal. But I explained how I didn't know about it. In the process I brought up Block's name, telling him me and Block had the same entertainment lawyer.

"Listen," he began. "Me and Block is cool. Let me holla at him about Joc, all right?"

I nodded. "All right."

"With the success of Boyz N Da Hood he could possibly make somethin' happen," he said. "And I know he's lookin' for somethin' new with Jeezy doin' his own thing now. Let me get at him and I'll get back at 'chu."

To me it sounded like a plan. "Appreciate that cuz," I said before we parted.

Well after my meeting with Carl Moe we continued to keep up what we had been doing. Ms. B's manager, Fats, had brought down this kid from L. A. to stay with him. He called himself Natural and was the brother of Shar Jackson who played on Brandy's show Moesha. Shar was also the baby mother of Kevin Federline, Britney Spears' husband at the time. Natural was trying to produce and make a career in the music business. He had a computer system with Q Banks and a mic set up in Fats's spot where he made beats and recorded.

Now Fats had a good location, so we would post up over at his spot a lot and record with Natural. We also had the girl Ms. S over there working on her R&B stuff as well. Fats still wanted to join us and try his hand at getting Joc some shows. I told him that whatever he could do we'd work it out. I explained how I had been working it out with some DJs I knew, that if they played Joc's song and it got hot, when they wanted to promote a show, we'd come and do it for free, and they could keep the door. But they had to do it before he got too big and his schedule was all booked up. Fats knew I did this to make up for having to lace their pockets with a couple grand.

During this time, Nitti called me to meet him at his studio, saying he had some really good news.

"So So Def wants to really do the single deal!" he said.

I wasn't enthused. "They still talkin' the same numbers?"

He looked to cut me off before I began, "Just think about it. I'm tellin' you, it'll be good exposure."

I left Nitti more turned off from the So So Def deal than I was before. To me what they offered wasn't even worth considering. Then after talking to John about a few things, he informed me that he had spoken with an attorney for the label and they were indeed interested.

Then I received another phone call from somebody I least expected: Eddie, AKA Skeeter Rock. From what I understood, he ran So So Def.

"Listen," Skeeter Rock said. "I'd like to meet with you and talk."

"All right, that's cool. When?" I asked

"Where you at now?"

I was at home in the studio, and when I told him he seemed surprised.

"I'm out South now," he said. "If you give me directions I could just come by there."

I saw no problem in it so I gave him my address and in no time he pulled up to my crib driving his blue Porsche. Me and Joc met him outside.

"What's up y'all?" He said as we greeted him.

He wanted to hear some of Joc's songs so I played about 10 cuts for him. Out of these, he really liked 3 or 4.

"That could be a single," he said of "Thousand Ones".

"That's one of our first ones," I told him.

When we were finished, Skeeter got straight to business. "So what's up with doing the single deal?"

I didn't want to bullshit him so I said, "Man five grand ain't enough money to do shit with."

He looked at me surprised as hell. "Five grand! We told Nitti twenty."

I said, "Well I guess he wants fifteen for his beat. And then after he gets that he wants to split the other five with us because he wants to do a joint venture with me."

Shaking his head Skeeter said, "All right, listen. What about twenty-five grand?"

"You gon' pay Nitti for his beat?" I was on top of my business.

"We'll see."

I was thinking. Twenty-five still didn't sound appealing. "What about fifty?

"And you pay Nitti?"

I said, "I already paid Nitti what I'm gonna pay him. Y'all pay the rest. Listen Skeeter, I was really lookin' for an album deal. Not just a single."

He nodded. "Well, it will have an option. If the single did good…"

But that wasn't good enough. "That ain't gonna get it."

Right then Skeeter Rock stood up. "Well fellas, let me see. I gotta run but I'll let 'chu know, All right?"

That day when he left, I had the feeling like shit was really getting close, like it was right around the next corner.

Block Business

The conversation I had with Carl Moe ended up panning out and he hooked it up for Joc to meet up with Big Block. Joc called me on Friday evening to tell me what was up.

"Block wants to meet us in the morning," he told me. "What 'chu wanna do?"

The timing was all off. "Man, Chris got a football game tomorrow," I said referring to my son. "But look, go ahead and holla at him to see what he's try'na do."

Joc agreed and that Saturday afternoon, after my son's team whooped some serious ass, I was back at home chilling when Joc hit me up again.

"Yeah, I let him hear some songs and shit. And I told him about what we had goin' on. He just said for me to give you his number so you can hit him when you get a chance."

He went on to run a few more details about their meeting and when he was done I told him that I was going to go ahead and call Block up.

"All right bra', get at me after you call and tell me what's up," he said.

"Fa sho." I hung up and punched in the number he gave me.

"Yo, this Block. What's up?"

"Yeah, this Chino Dolla." I said. "Joc's people."

"Chino, yeah, glad you called. I was really feelin' Joc. The music and all."

"True dat."

"Tell me, he continued. What kind of terms do you have him under? And how much have you already spent?"

I saw immediately that he was getting straight to the point, wanting to know my investments. "Well, I've spent around fifty grand from studio equipment, to paying for beats and a little promo. Right now my main thing is getting 50 percent of all Joc's publishing because selling albums is tough at the moment."

He laughed. "Yeah, you're right. I'm still in the hole with Boyz 'N Da Hood. They've sold over four hundred thou,' but the publishing is what's up."

Block went on to tell me to make sure all of my paperwork was done on Joc. I guess he was looking to give me his best advice. He explained that from his personal experience, artists didn't care who you were to them, or even what you've done in their favor . . . that in the end, when money got involved, they'd leave you dry in a heartbeat.

I told him we were indeed waiting on John to draw us up new contracts. "Oh, Imm'ah make sure the business end is all taken care of."

"Good," he responded.

Our conversation drifted on and he told me how he was thinking about approaching Lil' Wayne or some partner of his named Rick Ross to replace Young Jeezy in his group Boyz 'N Da Hood. I wasn't up on who Rick Ross was so when I asked he explained.

"Well, I've been knowing him for years," he said. "He's outta Miami. He used to sleep on my floor and vice versa. Rick's an ex-football player type nigga. Big as shit, but ended up getting into this rap shit."

"He played football professionally?" I asked.

"Nah, nothing like that," he said. "I just brought that up because he was playing down in Texas when I was fucking wit that nigga Tony

Draper from Suave House Records. When he was down in Texas, he did his first record deal with T. Draper.

He really ain't no street nigga, out there sellin' dope and shit. He's just try'na fuck wit' this rappin' so I'm thinkin' about puttin' him on."

Block told me how he used to manage 2Pac back in the day, him and another cat. I had heard he used to chill and smoke weed with them dudes but nothing about managing. I don't know if he was trying to boost his image up to me, or not. Either way I wasn't concerned about what he used to do. I was only concerned about what he could do now.

On that note I said, "Listen, we both got John as our lawyer and your partner Darryl is my big homie. We need to go ahead and meet up and chat."

My big homeboy Darryl's name carried big weight and he knew it. I just wanted him to know that niggas who were somebody in the city would co-sign for me. In the end we agreed that as soon as John got back in the country, we'd have him set up a meeting for us.

$$\$\$\$$$

News in the streets was buzzing about D4L's deal with Asylum Records. Their single "Laffy Taffy" had turned into a certified club banger and had taken them to another level. Their album was released on October 4th of that year and had marked a special moment of motivation for me. To be in the club that night their song was broke, though it sounded ridiculous to me, showed me how the right connections could take things to another level. And I knew if it could happen for them, then it could also happen for us.

When John got back, he put together the meeting between me and Block. Joc and I both went and met John and Block at this Chik-Fil-A Dwarf House in Hapeville. It was around nine in the morning so we all hit the breakfast line before sitting down to eat and talk about what we all wanted.

Finishing his meal, Block turned to me and said, "You can do nine out of twelve songs. I'll take care of the other three."

I disagreed, knowing he had a trick up his sleeve. "How about we do fifty-fifty on the songs? Or you can just come in for thirty percent, as a part of MasterMind."

He looked at me like I'd lost my mind. "Why would I do that?"

That's when John stepped in. "Look, how about y'all let me put something together that will be fair for the both of y'all?"

Me and Block looked at each other and nodded. "Okay," we replied in unison.

After we finished talking, we all parted ways. While riding back, me and Joc discussed what we thought of Block.

"I like that he's on his shit," I said.

"Yeah," came Joc. "His swag tells me he's about business."

"Yeah, and he seems to understand where we're coming from."

During the meeting, he told us how he could see if he could get us a deal through Bad Boy or the Warner Music Group. It would only be a shot. Nothing was for certain. I went on and told him about Nitti and So So Def and about my latest connect through my homeboy DJ Dre, and how he had been contacted by an A&R named Mike Garen from Atlantic Records. Mike had apparently been trying to get in contact with me.

As I replayed the meeting, I felt good about how everything was looking. One minute we only had open mics and now we had offers in the tens of thousands. Niggas wanted to fuck with us and that was real motivation in itself.

"I met with Block and he might wanna do something," I said.

Nitti just looked at me, obviously disgusted. "Boy, if you fuck with that nigga I'm gonna have to stick it to him for that beat. That nigga still owes me fifteen racks for my back end on the Boyz 'N Da Hood album. He was supposed to get me when he got the back half of the recording fund. That nigga ain't give me shit!"

Nitti was going off.

"Yeah Chino, it ain't got nothing to do with you but that nigga gon' pay me," he said.

I just listened to him. And yeah, he was right. But that shit he was going through had nothing to do with me. I never mentioned how

Skeeter Rock put me up on how So So Def offered us $20,000 because business wise it didn't matter. He did the beat and as long as we pushed "It's Goin' Down," he'd be involved.

BMF Takedown

Word on the streets was that it was over for Big Meech and his B.M.F. crew. Cats were saying that the Feds had arrested Meech out in Texas, laying low in a mansion in Dallas. Before, when he was in jail for a shooting in Buckhead, where he had gotten shot and Puffy's old security guard, Wolf, had been killed along with another person, a lot of people were wearing "Free Meech" t-shirts. This time, people seemed scared to even say B.M.F., let alone his name. That was except his real fam, who repped him hard. They rocked the "Free Meech" shirts and kept his torch burning strong.

But all in all, it was sad. Meech's fall was inevitable to some, for they felt it was coming. He had done it like no other in Atlanta since these cats named Danny Boy and Deck and their crew from the Westside got snatched up by the Feds. Meech had thrown birthday parties with ice sculptures that read B.M.F., parties with live zebras, giraffes, and monkeys and shit all up in Club Compound, way out the box shit! He had billboards all around the city of Atlanta and had thrown stacks and stacks of money at JD and Nelly and other ballers up in Magic City, making statements that said we got it! B.M.F. had done it B.I.G. for real!

But now it was time for the game to get back what it had given to him and his boys. And the city had been quiet ever since. The price of pussy was dropping to an all-time low and the dope climbing to an all-time high. Can you believe it? This nigga's fall caused the economy of pussy to drop! Shit, some dudes were doing really bad as a result. Cats that were eating good before, were now on the verge of standing in the cheese line.

But for others it was getting better. So I guess when one falls, the game makes room for another to rise.

When the bust hit, cats that were a part of BMF and still free, like Ill Will, held major beef with Jeezy. I mean it was gun play at certain clubs and everything. They said that Jeezy switched up on them, listening to Def Jam and backing up from supporting them in his music. But word was that Big Meech himself reached out from behind bars telling his crew to leave Jeezy alone, and that he was good. But the rest of the streets were waiting to see if Jeezy would soon be next on the Feds' list to be locked up.

Me, I hated to see anybody caught up. But I had to keep the momentum going on my own thing because that wasn't how I was trying to end up.

$$$

I was sliding through my hood on the Eastside one day with Joc. We had just left my baby mother's house in my '72 Cutlass—a classic vehicle. I loved its strong engine, and I pimped it out with a pearl white paint job and peanut butter brown insides. It was a convertible, and on this day, I had the top up riding and bumping my sounds. Low on gas, I stopped at this Amoco on the corner of Glenwood and Covington Highway. As I was at the pump I saw my man Gucci and his homeboy Courtney Cee pull up in his burgundy Chevy Lumina and hop out.

I called his name. "Yo Gucci!"

Looking in my direction he recognized me immediately. "Chauncey, what up?"

Joc had just come out of the store. Seeing us talking he approached and greeted Gucci and Courtney Cee. I hadn't seen Gucci in a minute and heard he had been locked up on a probation violation for beating some dude's ass with a pool stick at the pool hall. That's when he clarified the rumors.

"Yeah, I just got out," he said. "But hey, shit happens."

"Well glad to see you out," I said congratulating him.

"You still fuckin' wit' that music," he asked.

"You already know," I looked at Joc. "Aye, grab one of those CDs for him."

Joc went to my car and grabbed him one. When he came back, he gave it to him.

He said, "Nigga, that's you, Yung Joc, that I've been hearing all on the radio, in the county?" The CD had the name written on it and Gucci was looking at it.

Joc replied, "Yeah that's me."

"Damn boy, you on fire. That shit goin' hard."

That's when I said, "Look, we gotta do somethin' together."

Gucci said, "Cool, I'm wit' it. Matter of fact, I'm on my way to the studio right now. How 'bout I give you my number and you hit me in a couple hours."

And so that's what we did. We exchanged numbers right then. Now at the time it was around 10 a.m. so when 3 o'clock hit, I called him up and he told me he was at Big Cat Studio between Marietta Street and Northside Drive. He gave me directions and me and Joc jumped in my truck and were there in 30 minutes.

Gucci was standing outside when we pulled up. We jumped out, hollered at him for a second, then we all went in together.

The female receptionist working the desk tried to stop us from going in. "Excuse me guys, unless you have an appointment... "

That's when Gucci spoke up. "Oh, they're with me."

That was enough to send her back to her job.

As soon as we got into one of the studios, Gucci introduced us to another artist on Big Cat Records that he had in there with him. Gucci told him, "Pull up them Zae beats."

Right then, dude began flipping through a couple tracks. Every one of them was jamming.

I asked him, "Who did you say did them beats?"

"Oh, that's my producer," he said. "His name is Zaytoven."

"I remembered the name from when he did the song "So Icy."'
I said, "Man, I need to holla at him for some of dat heat."

He said it wouldn't be a problem.

Me and Joc settled in and in no time, Gucci found a track we all started feeling. Him and Joc started messing around with it. Joc was giving Gucci some things he could do with the beat. I thought this was strange but I didn't dwell on it. Then Joc said something about New Joc City. Gucci turned around and started saying Gucci world. But as we got to vibing, something came up where someone had studio time slotted for the room we were in.

"Look Gucci," I began, as we started to roll out. "We're gonna have to hook up again."

"Fa' sho," he told me and Joc.

"It's good to see you out and doin' ya thang again," I told him.

"Yeah," came Joc. "Bet, this is only the beginning."

For the next couple of days, Joc didn't mention anything about going back to the studio with Gucci. So one day I brought it up.

"Man I don't know about recording with him," Joc told me. "All that shit between him and Jeezy, Block might not want me fucking with him."

His comment showed me how his way of thinking might bring him problems down the road. First off, I knew he didn't have a clue what Block felt. Block was having his own issues with Jeezy, trying to get him to do another Boyz 'N Da Hood album. And Jeezy clearly showed he didn't want to do it. Block had told me, basically, "Fuck Jeezy." But I didn't say anything to Joc. I wanted him to make his own choices... but I knew sooner or later Gucci would be on fire and niggas would be doing back flips to work with him.

I knew you couldn't let other people's problems get in the way of you doing you and building your own relationships.

The following week, after meeting Block and John at the Chick-Fil-A, I spoke with him and he told me that he talked to Mike Caren at Atlantic Records. He said that there was no need in speaking to Mike anymore because he had plans to go over Mike's head. Then the week after this conversation, on October 28th, all four of us met back up at the same Chick-Fil-A.

"Listen," John said to all of us. "I've come up with a joint venture contract between MasterMind and Block Entertainment. In it, Block, you have six months to try and find a deal for Joc's music, with a major label. If you fulfill this duty, then you and MasterMind will do a fifty-fifty split on all revenue, advances, and credits. You'd also share as executive producers."

John went on to explain how Block was not given any exclusive rights to Joc or to sign any deal on our behalf. I had to sign any deal before it became valid. Publishing also was not included.

All three of us read through the agreement. John hadn't yet made changes to the contracts between MasterMind and Joc so he had us initial each page, saying we fully understood. Then he had us sign to acknowledge that Joc was in agreement to being signed to MasterMind Music.

During this meeting I said something that led Block to say, "You can take management if you want. And I'll be the label."

I just laughed and said, "Nah, that's okay."

Then with the ink dry on the agreement, Joc made a request. "Do y'all think I could get an advance? I got some things I'd like to take care of."

Block said cool and asked me if I wanted to go half. I was down so we gave Joc $7,000. And with that finished, we mounted up and left.

The first thing Joc did with his money was go and put down on a Ford Expedition. His days of dealing with his busted up Cadillac were over. Now he had a vehicle he could maneuver in.

"I'm tellin' you," I said proudly to him. "Patience. This ain't nothin'. We gon' make this shit work."

"I already know," he said confidently. "I already see it comin."

That Wednesday night we had it lined up to perform at The Peacock. Akinee The Black Mack was doing a showcase and we were on the bill. We told Block to come out so he could see how crunk the crowd got and to see Joc's stage presence. DJ Brad from the Legion of Doom deejayed the event every week and would always shout us out. That night the club was packed, and I couldn't wait to do our thing.

Akinee did his "Best of the Best" show and crews from all over the city were up in there. He had Joc as a special guest performer, so you know I had the squad out. M.M.M. was deep as hell in the club! When the time came, we didn't disappoint, turning the spot out. And by its end, Block had a good idea of what we were working with. Definitely this show fueled his fire to make something happen in the 6-month time span.

That Saturday night, Block hooked it up with the infamous Greg Street of the Hitmen DJs, for us to appear live on Greg's V-103 radio show. Block wanted to announce officially Joc signing to his Block Entertainment. So we all shot to the station to make that happen.

"Imm'ah just tell you," Greg said to us once we made it in. "JD played Joc's song last week and told us in the station, "Yeah, this new So So Def shit right here."

"Oh yeah," Block asked.

"Yeah. I was just laughin. You know how JD is."

When the time finally came, Greg got on the air and started the interview. Block and him spoke for a while, building up some suspense about the "new kid" Joc and how his song was blazin' in the streets. Then without further delay, they called Joc to the mic to make it official to everybody as to what the decision for his future was.

"Yeah everybody," he said over the airwaves. "I just signed to Block E-N-T!"

And immediately my cellphone blew up. I swear, people from everywhere started calling me. "I hear y'all on the radio. . . " "Ahh shit! Ya'll signed wit' Block?!" It was crazy! Street niggas, old friends, old hoes, haters. . . everybody called to congratulate us. I just thanked them quickly and got off the phone because Greg Street was signaling me to say a few words on the mic.

Greg asked me a few questions and I told everybody the details about the deal and thanked the streets for their support. I promised everybody we'd rep the A to the fullest and that they could expect nothing but heat in the future.

Greg's show was really poppin' so we kept it brief, thanked him for supporting us and we left there really feeling good.

After we did our radio appearances with Greg, me, Joc and the crew went out to this jumping ass club in East Point called Central Station. As I was pulling up a call came in on my cell that I didn't recognize. I said fuck it and picked up.

"Yo, who's this?"

"Damn Chino, what happened?!" A voice boomed in my ear. "I thought we were locked in to do something!"

Dumbfounded I asked again, "Who is this?"

"Skeeter Rock!"

I jumped out of my truck and into the parking lot amidst a crowd of party goers. "Man, you never got back at me about the album deal. And that lil' bit of money y'all talk . . . I spend that on shoes in a month."

"I just thought we were on," he continued. "JD thought Nitti straightened things out."

I told him, "Nah, he didn't." Then I told him about my agreement with Block.

"Damn! Look Chino, let me see if I can still do something," he said. "I'll get back at 'chu later."

"All right," I said, ending the call. I set my sights on the club, finally ready to relax and enjoy the progress we were making.

More support came from the same station's DJ Ryan Cameron. Soon after the announcement with Greg, we were invited to Ryan's show, between 12 p.m. and 6 p.m., to make the announcement there. For those who had missed it the first time, we told listeners that we had an important announcement and that Joc was the newest member of Block Entertainment. Ryan's daytime audience was big so we felt covered on all bases with this.

With everything going how it was, I felt like it was time to record with some more outside producers. I hit up my dude Mr. DJ to see if he was available and he told me he was. So me and Joc slid through to his crib and he played us a couple tracks. One immediately jumped out as us.

"Whoa! I'm feelin' that," Joc told him.

"Oh yeah?" DJ asked.

"Yeah, put that on loop for me. Imm'ah see what I can do wit' it."

So DJ went ahead and looped it while Joc went right into jotting down lyrics.

That night we cut the whole song and, to me, it sounded like it was calling for U.G.K. to bless the track with Joc. We told DJ we would be back the next day and he said he was down. We followed up and dropped one with him called "Unh, Unh, Unh" where the beat was a rendition of Tip's "Rubberband Man" and Jeezy's "My Hood" songs. It was a hit and we knew it the moment we finished. I figured two songs was enough and that we'd gotten what we were looking for.

A few days later, Joc called me. "Aye, MTV is doing somethin' for everybody in the A who's in the music business. It's down at the park off Metropolitan, we gotta go."

I said, "Cool, let's do it."

I had just left Jeezy and Lil' Will and I figured I'd see them up there as well. So I got dressed and shot out to the park. As soon as I pulled up and parked, I noticed that it looked like a family reunion. I got out my truck and made my way over to the action.

MTV had camera crews filming and everything. I found out that this was to be a photo shoot of all the pioneers and current artists in the music business in Atlanta. I had no idea pictures were being taken. I had just thrown on anything. So I ended up ducking the camera, trying to stay out of the spot light. They were telling cats to say their names on the camera, so they could know who we were, but with me being so programmed to stay away from cameras and out of the spotlight because of my street lifestyle, I kept ducking them.

Then the time came where everybody who'd shown up gathered in one big group to take a photo. I went to the back of the group, standing next to my boys K.P. and Tip.

"Listen," the cameraman said, after taking a couple flicks. "Some of you I can't see. You're just swallowed up in the back."

By this time, I was a little relaxed with the idea, so I moved to the front next to Young Jeezy. The cameraman snapped off two more pictures, one being the actual photo that was later used. Because I never gave my name and was ducking the camera the picture listed me as "unknown" on MTV's website for the picture.

During this shoot, a lot of people were out of town and a lot were not contacted. People were making jokes asking JD "Where's Kris Kross? We want Kriss Kross!" I ran into my boy C-Bone, who was glad I'd made it.

"My boy Chino," he called teasingly. "Boy you made it to the picture. Yeah, my nigga faked it 'till he made it!"

All of us who came from the streets busted up laughing because we knew what that meant. I didn't have to use the line "I'm a producer!" anymore to cover up the fact that I was dealing drugs. C-Bone was saying I had finally made it and was going down in history with all the greats from Atlanta. And though I appreciated the sentiment, until a major deal was done, and I had a few platinum plaques under my belt like a lot at the shoot, I wouldn't rest.

"Hey y'all! What's up?"

I turned from C-Bone and the group to see Lil' Will running up.

"They get started yet?" he asked.

"Yeah man, it's over," I told him.

Lil' Will missed out that day all because he made too long of an event getting fresh for the shoot.

I was constantly looking to upgrade my team, and I figured it was time for us to take some more photos. So I put a shoot together with my dude G Gleeze, whose people owned this club off of LaVista Road. Gleeze had this photographer named Earl to do our photos. In preparation, I got with my dudes Courtney and Trent who owned a management company called Red Oak Management. They had a host of clothing sponsors and I figured a free photo shoot to wear their gear wasn't bad. I also got my partner who owned a salon to silk screen some t-shirts for us. I had our logo placed on the front and Yung Joc "It's Goin' Down" on the back. I also had Low Down and Duddy under that and a single we had recorded for them.

Sticking to what I'd told Duddy that once the time was right, we had to bring him and Low Down back. Duddy had been coming to my spot when he wasn't on the road with Bubba. We had clicked back up at Bubba's video shoot for "Ms. New Booty," and since Bubba lived all the way north and I lived all the way south, Duddy would stay with me instead of trying to get all the way back to Athens before having to get back to Atlanta again to go back on the road.

So at the photo shoot, we had the club open up on a Sunday evening and had a few models that Gleeze had gotten from his promotion company called Stomping Grounds. Me, Joc, Low Down and Duddy, Flame, Elvis and some of the Goon Squad, like Mike "Caleto", Vick, A.K., Roc, Redman and some more of the guys, all flicked up. Block had come through as well and put on a MasterMind shirt and flicked up with me and Joc.

While in the middle of the shoot, Duddy and a few more homies got a bright idea and got a bottle of liquor from behind the bar. The owners ended up finding out and they quickly threw us out because we weren't supposed to touch shit.

"Damn," I said frustrated. "We need to finish."

"I know somebody," Chris Flame said whipping out his cell phone.

Chris called Phil, a cat who'd taken Chris in like a nephew to make tracks for a few artist he had. Phil owned this big ass club at the corner of Buford Hwy and North Druid Hills as well as The Eastside Bounce. Chris told Phil Joc was doing a photo shoot and that we needed a place. Phil was real fond of Joc, meeting him when Chris had taken him over to his spot a few times to write for his artist named Amanda, aka Sage. Phil would pay Joc a few hundred and Joc would come back to the studio flashing the money saying how Phil paid him in "lil faces" with that old money.

Phil agreed and we shot over to his club off Buford Hwy. and did the shots in these VIP rooms that were upstairs overlooking the dance floor.

Earl told everybody, "All right y'all, I wanna get some private shots of Chino and Joc modeling this free gear some sponsor must have given them."

Everybody left and Earl had these two chicks laying all over me and Joc in some sexy ass bra and panty outfits. They even did some half naked shots! The girl who was on me struck my curiosity being all over me like that. "Damn baby," I asked. "What's your name?"

She smiled and said, "Shay."

I went on and tried to holler but came to find out she was Earl's girl. Years later, she went on to be cast on a show on VH1. She competed with other girls for the attention of hip hop great, Flavor Flav, on the show *Flavor of Love*. Her name was Shay "Bucky" Johnson.

No Diddy

Still grinding, Joc was up at Soul Messiah Studio with Sunny, going through some beats that Shawn J from the group Field Mob had left. Both of them found a track they liked and redid the song "Fuck U Pay Me." Although they didn't know who did the beat, they felt it and did their thing on it.

When they finished, Shawn J came in and said, "Y'all used my track? I was gonna use dat track. Nitti gave me them beats to fuck wit."

So now they knew who made it.

"Man, we didn't know," Sunny told him.

The next day Sunny told me about it. "Look," I told him, "I'll hook you and Big Rick up with Nitti. Y'all can holla at him about the track."

Big Rick ended up buying the beat from Nitti, and I told Sunny he needed to give me 3 to 5 percent for my concept on the hook. But he acted like what I said went in one ear and out the other.

One day I got a call from Block. "Man, I let Puff hear the song," he said.

Excited I asked, "Is that right? What'd he think?"

He paused. "He ain't feeling it."

"Oh yeah?" I was a little disappointed.

"Yeah, but don't trip. Imm'ah see what else I can put together."

"All right."

Maybe I expected it all to come easy. Like "Snap!" and everybody would jump to sign us. But I remembered to be patient, cool and optimistic. Bad Boy was just one label. There were many others.

We had been booked to do a couple of shows; two were pretty big. One was out in Marietta at this club called Studio Seventeen. DJ Southern Bread was hosting it, and I worked it out where we'd perform in exchange for him to bump the song on a regular basis. From the way the crowd reacted when Joc hit the stage, Southern Bread had lived up to his end of the bargain and so did we 'cause Joc rocked it.

The other show we did was down in Macon, Georgia. It was at this college called Fort Valley State. My partner DJ Smooth was throwing a concert in the gym with one of the college organizations and had several acts lined up. He had D4L as well as Ms. B as the headliners. So again, we hit the spot deep.

At Fort Valley, we did our thing. After Ms. B and Joc's performances, we received star-like responses from the crowd. "It's Goin' Down" was a smash. At this time, I had my boy with us recording everything on video camera. When all of the excitement was at its peak, my boy put the camera on me and I pulled out a wad of cash, faded off of the Patron.

"This MasterMind Music niggas!" my voice boomed loudly over all of the commotion. My eyes focused on the camera. "Fuck JD! Fuck Puffy! If niggas don't wanna fuck wit' us, fuck 'em! We gon' do us anyway."

After my outburst, everybody jumped in front of the camera going ape shit. MasterMind had turned into a real movement.

$$$

Me and Joc were out and about taking care of business when

someone we knew told us they had heard a new song at Platinum 21 with Joc on it. According to them, the song wasn't "It's Goin' Down" or any of his others, and that the club had been bumpin' it a lot. We downplayed it thinking that the song was one they hadn't heard, because we were recording so much.

Well, a few days later, me and Joc ended up sliding through Platinum 21. We went to relax and to see about getting the DJ to play our music. When the DJ saw us hit the door he instantly started playing "It's Goin' Down." Then he proceeded to shout us out.

He told Joc, "Yeah, I got this song I want you to hear, that they likin' in here. The night DJ made it."

Curiously, me and Joc looked at each other as he went on to play it for us. The beat came on and the girls instantly started jamming to it and reciting the words. Then, the hook came in shocking us both. The DJ who had made the song had crafted it by inserting some of Joc's lyrics from "It's Goin' Down" to make the hook, using Joc's voice as well.

"Aye man, who made this," I asked over the music.

He smiled. "DJ Styles."

"When does he work?"

"He'll be here tonight, at eight," he said looking at his watch.

"Cool."

Joc followed me as we left out of the booth.

"Did you . . .? "

"Yeah," I told Joc as we exited the club.

"We gotta holla at him."

I gave him that look and said, "You already know."

We burned up a couple hours making our rounds and returned around 10 p.m. And as soon as we made it in the door, we heard DJ Styles's version pumping over the speakers. After hollering at my cousin Twon aka Snake, aka Angel, and Kamal who were managers at the club, we instantly made a B-Line to the booth, noticing that the new DJ was on. Joc then waved and got his attention.

"Yo pimp, what's up?" he said to us.

Joc asked, "Who did this song?"

He said, "Well, that's me rapping and my partner and I did the beat. I did the sample too."

I stepped in. "Look man, I'm Chino Dolla and this is Yung Joc. Big dog, y'all can't use that sample. We need to sit down and come up with something."

He gave us a knowing look, like he understood, "All right."

We exchanged numbers and I told Styles I'd give him a call.

The next day I hit him up and he told me and Joc to meet him at this nice subdivision of new homes off of Camp Creek. This was where his partner who made the beat, named Cochese, stayed with his pops.

"What's up y'all," he said, meeting me and Joc after we parked.

"Nothin' much," Joc replied.

"Let's go inside," Cochese said.

Cochese led us down to the basement where he had his studio. We all took chairs, and I got straight to the point.

"Listen, y'all can give Joc the song and I will put it on his album," I said. "If not, it would be a waste of a good song because we'd never clear it for y'all to use."

I stopped to see if they followed me.

"Now," I continued, "Me and Joc talked about this and he's willing to do two verses and leave Styles on the song. I will do a little to the beat and give y'all full credit. Just give me ten percent publishing. I'll also give y'all thirty-five hundred in advance for the beat, when we do the deal."

Both Cochese and Styles nodded. They were all for it.

This little misunderstanding with the song ended up turning into a good relationship between me, Joc, Styles, and Cochese. Styles would go on to blow "It's Goin' Down" up at Platinum 21, and we started going over Cochese's spot and recording. While there one night, Joc came up with a drum pattern on the M.P.C., which led Cochese to put some sounds to it. Brandy came in the next day and recorded a few lines with Joc, and they came up with a song called "I Know U See It."

Still grinding, me, Joc and the crew had been hitting spots deep. One night we hit a small strip club called 24k to holler at my boy DJ Outlaw. While there, a promoter named Cool Runnings approached us.

"Cheeeenooo Dolla!" Cool said in his signature tone. His voice sounding like he pinched his nose when he talked. "Bo'eeee, y'all blowin' up! An' Cool wanna promote y'all on de' radio."

"Oh yeah," I said, holding back a laugh. Although I knew Cool was about his business, his voice always cracked me up.

"Dat's right! Live at 24k . . . Yung Joc, MastaMine Musik C.E.O. Cheeenoooo Dolla. Dis Saturday! Yep y'all get da' VIP an y'all own section. And Joc don't gotta perform. All y'all gotta do is show up, 'cause y'all get it crunk!"

We thought it was a good look so we told him cool. And that Saturday it was on. After his promise to promote it on the radio, we showed up to a live setting. Me and my cousin Kenio both got $5,000 in ones and covered the VIP floor with them. When we left, Cool Runnings called me every week for us to come back.

"My boiii, Cheeenooo Dolla!"

Cool Runnings, one crazy muthafucka. . .

$$$

Well, the holidays had rolled in and it was time for me to throw my yearly Thanksgiving Day Feast. All my family showed up. My mom and her twin Nancy, my aunt Blondeen, my kids and the numerous cousins and other relatives in between. My mom and aunts ended up throwing down, putting together a meal that always outdid the previous year's, and in the end, the event brought my sprits back up. Having family around smiling and looking happy always cheered me up. It's times like these that motivate me to do something that would keep smiles on their faces every day. During the holidays, I enjoyed fucking with family.

One night I was out kicking it with my cousin Kenio on the Eastside. Whenever I was out that way I would crash over at his lay low apartment. Nobody knew about this spot except for me, his mom, his girl and his uncle Danny Man, who stayed in the same complex. This night me and Kenio hit Pinups and had DJ Outlaw playing Joc's music and shouting us out the whole time.

Well, one of these chicks in the club walked up to me and out of nowhere handed me her phone. "It's for you."

Confused I just looked at it. "Who are you?"

Smiling, she said, "Just take it and say hello."

At first I didn't know what to think. But then I said 'fuck it' and took the phone. The music was loud so I had to bend down and cover one ear. "Hello."

A voice on the other end said, "I've been calling you and you ain't been answering your phone."

I really couldn't make out the voice but I knew it wasn't my girl because I hadn't heard a hundred million curse words. "Who is this?"

"It's Christina."

I laughed. I hadn't heard from her since me and Joc tossed her up at Travis'. "You haven't been calling me."

"Yes I have," she said. "I've called and chirped you."

I said, "Why didn't you call my other phone. You know Nextel be trippin'."

"I don't know. . . forgot. Anyway, I'm in town. Hit me when you leave the club o.k."

I smiled, knowing what she wanted. "All right, I will." Then I hung up and handed the girl her phone back.

For the rest of the night me and Kenio chilled out. Then after getting good and fucked up, me and Kenio left around 4 a.m. When valet pulled my truck up, I could hardly walk. I knew I had to tighten up because I wasn't a fan of drunk driving and the DeKalb County Police loved to fuck with blacks, especially the ones riding cleaner than they were. A lot of times they would pull you over just to see who was driving so fly, or try to lock you up in jail for anything and holler at your girl when she came to visit. I was so glad I had moved out of Decatur and Lithonia before they could give me life in prison. And I wasn't about to let them give it to me tonight. I had to get myself together before we pulled off.

Getting Kenio to drive was out of the question. He was on about 5 ecstasy pills, rolling his ass off. He was also high off about 10 sticks of Cush, and he had no license. He was definitely no good. Plus, Kenio had priors that didn't sit well with me.

The week before, Kenio had been in a hit-and-run when we went to a club in Conyers. Some dude had hit him and Kenio jumped out of the car with his pistol, approaching the dude and his girl as they sat shocked. Kenio had the pistol's green beam on dude. Immediately the guy started apologizing and saying he'd pay for the damages. Kenio ended up jumping back in the car after scaring them half to death and went to an afterhours party at The Cave in Decatur.

After leaving The Cave around 5:30 a.m. that morning, on I-20, on his way to some chick's house, he drove into some old white dude's car while getting off on Panola Road. Well, both of them pulled over and when the guy saw no damage was done he said everything was cool. But before they could settle the matter, the police pulled behind them and told Kenio that his car matched the description of another car involved in an altercation at a club—an incident where someone pulled a gun. Long story short, the police ended up searching his car and finding his pistol. And Kenio found himself on a first class trip to the DeKalb County Jail. So he definitely wasn't driving my truck.

Getting my truck from valet, I pulled it to the side and called Christina. Trying to make it home to the Southside was out of the question, considering how fucked up I was. I told her to meet me in Decatur, off of Memorial Drive at this Waffle King across from the DeKalb County Jail. Then I took my time and headed there myself.

At the Waffle King me and Kenio chilled out, trying to get ourselves together. I swallowed a steak and eggs plate. Kenio couldn't eat because the pills had the best of him. Not too much time later, Christina walked in looking good like always.

"Hey Chino," she said. "Who's your friend?"

Kenio was sitting there drooling. It looked like his eyes were rolling to the back of his head like a jack pot slot machine. "This my cousin Kenio," I said.

I introduced them and on the slick Kenio asked me, "Cuz, how much she want for some of that?"

He was a big trick and I knew it. I mean, a 12 p.m. in the strip club buying pussy trick. "Just fall back. I got 'chu," I assured him.

After exchanging a few pleasantries we left. Christina followed us to South Hairston where Kenios' chill spot was. As soon as we got in the one-bedroom apartment and she saw the big flat screen on the wall, the king sized bed in the bedroom, she realized Kenio wasn't just some tag along. We went straight into action.

As soon as I got her naked, Kenio was right there naked before I could unbuckle my belt. We beat the pussy up nonstop and I didn't get any rest until 1 p.m. That morning, Christina finally came out of the closet with her addiction and asked us if we had some soft (power cocaine). This was right up Kenio's alley and he fed her all morning. Her snorting and him rolling off ecstasy, sleep was not in the picture. When I left that day I told myself I was done fucking up. Though me and my girl were having our issues, I didn't want to lose what I had in her.

At least, I was still willing to give it a try before I went broke fucking around in these streets. Money was tight, the houses I had bought hadn't made a dime. Actually, they were costing more to keep up than anything. I needed cash! I know you must be thinking of all the money I spent since my loss and saying "you ain't broke!" But you must understand my expenses. Remember I have a home, kids and other luxuries. So when I say I need cash it's because if I can't pay for what I've amassed and my lifestyle, then Imm'ah have to sell shit. Either that or go back to the block .

And I wasn't trying to do neither.

Puffy Wants To Deal?

The famous Club 112 had relocated to a new spot off of Peachtree and my home girl, Candy Coated, hooked me up with this promoter named Bitty who wanted to pay Joc $1,000 to perform. This paid performance helped to make shit look a whole lot better for our efforts.

We agreed and showed up at 112 right at the end of the night. Usually this is the time when shit is jumping but by the time they finally got Joc on the mic, the club was emptying out. But he still did his thing and when the club closed, Bitty started trying to play some games about paying us. I talked to this cat named Alex from AG Entertainment, to settle our differences. He had come across the street from his club Visions. I concluded that Bitty worked for him because he's the one who ended up paying us.

That night I thanked Alex and I thanked God that we got that paper because I had the squad with me and they were out in the back of 112 telling security that they were going to spray that bitch up if we didn't get paid. I didn't wanna catch a case over a funky ass thousand dollars but I had to let these niggas in the music biz know that I didn't play any games about my paper. Now I saw what my partner Bobby meant when he used to tell me "Get 'cho money before you perform. Because you never know what'll happen later."

Despite all our obstacles, we had begun to pick up a major buzz in the streets. And I could see that my whole team could feel it. Although I knew our hard work would pay off sooner or later, I was glad that Elvis, Chris, Shawty Slick, Sunny and Joc were seeing the results, because I needed them to continue grinding.

This was only the beginning.

One early Saturday morning, I got up after a long night of being out. My normal routine was very exhausting, but necessary. I was still in bed trying to get enough strength to go and shower up. That's when I received a call from Block.

"Yo Chino, last night Puff was in town and he went to Body Tap," he said. "Man, X-Rated played the song and Puff saw how crazy the club went. He said they kept playin' it and it gave him a chance to really feel it."

"Oh yeah," I said, wondering where he was going.

"Yeah," he continued. "And so he gave me a call sayin' he wants to do a deal."

I couldn't believe my ears. "You said what?!"

He laughed. "He wants to do the deal, Chino. He wants to sign Joc to Bad Boy South. He wants me to meet him after I talk to you, about a joint venture. What 'chu think?"

I couldn't focus, let alone think. I had a feeling something was going to pop, but this caught me off guard. I said "You ain't meeting wit him yet, that's what I think. Let me know what he's talkin' about."

Block agreed and we ended the call on that note. After that, I laid there in bed stuck, paralyzed and unable to move. After Block's news, I got Joc and the crew together and I told them about Puffy's interest. We weren't going to get all overly excited but I wanted them to see how close we were to reaching that next level.

"We're this close," I told them. "All we gotta do is keep pushin'. And once one of us gets in, we all make it." Shit was feeling good and I could already tell Joc was feeling a lot of confidence. The shows we were doing were helping him to grow as an artist and it had gotten to the point where his shows were just as good as anybody else's. He had turned into a true performer.

My boy Cool Running gave me a call one Friday saying how he wanted us back at 24k the next night. "Cheeenooo Dolla! I need 'chall ta come back. Y'all turned da club out."

His voice killed me. "I'll let 'chu know Cool."

"Liss 'en," he went on, "I got 'chu and whoever you want on da list. And of course da VIP"

"All right Cool. Let me get back at 'chu."

When I got off the phone I called my cousin Kenio and told him about Cool's invitation, to see if he wanted to go with us.

"Cuz I might be out of town," he said. "I'm try'na get this chick to drive me out to Knoxville, TN."

Kenio went on to tell me he had to go out there so he could make up for a loss he took. He said some dude he had been serving work to from the hood had been goin out to Knoxville with his family getting money. The week prior, Kenio had went out there with this cat and the dude introduced Kenio to this smoker he kept around to help bring customers. He said he took a brick so they could work it.

"Man, I was in the hotel room with the smoker," Kenio explained. "And when I went to sleep I woke up the next morning only to find him and my dope gone. Shawty, he got the whole brick!"

I couldn't believe he let himself get crossed like that.

"So I called my boy and told him," he said. "This nigga acted like he hadn't seen dude. So we met up and rode around lookin' for him but we couldn't find him."

"Do you think he was in on it? You know ain't nothing worse than the cross then the double cross," I told him, already seeing the move.

"Maybe. . . Naw, I don't know." He said. "He told me he'd cover it though. He'd just work it off on every trip I made. He'd give me like four-five stacks over. So now I'm just try'na shoot back out there and make up, because I still gotta pay Earnest."

Earnest was Kenio's big homie, who had always looked out for him. Earnest had been dropping work on him ever since we were young. Back when we were trapping in Lithonia, off of Bruce Street and Conyers Road. Kenio played middleman between me and Earnest when we got older, when I had people that wanted to buy a couple bricks. He was a real O.G. and I knew Kenio didn't want to disappoint the one who always had his back.

After he explained, I told Kenio I'd call him back the next day to see what he was going to do.

"All right," he said. "If I can't get a ride, shit I just might roll."

Thinking about how we balled the last time at 24k, I really wanted Babe to go, so that Saturday, after I got everything lined up, I called him back.

"I don't know if Imm'ah make it," he said. "The home girl Nicole rented me a whip and I'm waiting on Shawty to drive me down there. I just came in from the Westside, getting eight pounds of purp' from them P.C. niggas. Man they got that bubble gum for six stacks a pound. And shit, other niggas be wantin' sixty-five to seventy-five hundred for that purp'. So I snatched up those to take wit' me."

When he told me, the numbers on the purp' my toes curled. All those pounds that got caught up on that deal with Reece would've called for a shit load of rubber bands.

Well, trying to stick to the subject and save my heart some pain, I told Kenio to let me know before it was too late. When I didn't hear from him I called him back but he went on to tell me that he was indeed leaving for Tennessee. The girl he had driving had not shown up so he insisted he drive himself. I told him I thought he was crazy for doing so but he insisted he was straight. He said he'd call me when he made it. He needed to do his thing and he said he'd be back in no time. That night we decided not to do 24k. Instead, we hit up a couple other spots to politic with the DJs.

Sunday evening, I tried to call Kenio because he hadn't called me, but I couldn't reach him. Then two days later I found myself still unable to find him. That's when my Godmother, my aunt Chris, Kenio's mother called me.

"Baby, have you seen or heard from my other son?" she asked.

I said, "No ma'am. But I've been trying to call him."

"It ain't like him to go this long without calling or coming by here."

I knew she was worried. "Let me make some calls, ok? And I'll let you know what's up."

Immediately I called my boy Dee, who went to boot camp with me.

"Shawty, I just heard that Kenio was locked up in Knoxville," he said.

This was my worst fear. "What?!"

"Yeah," he continued. "Niggas in the hood were talkin' about it."

"All right," I told him. "See what else you can find out and get back at me."

I hung up and made some more calls.

My partner Japale, who used to serve cats in Lithonia and cut hair back in the day, was my second call. Japale had gone 100 percent legit and had opened a clothing store in Conyers. Everybody from Lithonia shopped at his spot, Fashion Industry, and if anybody heard any gossip, he did.

"Yep," he told me when he picked up. "It's true. Your road dog is fucked up. That's all these niggas is talkin' 'bout. But I don't know too much. When I find out more info I'll hit you."

Then Dee hit me back. "Yeah, they say he was set up by his partner from the hood. That Kenio went to this hotel to meet him and dude called and said for him to come to another place. As Kenio was on his way there the police tried to pull him over and he punched it. He ended up crashing into somebody's house; then he tried to run. But they got him. They're saying it was the Feds."

"Damn," I said shaking my head.

Dee continued, "They say he had a brick and two pounds of purp' or fifty stacks."

My line clicked. I looked at the caller I.D. and saw that it was my Godmother calling back. "Look Dee, keep me on point. I got his mama try'na call. Let me hit you back." I clicked over.

"He just called Chauncey," she said. I could tell she was crying. "He's locked up. But at least he's alive, because I was beginning to worry."

"I was just about to call you," I explained. "I heard too."

"Well, he told me to tell you to meet me at his duck off spot."

"O.K." I already knew what that meant. "I'll be there in twenty minutes."

I jumped in one of my undercover whips and met her off South Hairston. As soon as we got to Kenio's apartment we noticed his door was cracked open. Somebody had ransacked this place. I immediately saw that his big flat screen was gone off the wall. I found that all his shoes were missing as I searched for the shoe boxes he stashed his loose money in. He always kept about $50,000 in a fireproof safe box hidden in his closet. Now it was gone as well. I knew he had just bought those eight pounds from them P.C. niggas and hearing he only got caught with two, I knew six were hidden somewhere. Lookin in his other stash I found that those were gone as well.

In his position, I knew that Kenio needed everything he could get. But it seemed that now the game came to take back from him what it had given, just like it had done me. And I knew of only one muthafucka who could've done some scandalous shit like this. His Uncle Danny Man.

Or so I believed.

It seemed that everybody around me was taking a fall, fucking around in the game. All I wanted was for a relief from the struggles and hardships that caused individuals like me to resort to robbing and selling drugs just to live. Kenio meant a lot to me, I envisioned the day when this music shit popped, and we could enjoy a different life. And just when it was slowly coming into fruition, he got snatched up--another shattered dream.

Block had reported to me that Puffy had come up with an agreement. He told me John had the contract and that it was a good deal. So, we called up Joc and lined up time for us all to meet.

Now Joc and his family had moved from Acworth and stayed with his cousin Vick and his brother Darius in a house off of Cascade Road. The song was still gaining momentum and Acworth was too far, so now he was closer for us to be in the streets. Being that his wife was using their vehicle, I shot out there and got him. We were both eager to see what Puff's deal looked like.

"Just remember," I told Joc, "We came too far to settle now. I'm not signing shit if it's not in the best interest for your future."

He agreed. "I'm down with you," he told me.

We were to meet up at Block's studio, at this building next to Ms. Ann's famous burger spot off of Memorial Drive. When we arrived, John and Block were already outside the place. The studio was still under construction. "Hey you two," John said, shaking me and Joc's hands.

"What's up?" we asked them.

"Try'na make this shit work," came Block.

We went inside the building and I saw how walls had been knocked down to make more room for what Block was trying to do. There were no seats or anything so me, Joc and Block sat on some cinder blocks while John stood before us. In his hands was a stack of papers.

"This is the contract that Sean Combs had presented," he explained. "I've been over it and now I'm going to explain it to you all in layman's terms, so you all can make a conscious decision on whether you'll agree or disagree with its terms. I also have the new MasterMind contracts you requested Chauncey, for you and Joc, with all the changes you requested."

Wanting to get that out of the way first, John went over the changes in me and Joc's agreement, and then we both signed it.

"Now let's see what Puff talkin' 'bout," I said.

Bad Boy wanted to do a six-album deal. The first budget would be for $500,000 with $25,000 in promotional money and a couple million as needed on the label side for its promo. I had the album almost done and everybody I had to pay, including myself, was $5,000 and under per track. The money left over from the budget was to be split between me and Block 50/50. As far as the points on the album, we were giving Joc twelve and Block and I would split four.

"All three of you will also get fifty thousand dollars advance on this deal," John explained. "You'll get half of that as soon as the contracts are in, if you accept."

"I'm tellin' you, this is by far the best deal on the table," Block said. "With Puff behind this project we're sure to blow."

I didn't like the contract, but I did agree with that. Puffy's ability to push a project was undeniable. "All right," I said. "But I need some time to read it and see."

Smiling like his dream had finally come true, Joc signed the contract. Then Block. When it was handed to me, something strange happened.

"No, no, no! Don't sign it," Block and John said over each other.

I looked at them confused. I didn't want Block over anything I'd done but then I figured that he couldn't do anything without me. "O.K.," I said putting the papers down and figuring that this was how it was done.

John collected the paperwork and again reminded us that as soon as he got them processed we'd begin getting our money. I needed the $50,000 bad. That day, me and Joc left headed to Hooters on Peachtree St. feeling like we were on top of the world. We had finally made it!

The Deal

The reaction of everybody to us signing was crazy. My family and crew were ecstatic. Even my girl couldn't complain. But I knew I couldn't get caught up in being too high off of it. I had to stay focused. Until checks started rolling in, we hadn't made it yet. Still another step up the ladder waited for us. My goal was to blow the fuck up!

I took the days following in stride and rested up, because I knew our grind needed to be on one million. One night I woke to the sound of my cell blowing up. It was Joc. He went on to tell me that he was on his way to Body Tap with Puff, who had sent a driver to pick him up.

"Man come up there," he said.

"All right," I said. "Let me get dressed."

I got up, but because it was already late when I arrived, the night was already over. I saw Joc, Puff, Big Boi, C-Bone, and some more niggas in the parking lot by Puff's Phantom, smoking on a stick of that loud.

I got out my truck. "What's up y'all?"

Puffy looked over toward me and said, "I see you, playboy."

C-Bone looked around as everybody spoke and said, "Chino mutha 'fuckin' Dolla, Mr. Dope Boy Magic himself." We shot the shit for a minute and it seemed as if Puff was looking at me trying to place my face from somewhere then Joc came over to holler at me and we stepped off to the side a little.

"Shit bra', Puff picked me up from Vick's. Check out what happened." He explained how he had brought the new music he'd recorded and the video camera we used to record some of the shows we did. He said Puff went to cut on the camera to see how it was going down at our shows and it so happened to be on the part where we were leaving from Fort Valley College and I was like "Fuck Puff! Fuck J.D. . . we got our own money and ain't shit stopping us."

"I tried to stop him," Joc continued, "but he kept watching. Then after that part he asked who you were and I told him."

"What did he say after that," I asked while cutting my eyes at Puff, who was looking at me.

"He said he felt you. That that's how you gotta be in the business."

Joc went on to detail the events of the night. He said they made a lot of small talk on the way to the club. Puff wanted to know what he planned on titling his album. He told him *New Joc City*. Changing it from a graphic which meant, "stop, rewind, play" and showed him his tat of it.

When they got to the club they entered upstairs through the VIP. Puff got $15,000 in ones and hollered at the DJ and asked him to play "It's Goin' Down." Then they headed downstairs and the DJ started shouting them out.

Then the song came on and Puff gave me some bricks of ones. We took the wraps off and threw the whole fifteen bands. It looked like a blizzard! The hoes went crazy. Puff got a mic and was talkin' about 'This that Bad Boy shit'."

After Joc broke it all down, we chilled with Puff and them. Puff was talking to Big Boi about a song he had written for him. Then Puff called himself introducing Joc to Big Boi and that's when C-Bone told him that Joc was my work. Meaning I was the man behind Joc and that we all knew each other already.

Now this little gathering was major because of the history that existed between C-Bone and Puffy. See, C-Bone had been messing with Puff's baby mama, Kim Porter, and they had had a run in or two, one being at Club 112 where me and Bone and some partnas were at and Puff came throwing money from upstairs over the table we were seated at below.   Bone got mad that night and tried to go up the stairs, but Puff's security stopped him.   But on this night all seemed to be forgiven. I guess that phone call Puff made to Big Boi asking him to ask Bone to leave his baby mama alone was enough.   Whatever the deal, we just chilled out before finally going our separate ways.

That night I thought about how Big Boi let us slip through his hands, by not signing us to his Purple Ribbon label.   He had a song with C-Bone and Killa Mike called "Kryptonite," and it was blowing up.   "It's Goin' Down" would've been a good look for him.

Our work ethic was already strong and now with the deal it only became stronger.   Block had begun talking to Joc about management, asking him who he had in mind to use.   At the time we hadn't discussed any management, so Block insisted that he use this cat named Rico Brooks.   Rico used to work at this record store before Greg Street hooked him up with Block.   From there, he went on to manage Boyz N Da Hood.   Block told Joc that he wasn't letting an outsider come into the mix, and in the end, he basically "Debowed" Joc into signing Rico.   Me, I figured something was up but I couldn't put my finger on it.

So Rico came on and immediately he looked to get Joc involved in some of the big ticket events going on in the city.   One event was at Club Vision.   Keysha Cole, 8 Ball and MJG, D4L, and Joc were to perform.   So we got the whole crew together and shot up there to represent and show everybody that we were indeed on our way to the top.

At the club, all of us had VIP sections next to each other.   In the back of the establishment was a VIP where we were, and another was right across from it.   The dance floor was in the middle.   Keysha Cole was at the end, by the wall, right above the bar.   We were next to her, then 8 Ball and MJG and then D4L.   When the party got crunk, they brought the mics to the VIP and let everybody do their song from their own section.

That day me and Joc had hit Lenox Mall and got fresh to death. We chilled with our crew as Keysha sung a hit she had called "Love." Then she did the Mary J. Blige song "I'm Going Down" a cappella.   I mean she killed it!   That girl's voice was one of the best I had ever heard in person, despite what a lot of people say.

When they brought the mics to our section, Joc had Rico give me one to hype man for him.   When they started the song, me and Joc climbed over the rail to the section, got on top of the bar, and performed. I had a bottle of Patron as we did our thing. I was pouring shots in girls' mouths and glasses. Then when the hook came in, we took the place over with this dance that the youngsters in the A had given to the song. In the streets it was known as the "motorcycle," but they were now calling it "The Yung Joc." The whole club started doing it with us, rocking side to side. When we got finished and climbed back up to our section, I heard Keysha ask somebody, "Who was that?" She was like "Damn, why haven't I heard that song before?"

$$$

With money on my mind for a side hustle, me and Nitti rented out the Club Atrium where BET used to host the show Comic View on every Monday or Tuesday, and we put on a comedy show. We had a guy named Henry Welsh hosting and we'd get around four comedians to come out and perform. We worked it with the owner of the club, Mr. Brantly, that he would get the bar while we got the door. We also had the kitchen as long as we brought the food. I had my God Uncle Tank and his wife cook everything. That winter was cool but the show never really took off like we wanted. We had flyers that read "PlayMaker and MasterMind Music present Comedy Night," but we didn't do any real promotion, just word-of-mouth. Some nights we paid comedians more than we made. It lasted about a month.

Christmas was rolling in and with our new deal so was the festive spirit. I had done my usual thing, getting all the kids stockings and hanging them over the fireplace, decorated the tree and outer house. My daughter Chanell, and my two sons Christopher and Lil' Chauncey always expected the most for Christmas. And that's just what they got. Also I had my girl's son stocked up with plenty toys. I bought the boys power wheels and real motorcycles. My daughter already having power wheels and stuff got a new bike and plenty of the dolls called Bratz.

I bought my girl a laptop, along with some other shit. My mother and aunts came over for a few days and enjoyed the holidays with us. I'd already helped get them a 5 bedroom home and gotten my Aunt Blondeen a big screen T.V. and anything else she wanted. I did this because she'd done the same for me all my life. So I just broke them a little cash.

A few days following Christmas my girl's mother, father, sister and nephew came to enjoy the holidays. Now I'd seen how they interacted when we went to San Antonio to see her family. And when I say they went hard in the paint, I put that on everything. They argued sun up to sun down, all of them. Seeing that I was taking damn good care of her daughter, my girl's mom complained that she had gotten lazy. Once a basketball player, my girl had become out of shape, picking up extra pounds in her stomach and thighs. Don't get me wrong, she was tight but her mother's argument insisting that she was letting herself go was right. I already felt that the money, good dick, and the lifestyle had her spoiled. She even carried it like she knew she had it good. And as long as she was mine she would always have it this way.

Now her mom was a white woman, her father dark as me. Her dad loved to smoke that fire green and he used to say how he wished they had it out in San Antonio. He brought some from out there that looked like burnt cigar tobacco. He loved smoking joints and couldn't handle blunts. Pop was cool as a fan. That summer he had come down to pick up my girls' sister's son from his grandparents and we had a good time. I took him with me to the convention center where V-103 had their car show. I had him kicking it with Lil' Will, Jeezy, and some other C.T.C. members. I also had him backstage smoking Cush with Jeezy and Will. He had the time of his life as Jeezy ripped the stage. From that day forward, Jeezy became his favorite rapper.

You know, that night in the summer my girl called herself going off on me and her dad straight checked her. He told her to cut her shit out or she was going to run off a good man. That all I was doing was working and he was with me the whole time. He told her she was acting like I had another woman in her bed. Dude had my back.

During the days her parents were down, my partners Blue, Bodybag, and Lil Will had come by. When they knocked on the door, my girl's mom answered. As soon as I came we all walked outside.

Blue busted out and said, "Damn nigga, you done came up! You gotta maid now?"

I said, "nigga keep it down, that's my girls' mama." We all busted out laughing.

During the holidays I took them and the kids out to have some fun. First we tried to go to the largest aquarium in the states to see the fish but when we couldn't get in since it was new and the crowd was crazy, I took them to Centennial park and to the Nickelodeon Science Building. During this outing Block called me up.

"Are you ready for this?" he asked.

"Man, I've been grinding for this for some time now."

"Well, he began, I'm gonna tell you, Puff is really excited about this. He told me he wants to blow Joc up. By Jeezy doin' what he did leaving the group and signing with Def Jam that is motivating the hell out of him. I'mma show Jeezy he ain't stoppin' nothin' by not being in the group."

That let me know that Puff was gonna put 200 percent behind Joc. This was good news. "Well, we're ready. Like I said, this is only the beginning."

Staying busy trying to build the brand we kept doing shows. One was at a club off of Campbellton Road that used to be called Club Illusions back in the day. It seemed the whole Ben Hill, Adamsville and S.W.A.T.S. community was there. People I hadn't seen in years had come out to show love. When I saw this I knew we were on our way. I got so twisted that when we got back to Joc and Vick's crib all I kept thinking about was how good '06 was going to be to us.

A New Year and a New Deal!

Still on his grind, the Big Snoop D-O-double G came through Atlanta and showed us major love. First he was on the radio saying that he had heard "It's Goin Down" and that he loved it, telling the DJ to play it. Then he hit Club Vision for a performance and live on the air he told the DJ to play it again. This was huge promotion for us because Snoop was from the Left Coast. His showing us love it just gave us reassurance that it could blow up bigger than just the South.

The whirlwind of activity had Joc moving around nonstop. Rico had him in the studio with different producers. Block had gotten his studio halfway complete so we started recording up there. He told me one day when we were on our way to the Infiniti car dealership behind

North DeKalb Mall that Puffy told him to take $100,000 out of the budget to build his studio. I didn't say shit but wondered how in the hell could he do that.

In his studio, Block had his producer DJ Dana running the board, which was a Pro Tools Control 24. It was the same Control 24 that Nitti worked with in his studio. It was the new "IT" Pro Tools Controller. Also Tom Cat was a part of the team. He didn't have his studio anymore so he worked out of Block's. Block was having his team put together his issue of tracks and I had to say Dana was cooking up that heat. So with Block doing his part, it looked like we were making good progress.

Exactly what I liked to see.

New Year's Drama

We started out the New Year of '06 by announcing that Joc was now the new artist of Bad Boy South. I really didn't like the idea that my MasterMind imprint wasn't included in the promo but Block insisted that everything was straight. And that he had my back. We hit both of the big stations in the city, from Ryan Cameron's show and Greg Street's 6 to 10 show at V-103 to HOT 107.9's Duddy Boys show with E-Dub, J-Nix, Emperor Searcy, and Mz. Shyneka. We did the Morning Show from a live remote at DeKalb Technical Community College with Hot 107.9 morning crew. We were everywhere.

At the live remote morning show a pep rally was going on for their basketball team. Me, Block, and Joc sat at a table with the morning crew. As they interviewed Joc I noticed that Block had on a new watch. I mean that muthafucker was iced out! Well, during the break from being on the air, one of the hosts asked Block if he could remove his watch because the sun that was shining in from behind us was blinding her. That's when I really took notice of it.

"Damn boy, you doin' it ain't 'chu playa?" I said to Block.

Smiling he replied, "For eighty six stacks, this bitch better do it."

In my mind I wondered how he could afford that kind of watch. Especially after he told me how he hadn't made any money off the Boyz

'N Da Hood album, because it still hadn't recouped. I guess he knew something I didn't.

Meanwhile, Ms. B was going through her thing with Nitti. She wanted to get out of her deal with him because she felt he wasn't doing shit for her. She told me all he was doing was trying to get her single deals.

"He don't know how to run a label," she said. "He just knows how to make beats."

She went on to tell me how Nitti's other artist Young Capone was also still waiting on a deal and that JD wasn't helping out at all. See Jermaine left the parent label, Jive that they were at, for a 100 million dollar job at Virgin Records. When he did this they got left on Jive and it was slowing Ms. B's career up. At the time I would give her advice to keep her motivated but I didn't want to get too much into it. I just wanted both her and Nitti to work out their own differences.

Me and Nitti were still doing us despite the fact that he didn't like me going into business with Block. On Wednesdays we still hit Body Tap and fucked with Purple Ribbon. Well one night T.I. showed up there and some things got out of control with him and his crew versus some local guys. Man they tore the club up! Me and Nitti were standing in the back of the club watching chairs fly, people running and Tip at the center boxing some dude. Then all of a sudden he flew backwards onto the main stage with one shoe on, one shoe off.

That's when fights broke out everywhere.

The A.P.D. and club security came in bulldozing niggas and women. I took that opportunity to slip into the girls dressing room. I'd met this little broad and seeing her dip in there I followed to seal the deal. The night at the club was over so I was trying to make other plans.

Time was rolling and Block, Joc and Rico flew out to New York to meet with the staff at Atlantic Records and Bad Boy to go over their vision for Joc's album. The funny thing about it is I didn't find out about this meeting until they got back and Joc told me. "Block said it wasn't necessary for you to be there," Joc said.

"I don't know," I told him. "I'd just like to be involved with stuff like that. We came way too far."

Joc nodded his head. "Anyway they told us they're ready to push, so it's only up from here."

At Block's studio the construction was still underway on a few minor areas like the kitchen, lobby, bathrooms and stuff. He had his wife key up on their construction guys. A chick named Tomeeka was running the office with a guy named Kerry. Me and Block would oversee the recording that was being done. I would sometimes bend a couple corners with Block in his burnt orange Infiniti Q56 SUV, with matching 22 inch rims, or his black Dodge Magnum and chop up game. One day he told me while we were riding, that the checks should be in soon and that Puff told him to keep $100,000 to build him a studio. I was thinking why did he keep telling me this and how was he going to do that and get the $50,000 advance at the same time. If that was the case the studio should be ours since all of this was because of the joint venture. But I didn't say anything, just listened.

Well two days later, Tomeeka called and told me to stop by the studio. When I got there she gave me a check for $25,000 from Block Entertainment. After all I'd been through I needed it. I went straight to Sun Trust Bank, cashed in and gave Chris and Elvis a few dollars to help them out. I had to keep it real with my crew. If one of us ate then we all did.

My Uncle Otis came over my house for his usual Sunday visits. When I was little I'd stay most summers with him in Decatur. Well this Sunday he came with a little more excitement than usual. He'd heard on the radio that Joc signed the deal. Plus my aunt told him as well.

"What's up Unc?"

Smiling from ear to ear he said, "Boy, I'm proud of y'all, you know, when Blond told me I didn't think nothin' of it. But then I heard it on the radio...and well, I'm just proud of you boy."

I had never heard my uncle say that to me. Even though when I was young he'd brag about how fast I was in football to his partnas but I can't recall him ever saying he was proud of me.

"I saw one of your friends," snapping his fingers to remember the name, he continued, "him and his mama stayed in Decatur off of Tilson, not far from us. They used to live in Athens and ya'll played football together too. Ya cousin Tyrus used to be with y'all."

"You talkin' about Andre?"

"Yeah," he said excitedly. "He told me to tell you congratulations.

I hadn't seen Andre since his mother Mildred died. It was good hearing he was still holding up. Me and Unc went into my living room and took seats.

"Yep boy, I knew you could make something of yourself. Them streets was beneath you. I mean, you could've been a professional football player like your cousins Jeremy Stevens and Maurice Jones-Drew. You was that good."

"You think so Unc?"

"Shit boy, I know so." Unc sat back and said, "But I knew from when you was young that there was a chance you'd end up in them streets. You wasn't afraid of nothin'."

My uncle went on to tell how I loved running with the crowd. That's why he didn't keep me full time because he was busy working and stuff and when he'd come home me and my cousin Cedrick would be at the pool in Gresham Homes fighting or all the way up the street in East Hampton Apartments where a lot of drug dealing was going on.

"Keeping you was hard, with me workin'. Sometimes I'd drop you off in the Pittsburg Community, over ya Aunt Sara's house, with Boo Boo. But Boo Boo was older so he'd have you all at that park while he would be playing basketball and you'd just be running around. They would be selling dope and shootin'. And then by Carver Homes, over your Aunt Beverly's house, it wasn't no better."

He explained that was why he sent me to Athens to live with my granny. He thought that the inner city street influence might miss me by me being in a smaller town.

He continued, "Smaller town my ass! Athens wasn't no different. I guess black neighbors across the world have problems. But I should've known you'd be a salesman. You'd sell the shirt off yo' back for a dolla. I can remember you and Cedrick goin' to that pool with those book bags full of candy. Yeah, real hustlaz."

I laughed. "Yeah, we was try'na be millionaires way back then. Counting every penny over and over again."

He laughed with me. Then he turned serious. "Chauncey, you

didn't have to turn to them streets. I swear you didn't."

I just looked at him. I knew there was a lot he didn't understand, about how I felt about all of that.

"You know," he continued. "You had a lot of people who loved you. Your granny, Blond, Nancy and Norma, me, your uncle Dewey…we all loved you. Everyone helped raise you like you were their son." He went on to tell me how my uncle Dewey made sure he did what he could for me by taking me to football practice from age 5 until I was old enough to drive myself. He said me and Dewey's two daughters. Tameka and Melaine, and his daughter Beverly, we all were raised like sisters and brother. "I don't know why you turned to the streets and they did so well, at becoming professional career people."

His comment caught me off guard. I told him from his point of view they did a lot but that the only person that made sure I had what I needed was my granny and aunt Blondeen. I explained how they all let her lose my granny's house because she had to do for me and didn't have the money. "Come on Unc, you know shit was rough for me back then. It was five of us in a 2 bedroom apartment with one bathroom, eating government cheese out the brown box, peanut butter out a jumbo can and cereal out a bag. Then it looked like things were getting better, but they got worse when we moved into a house with no heat or A/C and not knowing when the lights or water would be turned off." I paused and let what I'd said sink in. Then I looked deep into his eyes, "When Beverly turned sixteen," I continued, "You bought her a car. Uncle Dewey did the same for Meeka and Melaine. But when I turned sixteen I couldn't get a ride to school when I missed the bus. So I had to do what I had to do."

He just looked at me.

"When Granny passed away my own mama told me I worried her to death and that I wasn't going to do the same to her. She said this standing in the doorway of my grandmother's house. I just walked out and she kept yelling at me, high off of whatever she was on. Unc, this pushed me all the way out there. And I promised myself not to ask her or anybody else for help—ever again.

My uncle listened as I bared my soul to him. I could see he didn't expect to find so much going on inside of me.

"You know," he began, "the day my mama, your granny, died it hurt me when I came to the hospital and saw you standing there crying. You were just talking to her, all alone. I told you everything would be all right but when you told me 'that's all I got and now she's gone' I felt like I'd abandoned you all those years. And when you got in those streets I always knew you'd get it together before you ended up dead or in jail."

The look in his eyes told me what I had already known. He cared and was now very proud of me. "I didn't mean any disrespect when I said she was all I had. I just knew I needed to man up. Before you came in I confessed to her and apologized. And I promised to get my life together." As I spoke, I remembered sitting on the front pew of Fair Play Baptist Church listening to Tellas, Jeremy, and Brantley sing "Precious Lord Take My Hand." That day, as I walked up to that pearl and gold casket and viewed my granny's body, I passed out. When I awoke, I was at the back of the church with my Auntie Olivia. "When they buried her," I said, "I felt lost, but at the same time I swear I had direction."

He nodded, understanding me. I stood up and he did too. Together we embraced and I told him I was glad he stopped by for our little chat.

"Soon we can take us a good trip to gamble, all on me," I said with a smile. "Once we sell these million albums Imm'ah treat you to a good time."

His smile was bigger. "I'm waitin' on it."

$$\$\$\$$$

Still hitting bars and clubs to keep up with the nightlife scene, and to see how the song was picking up, I ran into another Grand Hustle show. It was live like always, and one of Tip's crew members, a cat named Clay, slapped some dude at the bar like it was nothing. I said to myself, every time I'm out with them some shit jumps off.

I had to stay on point whenever they were around. . . .

$$\$\$\$$$

Block set up a photo shoot for Joc at a studio next to Zack's Studio off Northside Drive. This was Joc's first taste of a professional shoot with a stylist. It was a private setting and I could tell he was loving it, and could get used to it. Crystal, the stylist, did her job styling Joc and Block as we chilled in this little room listening to some of the music we recorded.

During this time there was an issue with Nitti who was feeling a certain way for not being a part of the situation. With Diddy now a part of the situation, he'd adlibbed Nitti's intro bringing the Bad Boy flavor to the song and chopped off the So So Def tag Nitti had onto the outro of the song. Upset, Nitti had taken it upon himself to demand $150,000 for the track on 'It's Goin' Down," and if Block didn't agree he threatened to file a cease and desist to stop the use. Now remember, when I paid Nitti we had an agreement that he'd get ten percent of the publishing for his input on the lyrics. It was registered that way with ASCAP. But now he wanted his fifty percent for the beat and twenty-five percent for his input on the lyrics. Meaning 75 percent of the song's publishing.

Imagine that!

Now, at the time we were to get the producer agreements done, Nitti's manager, Ian Burke, hadn't gotten them done but had my receipt for the track. Ian didn't know anything about me paying Nitti. Nitti didn't tell him because he didn't want to pay Ian his twenty percent fee. I found all this out when I contacted Ian about the producer agreements. Well at this point in time, Ian was no longer Nitti's manager; Skeeter Rock of So So Def was. And they flipped the whole scripts.

Now in comes Block to the situation.

Taking matters into his own hands Block, without telling me, let Nitti back him into a corner. When he told me about it, I explained how I could get the receipt where I paid Nitti for the track already. Block never told me okay, get it, or nothing.

"I got his bitch ass," was all he said.

I was in a triangle.

On the other hand, Nitti was saying "I told you shawty, fuck that nigga! He gotta pay me for the way he did me on my back end of the Boyz 'N Da Hood situation."

I just told him, "I hope we can work it out."

The next thing I know, I'm reading an article with Nitti dissing Joc and saying he wrote half of the song and some more shit. Then Block tells me that label executive Kevin Lyles was handling Nitti so we didn't have to worry about him.

"Shawty, I told you I can get the receipt," I told him.

But he didn't listen. "Nah man, it's cool. But you know I'm going through all this for you, since you ain't got the receipt."

"Nigga is you crazy?" I said. "I told you I can get it from Ian."

"Well, it's too late," he said. "I already got Kevin on it."

It's like drama came and invaded our success before success could even root itself. All I could do was pray for the best.

After hearing what Nitti said about Joc, and the fact that she had been trying to get Nitti to sign a release for her from PlayMaker, Ms. B took her frustration to the mic.

One night when we were at my crib recording, Ms. B. heard this track I had with a sample of Puffy saying "Get Live Muthafucka!" and she liked it. "Let me get that beat," she said.

I shrugged and said, "Do yo thang."

Right then B grabbed a pen and pad and started writing. When she got done, she got on the mic and all I heard was her talking about how Nitti looked like Eric Sermon from EPMD and wanted to be like Diddy . . . she just went hard. I knew then that even if Nitti could land her a deal it was over between them.

The beef had begun.

That night, I gave her a copy and hid the file safely in my drive just in case I ever needed it. The way things were going, you never knew.

Game Time

Just when I was getting accustomed to having the privacy of my own home, my girl informed me that her baby sister was moving in to try to get herself together, and she was bringing her boyfriend. At first, I was like damn! But my girl explained that her sister was giving her dude some time to get a job or he had to go back, and that her sister would babysit so she could save some money from that expensive ass daycare. I rolled with it, trying to understand that everyone needed help sometimes.

The day they flew in, I found her sister's boyfriend to be a cool dude. He said he was from the Austin, Texas side and that he rapped as well. He also loved to blow trees. Like my girl's pops, he was amazed at the kind of green we blew in the A. It wasn't that "dirty weed" he said he was used to.

After getting his advance money, Joc went and bought a Black Yukon Denali making me, him and Elvis look like the Denali Boyz: a promotion company for GMC.

Joc, his wife, Vick and Vick's brother Dog moved from Cascade back to College Park into Vick's mother's house, which she left behind for a new one. This became our new hangout.

Joc's shows began picking up while we still recorded, trying to find the right direction to take his first major released album. He told me how he wanted to do his like the cats done back in the day with skits. So we hooked up with Eric Miller to use his spot and got with Hot 107.9 radio personality Griff to do some skits for us. Griff went in on some funny shit and I sat there drunk, laughing my ass off.

Joc recorded with a couple of producers Rico lined up and finally recorded with Carl Moe. Carl's tracks were cool but Joc's style didn't bring them out.

One night, we had to do some work with a producer, so I met Joc at dude's spot. His studio was inside his crib in Ellenwood. I'd brought this chick who rapped named Queen that Chris Flame turned me on to. We were all chilling as this cat ran through his tracks when one jumped out at us. Joc went in and after a couple minutes he came out with the hook:

Yeah, I been there, done that/use to knock the pussy out . . . Now she runnin' back/so I knock the pussy out/knock it out . . .Knock it out . . .

I knew we had another one cause 'ol girl I brought along was loving it.

Joc hit me with another song he'd recorded. "This that shit right here," he said.

"I don't know, it gotta grow on me," I said by the middle of the first verse.

"Just listen some more, until the hook comes in," he said persistently. Then the hook came in: I'll do ya/do ya bad do ya bad…"

After listening to it twice, I found myself rapping along and bobbing my head. That's when I knew he had the ability to make people feel him.

Joc had been spending a lot of time at Block's spot along with the remaining members of Boyz 'N Da Hood. Block's in-house producer, DJ Dana, hadn't made any magic with his tracks, but he had some fire. Plus he was a funny muthafucka, with his powder-snorting ass.

While shopping for some more beats, we ran across Mr. DJ up at PatchWork. DJ and Block weren't acquainted, so I introduced them.

"Playboy, what 'chu chargin' for those two beats," Block asked about the tracks Mr. DJ had given to Joc.

"I get fifty," he told Block. "But for my niggas I charge twenty grand. But since you wit' my boy Chauncey I'll do ten."

Block busted out laughing. "Ten grand! What you done produced?"

DJ told him, "I got three Grammy's and plenty of platinum tracks." Then he ran down a list.

Block looked . . . well basically, stupid. Then he said, "Well I'll do seventy-five hundred."

"I'll just keep 'em Shawty," DJ said. "Ten stacks is a giveaway, with a four percent escalation royalty rate."

Block didn't budge on what I knew was a really good deal. And the songs were good. At the end of it all, I saw how Block wasn't taking my opinion into consideration—like it was his way or no way. Mr. DJ's songs wouldn't make the album and that was it. Case over and done with.

Before we left, I told DJ, "I appreciate it anyway folk. And don't trip, I still got 'chu when shit pops off."

He smiled knowing I was sincere. "I ain't pressed lil buddy. You know that."

Me and Block left the building. He said how those songs wouldn't make or break the album. Though it could've been true, I thought, who knows? They may have pushed Joc's album all the way over the top like Outkast's album had done.

Elvis called me one day. "Chino, man Polo wants to work something where I play the keys and help produce for him on his staff."

"Work a deal like what?" I asked.

Elvis explained how Polo Da Don wanted to pay him a fee for every song he did like a song deal. I told Elvis to tell him we wanted publishing and pub credits and that he could get producer credits.

"How much pub?" he asked me.

"Depends on how much work on the song you do," I said. "And tell him you still want a fee per song."

I told him we'd chop it up some more that Sunday when he brought his wife and son to my house for my stepson's birthday party.

Chris was working everywhere, spreading the MasterMind hustle. He stayed in tune to the latest spots and functions, looking for the next hot artist. One night I was with him out in Buckhead checking out the local talents when this young chick came up to me.

"What's up?" she asked.

At first I couldn't recall and then it hit me. "China? Damn lil mama what's up?" I hadn't seen her since we met at the Legion of Doom cookout.

"Nothing," she said, "I see you've been busy."

"Yeah, you know," I said, knowing she was talking about Joc signing with Bad Boy. "Try'na make it do what it do." We chopped it up on a professional note and I told her to keep her ear to the streets, so she would know when we were going to shoot Joc's video.

"Just in case I forget to hit you Shawty."

"O.K., I can do that."

"That's what's up," I said. "It should be soon."

$$$

My stepson's birthday party came and Elvis was there with his family. Me and my girl did a Shrek theme for the party where we all had on masks. The kids were all having a good time and my stepson was as happy as could be.

"Chino, check it out," Elvis said as we took some time to chill out. "I got this cat who wants to manage me. I got him drawing up some agreements between me and Polo, on what me and you discussed. We should be good soon."

I said, "Cool." To know Elvis was on his business made me feel good.

Now, to get Joc's song hot, I cut a few deals with some DJs like DJ Styles, DJ King Arthur, DJ Smooth, DJ Cloud, DJ Cool Aide, DJ Hershey, DJ Bill Gates and Princess Cut. I told them if they played the song and it blew up, I would give them their first show for free or we would do a door split.

The first show we did was with DJ Smooth down in Barnesville, GA at this small club. We loaded up the MasterMind crew and went down there, did a 50/50 door split and let Joc rock the house. Smooth was happy and it was a nice turnout, but he wasn't feeling Rico, Joc's manager.

"I didn't like how he posted up at the door with my head counters," Smooth complained.

I had Joc's wife Alex head counting with Smooth's girl, and Smooth said they said that Rico hounded them. Smooth was a little tipsy so I really wasn't paying him much attention. But he kept talking.

"Boy, I still remember that night at Peacock when Ms. B introduced us and you were sitting in the back away from everybody," he went on. "When everybody in the VIP stood up, you just stayed sitting on the couch sippin' yo drink."

"Yeah, just another hustler behind the scene tryin' his hand," I said.

Smooth didn't think so. "A lot of dope boys try their hand, but there's somethin' different about you," he said. "You gave up the game and went in for real, and us DJs seen it. I know you gon' make it, because how you speak. You talk like you gotta plan, and not just try'na be seen. I knew back then that I was gonna be a part of the team."

After DJ Smooth, the other DJs we made the agreement with weren't so lucky. Block told Rico that instead of us doing the free shows, the other DJs had to pay a fee of $5,000. I put the DJs in contact with Rico from the beginning, so when they got this news they instantly called me.

"If we played the song, then Joc would perform," they all complained. "That was the deal!"

And I had to agree with them. All I could do was tell them all I'd find a way and work something out, that my back was against a wall.

Another turn of events transpired when I found out that Block was taking DJ Styles off the song him and Joc had done called "Patron."

"But don't trip Styles," I told him. "The track is still going on the album so that means production credit for you and Kochese."

Two people who weren't tripping were KoolAid and King

Arthur. They were cool. DJ Cloud on the other hand, was tripping. "I was playin' Joc's shit when nobody else was," he went off. And he was right.

"Cloud, look," I said. "You know where ever you workin' all you gotta do is call and me and Joc will be there. And when shit pops off you know Joc's gonna break you off somethin'."

DJ Hershey didn't trip. He just said he was glad to be the first one to break the song on the 5 o'clock mix at Hot 107.9. I was glad he understood.

I didn't like the way Block intervened in my mix. It was my maneuvering that brought us to the point where we crossed his path, taking him to Puffy with a product that brought checks into the picture. Not being egotistical, but my past relationships, business savvy and connections in the clubs with DJs and women helped to establish us in the streets. His cutting them DJs short like that wasn't gaining us anything. Why did he want them to pay? I couldn't figure that out. And why didn't Joc step up was another question I had. He knew the importance of having the heart of Atlanta beating for us. Maybe he was looking at the money. I could understand that. But Block? He knows once Joc blows we'd get four, five, times that amount and more. Hmmm . . . I just didn't like it.

Joc was doing a lot of paid and promo shows for DJ pools to get his song moving. The promos were for local stations. One show, 107.9 did a function at Banneker High School in College Park. They had him as a special guest and what made it even crunker is that it was his old high school. Now it was Deloreium and Chelsey's.

At the event, Block had gotten some white Kenlo t-shirts made up by a local guy famous for his thick quality tee's. They had Yung Joc "It's Goin' Down" on them in red and black. They had the Bad Boy South and Block ENT logos on the sleeves. Now I didn't trip about the MasterMind logo not being on them, but I asked Block anyway. "Oh, Bad Boy did those real fast," he told me, "just for some promo shit. I got you though, don't trip."

Normally when we moved it was Shawty Slick, Vick, A.K., Roc, Redman, Mike, Rico, Block, me and Joc. Joc started using this guy named Corey Williams as his body guard. They called him Biggs. I wasn't sure why they called him that being he was only 5'8" and 200 lbs. But I was told Biggs was something in law enforcement, or had been, and he was permitted to carry his firearm. Both me and Block were convicted felons, as were a lot of us, so it was good to know we all had legal protection around. Joc could carry his gun for protection, but being around him with it could've landed me or Block in prison for a lot of years.

At the Banneker High show, we had Vick and Mike as the hype men while the rest of us worked the stage. We was rocking and doing the Yung Joc dance that had grown to be the official dance for the song. And by the end of the song, kids were up on the stage with us, rockin' to the beat. It got so crunk we had to rush off the stage and out the auditorium's back door.

Yeah, things were picking up.

Next, we hit Tallahassee, Florida for T.J. DJ's record pool. I borrowed my cousin Mite's van so all of the crew could ride together, following Joc and Rico and 'nem. Joc had me and Mike as hype men for him. When we got off the stage the whole building saw we had a hit. A lot of label execs were present and they were giving out their material and had a panel of speakers giving out info on how to make it in the music biz. I took my girl's sister's boyfriend, Gutta, so he could have a good time and see what I do. He had become very useful around the house, feeding my Rottweilers and shit. He was cool. All he wanted was some good green to smoke and he would do him. He managed to get a job selling shoes not too far from the crib, so he had his own money, which made him even cooler.

Since the deal, Joc had been tied up doing whatever Block had lined up for him, so that left me with time to catch up with a lot of people I hadn't had time to kick it with. One of those people was my homeboy Big Hog from the Southside. I called him one day and he told me he was over this cat's named Big Floaty's crib on Creel Road. Big Floaty was a part of the Attic Crew, which was one of my personal favorite rap crews.

I hadn't spoken to Big Floaty in a while either, so I shot over there. While there, we kicked it and he played me a few songs he'd recorded. "Man we need to hook up," I said, being my usual self. We always said we would but never had.

"Yeah, y'all need to do that," Hog said. "But right now what you got up for the day Shawty?"

"Nothing," I replied.

"Won't you run me by the Northside, by this studio Blue and Body Bag are at?" he asked.

Both being from the Southside, Blue and Bodybag were doing their thing in music as well, with Bodybag making beats and Blue rapping. I knew Hog was still pursuing a rap career as well and was pretty good from what I was told. I told him cool, and I told Big Floaty I'd catch back up with him later and we dipped.

So we shot out north and ended up off of Howell Mill Road, at a studio that belonged to Vivica Fox's ex-husband, Six-Nine. Bodybag was there on the computer cooking up a beat while Blue was freelancing around the place.

"What's up y'all," Blue said.

We all got settled and I sat back and chilled. The place wasn't big and hardly had any equipment. But the one or two other guys working there seemed to have everything they needed. We just listened as they worked on the track for Blue. After a short while, Bodybag finished and he and Blue said they were going to dip with us. We loaded up in my car. That's when Bodybag said he needed to run out to Akon's studio.

"It's a dude I'm try'na catch up there," he said.

"All right let's roll," I said.

On the way, Hog went through his same ol' spiel about the music biz, whenever he got high off weed.

"I could've been that nigga," he said. "Bigger than anybody. When KP and them wanted to sign me to LA Reid. But I didn't do it, I kept it real with Akon and yo cousin Chino, Devyne Stevens."

"I don't know dude like that," I had to tell him once again, meaning Devyne. "I think we related somewhere down the line."

"Yeah, y'all kin folk nigga," Hog said. "Anyway, we was all broke living in the same apartment. Now they doin' it. It was just some funny shit happening in the game, some people they had me around that I wasn't feelin'."

Curious I asked, "Funny shit like what"?

"Faggot shit," he said straight forward. "A lot of them niggas in the game, you'll see. Ya'll just signed that deal. Just watch, you'll see 'em." I was ready to get into the conversation when we reached our destination. "I'll tell you more about it when we come out of here," Hog said.

We went into the studio and after hollering at who he came to see, Bodybag and the rest of us stepped out back to smoke a blunt. On our way in, Hog called me to the side.

"Man, I done caught niggas doin' some gay shit in here," Hog said. "You know I'm 'whatever floats ya boat' but that shit ain't for me."

"Who was it?" I asked.

"Nah, I ain't gon' put nobody out there," he said after thinking a second. "But I wasn't the only one who caught it goin' down." He called Bodybag.

"Man, tell Chino what we ran into that day. I didn't tell him who, just tell him what we saw."

"We came in the studio and heard some moaning and shit," Bodybag said. "So, you know us, we figured somebody had a little freak in here, drilling her ass out. So we lined up at the door, stripped down to our boxers and then busted in the room. And what we saw brought us to tears. We saw somebody getting' dug out from the back and it wasn't no chick."

This information had me thinking. Then on the ride back to the Southside Hog told me he found himself at a secret location, a mansion party where, when he looked around, there were no women in attendance, only a few big wigs in the industry and producers. He and the people he was with had been invited, but when they saw this they all dipped.

"I learned if it's ever a party that's a secret and hasn't been advertised, I ain't goin'," he said. "And you better not either if you don't want any surprises."

I told him thanks for the heads up. I dropped them all back off and Bodybag told me he was going to hook me up with Six-Nine because he sings and needs beats. I told him cool and headed home with the story he told me wedged in my mind.

A House Ain't A Home

Gutta had been maintaining his job and I was glad. That showed me he was trying to do something with himself. One night he wanted to roll with the crew to club 24k, and my girl's little sister started tripping. She accused him of just wanting to party and chase after hoes. She sounded just like my girl. He ignored her and went anyway. The next day when I came home from running errands, I found them going at it. They were beefing so hard they put a hole in the wall of the bedroom I'd let them sleep in.

So disrespectful.

When my girl came home I asked her did she know what was up with them. She informed me that her sister said she was leaving within the next few days. When she did, she left Gutta with us, two people he barely knew.

"Man Chino, this is fucked up I know," he said. "But as soon as I get my next check Imm'ah get outta your hair and get a bus ticket home."

I hated his situation had went sour like it did and told him I'm sorry things didn't work out. But that he had to do him and if a chick didn't understand, so be it. When he got his check, I dropped him off at the Greyhound and he went back to San Antonio.

For the next couple of days I missed ol' Gutta's company in the studio being that Joc, Slick, Sunny, Elvis and Chris were gone working all the time. Most days I'd go up to Block's studio when Joc was there but that slowed up too. But I never lost focus of our goal.

Shows were still picking up and it was time for the annual Bronner Brothers Hair Show Convention. It was a big event in Atlanta and they wanted Joc to perform. Well we all rolled and I took Ms. S with us to help network since she was a hairstylist. After Joc rocked it, him, Rico and some others left while me, A.K., Vick, Dog, Redman, Roc and Ms. S stayed to hear Keysha Cole sing her song "Love." When Keisha did her little rift on the hook, Ms. S was singing with her. She was so loud that she began gaining attention and people were clapping for her.

I can't lie. She sounded good.

After the convention, we all dipped and I dropped Ms. S off with a serious thought in my head of starting on her solo project. I bent a few corners alone because I didn't feel like having a fight with my girl, who had some of her girlfriends down from Tennessee. There was just too much estrogen in my house for me to be dealing with.

Elvis had finally gotten his business right with Polo Da Don. He said the numbers weren't in stone yet but they were talking fifteen percent publishing for him. I told him to let me know when the paperwork was done on it. Polo had been working with heavy hitters in the game and Elvis fucking with him let me know we'd make real good connections from their working together. I wondered what happened to the kid Rich Boy Polo had back in '02/'03, from Alabama. Polo hadn't gotten time to do anything with him yet because of the time he was spending producing other artists.

$$$

One day Nikkia called and said she had two vans for sale. "They're in good condition if you know anybody who wants one." She told me that her dad got them at an auction and how he rebuilt the motor in the big van. She had them both at her house and wanted me to come see them.

"Give me a minute and I'll be through there," I said. I figured

they'd come in handy for Joc and the crew for shows and stuff. I just
needed to see how they looked and if I could get them for a deal.

I shot over to her house and when I got there I saw a dark green
'97 Dodge minivan and a '95 Ford Mark IV conversion van. They both
had a good interior and body and the conversion van had a spot for a TV
and a bed for those long trips.

"What does he want for both of them?" I asked Nikkia when
she came outside.

"Five thousand."

"I'll take 'em," I said.

I had her follow me home in one and told her to sign the titles
and to get the tags. I'd put them on my insurance plan with Progressive.
I knew this would be a good investment.

Speaking of investments I hadn't really spent any of my advance
money and things were looking like they were only going to get better
at the rate Joc's single was picking up. I figured I'd do a little home
improvement. The previous year, I spent money on what everybody else
wanted me to, this year I'd get what I wanted.

I attacked my home by laying some hardwood from the front
door to the back sliding door, through the dining room and kitchen.
Then I started on remodeling my cabinets, counter tops and appliances.
Shawty Slick hooked me up with his partner who was from Oglethorpe
County outside of Athens. He gave me a price I couldn't refuse to do
my floor. He was also my partner Fred Mitchell's cousin, so I didn't have
to worry about any bullshit coming to my home.

$$$

While enjoying our new success one night at The Ritz, me and Joc ran
across this cat who called himself Freeze. He said he made jewelry, along
with doing eyebrows and facials for women. After noticing the jewels he
wore, Joc wanted dude to make him a charm for a chain. When he made
it over to the crib, we sat and discussed what he could provide.

"Yo, I can do shit with real diamonds and fake stones mixed, to save your pockets a few chips," he told Joc.

"Tell me first what you got in mind."

"I was thinking about goin' with the letters J-O-C."

"How big?"

"About the size or a little smaller than Chino's C-S chain."

"What size stones? And what clarity?" Freeze asked.

Joc described everything to him, and when he was finished Freeze told him some prices: $7,500 one way, $2,500 another way and about a $1,000 with some fake stones.

When he was finished, Joc said "Damn! I'll let you know in a day or so. But that stack sounds cool. . . . and that twenty-five."

"O.K., just let me know. And Chino, if you want something holla at me too. Y'all don't know how much of the costume jewelry I make for these niggas out here. A lot of them be doin' their videos and shows, just sportin' it and people just can't tell the difference," he explained. "My work is that good. Plus, if somebody take it at a show you ain't lost nothin' for real."

"You know I can holla at Torose, up at the Burlington Coat Factory in Greenbriar Mall. He made Nard's shit," I told Joc after Freeze left. "He keeps VVS one and two on deck. He let niggas owe him racks and he rented out shit. Even though he kinda chilled out on that, since niggas was owin' him twenty to eighty racks."

"Nah. I'm gonna mess wit' Freeze," Joc said.

In my mind I was like *All right if that's what you want. But it just wasn't for me.*

Chris Flame didn't stop networking and told me he was going to lock in a pub deal at EMI with a dude named Big Jon.

"I told him about you and he wants to sit down and talk," he told me. "He's coming to town soon and he wants me to get you and him together."

I told Chris I was down as we talked in my kitchen, with half the floor done in plywood. Dude could only work every other Saturday on my home because of his main job, but I was cool with it.

"As soon as Big Jon comes to Atlanta, let me know," I said.

Well one day he called Chris while me and Chris were working on some material. Chris hollered at him for a minute, then he shot the phone to me. We made our introductions and he told me he heard we were doing big things and that he was flying into Atlanta from L.A. at the beginning of the week. Then he'd be headed back to New York.

"I'll call you guys when I get there," he said.

We exchanged numbers and email info before we disconnected. When Big Jon got to town, we set up to meet for dinner at his five-star hotel across from the Lenox Mall in Buckhead. When we arrived, we met him at the restaurant, shook hands, ordered a round of drinks and appetizers, then had a little small talk before getting right down to business.

I gave him the history of MasterMind Music and who my attorney was.

"Me and John Christmas are friends," he said. "I'll make sure to call him about you and tell him we met. Tell me this Chauncey, what kind of arrangement do you have worked out with Block? And what was done with Bad Boy?"

"Well, me and Block did a joint venture," I said. "But I still got all my rights to Joc, and my fifty percent publishing on him. I'm still trying to figure out what Block actually arranged with Bad Boy. I'm not sure right now."

Big Jon told me how he had been following the single and that it was picking up momentum.

"There's two things me and you can work out, a publishing deal for your production, and I'll work the splits out with John Christmas; and an administrative, or co-publishing deal for Joc's work," he said. "And I'll base a monetary advance on how big the album looks like it's going to be. Also if you have any other producers on the album that you have pub-interest in, we can also do something on that."

I then explained to him the situation with Elvis and Chris. He said, "Don't trip. Chis is already signing. And if you have any interest in some of his songs we'd just add it to your song catalog as well."

We ended our meeting with him saying he liked me and thought we'd make a lot of money in the future. I felt the same way.

Like he told me, Big Jon got right on it. While I was out handling a few things, my lawyer called me and said he spoke to Big Jon and they indeed wanted to move forward. He told me they'd do $100,000 for me as a co-publishing deal with a fifty percent split for three full songs. He said we'd do a conference call with Big Jon to go over all the details for my share of Joc's publishing and interest. I said cool.

After talking to John Christmas, I was pulling up to my house when my Blackberry rang. Without looking at the caller ID I hit the 'talk' button and was greeted by both my lawyer and Big Jon.

"Hey Chauncey," Big Jon said cheerfully. "So John told you what we discussed?"

"Yeah, he did. As soon as I was about to say another word, I heard my phone give the signal that my battery was dying out. Quickly I said, "Hey I gotta switch phones and call back. This phone is going dead."

I hung up, switched to my Sprint and called my lawyer back, who then connected me with him and Big Jon. 'O.K. now where were we?"

Sitting in my driveway, I noticed my girl pull in and park next to me. Knowing she couldn't see me through my tint I rolled my window down halfway, put up my index finger, and mouthed that I'd be inside in a minute. Then I rolled my window up. She turned and went in the house as I continued on with my business discussion.

Big Jon said we would do $100,000 or $150,000 for Joc's stuff and asked me what I thought. I asked a few questions like when would I get my money and how would it get paid. He explained that I would get my money for Joc all at one time. My personal work would be 60/40: 60 up-front and 40 on the back end when he recouped the sixty he put up. As we were getting into it, I heard a knock at my passenger side window and looked up to see my girl. I asked them to hold on.

I rolled the window down. "What's up babe?"

"You can't talk to yo' little bitch later?!" she busted out with her face twisted in disgust.

Shocked (and not in the mood for her bullshit) I fanned her off. Here I was talking about major licks on some legal shit and she thought I was on the phone with some chick. "You're trippin'! This is a business call." I then rolled the window back up.

"Excuse me guys. Now where were we?"

Big Jon went into everything I needed to know and we wrapped the call up on a good note. Then I heard a loud pounding sound on my window. It was my girl again, beating her fist hysterically.

To my lawyer and Jon I said, "Well all right then let me know when we get everything in writing."

"I sure will," John assured me.

I disconnected and pulled my keys out of the ignition, hopped out my truck and headed toward the front door. My girl was storming behind me hollering about some "bitch" I was talking to.

"Yeah," she pushed. "You could've talked to the hoe inside. But no, you wanna be all in the dark about it. I saw you."

I turned around at the door. "That was a business call. My battery was low and if I would've pulled it off the charger it would've died."

Then out of nowhere she hit me with a blind shot to the arm. "I'm tired of yo shit. Leave! Go and be with that bitch!"

First, I was stuck, because she really believed I was on the phone with another woman. Shaking my head at her, I just turned around and went in the house. And as I started walking up the stairs, my girl pushed me from behind and snatched me by the collar of my jacket.

I pulled back roughly, snatching myself from her grasp. "Watch out. You trippin' I told you." Then I continued up the steps.

About four minutes later, I'm in my room undressing with the door locked when I saw the biggest knife from the kitchen sliding through the door seam.

"Fuck you! You 'ah no good nigga," she yelled. I opened the door to see what was wrong with the brawd when she heaved an overhand swing with the knife. "Just leave! Get out!"

The swing made me step back and as she took another swing I shot my left hand up and it caught the tip of the blade. The side of my hand immediately started burning. "Bitch is you crazy?!" I was mad now. "Put that knife up!"

When she didn't listen, I bum rushed her. I popped her like Troy Polamalu and knocked her into the hall. She flew into the wall leaving a large hole in the drywall. "You muthafucker!" Her voice full of anger. With the knife still in her hand she got up. I went into our bedroom and locked the door. Then from behind the door she hollered out, "I'm callin' the police."

I couldn't believe she was trippin' so hard. Then to say she's calling the police was the icing on the cake. I was standing there with blood dripping down my knuckles knowing I couldn't possibly continue in this relationship. Looking at the door, I just dropped my head, turned and went to wash and clean my hand in the bathroom.

I was just finishing up putting a bandage over my wound when I heard a loud knocking on my front door. With my bedroom door locked, I didn't move from lying on my bed. But I did turn the TV volume down to hear what was going on downstairs.

"We got a call of a domestic dispute from this address," I heard an officer say. "Yeah, I need help making my boyfriend leave." I heard my girl tell the officer.

Sitting up, I heard the footsteps climbing the stairs quickly. Boom, boom, boom! "Sir could you please open the door," an officer yelled. Without saying a word I opened the door. Standing in front of me were two Clayton County officers. A short fat white guy and a tall slim one. "Sir, we're trying to see what's the problem here." Fat boy asked.

"He hit me," my girl said all of a sudden.

Then I saw fatty take an aggressive stance while the other one spoke up. "Would you please put your hands behind your back, sir?"

"Man I ain't touch her!" I said finally. "This crazy bitch is the one who attacked me with a knife." I held up my hand in front of them.

I saw a look of contemplation on the two officer's faces. Then out of nowhere they looked at each other and the one in control said to my girl, "Ma'am, put your hands behind your back."

The shock on my girl's face was of agonizing pain. "No please," she cried at the realization of what she'd done. "I'm sorry, I don't want him to go to jail. I just wanted him to leave. But now, he can stay."

"Not today," the officer said. "You're going down."

At the end of the day, they concluded I needed stitches, gave me a ticket for some shit and dropped me off at Southern Regional Hospital. While I got stitches, they took my girl to the county. I got out at 7:30 a.m. and like a damn fool, I bonded her out thinking it was the least I could do being that I was done with her ass.

Time To Lay Low

Two weeks or so had passed since me and my girl's fight. We had been around the house acting completely frustrated with each other. I stayed on my biz and she stayed on some little girl shit. Our attitudes had us sleeping in different beds and all. When we did sleep in our bed together, we couldn't tell with the Grand Canyon space between us.

Well one night I jumped up to take a piss. I went to the bathroom half asleep, drained the snake and flushed the toilet. Now my toilet was the kind with the chain on the inside and sometimes you gotta jiggle it a few times, to get the water to fill up in the tank. So, I jiggled the chain and stumbled back to bed.

It was around 6:30 a.m. when I heard a loud scream.

"Chauncey!"

It was my girl. She sounded frightened. I jumped up quickly, grabbed my .40 Cal from between my pillow and headboard and dashed in the direction of her voice. She was in the bathroom. I shot through the door and instantly saw her concern.

"What the. . . "

Everywhere in my bathroom there was water, wall to wall. The toilet was still running and water was coming out the toilet. My girl stood there with water to her ankles. "This shit's been running all night," she said.

Immediately I went for the chain and jiggled it to make the flap on the inside close, to stop the running water. My girl went and grabbed some towels to soak up the water and the mop from downstairs. That's when I heard her scream again.

"Chauncey!!"

Her voice made me hurry down the stairs. I bent a left to my den and saw another tragedy. Water had bled through the floor and made a big hole in my ceiling in the kitchen. Water streaks stained my walls and water was all over my new floor. That's when the alarm went off in my head to go check the basement and all my music equipment. I shot off to the basement with dread. As soon as I got there I noticed a few of the drop ceilings had fallen out, the carpet was soaked and the back wall was drenched. But thank God that none of my equipment was damaged. I checked the mic booth; it was straight too.

For the next twenty minutes, I did damage control. My girl called our insurance company and made a claim. The next day they came out, put the big fans in and dried my house out. They told me they had to repaint, do the floors and cabinets again and that I could re-carpet the whole house through the contractor for a deal. I paid the deductible and told my girl to pick out whatever cabinets she liked and beige carpet. I told her to do my basement black, to match my black and silver walls. All this was going to cost, but it didn't hurt so bad knowing me and my crew were finally getting checks.

$$$

With my place torn up and Block's studio still under construction, I found myself hanging at Vick's. Shawty Slick had been down to my cousin Nard's spot recording. He had STR8 Drop Records back up and running with a studio on his mom's property. Slick told me Nard wanted me to call and so I hit him up to see what he had going.

"Yo, what 'chu know about this cat named Frazier from Athens?" he asked. "They call him Bump."

"I knew of him back in the day," I said. "Why, what's up?"

Nard told me Bump had a trap spot that was rollin' near my grandma's old house, and that one of our people told him to get the word to Bump that the police were watching him.

"You ain't been messin' wit' him, have you?"

I said, "Hell naw! I ain't been doin' shit but this music!"

"Our dude said some Feds went to his sister's house and asked if they could use her house to watch his spot. I really don't wanna call him if he's that hot. But I wanted to get at 'chu first, to see what you thought."

"Look, if you do call make sure it's from a throw away," I said. "Because you don't need that bullshit on you."

He agreed and we hung up. Hearing them people were on Bump made me ever more glad to be out the streets.

The next day, me and Slick were pulling up to my house when my neighbor, an older lady who barely even spoke to me, called me over to her front yard. "A lot of police came to your house, they showed me a picture of you and asked if I knew you. I just thought I'd let you know."

"Let's go back to Vick's," I told Slick.

My mind was racing, and because I wasn't in the streets, all I could come up with was how I'd missed seeing my PO the month before. Not really buying into the PO sending "a lot of police" to my house, I really couldn't put my finger on why they came. Not really feeling this was the time for all of this I said *fuck it*. They were going to have to catch me. I'd just have someone call to see what the warrant was for. I called my girl, told her the scoop and stayed over Vick's that night. I just didn't need any surprises.

The next day I went home around ten that morning. I stayed inside all day. The following day, I planned on doing the same thing. I got up around eleven, made some calls and made sure I kept the noise down to a minimum. For some reason, I had to go into the room I had over top of my garage to find something my girl had boxed up. Now I never went into this room. But as soon as I got up there, I heard some commotion and a loud commanding voice coming from my back yard.

"Get down, now!"

Instantly I fell to the floor. That's when I heard the voice say again, "Go on, get from back here!"

I knew it was the police now and I figured that the officer came across some of the kids who be riding along the path at the back of my place. Now I started hearing boots and the crackling of walkie-talkies and I knew they were trying to surround my house. I put my phone on vibrate and called Vick.

"What up boi," he said cordially.

My voice dropped to a whisper. "Nigga, come get me."

"Why you whisperin'?" he asked.

I told him what the deal was. And while I was explaining I peeked out of the window and saw no police were visible. Creeping through my house, I made it downstairs, ducking the windows and managed to get to the back door. No police were still in sight. "Listen, hurry up and get here Shawty."

"I'm fifteen minutes away. I'll be there. In the meantime just calm yo ass down."

It seemed like it took Vick twelve hours to save me from my own confinement. Becoming more claustrophobic with every passing second, I hit Vick about twenty times! Finally, he made it. Checking my surroundings, I bolted out my front door after seeing they were gone and jumped right in Vick's Expedition, ducking low in the passenger seat.

"Yeah, stay low," he said. "There were two Clayton County police cars right at the top of your neighborhood."

I stayed down and as soon as we were in the clear, I came up. When we got to Vick's I told him and Slick to go get the conversion van I'd just bought. I called my girl and told her what was up. I explained how it was too hot for me to be over there and I'd slide through when I could. But for the most part, I'd be at Vick's.

Joc had a couple of shows lined up in Alabama and Dallas and a DJ Pool in Houston. I figured it was right on time, with all my drama with the police. I really needed a getaway. I went and got my van ready for the road. I bought a CD player, new speakers, a new 27" flat screen, DVD player, PlayStation and everything else for it. Now I was ready.

For the days I stayed at Vick's, it became a headache. With Joc, his wife, my niece, Vick's brother Dog, Slick, A.K., and Roc basically living there, it was too much. I really missed home. The only peace of mind I got was when I would go over my home girl Ms. S's house. I told her my problem, and she told me I could chill at her place anytime I wanted. There had never been anything between me and Ms. S even though we flirted from time to time. We had been friends and I accepted that.

What started out with me at Ms. S's innocently sleeping on the sofa, having talks about life, and venting my frustrations concerning my girl led to us clicking. Soon I went from the sofa to her bed. That first night I laid enough pipe in her to run water all throughout Africa. This became my spot for my whole time on the run.

The time had come to go on the road with Joc. He had laid another track by two producers that went by DaDa and Vegas. Vegas had written and sung a fly hook for the song. It was called "1ˢᵗ Time."

"We need to get that boy Trey Songz for this," I told Joc.

"Or maybe Lloyd," he said.

I told him I'd holler at some of my people in Virginia that messed with Trey Songz, to see what was up. "See if we could get a street price, and not a label price," I explained.

When I talked to Block, he told me he liked the song as well. I told him about how I thought Trey would do the song justice, but he said he didn't think so.

"Let me see what I can come up with," he said.

I knew he wanted to make sure he fulfilled his issue of songs but overall we needed to make a good call on everyone. He just shrugged off my opinion knowing what I felt was a hit.

When we packed to leave, we had my van and one Joc rented. The whole crew mounted up: A.K., Vick, Mike, Slick, Roc, Redman, Rico, Biggs the security, me and Joc. Headed out to Birmingham, Alabama, I called up this chick me and Nitti met at one of the football classics. As soon as we arrived, we hit the local radio station, did a quick interview and told them how we were going to hit the club. Then we checked into our rooms. As soon as I settled in, I called ol' girl to tell her where we were.

"I'll be right over," she promised.

That first night in Birmingham me and Joc twisted baby girl like a pretzel. We put dick in every hole in her body. My girl had my mind on "fuck-ah-bitch" and I needed to have some fun. After taking pipes in her pussy and ass at the same damn time, lil mama hopped up like a pro, got dressed and straightened her hair out.

"Well, she began, y'all can call me after the show, if them other bitches can't put it down," she said, her hand on one curvaceous hip, ass all poked out in the back.

I knew that night was only going to get better. We hit the club, rocked it and went back to the rooms with some chicks we'd met. The party continued on as some of us got some head, high and drunk, hitting and switching on them girls from room to room. By the next morning, we were all back up and out of there. Our next city was Houston.

And you know how live it is out there.

On The Road

On my way to Houston with the crew, I called my boy Jamie
Fair. Me and him grew up together and he had went off to Southern
University in Louisiana to play football. Well, he blew out his knee and
was now working a corporate job in Dallas.

"Chauncey, what's up?" he asked.

"Man, I'm headed out your way; on my way to Houston first. I
know you know some people out there I can network with."

"As a matter of fact I got a home girl you can get at," he told
me. "She's in the modeling industry. She keeps bad hoes on deck. Her
name is Tonya Terrell."

Interested, I got Tonya's number from Jamie, and he hit her up
to tell her I was calling.

"Good lookin' out," I told him.

Well, Jamie plugged me and Tonya together. I got up with her
and assured her I'd call her when I got to Houston. She said her and her
home girl Diamond could fly down there together. We made plans for
them to stay with my crew.

When we made it to Houston, Tonya and her girlfriend flew in
from Dallas, caught a cab to the hotel and joined us. They both set up

to stay in my room. Both ladies were nice looking and my boys were looking. I intended on keeping it strictly business. Messing with the women in Birmingham had me on chill, plus I knew that later on I'd want to mingle in the Houston nightlife.

I got my crew rooms like I always did. The promoter paid for rooms for Joc, Rico, Biggs, and Mike. He also paid for their travel. I didn't mind paying for the crew because I knew the importance of having a road presence, the support of real (day one) homeboys. Some say they're street but don't have the streets with them. So with A.K., Vick, Slick, Roc and Redman, I was keeping it one hundred percent. Paying for gas, rooms, food, liquor, etc, I just looked at it as an investment, even though they were simply there to support Joc. I mean, their support is what got us here.

While in Houston, we hit a couple spots. The strip club Harlem Nights was a spot I knew. I hit up Onyx. Tonya and Diamond were along, as she gave me the insight on what was going down in the city. While at the club for the record pool, mingling, she grew surprised, grabbed my arm and tugged me toward the bar.

"Oh my god! My boyfriend's here," she said as if she didn't expect to see him. "Come on, I want you to meet him."

She walked me over and introduced us. His name was Trae Tha Truth and he was an aspiring rapper who had a small buzz in Houston. Tonya told him that I was Joc's people and we made plans for him and Joc to hook up.

"All ready," he said as we dapped up. "Dat will be love mane."

"Dat's what real niggas do shawty. Matter of fact let's go find Joc, he's somewhere in this bitch," I told him as we took off to find Joc.

That night I bumped into my boy Attitude after finding Joc, and we got a chance to catch up. He and Joc discussed what he had going on and said they needed to finish up the song they started at Attitude's spot. Attitude said how he'd been doing a lot of writing for Timberland and Puffy and how he'd inked a song for Nelly Furtado called "Glamorous."

I'd collected a lot of CDs by new artists, and on our way to Dallas, I was bumping this one jam by an artist Tip had. His name was Young Dro, and his song was called "Shoulder Lean." It was a banger. I played that shit so much my crew wanted to toss the CD out the window.

In Dallas, we checked into a hotel in the downtown area. Tonya and Diamond went home after driving back to Dallas with us. With a full schedule, we met up with a record exec from Atlantic named Yancee. He took us to meet a few mom and pop record stores and a luncheon with some radio PD's. We also got up with the promoter for the show.

Back at the hotel, we were trying to get ready for a visit to the radio stations, but after not being able to find an open barber shop, we found ourselves badly in need of haircuts. My partner Jamie knew a couple barbers who did celebrities' haircuts, so we called them. And boy did they charge. It was $50 a cut and $20 for a line up. I made Joc kick out with me on this bill. There were just too many heads.

Finally, we hit the station up. Joc did his interview and on-air he told the people he intended on hitting up the hood in Dallas. Afterwards we had the promoter take us to this car wash in the hood. We could tell it was hood because we saw smokers wandering around and everything. We had them wipe down the vans while we went out to mingle. A lot of people responded to Joc's announcement and we wanted to interact with them. Biggs tried to keep us close, not wanting us to wander too far.

"Man, we from the hood," we all told him, still intent on doing our thing.

Joc signed some autographs and it was clear everywhere we went that the song had grown. He told a few hood cats to come and check out the show and kick it with him.

"Fa sho' mane," they said in their Texas drawl.

I was thinking, damn this nigga Joc is a true politician, shaking hands and kissing babies. Now that's how you sell records!

While at the car wash, Roc had gotten in touch with his cousin who lived in Dallas. He was from Atlanta but had been down there for a long time, picking up the accent and everything. He came through the hotel when we got back, brought us some green and kicked it over dinner at the hotel's roof top restaurant that rotated, giving us a perfect view of the town.

The show was at this little strip club on the outskirts somewhere. Joc did his thing and rocked the crowd. Jamie had called up three chicks and had them come out with us. One of them was this red bone and we hit it off instantly. That night we headed back to the hotel to relax.

The next day in Dallas, Jamie came back through and said he wanted me to meet this guy named Mel The Mack, who worked at one of the radio stations. So we hit this strip club, and I met Mel and the DJ. I wanted to have connections in every city we hit because I knew how important it would be for us in the future. After that, we dipped and hit another strip club.

"This is where ol' girl and them work," Jamie told me. "The three from last night." He was talking about the red bone chick I hooked up with and her friends.

As soon as we hit the door it was like in the movie Playa's Club when Dolla Bill hit the red light: strippers came out the backroom somewhere and swarmed us as if we were Uncle Luke. Ol' girl and her friends were a part of the group. Being that they'd already kicked it with us, they knew how we got down. The rest of the girls swarmed, but when the dust settled we just chilled with baby girl and her friends.

"I gotta dip," Jamie said after about an hour in.

"Don't trip, we'll be back in Dallas in about two weeks."

When Jamie left, me and Vick finished off a bottle of Grey Goose, getting real fucked up. Vick was a trip whenever he got faded, and he liked to crack jokes. He loved to do this Tony Ya Yo impersonation where he'd wave his hand under his nose and make a stinky face saying, "I smell pussy," while rocking side to side like Flava Flav. Well this girl was dancing in front of him, bent over at the waist, with her ass in his face. Vick stopped her, shot a few bucks to her, all while doing the "Tony YaYo" move. Me and the chicks were cracking up the whole time.

For the most part, Dallas was jumpin'. They loved Joc and the nightclubs, we loved them. But it was time to get back to Atlanta. Time to get back on the grind.

$$$

Back in Atlanta, I took time to get my wardrobe together. I talked to Block at the studio, and he told me Kevin Lyles had worked out a deal with Nitti that included Nitti getting $70,000 for three songs and seventy-five percent of the publishing for "It's Goin Down."

I shook my head and said, "Man, I told you I got the paper where Nitti had already agreed to only ten percent for his little input. Shit, he didn't do no more than I did. I even had him switch up the track by my input. I should be asking for production credits then."

"Don't trip," Block said. "I got him."

I left it at that. But I wondered, why didn't he want that paper?

That day Block told me we would be shooting the video for "It's Goin Down." I was excited that we were about to take it to another level. Some days later, I hit him back up with an idea for the video. I explained that it would start with Block pulling up in a Chevy in the hood at a stop sign. Me, Joc and the crew would be standing on the corner. I then would go to his car, hand him a DVD and tell him to check out our video for our song. After that he'd pull off, pop the DVD in and then it all flips to what he sees:

1) Nitti begins with the intro
2) Different shots of Joc performing in the club, killing the stage, and doing the dance.
3) Puff and Block in the club peeping how Joc's killing it.
4) Joc in the mall with hella bags, walks by Puff and Block and they see how he's doing it.
5) Joc in the hood, Puff and Block drive by and see how he's got the block jumpin'.

The concept would be, everywhere Block and Puffy saw Joc, it was goin down. Then at the end, the video would zoom back out of Block's DVD player's screen and all of us would be sitting at a round table, with Joc signing the deal with Puffy. Then it's really like "It's Goin Down!"

"I like it, I like it," Block said after hearing the concept. "I'll see about putting that together."

But as I was slowly seeing, these were only words. He never brought it back up to me again.

Still on my wardrobe, I had my man who made custom clothes do me a few pin-striped baseball jackets that Jeezy and a few more cats from NY and ATL be wearing. He did one white and trimmed in blue with a dollar sign on the back, and a white zip up jacket with red trim with Chino Dollar across the front—just a little something to insure my brand, even though my intent was to mostly play the background.

For the next few weeks, we were mostly on the road. By now, we were rocking shows all over the Southeast. We'd hit a city, hit the hotel and then do radio and talk shit. Joc would say shit on air like "We'll be at such-in-such club tonight. First fifty ladies, free drinks on my bro Chino Dollar." Then I'd be like, "A thousand dollar giveaway from Yung Joc for the finest lady in the club." Sometimes we'd race to see who could put who on blast first, over the airwaves.

In each city, we'd hit the malls and buy fresh tees, boxers and clothes. People were recognizing Joc, calling him out and taking pictures with the crew. After the shows we would take chicks back to the hotel, knock 'em off and leave the next day. Leaving nothing behind but old boxers, socks and tees shirts for the maids to throw away. Some cold ghetto nigga shit!

During shows, Vick would sometime hype man with Mike. Joc would do a few verses from other songs before doing "It's Goin' Down." He'd also do "Patron," and I would throw a few dollars when he said, "Ask Chino Dolla 'bout that Dope Boy Magic." This was our routine.

During this time, my van earned the nickname "The Late Van" because I always seemed to make it to our next destination hours after Rico and them. But I always made the shows. The scene at each event was cool for us not to have a video out. And we could only imagine how things could only get better.

One night while at a hotel me and Joc found some time to chill out, just one on one.

"Bra', I can't wait to shoot this video," Joc said. "I think they got that shit straight with Nitti so we should be good soon. What 'chu think?"

"All the paperwork should be finished by now," I informed him.

"The video's gonna put us all the way out there."

I could tell he was loving the outcome of all our hard work, and I was glad. The times we found to chill out were priceless because there was always so much going on. Talking about how far we came and how possible our dreams were becoming only motivated us more. But what seemed to intrigue Joc as much as our success with the song was the attention it was causing with the women.

"Man I can just imagine how these hoes gon' be actin' when we drop this video," he said eagerly.

I listened, thinking how dangerous it was to trust these women. He must've read my mind.

"Do you see how these chicks be having us in here, freakin' all of us? Then they turn around and go home to they nigga!" Joc sat looking at the ceiling of the room we were in, shaking his head. "Just to kick it with the crew for one night. Man, that's scandalous."

"You ain't lying," I said, "I'm starting to think that it ain't no good chicks out there. They all act like groupies when they're around the one who they think is the big man."

And even though my assessment was harsh, it was what I said as the truth from what I was experiencing. Money and fame seemed to bring the "inner ho" out of the best of them.

Finally, like promised, we ended up back in Dallas. The promoter had gotten Joc, Rico, Biggs and Mike some nice rooms. The rest of the crew was with me. We pulled in late because of a long night. The hotel required a credit card deposit so Rico had the promoter add the rooms for us and I paid cash for them. I got the usual, two doubles. We called up Jamie to come out and chill with us while we did our thing.

Tagging Jamie along, we did radio and hit the mall. We did an in-store for some autograph signings before heading back to the hotel. Jamie called up the girls we'd met on the prior visit. They came through and then we hit up Club Blue. At the club, we hit the VIP before taking the stage. Joc rocked that bitch and then we headed back to our rooms with a bunch of chicks.

Back at the hotel, Joc was on another floor so I didn't know what he had going on. It was like three or four chicks following him and one of the chicks with us had run off behind him too. Me, Mike, Roc, Slick, A.K., and Vick mixing three chicks. We woke up late and behind schedule. Dallas was definitely accommodating us in a major way. And we couldn't complain.

Video Smiles and Tears

I was staying between my boy Vick's, Ms. S's and Rod's place. At Rod's I had turned the extra room he had into my bedroom, with an air mattress. There, I had a view overlooking the city skyline. I hadn't talked to my so called "girl" and didn't want to. The only conversations we had was about the house. I gave her money to buy new appliances and for the extra carpet. I told her she could do it however she wanted. I didn't know if I was going to be living there much longer. I also gave her money to feed my German Rottweilers. That way Nikkia didn't have to keep driving all the way over there to do it.

The video had been scheduled to be shot within the next few weeks. In the meantime we kept performing. One city we hit up was Florence, South Carolina, and I let Ms. S come along with us. Once we arrived, we met up with D. Woods, who had been a part of the Bad Boy family. She'd come out to support Joc as a friend because Joc used to go with her sister Shanel (Young Money) back in the day. So once we all came together, we all kicked it and got reacquainted.

That night in South Carolina, we did the club and came back to the room. Me and Ms. S had a room, a double, but I had plans on staying with the fellas. We were doing so much bouncing from room to room that it got crazy. I found myself over in the room with Vick and theothers as we entertained six girls we had with us.

That's when a knock came to the door. I got off the bed to answer it, opening the door immediately.

"Yo, what's . . . ." I was cut off by the sight of two strange looking black dudes dressed in black jackets and beanie's. Instantly I went from cordial to defensive. "Who y'all lookin' for?"

One dusty looking cat said, "I'm lookin' for my sister."

"Your sister? How you know she's in here?" My eyes shifted to his partner who looked just as thirsty as him.

"She called me," he explained like it meant something.

I saw through all the games. Without hesitating I pulled the .40 caliber pistol I kept on me at all times, out of my pants pocket. "Ain't nobody used no phones in here. Bitches been getting' fucked," I said matter of factly. "But I'mma get these girls to the door so you can see if she's in here." I called all the girls to the door.

Dusty number one and two looked crazy as the girls came to the door. By now, everybody was curious as to what was going on. I was curious myself to see which one of them called these niggas. But after looking at the girls, they quickly stepped out of the doorway.

"I don't see her," dusty number one said.

"All right then," I said, waving the pistol for them to head out.

Both cats obliged my request and made their way down the corridor of the hotel. Still not satisfied, I followed them to make sure they knew I meant for them to get ghost. But as I followed them around the first corner by our room I saw them meet this little bitch that was with us earlier, who left because she didn't want to fuck. I knew something was fishy. All along it was this little bitch.

Being that they saw me lurking, both cats and ol' girl bounced as if they were leaving. But to be safe I went and put the crew and Biggs on alert. Joc came down and I ran it to him. We dismissed all the chicks, stripping the crowd down to just the crew.

"Where's Ms. S?" Joc asked me.

"She's in the room."

He got up and headed for the door. "I'm 'ah go see what she talkin' about.

"Shit, I don't know what's up wit shawty," I said. "She might be a groupie for a young star like the rest of them hoes."

"Let's find out," he said as a challenge. "If you hear some noise, come on in. You got a key right?"

"Yeah, I got one. Go see if she's try'na go."

Thirty minutes passed with me wondering if Joc had accomplished anything with Ms. S. Finally, I headed down to the room and put my ear to the door. That's when I heard Kara's voice echoing softly inside.

"No Joc . . . I can't do this."

I stood there quietly, listening. Five minutes later, I heard some moaning. She gave in, which was no surprise to me. Figuring it was going down I stuck my key in the door and unlocked it. But as soon as I pushed to open it, my access was denied because the chain was in place. That's when I heard fumbling inside, before Joc came to the door and opened it. He was wiping his mouth with a face cloth.

"Oh, what's up," he said casually.

I went in the room and Ms. S was laying on the bed, on top of the covers. She was looking at me crazy as hell. Thrown off by Joc, I acted like I had to grab some things and then me and Joc dipped back to Vick's room. Once we got there, I turned to him.

"I thought you were hittin'."

"Man, I was just trying to get in that hairy pussy."

Dumbfounded I asked, "Why you put the chain lock on the door?"

"I didn't do it. She must've done that shit. I'm about to call and tell her I'm coming back."

He called and after trying unsuccessfully to convince her, got off the phone. I had fucked off the move. But the answer to my question was answered: Ms. S was no different than the rest of them we were picking up at the clubs.

That night I went back to the room with her and she acted like I was supposed to be mad at her. I wasn't tripping and got in the other bed to go to sleep. She climbed in with me, intent on explaining herself even though I had said nothing.

"We weren't doing anything, we were just talking."

"I don't care. If I did, I got mine and that's a rap."

The next day Ms. S and D. Woods were my designated drivers for the late van. I kept rapping along with certain songs whenever it talked about hoes being hoes. Ms. S caught on after a while and out of nowhere she broke down crying while we were on the road. After D. Wood kept saying I was wrong for my behavior, I finally let up on her. I just wanted her to know that I was no fool. So I settled the whole thing by telling her everything was cool between us and we left it at that. For the rest of the ride I enjoyed her and D. Woods entertaining me with their singing.

$$$

It was time for the video. A day before we did a casting call. We had been announcing it on Hot 107.9, V-103 and Greg Street had been pumping it real hard. We also had the announcement online. At Block's studio females showed up running a line from the front door to the parking lot, on down Memorial Drive. Joc, the crew, Boyz N Da Hood and a few partners of ours chilled outside. Me, Kerry, Ke, Tomeeka and Rico sat in the office going over each girl's headshots, reading their info sheets. We'd have them come in and dance for us to see what we liked. After a few hours, I had seen enough and headed back to Ms. S's spot to get ready for the next day.

When the morning finally came, Ms. S woke me all amped. "Boy, it's almost seven! Get up before you be late!"

I jumped up. My clothes were already laid out. The night before I called all the homies and told them where to meet us. Our arrangement was for all of us, Joc and everybody, to meet off of Columbia Drive at the Kroger Plaza between 7 a.m. and 8 a.m. I told the homies to drive their old school Cutlasses. I also told Quet to pull out either mine or his and to tell Nard to bring his. He said he was bringing his and so was Nard. This dude Mike had a rim shop and was bringing out custom Cutlasses as well. The only thing left for me to do now was hop in the shower and get my ass down there.

By the time I arrived, a crowd had already formed. Joc had an old camper parked for a dressing room. As soon as I parked, Tomeka came and got me.

"Joc wants you. He's in the camper."

I made my way in that direction. But before I could reach the doorknob, Rico called out to me.

"He's in there trying to get dressed Chino."

I detected he meant for me not to interrupt or go in. But before I could reply the door flew open.

"Damn bra'," Joc said to me. He was standing there in his wife beater, almost finished dressing. "Where you been?! I was about to start blowing up your phone. Come on in."

I looked at Rico, really wanting to check his ass but it wasn't the time. So, I brushed it off and went inside with Joc.

"All right, what'chu wearing?" he asked.

I had a few options but I wasn't sure. "I haven't made up my mind."

"Well I'm rocking my New Joc City jacket," he said, holding it up.

"Cool. I got something red and white," referring to my custom made jacket with Chino Dollar across the front.

He smiled his approval.

"You know, that's probably my old wing stand I sold." I told him referring to the stand in the parking lot. It still had the Wings on Wheels sign on it.

He nodded. "Yeah, I saw that."

"You know it's crazy that we're shooting on the Eastside and on the song you're screaming College Park." College Park was on the Southside.

"Yeah, I guess it's on you and Big Block."

"I don't have any say in the matter." I said.

"Well, let me go to my dressing room," I said as Joc just let my response drift, with no reply.

"O.K. I'll see you in a minute," he said.

This wasn't my first video set, as I had been in Bubba's, Jeezy's and Gucci's. But this was the first for a member of my own label, and I can't explain in words how excited I was. Everything was set up. The camera crew and light hands were ready. The set had professional stylist, makeup artists, and models to go along with the professional video producer. Executives from Bad Boy were running around, making sure everything was in place so we could have a successful shoot. And with the whole city out to support us I knew we couldn't lose.

The first scene we shot we had a few old school cars parked in front of the wing stand. There was a '72 convertible Cutlass that was black and white, a blue and white hardtop and a burnt orange hard top Monte Carlo. Nitti showed up despite saying how he wasn't going to deal with Joc anymore. We all dapped each other up and brushed whatever feelings under the rug. Then we caught up on a few things as they got the cameras ready to film.

All our homies were positioned behind us. Duddy, Shawty Slick and DJ Smooth were some people we made sure got some video time, so they got in the front line. Chris Flame and Elvis didn't care for the exposure. Vick, Mike, A.K., Redman, Roc and Nard and others made up the rest. When the time came to shoot, they dropped the track and Joc went into his mode as the rest of us bobbed and swayed to the beat, with me and Nitti right next to him flanking his left and right.

It truly was Going Down!

The next scene we shot we did at a shoe store in the Kroger Plaza. Quet had just got the '72 convertible Cutlass he'd bought painted a Georgia Tech yellow (after the university's mascot, the yellow jacket). They parked it in front of the store and had me post up on the hood. In the scene Joc would pull up in the black and white 'vert, jump out, dap me, and from there we'd go in the store with a group of girls. For this shot, I changed into my black and yellow custom made shirt, by my homie Shay. Joc had on his blue and white windbreaker. Together we hit the store, shopped, then came out and jumped in the 'verts with the girls and plenty of shopping bags. We pulled off with a line of old schools following us.

Next we headed to Kirkwood. Old schools on big rims were lined up as far as the eye could see. One cameraman drove in front of us, filming from a van, to catch all of us in succession. Another filmed from the lane next to us as we passed him. When we finally arrived at the shotgun house we were to film at, it was jammed packed. Atlanta Police were everywhere, and with the warrant over my head I was on pins and needles. The streets were blocked so only a few cars were allowed on the street. I saw the "late van" by the house, which told me Slick had made it. I was glad because I felt like I might need a low-key escape route.

Because the shotgun house had no front yard space, they changed the shoot to another house down the street. Me and Joc jumped out the 'verts at the new location. They set up the cameras and again we got together. It felt like the movies.

"This is what we've been waiting on bra'," Joc said.

"Yeah," I said smiling, "Now let's finish it off."

Me, Joc and Nitti did our thing as the music played loudly through the speakers.

By the time we finished shooting the scene, it was all eyes on us. There were so many people that it seemed the whole ATL was there, and it seemed like half were APD. Instantly, I got paranoid. I noticed the Red Dogs (Atlanta's Drug Task Force) and everything. I was thinking, what the fuck is a drug task force doing at a video shoot?

Now, I was really spooked. I told Joc, "Boy, I gotta get outta here. You see the Red Dogs?"

He was already on it. "Yeah."

Tomeeka came and interrupted us. "Chino, Block said you and Nitti were shootin' the intro next."

"All right," I told her.

"Listen," Joc said after she left. "When we leave, we'll have everybody crowd around us and then you just get gone."

"That's a bet and I'll go change for this last shot," I said.

With all the commotion with the police, I guess I took too much time changing in the late van because when I returned, Block told me they'd already shot it. He used Young Capone to do it with Nitti.

"Man, we was looking for you," he said.

"Nah, y'all didn't want me. I was in the van," I told him.

"Well you took too long," he said. "I even had to wait for them to find me a Chevy to film my cameo. You know I'm the Eastside Chevy ridah."

I shook my head. Block was full of shit.

Block did his scene in an SS Impala truck, with my main man Darryl in the passenger seat. They had Lil' Duval, the comedian, in it doing some funny shit, fucking with them.

Next, we took the shooting inside the shotgun house, where Joc acted like he was getting dressed and pulling out in the 'vert for the day. After that we packed a crowd into the house and let "It's Goin Down" pump through the speakers, creating the set of a jumpin' ass house party. It was off the meter.

During this shot, to add to the flava, the models, like Maseeka, Tanesha and a few others were bringing to the set, Block brought out this young chick named Ebony. She was sporting a mean Mohawk with plenty of swag. She made the whole party scene stand out. That made me think about the young chick China Doll I'd told to come.

After that scene, it was a wrap. It was dark, and before we dipped, cats had been coming up to me complaining. Unfortunately dudes cars were getting stolen. One of the people was my cousin Deon's little brother, Big Green. He had a box Chevy Caprice sitting on 24s.

"Damn cuz," he said, still with his steering wheel in hand. "These East Atlanta niggas is roguish! Man, you owe me. Imm'ah come to your house tomorrow and get some of them pounds you got."

"I don't fuck around no mo' shawty," I said.

He wasn't trying to hear that.

That's when the pretty girl who'd just crossed my mind and who I'd invited to the shoot, China, walked up.

"I see you made it." I told her.

"Yeah and I'm glad I did," she said, smiling. " It's good to see you guys puttin' it down."

"Thanks."

Me and China went on to discuss a little business. Finally, I told her I had to be going but that they should come and celebrate with us in Buckhead. She said cool.

The whole time my eyes stayed on the APD. Joc's plan to get me out of there turned out to be a good one because it worked. That night we all bounced, headed to Buckhead to party. Buckhead wasn't poppin' so after a few drinks we all decided to take it to the Southside to The Ritz, where I ended up drunk as hell.

What a wonderful way to celebrate. But the next morning I woke up to some of the worst news I could ever imagine. I got a phone call from Ms. B telling me that the lovely girl China had been killed that same night in a car crash.

"It happened downtown while she was with The Bishop of Crunk after they were leaving the club." Ms. B said in a stricken voice.

My heart dropped.

What a beautiful life to lose. Rest in peace China. This chapter is dedicated to you . . .

A Hard Decision

Now that the video was over, I figured I'd keep a low profile. But I needed to figure out what I was going to do about the warrant I had. Joc had been spending lots of time at Block's studio recording, in between the shows we were doing. On the road, it was getting even crazier. Girls were lining up for miles. There were girls trying to fuck Joc or simply anyone in the crew. For Joc, this was all new, and me and Vick were giving him hell on it. There would be occasions where he'd have a chick in his room and we'd hit the door and he'd be like "Nah man, she ain't wit it. I already asked her."

We'd just laugh. As soon as she left his room we'd catch her in the hallway and like magic she was naked in our room. It got to the point where we had to tell him in front of the girls, "Joc, she's wit it," just for him to see she wouldn't protest. And always he'd look at the girl he was with, only to get a smile back, except for the ones who felt he didn't agree and felt they didn't want to blow their chance of being with him.

But let us tell it, yeah, she's wit it . . .

After a few spot dates, we ended up in Dothan, Alabama. I'd heard of the place because back in the day my cousin Mike had partners moving a lot of bricks out there. When me and the crew hit the city we checked into our hotel, chilled out, then hit the radio station where Joc did his interview and announced where the party was going to be that night. When we were finished the promoter told us that he had rented out a part of some Italian restaurant for us, for dinner. He said it was his homeboy's birthday.

"Y'all are the main attraction," he said. "All meals and drinks are free."

Free food and drinks? Of course we went . . .

Like promised, the whole left side of the restaurant was reserved. I managed to get the table at the back, in the corner. As we got comfortable, two or three guys hit the door, iced out. I mean, I saw diamonds shining from way across the room! We were informed that the shorter one was the birthday boy. I watched as the guys were greeted by the promoter before finally making their way over toward us.

The short one came and dapped us up. "What's up y'all, I'm Zeene Man."

Instantly I peeped that these niggas were hot as firecrackers. Ol' boy had diamonds in his mouth, top and bottom, a diamond chain, another chain with a charm, a big diamond bracelet and a diamond pinkie ring. All his shit was white gold and had some good quality stones. Not that cloudy, diamond chipped shit.

Halfway through introducing himself to us, I heard this Zeene Man cat fucking with Joc. "Joc boy, where dem bricks at, you be talkin' 'bout? Meet you in the traaap! I know you know where they at in the A."

Joc laughed him off.

The night rolled on. I enjoyed myself and ate a healthy meal. Zeene bounced around getting acquainted with the crew before he finally made his way back to me.

"Ayo Chino," he said, taking a seat next to me.

"What's up playboy," I said. "I 'preciate the meal."

"Ahh, it's nothin'. But look, Joc said I need to holla at 'chu," he said. "I heard him on the song, when he say 'Ask Chino Dolla bout the dopeboy magic.'"

"Man," I told him straight out, "I don't know nothin'."

He smiled a diamond encrusted grin at me. "Boy, I'm the Zeene

Man. Call me the Geenie Man. I'll make 'em disappear man!"

I thought to myself, this nigga is either crazy or the police.

When we were done eating, we went outside. Zeene told Joc, "Boy don't worry about shit. I got y'all some hoes, green, liquor . . . whatever y'all want."

I noticed Zeene had a brand new black on black Q56 Infiniti truck, with some chrome 26" wire rims . . . clean as hell. We told Zeene and his crew we wanted to hit the mall, so that's what we did next. At the mall, we bumped a few chicks, shopped and headed back to our rooms.

By the time the show came around, we were more than ready to perform. Rico called and said we were getting picked up at midnight by a party bus. He said he didn't know if everybody would fit, but I told him someone was going to drive my van so it didn't matter. At twelve, a mini bus with limo lights in it pulled up to the hotel. Joc, me, Brandy, Rico, Biggs and some Bad Boy reps, Amir and Yancy, rode on the bus. That's when I met Amir. He kept peeping at me because of how all our crew kept coming to me, asking stuff concerning Joc, when Rico was supposed to be his manager..   On the way, Joc took the time to tell me about the talk he had with Zeene Man. "I just told him to holla at you," he explained. "It looks like these niggas is ballin' down in this little muthafucka."

"Tomorrow Imm'ah make some calls and see what's up with dude and his boys," I said.

When we arrived at the club we all went in together, straight to the VIP. A short time later Zeene and his crew had made their way in. They went up to the stage and his boy named Red got on the mic, announcing it was Zeene's birthday.

"This how we do it," Red said with Zeene standing next to him. Red then presented his partner Zeene with a diamond watch. "Happy birthday homie!"

Zeene accepted the watch and then the mic. "Good lookin' out." Then to everybody in the club he said, "But this ain't only a night for me. It's for y'all too. So I gotta little gift for everyone. Yo Joc, come on down."

Joc took the cue and made his way to the stage. Then as soon as he made it, the beat dropped and he went into a few songs. I did my usual and threw like $200 worth of ones into the crowd. When Joc did "It's Goin Down" Zeene got in on the dance during the hook and enjoyed himself. We had a helluva time.

At the end of the night, the line of cars following us was crazy. So many chicks flocked around us that it was complete mayhem. We partied until 6 a.m., hitting up the Waffle House and another club before finally hitting the hotel for some much needed rest.

The next day I called to get the 411 on Zeene Man and Red. Come to find out, they were pressed to get some work because of a conspiracy that had snatched up some of their connects. Cats as far as Fort Myers, Florida all the way to Albany, Georgia had been locked up. While I was with them, I peeped how big they were doing it in that small ass town . . . like Red, with his aqua candy blue Mercedes Benz chicken box truck. It was sitting on some chrome 26-inch rims with four 15-inch woofers. He had to put Plexiglas to replace the windows. Zeene and Red were flashy and known by everyone. I wondered what was really up with them.

Back in Atlanta, I took some time to see my kids. My girl called me too. She wanted us to try and work things out. She claimed to miss me, so I got a room on Old National and had her come by. I just told her I couldn't accept that police shit and her fussing about what it took for me to make my dreams come true. I told her she should understand and how being in the clubs all night was just work for me.

My girl told me that she was sorry and would try to do better. Her side was about me coming home at night. She said that she found an apartment if I wouldn't change. I told her I understood and would call when nights got too long. I really loved her and didn't want to disrespect her. We made up and I told her I'd be home after I took care of the warrant.

Joc and his family found a nice two-story house to rent off of 138 in Union City. When they moved, I slid over to Vick's. Even though I wasn't tripping with Ms. S, she was still acting guilty about what went down with Joc. So staying at Vick's was more comfortable. My goal was to turn myself in after the video aired so I could go home.

With time on my hands, I caught up with a few friends. A home girl of mine named Keisha came by and we chopped it up about what she had going on. Come to find out I, wasn't the only one with legal

318 A Hustler's Dream I

problems. She told me that she got busted driving from Arizona with fifty pounds of weed. She was stressed but I told her not to worry about the Feds, and that it was some state shit.

That's when Vick came in. "Aye boy! We on TV!" He was all excited. "They got us as the Jam of the Week. It's gonna play every hour, all day-all week."

For the next three hours, I watched television in Vick's room, watching as me, him, Joc, Nitti and all our friends entertained the world. I called Joc who said he had received a million phone calls. I told him to tie his shoes up tight because it was going to be a long ride to the top. When we got off the phone, I had a feeling of accomplishment, like I'd finally made something of myself . . . something my grandmother would've been proud of.

Vick's brother Dog was in the living room chilling, laid back on the sofa when I threw him the keys to my van.

"What's this for," he said looking at the keys.

"I want you to drop me off at Clayton County," I said, referring to the jail house.

Dog's eyes bugged out. "Man, you bullshittin'. You on TV and shit and you want to go to jail. Boy stop!"

I gave him a serious look. That's when he knew I wasn't playing.

"All right, I'm waiting on you."

And with our video airing all across the nation, I turned myself in to the authorities. I couldn't believe I was doing it myself. But I knew I needed to do it, in order to really be free to enjoy all that was going to come. The sky was the limit and I didn't want to miss it for the world.

Try'na Build A Future

From designer clothes to an orange jumpsuit, from a mini mansion to a small cell, no TV, and a max style 23 and 1 lock down program. The Clayton County jail was a world away from the one I was used to.

My old lawyer Bill clarified for me that any warrant was because of a probation violation and for not completing the anger management class for the fight with my girl. He told me I'd have to sit 15 to 30 days before a hearing. I was stuck.

During this time, I reflected on how things were moving with MasterMind and Joc. I called the crew and it made my time that much harder. They would be in different cities in North Carolina, Alabama and other places doing their thing. They still used my van and Ms. S was still hanging in there doing the driving. Joc had stepped up and started footing the travel expenses for the crew, and my cousin Quet bought Torrey everything he needed to film for a DVD. Now Torrey could use all that schooling he had for film and put it to good use. Quet got him a Canon XLR camera, a Mac G5 with all that Final Cut Pro editing and special effects software. Torrey was ready to perfect his craft.

By the time my court date came, the judge released me with

time served. My girl came and picked me up and I went home. It felt good to be back in my own clothes, and my own bed. She had gotten all the appliances and redone all the cabinets and counter tops. Everything looked good after the damage was fixed and it almost felt like I had bought another place.

For the next couple of days, I chilled around the house. Needing to get busy, I finally went and got my van from Vick's. Joc hit me and told me to come up to the studio. Dog was with me so we both headed up there. That's when I got a call from a strange number. As soon as I answered I heard an unfamiliar voice. It was a female.

"What's up Chino? I've been try'na get in contact with you."

Confused I asked, "Who's this?"

"NyKeisha, from Ohio."

I couldn't place the name so she told me we had met at a club in Buckhead. After explaining that night's events, I remembered. She was calling to see if we could hook back up and chill.

"Imm'ah keep it real wit'cha baby girl. I'm kinda in a situation right now, with someone. And I wanna see how it turns out."

She understood and told me if things changed I could call anytime. When I hung up Dog just looked at me like I was crazy because he was with me that night and remembered her.

When we got to the studio everybody was there. The construction was still going on with Block overseeing it. Everybody welcomed me back and it felt good.

"Damn bra'," Joc said, happy to see me. "You're not gonna believe the shows now. Everywhere we go it's crazy. We got one out in Montgomery, Alabama at Club Rose this weekend."

I said, "Cool, I can't wait to get back on the road."

Joc let me hear some new music he had done. They had changed the second verse on "Patron" and put this cat from Houston named Short Dog on it. He had a song with Lil' Wayne called "Play Wit It" that my partner Diesel produced. Diesel was from New Orleans and he used to produce for Cash Money back in the Hot Boy days. He moved to Atlanta after Hurricane Katrina. I always bumped into him at the open mics we used to do.

"I like that one," I said about the song with Wayne.

"Yeah, me too."

That weekend we loaded up the vans, the whole MasterMind/ Block ENT team and headed to Alabama. When we got there we got hotels, hollered at the promoter, did radio then hit the mall. Before we could even begin shopping a humongous crowd gathered around us. It was crazy! Bad chicks were everywhere and of course we made our selection to kick it with us later. It felt good to be back in the game.

At the club, the place was packed. Ms. B performed there back in the day and I knew exactly what type of crowd to expect. When she finished her set niggas had torn the club up and was outside in the parking lot standing on cars and shit with sawed off shotguns and choppers. Montgomery niggas was gang banged out.

Well this night was no different.

The club was small. We hit the VIP, got drinks then finally hit a stage big enough to fit only one and a half people. But it was crunk. Two or three fights broke out. We did our thing and got out of there having to leave behind the chicks we'd bagged for the crew. This show showed me how much had changed. All the hard work over the years was finally paying off.

One day Elvis called me and asked me to come to Doppler Studios because he was working on a project and needed my keyboard. Me and my girl hadn't been having any problems, although I felt a little distance between us. Nevertheless I told her I'd be going to the studio and that I'd call to check in if it got late.

At Doppler , Elvis and Ralph had been working on some stuff with a few artists and Elvis tricked me into coming to the studio by saying he needed the keyboard because they wanted me to do some arranging. The work was consuming and time was flying by. Around 2 a.m. I called my girl to check in but I got no answer. I left a message and explained how my phones were in the truck because my Nextel would interfere with the Pro Tools if it rang and my Sprint phone was on the charger. After that I returned to my work.

Finally finished, it was 5 a.m. when I made it to my truck. Elvis and Ralph were still at work but I was tired, barely able to stay awake. As I began driving, I noticed my girl had actually called like 2 or 3 times.

I immediately hit her, hoping her voice would keep me awake but I got no answer. I then called Ms. S who had left some messages as well, and asked her to talk to me while I drove.

"I don't think Imm'ah make it," I told her as I was threatening to doze off.

"Where you at?"

"The Grady curve. Look is it all right if I crash over there, because I don't wanna crash try'na make it to the house."

Ms. S told me it was cool so I headed over to her place. She kept me up and I made it safely. As soon as I got inside I fell straight to sleep. I woke up around 9 o'clock that morning, got up and shot straight home.

I noticed my girl had called but when I hit her back she didn't answer. I was sort of glad because I didn't feel like arguing. I pulled up to my house in no time, got out and when I opened my front door it looked like I'd been robbed of all my shit. I could hear the echo of my footsteps on the wooden floors. My furniture, paintings, and even some of the paint off the walls was gone. My big screens were gone, all my plates gone, cups gone, spoons gone, forks gone. . . everything gone. I went upstairs and saw my bedroom set was still there but my guest bedroom set was gone.

I'm thinking...what the fuck?

Hurrying, I went to the basement but thankfully all my equipment was still safe. I went back to my bedroom and something told me to check the closet. When I did, I saw my girl's clothes were indeed gone. Also, her son's clothes were gone. Seeing this, I went and laid down. I didn't even feel bad. Actually I was feeling like a huge weight had been lifted off my shoulders. It was then that the famous quote of Dr. Martin Luther King, Jr. popped up in my head.

"Free at last, free at last, thank God almighty I am free at last!"

Then I passed out.

When I woke up, Joc, Slick and Vick had all called to tell me they were up at Block's studio. I called Slick and Vick both, told them what happened and they both came to help me move some furniture from the basement to the den area. That day we all laughed at all I had been through. Slick clowned about how I didn't even have a cup to drink out of. I ended up going to Family Dollar and Wal-Mart to get shit for the bathrooms and kitchen utensils. Once I had things organized around the house and Vick and Slick left, a sense of loneliness came crashing down upon me. Just needing somebody to talk to, I said fuck it and called baby from Ohio, NyKeisha.

$$ \$\$\$ $$

Joc was performing in Nashville. We got there, got our rooms at around 9:30 p.m. and was due at the club around 12 midnight. The promoter and his people came and fucked with us and one of his boys brought a video camera to film us. When the time came to hit the club, Rico got a call and said the club was too packed and that the fire department had shut it down, causing a fight to break out. Disappointed that we couldn't give the fans what they wanted we just headed back to the A with Joc making some of the easiest money in his life. The hype was truly building.

A few days later we headed back out to Tennessee because Joc had a show in Memphis at Club Premier. We did the usual radio station promotion, meeting the host named Little Larry. We took live callers, pumped up the night's event and did a live call with local artist Yo Gotti. Gotti was slowly blowing up after generating a massive following in Memphis. He told us he was up at Tunica gambling and said he'd hook up with us later that night at the club.

Club Premier was packed. It felt like the floor was about to cave in, bouncing like a trampoline. Joc rocked it, and afterwards, him, Rico, Biggs and the DJ he'd hired (DJ Black from the Hit Men DJs) left while me, Vick, Slick, Roc and A.K. chose to stay. After they bounced, the rest of us chilled out in the VIP

Bun B was in the building. So was Yo Gotti, who had made it as promised. Gangsta Boo walked up in our section while we were standing on the sofa drinking and having a good time. Then two little chicks, one black and one Asian, approached Boo and commenced to throwing blows at her. Everybody formed a circle around the three girls who were fighting like cats. In a matter of seconds, Boo was laying halfway on the floor and sofa holding the black chick, while the Asian continued to swing away on her with exposed titties bouncing everywhere. It took security ten minutes to get through the circle to break it up. That shit was crazy— hands down the best performance of the night.

The next day I got a chance to get to know the dude Amir from Bad Boy. He handled a lot of business for Puffy. See you've gotta understand, I played the background so much a lot of people didn't quite know what my position was with Joc. They just assumed Block was the go to man. But me and Amir spent time talking at the hotel's bar before hitting some of Memphis's hottest strip clubs. It was my treat, with all expenses on me. Amir was cool and I formed a cool relationship with him.

I was back in Atlanta and hit up Platinum 21 to get at DJ Styles and guess who I ran across: Gangsta Boo. When she saw me, I could tell her mind went back to the night I last saw her and the fight she had with those two girls. I put my finger to my mouth and made like I was turning a key as to say, "I didn't see anything."

$$$

John and Big Jon worked out the details of my Pub deal with EMI, and I was to have the contracts soon. John called and also informed me that Block had figured out he hadn't gotten any interest in Joc's publishing, through our joint venture. I called Block about it and he said if I didn't want to give him any of the publishing then he'd just take all the royalties from the sales.

"Listen," I told him, "I'll be fair, even though I don't have to give you anything."

He said he was cool with that. So we had John draw everything up and he came over my now empty house with a one-page agreement stating me and Block would co-administer and split Joc's publishing. John said it was so Joc and Block could go and do them a pub deal themselves. I signed the agreement on the only table I had, which was an end table. My boy Eric Miller had come up and gotten a part in the

NFL complex center for kids. He'd gotten the basement, from the gym and was putting a studio down there. He was using two rooms, and so far he had one of them done up with his old equipment. Me and Slick was stopping by and fucking with him. He told me he wanted to manage M.M.M. for twenty percent and said he'd stay on top of what Block was doing. After going over the details, I said cool and we had John draft an agreement that stated his duties, how he'd receive his payments, and terms of termination.

John called me one day and told me to meet him in Union City Mall, for lunch. He had the EMI contracts for me to sign. I made my way to the mall went and hollered at Wingo (from Jagged Edge) at this candy store he'd opened up. While I kicked it with him, John called and told me to meet him at this little restaurant inside the mall called Buffalo's.

The contracts were pretty much what we'd discussed. John explained everything over lunch and I had no complaints and signed.

"I wanna bring Elvis in also," I explained to him. "His production work has potential to generate a lot of success."

"That's a good idea. It would also be a good start financially, for you all to make some big moves. That would give between the three of y'all, four hundred to four hundred and fifty grand of capital to work with."

"Yep," I said, but I was thinking how bad that money was needed for me to survive. I wasn't broke but I was sure fucking up the church's money.

$$$

The company responsible for fixing the water damage to my house was almost finished with the ceiling in my basement. They were down to doing touch up and I was looking forward to getting my studio back running. With Joc up at Block's, Elvis at Zaky's and Chris everywhere in between, I had some down time to arrange a few tracks.

One day while running through some beats, my boy Bodybag fell through with Vivica Fox's ex-husband, Six-Nine. He sang R&B and wanted to hear some of my tracks so we listened, and after hearing a few he liked, he asked me if he could sing some hooks on a few. I was thinking how wild this cat was. He was a giant and I couldn't imagine him doing R&B. We talked a minute about doing some recording on a later date before the time came for him to go. We promised to keep in touch.

Watching Six-Nine duck through my doorway I closed the door and turned to Bodybag.

"Man, the only singing that nigga gon' do is in the circus," I said. I busted up laughing.

"Yep. The world's largest singer."

Show Me The Money

Shawty Slick had been staying at Vick's so he would be closer to the action and not way out in Athens. With his car broke down, I let him use my van. Somehow Mite got his hands on the keys, saying he needed to use it for a family trip. When I called him about my van, this nigga tells me I owed him two or three stacks from some old shit I had taken a loss on. In other words, he was holding my van hostage.

Out of a van, I missed a couple of Joc's shows. His manager was acting like a little bitch, complaining to Block about him not being able to handle everybody at the shows. I was already thinking, *who the hell this nigga think he is?* But I was trying to keep calm for Joc's sake.

Being that we hadn't been spending much time together, Joc called me and asked what I was up to. "Nothing, chilling at the crib."

"Cool, I'll be there in fifteen minutes."

When Joc pulled up he called and told me to come outside. The first thing I saw was some bright hologram blue headlights. When I got up to the car, I saw he was sitting behind the wheel of a silver CL 550 Coupe, with chrome rims. The windows were down and he had the brains busted.

I jumped in. "When you get this?"

"I just got it today. You like it?"

"Yeah," I said. The muthafucka was fresh.

"You can get it whenever," he said. "Let's roll out."

We hit downtown and rode by a few spots. We bumped into Roc, the guy Joc had worked for, and LaTocha from Escape. Roc was feeling the Benz, seeing how far Joc had come. After that we hit Body Tap and got a chance to kick it, just me and him.

Kicking it this night made me and Joc realize it would be our last time kicking it as Chauncey and Jasiel. Though it wasn't said, we treated it as such. And so we lost ourselves in having a good time, poppin' bottles and flirting with the girls.

Since my girl left, I had received only two calls from her. One was to tell me to finish paying the people for the carpet, and the other was because she'd taken some of my computer stuff. During one of those calls she had the nerve to say her leaving might teach me to appreciate her more. I thought, *what was it to appreciate? She didn't cook, clean and only complained.*

Anyway, Elvis called and I told him about the Pub deal with EMI and asked if he was interested. He told me how he had been talking to people like Sylvia Rhone, but he wouldn't mind getting at Big Jon. I called Big Jon on the spot via 3-way and plugged them together. During the conversation, I promised Big Jon that Elvis would have a song on Joc's album, and Elvis explained about the stuff he was doing with Polo. When we ended the call, it all looked promising for Elvis.

Then Big Jon hit me back.

"If you can get him over here, I can get you fifty percent of the deal, which would be twenty five percent. So holler at him and let me know."

When I got off the phone with him I wondered if 25 percent of my 50 percent was going elsewhere. Shit just got slicker than duck shit in the music industry.

The day I had been waiting for finally came. John called me and asked me to meet him at Union City Mall again. I made it in about 30 minutes and found him in the food court.

"I got something you want," he said.

I opened the envelope and found a check for $57,000.

"Now that's minus my percentage. You'll get another forty thousand when you fulfill the terms of the agreement."

I nodded.

"Also, we weren't able to do the deal for your interest in Joc. Apparently Block had already did his deal with Warner/Chappell and two companies cannot collect for the same catalog."

I was caught off guard by this news. "Well how will I get my money?"

"Oh, Warner/Chappell will pay you your share."

"I wish I would've known all this beforehand," I said.

John nodded, understanding how I felt. Then he gave me a serious look and said, "Now don't go and blow your money on cars and clothes . . . things of no value. Chauncey, you should invest your money. You know, I'm doing research with the HBCUs and a lot of black racecar teams dealing with fuel. We're making gas out of vegetables for racecars. Also, I'm doing lucrative things in Brazil, selling books and different stuff online . . . a lot of things to invest in."

He had me thinking. "Sounds good."

"Also you gotta come over and check out my place in Brazil," he said. "I can get you a nice apartment for very cheap so you can see the opportunities available to you. If you wanna really build your financial base you're gonna have to minimize your spending Chauncey."

I knew he was right. I did need to start looking into investment portfolios. I told John what was on my mind and that I'd get back with him on it after the album came out. When I left the mall, I headed straight to the bank and deposited the check. I hated I didn't get the other $150,000, but something was better than nothing. Time was rolling. Joc called and said he had a photo shoot for his album cover. Eric also hit me trying to get me some split sheets he had for MasterMind. I told Eric I was on my way to Joc's album cover shoot and I'd catch him later.

At Joc's shoot, I found a camera crew setting up and getting him in place. He was posted up in front of my partner Lil Dave's blue '73 Chevy dunk, mounted on 26-inch floaters with a few chicks in the background. A cameraman was snapping away flicks. After we changed locations, Eric Miller caught up with us and handed me some fucking split sheets with MMM as the heading like he had done something.

"How come you didn't know about the photo shoot?" I asked.

"I gotta holla at Block and Kerry and see what's up with that," he replied dumbly.

Right then I began wondering if his services were really needed.

In preparation for the album, Block decided to do a Gangsta Grill mix CD with DJ Drama. He told me I needed to go in the booth and do some drops. He also asked what Eric was supposed to be doing. I told him "managing."

"I'd get rid of that nigga," he said. "He's in the way."

Dana was running the boards so I went in the booth, dropped a few drops and made sure I plugged MasterMind Music in there.

"Boy you got some playa shit down," Dana said when I was finished. "Niggas need to pay you to talk on their CDs."

"Nigga you just high," I said.

As soon as I left, I called my cousin Nikkia and told her to type up a letter to Eric and fire his ass. According to the agreement we had, termination had to be done through a written notice. I couldn't accept slacking, especially when money was involved.

Saturday night Carl Moe called me and told me that Body Tap was jumping. Not having anything going on I got dressed and shot up there. When I arrived, I saw how packed it was, with valet parking full and the side streets as well. I got lucky and found a parking spot in the club's lot.

Making my entrance through the upstairs VIP section, once inside I hit up the DJ booth to see who was working. As soon as I stepped in the booth I saw Carl Moe there with my boy DJ X-Rated.

"What's up y'all," I said, dapping both of them.

X-Rated took to the mic and addressed the packed crowd: "Yo, my man Chino Dollar just hit the building and y'all know what time it is!!" "Then he proceeded to put "It's Goin Down" on.

"I'm good. What up wit'chall?" he asked.

Carl Moe said he was trying to relax. "I just stepped in to holler at X for a minute, then I'm try'na get some drinks."

With that being said we chopped it up with X-Rated a moment or two more, then made our way downstairs. We both ordered a few drinks and enjoyed the night.

Now when Carl gets off the drink he's a world of fun. Taking in the scene he began cracking jokes on a few busted-outfit-wearing hoes and a few wanna be ballin' fake jewelry wearing cats perpetrating in the club. He had me laughing my ass off. The alcohol had gotten to me as well, so I wasn't holding back, laughing good and hard.

Finally, exhausted of being hard on the crowd, me and Carl headed back to the DJ booth with X-Rated where the three of us hit a blunt up. I hit the strong a few times and got high super-fast because I really wasn't a smoker.

"Aye y'all, I need a Newport," I said. "Imm'ah step out for a minute."

Making my way to the little VIP lounge area, I lit up and let the cigarette boost my already mounting high. A few chicks were near and were enjoying themselves and it didn't take me long to strike up a conversation with them. As soon as we got into a good dialogue Carl Moe comes over high and drunk as hell, cracking jokes like he was on Def Comedy Jam. The girls walked off and all of a sudden he continued with me at the ass end of his jokes.

I snapped. With the Corona bottle I had in my hand I tried to connect with his head and I said, "Nigga who the fuck you think yo' broke ass talking to!" I was up in his face now. "Nigga, I'll beat yo mutha fuckin' ass!"

My words and anger drew the attention of a couple cats that knew both of us. "Man, y'all break this shit up," homie said, coming from behind and grabbing my arm.

Not heeding the advice, I continued to go off. Carl Moe said something slick, fed up at my shit, shoved me back then dipped out. The guy who separated us told me I needed to dip because I was fucked up. Still upset, I decided to bounce, feeling my night had been ruined by Carl Moe's overbearing sense of humor.

On my way out of the club a text message came through my phone: IM GONNA SEE U NIGGA

The message was from Carl Moe's number. At first I got heated and called his phone from my truck. But after several attempts, I couldn't reach him and just sat there. I thought about what happened and figured that I was dead wrong for blowing up on him like I did. Carl was only having fun. With this new outlook I tried to call him again to tell him I apologize for my behavior. This time he answered, but he wasn't trying to hear anything I had to say.

I felt like a fool for jumping to conclusions. We ended our conversation coming to no resolution. As I hung up I spotted Carl Moe on the side street standing next to his car. He was putting his phone away. I swerved over to him, jumped out and tried my hand with him face to face.

"Moe, my bad shawty," I said sincerely. But he still wasn't trying to hear it.

Seeing I wasn't making any progress, I said fuck it and asked, "Well what's up then? If it's beef let's cook it now. If it ain't no problems let's act like men and dead dis shit."

His only response while getting in his car was "I hear ya shawty." Not feeling he understood I just jumped in my truck and dipped. I figured that we both needed to calm down. Maybe that was best.

Since my girl left, I had been partying really hard. Hitting Buckhead with Lil Will, Jig, Cheese, the Jagged Edge twins who had just bought two new CLS 550 Benzes. I found us taking over VIP sections all over the city. It reminded me of the times I used to spend with Darius, Paul and Eric, or when me and STR8 Drop used to go clubbing, carefree. I began thinking how blessed I was because Darius was now doing a Fed bid, not ever guessing back then that he'd be there. In the game, tomorrow's freedom was never promised.

One night at the club Central Station, I bumped into my home girl Tericka. She was looking good and having a good time.

"Boy, I've been seeing you all on 106 and Park, doing ya little dance," she said. These hoes be all in the club askin' about who you is."

"Oh yeah?" She was trying to flatter me.

" They be like Joc cool but where that nigga Chino Dollar at?"

I laughed. "Girl, stop yo shit."

She started laughing too. "I ain't lyin'! They be all on Joc's MySpace with that shit."

For the rest of the night it was nothing but love from everybody I knew. They knew how far I'd come. I told Tericka I had to get me a MySpace page. I'd been on Joc's and figured it would be good to have something available for people to get at me through.

After my girl took my flat screen, I got one from Joc to hang in my den. With the renovations done, I figured it was time to do some decorating and quit living like I stayed in a trap house. So I hit the furniture store and got a beige living room set, some black paintings, a matching dining room set, kitchen table, ceiling fans and all. I went all in! When I was done I barely wanted to leave the house.

Things were going good for Joc. The DJ Drama mix CD had dropped. I was a little heated because not one of the drops I did were used. Instead, Drama just gave me a shout out. I hadn't had much time to talk to Joc about anything. He was doing a lot of flying to shows and I wasn't on his rider so I'd have to pay for my own flights. I figured I'd only go to the ones I really wanted to be at. Plus, we'd have a tour bus shortly and I'd just jump on there.

One day I was on my way to Block's studio when NyKeshia called me. For the last couple weeks, me and her had been talking a lot. She called to tell me her brother in Cincinnati wanted to holla at me about booking Joc. I told her it was cool and to have him call me. Anyway, he did and we ran it about how he used to get money in the A and about a few people we knew and how we had met at a strip club called Pink Pony back in the day.

"Look, I already booked Joc for two shows, through some lady named Amy at this booking agency," he said. "I paid twenty grand a show though and I was try'na get some love."

He went on to say how he had just gotten out from doing a bid and was trying to fly straight.

"I wanna book Joc for five to ten shows, if I can get him for fifteen to seventeen grand. And I'll pay all the front half on all the dates up front, at one time."

"Let me call Rico, and plug y'all up, All right?"

I clicked over and called Rico and briefly explained to him what was up and clicked back so all of us were connected. Rico listened as NyKeshia's brother told him what he told me.

When he was finished Rico said, "Nah! Twenty grand is the price. And I'm about to go up to twenty-five."

"I understand," he said to Rico. "Amy said she may be able to do nineteen, but that really ain't no love."

It was at this point, Rico started talking reckless. "Nigga that's the best deal, twenty thousand! And you better jump on it. Y'all niggas be broke, try'na do big thangs. If you want Joc, then you know what it is."

I just listened dumbfounded.

"Hold up," dude said, finally fed up with Rico's shit. "Who you think you talkin' to? You gon' be in my city in a little while. This shit real over here, nigga!"

Rico cut dude off, told me to call him back later, and hung up. Now it was just me and NyKeshia's brother.

"What's up wit'cha boy?" he asked me. "You need to holla at that nigga, for real. Before he gets fucked up."

"Give Rico a pass. He don't know who he's talkin' to."

"I might just have to show him, when y'all get out here. I heard y'all were gonna be on the tour with T.I."

"That's what I was headed to talk to Block about when you called. Look, let me know how things turn out with Amy, okay?"

He said he would. And being that he'd already paid the deposit for 2 shows, he felt confident that he'd see Rico face to face. When we got off the phone I knew I had to pray for peace. Because if dude was anything like I figured then Rico was in trouble.

At Block's he told me that T.I. had said Joc could open for him on his King Tour. It was to help Joc promote New Joc City. I knew Block hadn't hooked it up with Tip, but that Atlantic probably did, since it was the parent company for both Bad Boy and Grand Hustle. I knew if Tip would've had his way then his new artist Young Dro would've been opening up with his single "Shoulder Lean." Block told me the tour bus was ready and should be on the road soon.

I was at home talking to Lil' Will about his supposed deal with Jeezy's CTC label. Will expressed how he felt they were trying to play him on the deal. I really wasn't in the mood for the conversation, concerned about my own issues and the money being right for my own business. That's when Joc hit my other line.

"What's up Chino?" he asked. "Where you at?"

"The crib."

"Look, I need you to meet me at Salams, on Riverdale Road. I want you to help me pick out something."

I really didn't have any plans so I told him I'd be there in a minute. I told Will I'd holler at him later and I bounced out the door.

Salams is a used car lot that sold luxury cars and trucks. Me and Joc looked around. He liked this Range Rover they had and this BMW 745. We also saw this black Benz CL 550 that was like the silver one he already had. He was torn until he finally made up his mind.

"You know what, Imm'ah get the Rover and the Seven Forty-Five."

I said, "They cool."

So we got with the guy and went into his office to get the paper work done. Joc asked for a deal for the cars he liked. Dude said, "You only buying 2 cars, what kind of deal you want?" Joc told him depending on the deal he'd buy more than 2 cars. Dude asked how good his credit was.

"Imm'ah pay cash," Joc told him.

They worked out a deal on the spot. Joc hooked it up where the guy would work with him when buying more than two vehicles. He told me he wanted for us to do a luxury car rental service. I didn't know how it would work but Joc was confident. We ended up picking out three 745's, two Range Rovers and one black CL Benz.

"How much money you got on you?" Joc asked.

"Shit, I ain't got nothing but five or six stacks on me."

"Okay," he said, "and give me half on the cars later."

"Is you crazy?" It seemed he had lost his mind. "I might chip in on two of them, but that's it."

"Cool," he said finally. "And you know you can get any one of them when you want. You'll at least have the keys to one of them."

Joc's wife got insurance on all the cars and basically ran the luxury car rental service. She found this parking garage downtown Atlanta, parked them and put "Rent Me" signs on them. Joc had 22-inch Ashanti rims put on all of the cars and 26-inch rims on the Rovers. For the days that followed, I changed cars like I changed draws in the morning.

Things were paying off. All the support me and Joc gave each other had things finally looking up. Me being there for him and his family when they needed a place to stay and him believing in me to the point that he'd gave me a reason to leave the dope game, seemed all worth it now. We had come a long way.

The King Tour

It had been six years since my newly established brother Gino had gone to prison. That time had passed and now he had made it to a work release camp. Joc had shows in Savannah and then Florida. On their way to Florida, they picked up Gino from where he'd gotten a weekend pass to go see Joc perform. I told Joc to call me when they picked him up.

When Gino hit me he was all excited. "What's up bra'?"

"Everything's good," I said, glad to hear his voice. Gino was just at a loss for words as was I. "How you feelin' now that you're out?"

"Man, you just don't know bra'," he said, exhaling a long breath.

Gino went on to explain how he had been hearing the song on the radio but didn't know it was Joc at first. Then he called home, asking who was this Joc dude rapping about College Park, his second home.

"They was like, 'yo brother fool'. I couldn't believe it was him until I saw the video."

We talked about how things had changed and how everything was going to be all good now that the three of us were going to be busting moves together. Finally I told him I wasn't going to keep him.

"I'll catch up with you when you get done with the work camp," I said.

"We'll kick it then, All right? Until then you got my number. Hit me if you need anything."

I was glad fam was getting out of that hell hole of a prison. And to have Joc and me in a position to help him on some legal shit was even better.

With John spending most of his time in Brazil, I found myself without any legal counsel to assist me in handling my business. I needed to make sure my end was straight with my joint venture with Block. We agreed to do a letter of direction and send it to Atlantic so my fifty percent would come straight to me. So far that letter hadn't been written. I also needed someone to register all my songs with ASCAP and to make sure my share was listed with BMI on Joc's registration of songs.

To get it done I called Nitti to see what was up with Miryam. She registered "It's Goin Down" for us so I figured she could get the job done. But Nitti said she didn't work at the office anymore but he had someone named Pamela Johnson, Ian Burkes' assistant at ASCAP. I got her number and called and we made an appointment to meet at her office on Mitchell Street downtown.

On his grind, Chris Flame had met a lawyer while in New York. His name was Jeffery Wooten. He had done Chris's pub deal. I got Jeff's number from Chris and called him as well. Jeff said he'd heard of the things I'd put together and liked it. He thought we could be the next big thing out of Atlanta.

"You know, we as young black men have to stick together," he said. "In this music industry, everyone's trying to get over on each other, instead of helping each other. Listen, fax me the contracts that were in place and I'll see what I can do."

I asked him if I could give Elvis his number so he could get with him about working his pub deal also. He said he didn't mind. Jeff was cool and we ended our conversation without him once mentioning to me any kind of fee for a retainer.

Later in the week I turned around and finally met Pamela Johnson. We came up with an administration agreement where I would pay her every three months and she'd register all my songs. She would also make sure my credits were done correctly on the album cover and everything else concerning my publishing. I gave her the names of my ASCAP publishing company, which was Basement Funk.

She told me she had to set up one with BMI, since that was the company Joc was under, so I could collect my share. I told her to just set it and name it Basement Funk South.

$$$

The tour bus was finally ready. It was black and had a picture of Joc from the photo shoot we did with YUNG Joc in big yellow letters beneath it. It had a leather seating area in the front, TV and surround sound system, kitchen area, bunk beds with curtains, and at the back of the bus was a suite with a big screen and all.

When it came time for the tour, Torrey was assigned to film each show. Rico booked a club event after each concert on the tour. Tip wasn't doing any club events, which left all that money for Joc to make. Days where it would be a one or two day bus ride, Joc would just fly and meet the bus in the next city if he had an event in between. I would do some spot dates but I knew I couldn't stay gone like that. And plus, I wasn't getting paid from the shows and nobody really extended any invitation for me to ride along.

During the tour, my man G from Cincinnati, but who lived in the A, called and asked me if I was going to hit the show in his city.

"I'm try'na get'chu to ride with me if you ain't going with Joc and 'em," he explained. "I got some paper to pick up out there so I might as well hit the show while I'm out there and if you with me I can get some of that V-I-P treatment."

I was still contemplating on going but I told him I would, just for him. So when the day came me, G, and his partner Slim hit the highway. I was riding with them so all I needed to do was relax.

During the trip, we stopped and switched drivers and gassed up. Slim told G, "Man, pop the hatch to the trunk and let me put these shits in the trap in the back. You drive too fast."

Confused at what he was talking about I watched as Slim reached underneath the backseat of the Tahoe we were in and pulled out one SKS assault rifle and one Carbon 15. The second came from underneath the seat I was sitting in. I almost shitted on myself when I saw this. The last thing I needed was a Federal "Felon in Possession of a Firearm" case. Thinking about the caliber of these dudes I thought, man I hope they ain't about to hit no licks with me with them.

We arrived in Cincinnati and were at the show in no time. Tip and Joc killed it. I had seen some niggas do wild shit in their shows but Tip's energy level was out of this world. And his lyrics stayed on point, combining with an arrogance that helped him play the role of The King successfully. I'd seen him rip the stage and a female fan who'd grabbed his pants leg. He then told his road DJ, DJ Drama, to cut the music. He told the girl not to grab on him because she wouldn't like it if she walked through the crowd and a man grabbed her on her ass. Then he gave the cue to Drama and told the chick "don't be grabbing on me because you don't know me" as Drama hit his banger "You Don't Know Me." That shit just fell in stride.

Well at the show, while on stage, Tip asked the crowd, "Who's orange Charger is that parked out front? That bitch is clean!"

A few cats hollered out amongst the huge crowd.

"Well it's clean but it ain't got shit on mine. Cause I'm The King," he proclaimed. Then he began to perform his song "Look What I Got."

We had a good time. Torrey and them were going to the club event Rico lined up and I told him I'd catch up with them later. G had to go pick his money up so we smashed over to handle that first. I was praying all went well with his business, and when G did his thing and came back to the truck he confirmed that everything was cool. With that, we headed to the club.

Club Ritz was where Joc was to perform. While I was waiting on G to get his money, Torrey had called and told me Tip and Grand Hustle was coming out that night also. Now out of all the show dates, Tip had never hit the after party show with us. So I figured it was about to be one helluva night. I was a little pissed because G had over $220,000 in cash. Plus the rifles and an extra two pistols and didn't want to stash them. I asked if he was going to put the money and guns up but he told me not to worry. "Anything might pop off in the Nasty Natti and we might have to dump and run like '95 Madden."

Easier said than done. I didn't know about him but I didn't need a Fed case.

The Ritz was jammed packed. I had called Joc prior to tell him if I wasn't there when he performed to throw some money on the part in "Patron" when my name was said. Well when we arrived Torrey had someone at the door waiting on us. As soon as we made it in, Joc had just said "Ask Chino Dolla 'bout that dope boy magic" and I saw money raining from the stage. I pulled some bills out myself and tossed it in the area I was in.

"This bitch is crunk," G said as we tried making it to the VIP section.

When Joc made it to "It's Goin Down," Tip and his crew started throwing money. Tip also had a mic and started yelling out how he was The King. Finished, Joc exited the stage and went through the crowd dapping cats up until he made it to the VIP. That's when we saw commotion coming from Tip's security and a small group of local niggas.

"We got money too," some cat yelled out to the security. "We just try'na holla at o'boy."

A small fight broke out between the security and the group. By this time, we cleared out the VIP. We lost Joc in the mix and I called Torrey to see where they were. He told me Tip had left and that he and others in our crew along with DJ Drama were locked in some room, and that Biggs had lost the keys to the van they came in.

"Y'all get up outta here," he told me.

As soon as I dipped outside I got caught off guard when dudes started busting off shots in the air. Shit was crazy.

"Let's get the fuck outta here," G said. "I know these police gonna be pulling niggas over and shit."

I was thinking the same thing. With all the guns and shit we had, I began to really worry. We jumped in the truck and slid out of the parking lot without being detected by the police. We hit some back streets because we knew the main streets would be filled with cops. I tried calling Joc and Torrey but I got no answer.

Finally Torrey hit me. "Man we got up out of there and we gettin' on the freeway right now."

"All right, we on our way to the freeway now," I told him.

A few minutes later we arrived at the southbound freeway's on ramp and saw the Marshals had it blocked. My heart dropped as I thought about the guns. I just knew I was gonna be shipped to prison. Cars were slowing down ahead of us. That's when my phone rang. It was Torrey again.

"Man, somethin' done happened," he told me.

"Somethin' like what?" I asked.

"Well, I see Tip and his crew's van pulled to the side of the road. Hubcaps and shit are all in the street. The police are turning us around and giving us an escort."

I was confused. "An escort? For what?"

"They said they need to holler at everybody," he said. "Y'all need to get lost with them Georgia tags."

I told G what Torrey said and he told me not to worry, that we'd be back in the A in a couple hours. I ended the call praying for the Lord to help me to make it home safely.

I was at T.G.I. Friday's on Peachtree Street with my cousin Reece when Joc called me. "Shawty," he said in an exhausted voice. "Philant is dead."

"What?!?!" My mind went blank as I sat taking in what Joc just said. Philant Johnson was Tip's good friend, someone everyone knew as a good and humble guy. He worked as Tip's personal assistant and was an employee at Grand Hustle. He was just 26 years young. He went on to explain what all went down the night before in Cincinnati. Apparently some cats followed Tip and sprayed up the van, and in the end, four people from Tip's entourage were shot. Philant was one of them.

"The shit is all over the news," Joc informed me. "I'm about to do a live call in right now, about what happened, with radio in the A."

I told Joc to make sure he gave a shout out from all of us to Philant's family and to tell them we are praying for them. When we ended our call, I just sat at the table in the restaurant lost in my thoughts. My cousin Reece and I discussed how crazy it was that something like this happened to someone like Philant.

"Just when everything seems like it's going good, that's when the bullshit happens," I said.

Reece just nodded in agreement. He knew I was referring to all our situations just as much as to what happened to Philant. And though I was proud of what we were accomplishing, this tragedy reminded me that anything could happen in a moment's time to change all we've hustled to get. I knew then that it was important for us to stay focused and not let the bright lights blind us to who and what we were.

The Madness

"......the shooting on Southbound Interstate 75, one of two main arteries leading to Cincinnati's downtown area, at 3 a.m. The incident occurred after a show by Atlanta rappers T.I. and Yung Joc at Bogart's nightclub in the Clifton neighborhood near the University of Cincinnati. Following the show, T.I. and Yung Joc went to an afterhours party at The Ritz night club where an altercation began."

I was sitting in my studio listening to the news when my cell phone rang.

"Hello."

"Chino, this is NyKeshia."

"Hey, what's up?" I said, not expecting her call.

"I just wanted to call and say I'm sorry about what happened to Philant," she said with sincerity in her voice.

"Yeah, we're all tripping over this shit right now. How've you been?"

There was a long sigh before she spoke. "Honestly, I've been having a hard time."

"Really, what's going on with ya?" I asked.

"Chino, my brother got killed."

"What?! I just talked to him a few weeks ago when he was trying to get Joc out there to do the shows. Me, him and Rico were just . . . "

"I know," she said cutting my rambling off.

"What happened?"

NyKeshia explained how her brother had gotten pulled over by the marshals one night after leaving the club. Some kind of way he ended up shooting and killing an officer. He went on the run, and the police found him at this girl's house. They kicked in the door and killed him on sight.

"I don't know if he had done his shows with Joc or not and I'm trying to get in touch with his partner to see if he should get his money back."

"Damn NyKeshia, I'm sorry to hear this shit happened. Call me and let me know what you find out about his money and if Joc did the shows or not, All right?"

I hung up thinking how crazy everything was getting. It seemed like no matter how legit people tried to go, the streets were still claiming them, in one way or another.

That Sunday, Joc had a show at Prime Time in Atlanta. We all met at Vick's spot before jumping on I-285 from College Park to Decatur. When we met up with Rico, Bigg had a couple sheriffs with him explaining to us that we might not need to do the show because some death threats had been made on our lives. The police said they didn't know who made them, but they were coming out of Ohio and they were associating it with what happened in Cincinnati. The first thing that popped in my mind was that Rico didn't want to give the promoters their money back and that he had his hand in this some kind of way. So with the escort of the DeKalb County Police and helicopter, we were led back onto I-285 and escorted all the way to the Clayton County line. Later I found out the threats were really due to the shooting at The Ritz.

Time had come and Gino was finally released. We got together and rode around the city, chopping it up. Joc had hit him with a few stacks and had him pushing the black Benz CL joint. He was a wild hot head but was looking to get himself situated in the world.

"I'm try'na figure out what I'mma do now," he said as he watched the scenery of Atlanta, taking in all its changes.

"Just take your time," I said. "We'll put something together for you. I'll help you however I can."

This little bit of support motivated him and I was glad I could help. Especially since I saw he was serious about getting himself together.

Meanwhile, Joc was doing shows seven days a week. His fee was now up to $25,000 a show. Finally Rico made the decision to give him Sundays, off which gave him time to relax. He called me talking about how he bought himself a new CLS 550 Benz. He was on the road when he bought it, and was waiting on it.

"I've already paid, I just need you to pick it up if Alex can't," he said, referring to his wife.

"All right, I got 'chu," I said.

He went on to explain how he talked the dealer down from $75,000 to $60,000, telling the dealer he'd pay cash. The dealer negotiated the deal telling Joc if he paid cash then he would pay the insurance for a year. The dealer also said he'd ship it. Joc told the guy to put it all in writing. The dealer then went and got at his supervisor, who told him the deal was up to him, so he did it.

"When he said he'd do it, I went to the nearest SunTrust and got a traveler's check. When I went back and gave him the check he liked to shit on himself. He thought I was just some nigga off the street and wouldn't have to eat those promises. While we were doing the paperwork someone from the shop came up to me and asked me for my autograph. They said their son liked my music. Chino, you should've seen the dealer's face when he realized I was a rapper; it was like he wished he didn't give me that big break on the car."

"Yeah, if he knew that he would've tried to get the whole seventy five," I said.

"And he could've too," he said. "That's how bad I wanted it."

I told Joc I had him covered. I did what he asked and got the whip. Joc came and picked it up and had some 22-inch Ashanti rims put on it. I was glad to see him treating himself.

One day we were mixing songs at the studio, trying to get everything ready. We were working on "Patron" and the part came on where Joc says, "Ask Chino Dolla." The door to was slightly cracked and Block was in the other room talking to some of the crew. That's when I thought I heard him say something like "How to fuck Chino Dolla." The music was so loud that I wasn't sure, so I decided to ask him.

I stepped out of the room and approached him. "Aye Block, what'chu say? How to fuck Chino Dolla?"

He was caught off guard. "Huh, what . . . naw dog, ain't nobody say that."

But when he turned I thought I saw a smirk on his face. I decided to brush it off, but I kept it registerd in my mind.

June 6 was nearing and so was the release date for the album. It had been pushed back already and we still hadn't picked all the songs, mixed or mastered everything yet. Block had Niko from Patchwork mixing some songs, and Joc was in the studio touching up some shit as well. I was getting sessions from producers we'd recorded with to see if these songs would make the album.

One night I was at Cochese's house waiting on Joc so we could finish a song when Block called me and said the song "Beat It Up" wasn't going to make the album.

"Man you're crazy!" I said. "That's one I personally picked."

"It ain't me," he said. "It's the label."

"Man they're trippin'." I couldn't believe they were trying to cut the song. It was a sure hit.

"Look, let them pick," Block continued. "That's what I had to do with Boyz 'N Da Hood. I let them pick the second single. And then if it flops you ain't gotta listen to them anymore."

"I guess we won't have to listen, because it will be all over with," I said.

Me and Block went back and forth before we ended the call. He hit me back minutes later with Harve Pierre from Bad Boy, on the phone. I told Harve what I told Block and how much I wanted the song on the album. During all this, Joc finally pulled up to the studio. He got on the phone and told them he wanted the song as well. Joc doubled back and had a text conversation with Puff about it and it was settled: "Beat It Up" would be on the album.

"You know, it's on you if the song doesn't do good," Block said later. "You won't have to worry about picking another song again."

"You'll see," I said confidently. "I'm in the streets. I know what they want out here."

I was beginning to see that Block had no ear for what was hot. Either that, or he just wanted to limit my creative input. I was really beginning to wonder.

The album delivery date had come and we still needed one more song. Out of all the songs we made, Chris Flame didn't have any on there. The album was gone and we got word back that they didn't approve one cut so that was my chance to push a song produced by Chris. Having one he and Joc had done, I caught Block at his studio, and shot him the song.

"Here, this song we need," I told him. "Just drop it in your drive, go ahead and mix it and send it off."

Not having time to argue, he gave it to Dana who did some edits. I had tightened up the track already so when it was finished "I'm Him" came to life. And that was the closer for New Joc City, with my part of the agreement fulfilled. My seven songs included: "It's Going Down," "I Know You See It," "Patron," "Dopeboy Magic," "Picture Perfect," "I'm Him" and "Beat It Up." This gave my whole crew a spot on the album, except for Slick, who killed "Nan Nudda Pimp Like Me" back in the day, and it was too late to get him on a verse.

The guarantee I gave Big Jon that Elvis would have a song on Joc's album was satisfied. With that, Jeff went ahead and closed Elvis's pub deal, getting him the same terms as Chris's deal. I was just hoping I wouldn't live to regret I didn't take the back door deal Big Jon had offered me.

Although I was glad things were coming together, I wasn't getting comfortable; business still had to be handled. Credits had to be done, producer agreements had to be signed and some more stuff. The woman I hired, Pam, had gotten my BMI Publishing company set up, and now they had to go through each song credit and list Basement Funk South and Basement Funk on the songs produced or written by me.

Pam was also getting the producer agreements and split sheets signed. At the end of all the commotion, I was on top of my shit.

One day Block called me in his office to discuss some business. "We gotta find somewhere to put you, on the album credits."

I was confused. "What do you mean, my executive producer credits?"

"Nah, they won't do that," he said. He saw I wasn't feeling that.

"But don't trip, I got 'chu. We gon' put me and you as A&R. Is that cool?"

"Hell naw"! Now I really wasn't feeling it.

" Man, I'm try'na tell you that I got 'chu," Block said after exhaling a deep breath like I was being complicated. "When I get this label deal, you will have your own thing through me. Then you will just be the executive producer, along with me. Puff and them don't want to do that right now."

I just looked at him and shook my head. I turned my back to walk out.

"Do whatever," I said. I had to leave because I didn't want my anger to get the best of me. A&R belittled the work I'd put in, and I felt Block shouldn't have accepted it either. But I just let it go, praying it all played out in our favor.

Joc had been talking with Brandy. He wanted to sign her and when Block found this out, he wanted in. Block told Joc that they could sign her to Block Ent, and they could split everything. Brandy was telling me all of this and how she felt about it.

"I ain't try'na fuck wit them," she said bluntly. "I really wanna do my own thing Chino, and I want you to be a part of it."

"What's up wit' Nitti?" I asked.

"He still on some hoe shit," she said. "This nigga talking 'bout I'm still under contract. I just went ahead and served him with some termination papers."

I really wanted to see Brandy back in the thick of things. It's where she belonged. She was just like the rest of my crew and I wanted the best for her. Hearing that she wanted me involved with her next project made me feel good, and it showed me how valuable I was to her.

Her "Ms. B" image had a lane in the industry and I knew she still could build off the momentum she had begun with "Bottle Action." I felt like me and Joc owed that to her. She was the beginning for Joc, and I had learned a lot from her situation.

The time for all of my hard work to pay off was right around the corner, and I knew I just needed to be patient. Looking back on the long road I travelled brought a great feeling of accomplishment. It wouldn't be long now.

Miami

With the city's pussy price at an all-time low, due to the loss of BMF on the scene, me and Rod would hook up and hit mostly strip clubs. We didn't do Magic City too much because the Feds had that on fire. I had heard they'd put (or was putting) up a big screen where you could see yourself partying in the club, and that was too much for me. I didn't need anybody getting footage and looking at it, see me in it like that. It was bad enough the Feds were getting cats' photo negatives out of the club for investigations. Although I was transitioning myself into the music business, I still didn't need any misunderstandings concerning what I was doing. I just didn't need it.

Rod had bought a black Lambo with black and canary yellow insides and trim. Me and him would hit up Platinum 21, Pink Pony, Strokers, Pinups, Pleasures, Cheetahs, Gold Rush, Body Tap and Goose Bumps. We'd pull up and park out front. With Joc's video being #1 on the 106 and Park countdown, my face was kinda familiar to some people.

One night when leaving Body Tap a young black APD officer saw me and said, "I saw you in that video today, Yung Joc's. When they be doin' that dance."

"Oh yeah," I said as we hopped in the whip.

The officer was parked by the front gate and was on his way to his cruiser. "Yeah," eyeing the Lambo he said, "Man this muthafucker is clean."

Rod said, "preciate it."

The officer walked and got in his car and Rod started the Lambo. Just then we saw lights flash and quickly saw it was the officer. He pulled up next to us with his window down. "How does that thing run?"

"Oh she running," Rod said.

"Pull down here," the officer said, referring to a side street next to the club. We watched as he led the way, us following behind him. Once we got away from the crowd and pulled next to him he told us, "Let's line 'em up."

"What, you wanna race?" Rod asked.

"Yeah, down to that corner store," he said.

"All right, fuck it," Rod said after looking at me, then back at the officer.

Next thing I knew we were both flying down the street. The Lambo bolted out front and in seconds, we were four car lengths ahead of the cruiser. We made it to the store and had stopped by the time the officer made it.

"Damn that muthafucka's fast," he told us. He jumped out his cruiser and gave us a card. "If y'all ever have any problems give me a call. I do security too."

Rod got his card and we left. I told Rod to keep the card because dude might come in handy one day.

The time for the album release party was coming fast. Bad Boy set up a luncheon at Justin's restaurant for Joc and the staff. The tour bus was parked out back and me and Joc found time to chill and talk, just me and him.

"I think our next single is gonna be "I Know You See It," he told me. "It's crazy because all the songs we did are the ones they're liking at my shows."

"Our chemistry is right, that's all," I said. "This is what we grinded for."

"I'm just ready to get all these promo shows out the way."

"You know, that's gotta be done."

"I know," he said.

The next thing I knew he was fast asleep. I just looked at him lying there on the couch thinking, *yeah, he's living the life.* They were running him like a quarter horse at the Kentucky Derby.

$$$

Memorial Day weekend had rolled around and everybody was getting ready for the M-I-A. Miami was jumping this weekend and everybody was calling me and saying how they were going down there. Rod hit me. Joc called and said he had to perform at the Radio One show, and Nard called talking about he hollered at Torrey and they both wanted to roll out there. Everybody wanted to know what I was going to do.

"It's last minute as fuck, I don't know," I told Nard. It was already Thursday, which was cutting it close.

"We can fly out tomorrow," he urged. "You know it's gonna be jumpin'."

"All right, fuck it," I said finally.

"Well let's see if we can find some rooms."

I told him okay, and we set out to make reservations.

For hours, I was on the phone calling hotels but had no luck. I called Rod back and asked him where he was staying. He put me up on this penthouse that was renting rooms. It was located downtown and not on South Beach.

"I got a room there, call and they should have something for you," he said.

I got the number and hit them up. I spoke to a lady who told me she only had a few rooms left. I got Nard and me one. With this done, I hit Nard back and we made our plans to fly out the next day.

I called and told Joc I would be at the show. He was glad and promised me it would be a blast. Me and Nard packed up and hit the airport for our flight. I was glad I decided to go. I needed a change of scenery and to relax a little. Even though we'd do a show in Miami, it had a way of making work feel good. There was nothing like being in the party atmosphere of the M-I-A.

On the flight, me and Nard befriended two chicks who were also from Atlanta. They were heading down to Miami to party as well. They had made their plans last minute so they didn't have time to get any rooms. We told them we both had extra bedrooms and that they could post up with us. They took our offers saying they planned on being gone most of the time, like us.

In Miami, we found the penthouse and settled in. I called Joc, Rod and the crew and told them I made it. That night me, Nard, Rod and the chicks we met on the plane all hit the city together. Joc's show was the next day so we went ahead and club hopped, enjoying the night to the fullest.

The day of the show, Joc had been moving around a lot, doing promotions at radio stations and shit. We didn't get a chance to catch up with him during the day, but I knew we'd catch him at the show. Rod had gone out to handle some things as well. He'd been trying to catch up with this dude named Slam, who he said was Puffy's A&R. They spoke a couple of times and Rod told him he would be at the show. He also let him know he was with Joc and his people.

When the time came for the show, we all hit up this amphitheater where it was to be held. People were everywhere. Rod told me what time he'd be there and he met us in the back, at this gate they had for the artists to enter. In order to get in you had to have not only an arm band, but a ticket as well. Rico and Tomeeka had all the tickets and arm bands, so we had to wait on them. While we waited at the gate vans were pulled up, and artists jumped out left and right. One van pulled up with Duddy, Bobby and Bubba Sparxxx. When they all jumped out we immediately began dapping each other up.

"Man, what 'chall doing out here?" Bubba asked excitedly.

"Waiting on Joc and them," I explained. "Damn, it's good to see y'all boys."

"You too," Duddy chimed in.

"Why you out here waiting?" Bubba asked.

"Oh, we waiting on Joc and them so we can get our tickets and shit."

"Shit, y'all can just come in with us," he offered.

Bubba's people told him they didn't have any extra bands and tickets.

"Don't trip, I'll just wait." I said.

"All right, we'll see you inside."

In about twenty minutes or so, Joc pulled up. It was the whole crew: Boyz 'N Da Hood, Block, Tomeeka, Kerry, Ke, Biggs, Rico, Mike, Torrey and some Bad Boy personnel. Joc told the people at the gate that we were with them and they still wouldn't let us in. We turned to Block who claimed that they only had a few bands. Then some kind of way Tomeeka produced two extra tickets for me and Nard. I looked at Block suspiciously, like he was on some funny shit.

"Just go through the front, we'll get Biggs to get y'all back stage," Tomeeka said.

We did what she suggested, and in no time we were back stage.

The crowd was enormous. Acts were going on and off the stage like a merry go round. Backstage I caught up with Joc and the rest who were all grouped up and mingling.

"Duddy and Bubba are upstairs," Joc told me.

"Yeah, I saw them coming in," I said.

"Yeah, they told me."

I went upstairs to holler at them for a while and came down when Bubba's time to hit the stage rolled around. I stood backstage and watched Bubba do his thing. He still had it. After Bubba, Rick Ross performed a song he had out called "Hustlin." It was a banger and had the radio stations on fire. When Rick Ross finished, he brought out Block who introduced Boys 'N Da Hood. Word was that Block was going to put Rick Ross in Boys 'N Da Hood to replace Jeezy. After Block introduced them, he hurried off stage because he wasn't feeling well and sat down with a white towel draped over his head.

"Puffy's supposed to come out on stage," Joc said to me.

"Oh yeah?"

"Yeah. We practiced his Diddy walk, to go down the middle of the stage."

"The Diddy walk?" I asked jokingly. "Oh, you on your Diddy bop now?"

"Ya boy can get fly too, you know?"

We laughed.

"You wanna hype man for me, with Mike?" he asked.

"I don't care," I told him.

Right then Boys 'N Da Hood finished their set and Rico came and gave me and Mike microphones.

"Y'all go on out there," he told us.

"It's ah' Nitti beat" echoed throughout the amphitheater as the track started to play. Me and Mike hit the stage hyping the crowd as the intro sounded. The stage was huge. It had a middle section that ran out into the fans. Working the full stage was definitely a job for three people. When the first verse came in, Joc ran on stage and up the middle runway to do his thing.

The red, yellow and green lights flashed in sync with the music. I was in a complete zone. The Patron and energy from the crowd had me, Joc and Mike amped. During the first two hooks, we'd take a different area of the stage and join the fans in doing the dance.

Entering the third verse, the lights faded to dim and returned super bright, showing Puffy and Joc *Diddy boppin'* down to the front of the stage, where I just so happened to be. I fell back and let them do their thing. When the hook came we all came together and did the dance with the whole crowd leaning back and forth with us.

When we finished, we were rushed out of a back door, through a crowd of people out back where Puff had a Phantom parked with a driver waiting. He and Joc jumped in and rode off. The vans for us were parked and ready to leave as well. I told Tomeeka and them I was cool, as I saw all the chicks around. I figured this was the best place for me. So Torrey, Nard and me chilled until we finally hit the streets, mingling and partying with the finest women Miami had to offer.

Tomeeka called me later that evening.

"Puff called to see if any of us wanted to come to his house for dinner, on Star Island. Y'all want to come?" she asked.

I told Nard and Torrey, asking what did they want to do. They were cool with it.

"Yeah, we comin'," I told her.

"Well Imm'ah send the van to come pick y'all up," she said.

Me, Nard and Torrey told the chicks we were with that we'd catch up with them later. After escorting them out of the penthouse, we got ready. It wasn't more than 30 minutes later that a black caravan and a travel van pulled up out front to get us. I jumped in the black caravan with Joc, Rico, Tomeeka, Biggs and some Bad Boy staff. Nard and Torrey jumped in the other van.

"What's up," Joc asked in a good mood.

"Man, just enjoying myself," I told him.

"We killed the show earlier," he said. "But aye, listen to this right quick."

I watched as Joc inserted a CD into the van's stereo system and instantly the song we recorded called "1st Time" began to play. As I listened, the hook came in and a voice I didn't recognize was singing.

"What happened to getting Trey Songz?" I asked.

"Block didn't get him," he said. "Instead he got Marcus Houston to sing the hook and worked a deal where I'd be on his next single in return. We already recorded that too. Wanna hear it?"

"Yeah," I said.

After the song finished, Joc put in the single for Marcus Houston and being honest, it wasn't a hit to me. I told Joc his song had lost its original feel. He just shrugged and said we'd have to see how well it does. The whole while I was thinking, *why Block didn't tell me he was changing the plan?*

Traffic was heavy. We made a few runs and picked up some more people. Finally, we made it to the guard shack that stood at the entrance to Puffy's neighborhood. The driver of the van made way after we got clearance and entered the circle driveway to Puffy's house. If I say his house was extravagant, it would be an understatement.

"This bitch is fly," I said in the van.

The driveway was made out of brick cobblestone. An outer house, like a built-in pool house, was off to the left with a flower garden surrounding it. A brick wall was built up, knee high, in a circle directly in the middle of the driveway. A fountain was inside the circle. Phantoms, Bentleys and other exotic cars were parked in a semicircle behind the fountain.

After parking, we all got out and were then escorted to the side of the house where we kicked off our shoes and exchanged them for some all-white slide on slippers. We were told Puffy doesn't let anyone wear their shoes in the house. After this, we went back to the front of the house to go inside.

As soon as I got in I saw a big eating table shaped like the letter U. We all walked through the house and went into the kitchen where Puff had a serving line set up like a Piccadilly's restaurant, or a high school cafeteria. We got our trays and placed plates on them, moving along in a line filled with people who had arrived before us. Everyone was helping themselves to the varieties of food available. As I moved with the line, I couldn't help but admire the style in which Puff had. His success afforded him to present a wonderful environment, to be a host.

Biggs came up to me, Nard and Mike. He had Tomeeka with him.

"Puff said y'all are cool, enjoy yourselves," she said. "But make sure y'all don't be all up in people's faces, bothering them and shit."

"Tell that nigga we ain't no groupies," Nard blurted.

"Man tell that nigga we ain't even trippin' on even being here," I chimed in.

"Nah! Tell that nigga we got bread too," Nard said, pulling two rubber-banded knots from his pockets. "This is twenty racks right here, just for this weekend . . . and I got another mil to go wit' it."

"Chino, Chino," Tomeeka said, trying to get control of things. "Calm down." People were beginning to look in our direction and a security guard came over to our little crowd.

"Puffy said y'all cool man," he said. "Y'all have a good time."

I looked at Biggs. He should have straightened that shit and not even brought it to us.

"Why you pull that money out like that?" I asked Nard as we continued down the line. "That little paper ain't shit to Puff."

"Shit I just wanted to let the nigga know we ain't no street punks."

I laughed and told the servers what I wanted from the selection of food. When I was finished I went to the drink dispenser and got me some soda and sat down at this little table facing the line because the big table was full. I noticed to my right a double-door cooler that resembled the type you saw in a convenience store, the kind that held sodas and beers. This one had nothing but Cristal, Moet and some other shit. Just then somebody called me to the big table so I got up and headed over there.

As soon as I got to the table I noticed super producer Scott Scorch was just getting up. He had a beautiful Cuban looking chick with him who looked like an angel dressed in a white linen sundress. That's when I began looking around the table.

"Is that Beyoncé?" I asked Nard.

"Hell yeah, and look, there's Jay-Z."

I saw him and more familiar faces. That's when the waitress came and brought us our alcoholic beverages. Puffy had whatever you wanted: Patron, Grey Goose, Hennessy, Cristal and Moet. He even had them all by the bottles.

After we finished, we were all introduced to Beyoncé and Jay-Z, as well as some record executives. We all mingled in the living room together as Puff played Joc's CD through the house's stereo system. Puff had a big theater-sized screen on his wall and a long sofa and some end recliner seats. Some people went out and sat on the back patio, down by the pool. Me, Mike, Torrey and Nard went wandering out past the pool and found ourselves by a trail just beyond a gazebo Puffy had. Tomeeka told us this trail would take us to the channel water, where boats were docked. We followed the trail until we got to the water, where we stood admiring the scenery of boats and yachts bobbing on a large expanse of sparkling blue water.

"Man, this is hard," I said.

"Now this is the big life," Nard agreed.

All of us relaxed, taking time out to smoke some exotic weed.

Although I'm not a big chronic smoker, I felt the mood was right. As we smoked we all found ourselves on our cell phones, calling back to Atlanta telling our family and friends how we were at Puffy's house in Miami, eating dinner with Beyoncé and Jay Z.

When we came back from the docks I went back into the living room where I found myself talking to some chick. That's when someone came and told me Joc wanted me to come to the front, where Puff had a studio in the little building by the driveway. I excused myself from the lovely lady and found my way to the studio.

Puffy had spared no expense on studio equipment. I found Joc inside.

"What's up bra' . . . you good?" Joc asked.

"Yeah, what's up?" I asked. "What 'chu doin'?"

Joc told me he was helping Puffy write some new material for his next CD *Press Play*. Joc needed me to help him remember an old verse he used to recite. After helping him for a minute, I went back inside and bumped into Jay-Z coming out. He was dressed in some camouflage shorts and a black t-shirt.

"What's up man," I said casually.

"Nothin much," he responded. "You Joc's people right?"

"Yeah, his brother," I said.

"I like his style. Y'all keep up the good work."

I thanked him as he continued about his business.

Back in the house, I heard "Dopeboy Magic" bumping with my verse on. I went into this little room and sat on a sofa where I found Mike and some chicks talking. Then I went back into the big room where I sat on the floor in front of Beyoncé and the chick I'd met, when this dude began calling my name.

"Chino, yo Chino."

"Yeah, what's up?"

"I'm Slam," he said. "I just talked to Rod and he told me you'd be here."

I got up and went by him and we chopped it up. That's when Puff came in and announced that it was time for the Mayweather fight.

I'd heard Mayweather was supposed to be boxing. I watched as Puff hit a button or something and the back wall before us slid away, revealing the large screen, for everybody to see, even from outside the room. Then we all sat and watched as Mayweather punished some cat to win yet another fight.

After the fight, me, Nard, Mike and Torrey sat on the back patio drinking and talking to these fine ass white chicks from Sweden. Nard was tipsy and dropped the champagne flute and it crashed loudly on the concrete. Instantly, one of Puffy's maids came and swept up the glass, before bringing him another drink. That's when we heard a weird noise.

"Awwk! Awwk! Awwk! Vulture on the loose, vulture on the loose."

That's when I looked up and saw that it was none other than Puffy himself, flapping his arms like wings and swooping in like a large bird. He came and sat on the arm of the seat Nard was sitting in and Nard dropped another glass.

We all busted out laughing.

"Man, y'all got down today," Puff said, talking about our performance.

Me and Mike thanked him. Puff mingled with us some more then he moved on to his other guests.

"So, what 'chall doing tonight?" Slam asked.

We weren't sure but we finally came up with going to a strip club. Slam agreed to go. Puff had said he was going to chill and I figured out why: I'd seen him with a blonde haired white chick with a super fat ass. So his night was sealed.

It was getting around the time to leave. Everyone was starting to form outside and I got up with Slam, Mike, Torrey and the Swedish chicks. They were all out there going over plans for the night.

"Where's Nard?" I asked Torrey.

"Y'all look!" Tomeeka said while pointing to Nard out drunk in Puffy's immaculate flowerbed.

"Help me get him to the van," I said to Mike and Torrey. First, we stripped him of all his jewelry and money. Then we put him on the first row seat of the van.

Following Slam's lead, we ended up at a mixed-crowd, upper-class strip club. We had gotten a big VIP room. After about an hour, Torrey came back and told me he couldn't find Nard. He had wondered off from him in the club.

We were with the Swedish chicks. Slam had them lined up and was putting his tongue down their throats, one by one. When he was finished, he looked at me and said, "You want some of this?"

I thought, this nigga's enjoying life right now. But with a missing, drunken Nard on the loose, luckily I couldn't join in. I told Torrey "let's split up and see if we can find him." Thirty minutes later and still no Nard in sight, we headed outside to check the parking lot where we found him lying on the hood of the van.

Shit was crazy that night. When the next morning came, Nard woke up at the penthouse panicking: "Man, who stole my money? Somebody stole my jewelry!"

"Stop hollering, we got it before Baby did."

He started smiling.

"Baby who?" he asked. "Did y'all get my phone?"

"Nah, we didn't get your phone . . . you been got for dat," I said, shaking my head. I just started laughing and walked off, headed back to my bed where ole girl from the flight awaited. My phone rang and it was Joc.

"Chino man, I'm getting used to this," he said.

"I'm just glad to see it finally paying off for you."

"For us," he said.

I needed to hear that.

"They're flying me out to Dallas," he said. "Y'all should come down."

I looked and saw everyone in the penthouse finally up and moving around.

"We'll be there," I told him.

Nard was already eavesdropping. "And Imm'ah call the airlines," he said.

Self Treat

My partner Jamie picked us up at the Dallas/Fort Worth airport. Joc was staying at some hotel that catered to the stars, so we got a room there.

When we got to the hotel, it was packed. We met Joc at the bar and bumped into Chamillionaire, who's "Ridin' Dirty" song was bumpin' just as hard as "It's Goin Down." We screamed at him for a while then I dismissed myself to go back to my room to change clothes for the night. On my way back to the room, I ran into Chamillionaire again at the elevator.

"This shit throwed ain't it?" Chamillionaire asked as we stood waiting. "What 'chall doin' tonight?"

"Workin," I said. "We got a show in Shreveport . . . we just flew in and we're gonna take the bus down there then we got some shit to do here tomorrow night."

At that moment, we heard someone walking up and turned to see Pimp C.

"What's up Legend?" I asked Pimp C.

"I'm glad you back with us mane," Chamillionaire said from the heart.

"All ready," he responded before coming over to dap us up. Then turning to me he said, "I saw y'all earlier but I didn't get a chance to holla. I just wanted to say I like what 'chall doin'.'"

"Preciate it Pimp," I said. "That means a lot coming from you." Pimp C was legend in the South. A head nod from a real pioneer meant a lot.

We stood there chilling out for a while and then some young cat walked over. He had a video camera and was saying that he was recording a hip hop DVD.

"Would y'all give a few shout outs for me," he asked.

Not ones to turn down a young hustler, me, Pimp C and Chamillionaire gave some shout outs to each other, ourselves and finally dude's DVD. When we got done, the dude thanked us and we all said our parting words.

After I got dressed, I headed to the tour bus and was about to board, when I saw Nard just standing off to the side.

"Come on Nard," I called out.

Nard moved to get on and that's when Rico popped out of nowhere.

"Damn Chino," he said. "You just bringin' niggas now?"

"What?" I said, not believing my ears. " That ain't nothin' but my cousin Nard."

"You good but he can't come," he said.

"I know I'm good and as for Nard, if it wasn't for niggas like him, Joc wouldn't be where he's at now," I said, "which means you wouldn't have a job." My words were hard and direct. I had been seeing too much and not saying shit. I wanted to make sure niggas didn't start coming to think I wasn't a factor, and that my word didn't count.

"It ain't on me . . . it's the label," Rico said, switching his approach. "The insurance won't cover if something happens. Right then I saw a chick on the bus who was just sitting down. I also saw a chick following Joc around.

I called Joc out.

"What's up Chino?" he said.

I nodded at Nard.

"I ain't leavin' my nigga," I said, "so I'll catch up to you when y'all get back from Louisiana."

Joc gave me a confused look before looking at Rico. Me and Nard just spent off.

That night me and Nard ended up calling Jamie. The three of us hit a strip club and fucked with some girls we met. The next morning Jamie came with a few chicks and we took Nard to the airport. The whole vibe was dead for him and I knew it. Joc and them came back and I fought with the idea to check Rico some more. Torrey was doing his filming and Mike doing hype man, but Nard had been "in" in many more ways: money, support and loyalty. Niggas like Rico didn't understand keeping it real to those who helped you to make it to the next level. He probably had a small gang of niggas he stopped fucking with since being with us.

But why wasn't Joc speaking up?

<h1 style="text-align:center">$$$</h1>

Back in Atlanta after hitting a few more cities. It was about time for the album to drop. Block told me that Carl Moe was a little upset because he didn't get a song on the album. I told Block that I felt he should've gotten a song regardless of what happened between me and him that night at the club. At the end of the day he was a major factor in Joc's success.

In preparation of the album release, Greg Street pumped the hell out of the song one night. He played it on his "Top 8 at 8" in all of the 8 spots. The momentum was building for Joc. He had to be in NYC to do some promo for the album on 106 and Park. I stood in my living room when it aired thinking how I was supposed to be there, so I could crack at Rocsi. In the interview, Joc shouted me out and the team. DJ Smooth had shouted me out on Rap City back in the days but this was different.

With my phone ringing off the hook, I enjoyed the feeling of what we'd accomplished. Then when they played the song at #1 and I saw myself, Joc and Nitti, I thought back to when times weren't as sweet, when me and Joc had to go get his raggedy Cadillac and my girl, at the time, was hounding me about helping him and his family out. It felt good to see him living his dream.

Now that the album was turned in, I asked Block about the twenty-five racks I was supposed to receive. When I called him, he told me to come by the studio and I was there before he could hang up the phone.

Honestly, I was praying there wouldn't be no bullshit with my money. I didn't know, but I was beginning to feel uncomfortable with how cats were carrying it. Even though I knew I was covered from a legal standpoint, I didn't want to disturb the positive vibe of success in all of this. So, when I went to discuss my ends, I was glad when Block gave me my money without any problems.

After I hit the SunTrust bank and was heading home, something told me to stop by the Mercedes Benz dealer in Union City. Ju-Ju's uncle worked up there and I figured I'd just see what they had new on the market. But all that went out the window as soon as I pulled up. Sitting under a canopy right at the entrance to the building was a white Benz with chrome wheels, just calling me. *"Chino . . . Chino, come get me."* I hopped out like a man saving a beautiful drowning woman.

The CLS 550 Benz was clean with sand interior. After looking at it real good I went inside the dealership and stepped to the receptionist's desk. A young white lady was working.

"Yes, I'm looking for Mr. Harris," I said.

"Yes, I'll get him for you," she said smiling.

"Unc, what's up?" I said as I saw Mr. Harris coming from some back offices.

"Hey Cha', boy what 'chu up to?"

I explained that I was just stopping by to holla at him and that's when that new CLS started calling my name. Mr. Harris told me he could do the paperwork if I wanted it. I asked what would I have to put down on it.

"What 'chu lookin' like?" he asked.

"How's ten grand?" I asked.

"Cash?"

"Yep," I nodded.

"If you give me ten grand it will be waiting on you in the morning to drive off the lot," he said, "as long as you got your insurance to cover it."

I told him my insurance could cover it and he said it was a go. Then I went outside to the van and grabbed $10,000 in crisp $100 bills still wrapped in the bank wrap.

"O.K.," Mr. Harris said with a smile. "Imm'ah make sure everything is ready for you in the morning." He shook my hand and said, "Cha, before you leave I just wanna say I see y'all doing y'all thing. Tell that nephew of mine to holla at me."

"Dat's what's up," I said with a smile. "I'll let Ju-Ju know."

New Joc City

June 6th. The day of the album release. I woke up excited. I headed down to the car dealership and picked up my brand new trophy. I felt so deserving, after all my hustling and grinding, to have finally made it to this point. And with Joc finally dropping his album, I knew the sky was the limit.

After getting a fresh haircut at "Off Da Hook," I needed something fresh for the day, so after I picked up the Benz, I headed to Lenox Mall. After leaving the Benz with the valet, I hit up Neiman Marcus and the Gucci, Prada and Versace stores, only to come up with nothing. Figuring one could never go wrong at Macy's I headed there and settled on a white Sean John collared shirt with orange stripes stitched into it. I'd already bought some brand new white and orange Air Force Ones and an orange LA fitted cap I'd gotten from DTLR. The shirt was all I needed to complete an outfit for the day's events.

Joc was scheduled to do an album signing that evening at the Best Buy on the south side in Morrow, off of Mount Zion Blvd. I shot back to my house and got dressed and handled a few things like making calls and setting things up for that evening. When I was done, I hopped in my new Benz and headed for the event.

When I got to Best Buy, there was a huge line formed out front. There was a table set up to the right as soon as you entered the building where I saw Joc and Block sitting with Greg Street, who was doing a live radio remote. Harve Pierre from Bad Boy and Kevin Lyles were on top of everything. As soon as Greg saw me he called me over.

"Yo Chino. . . .yeah, y'all we got Chino Dolla in the building," he said over the airwaves.

"What's up Greg?" I went over and gave Joc some dap and tossed a head nod to Block.

"Aww, nothing but this New Joc City," he said. "Tell us about it. How you feel about the album?"

"I love it man. It's goin' to be big. The streets are going to love it."

"What about tonight? The album release party is at Club Vision. What 'chall got planned?"

"Oh, you know us," I said smiling. "We're gonna do it big. I'm thinking about buying the bar out for an hour or two."

Greg went on to Block to get some comments from him, and I turned to Joc.

"Man look at all these broads," he said.

"Yeah, I know," he said, referring to the various shades, shapes and sizes of females around us. Block had model chicks walking around wearing "I Know U See It" baby tee shirts to promote Joc's next single. The scene was unbelievable.

I sat as women, men and young teens came to have their personal copy of *New Joc City* signed by Joc himself. The praise Joc received was overwhelming. It was all a clear indication that our long hours in the studio had finally paid off. We took a few photos with the fans and models, which helped me to meet this pretty ass Spanish model, Liz, that was a must-have.

"I'mma be back." I told Joc. I went and bought a CD myself. I didn't have to but for some reason I wanted to experience it from a fan's perspective, despite my having everything in the world to do with its creation.

I was on my way back to the table when I stopped to look at the final product. Something caught me by surprise. I looked at the front of the CD, then the back, and then both sides over and over again. *"What the. . . "*

  With my eyes glued to the CD, I searched intently only to find two logos and names credited for the creation of Joc's album: BLOCK ENT/BAD BOY RECORDS. I felt the stab of disappointment. After all the blood, sweat and tears I had shed; I had literally lost my family behind this product: my girl and stepson I had raised, along with time from my own children, only for someone else to get all the recognition.

  "Fall back and play your role…I got 'chu. . . " I could hear Block like it was right in my ear.

  What in the fuck did that mean? Now I was really beginning to wonder.

  "I can't believe this," Quet said, looking at the CD back at my crib, "how these niggas ain't put the MasterMind Music logo on this shit?"

  I heard him speaking but my mind was running a million miles a minute. After seeing it for myself I kept my composure, not wanting to ruin the event at Best Buy.

  "That nigga Block is gonna answer for this," Torrey said.

  I didn't reply.

  Before we left Best Buy, I had gotten a few VIP bands from Tomeeka for the club that night. I knew I needed to holler at Block about the reason MasterMind wasn't on the CD. I'd give him a chance to clarify first, before I jumped to conclusions.

  At my crib, me, Torrey and Quet got ready for the club. I got a call from Reece and O, who'd just landed from Cali, telling me they were in the city and ready to smoke everybody in the club out. I told them to meet me at the club later and that I had VIP bands for them. After I got off the phone with them, Joc hit me.

  "What's up bra'?" he asked. "When you left it seemed like something was bothering you."

  I kept everything to myself for the moment. Even though it troubled me that he didn't notice.

  "Nah, I'm cool," I said. "Where y'all at?"

"We're on our way to the studio to load up to hit Vision right now," he said.

"All right. Me, Torrey and Quet are heading out," I told him. "Reece and O just called me too. They'll be there."

"O.K. I'll see y'all there."

The Album
Release Party

The time was 11:35 p.m. when I glanced at the diamond-encrusted bezel that laced my left wrist.

"Let's ride y'all, it's show time," I told Quet and Torrey while standing up from the sofa and grabbing my keys and phones off of the coffee table.

"Say Boi Boi," Torrey began, "where the after party at?"

"Wherever we want it to be," I said. "Why you ask?"

"Because if we ain't coming back here and hitting the Georgia Terrace or somewhere, I need to bring all these pills, cash and bottles. . ."

Torrey barely finished his words before Quet cut him off: "Man, we ain't taking all that shit. We might wake up in Vegas or somewhere."

In the car my mind drifted. Just nine months ago, I was maneuvering through Atlanta's underworld in my Denali, headed to Body Tap to introduce "It's Goin Down" to the city. Now I was pushing my brand new Benz up 75/85 North to introduce the world to *New Joc City*. Enjoying the new car smell while consuming our new product had me speeding and dipping in and out of traffic like Mario Andretti. I was on cloud nine, as I rapped along with my verse on "Dope Boy Magic."

Before I knew it we were engulfed by the city's bright lights and turning off of Peachtree Street into the parking lot of Visions night club. Benz's, Beamers, and Bentleys filled the line for valet parking. My boy

Alex G had come a long way with his entertainment company from back in the day. I remember when he used to valet park cars. Now he had the biggest clubs in the city. AG Entertainment was also making moves in Miami, Houston, and Dallas, expanding his brand. Not everybody got to do an album release party at Visions.

But we were . . .

Lines at the front and side were both filled with some of the baddest chicks in the city. While creeping forward, I watched all the women in body suits, miniskirts and low riding jeans with their hair all fly thinking which ones would end up as our guests for the night. Grabbing my phone, I called my dude Ced and told him to meet me at the valet parking. Ced was my security for the night. He was 7 feet tall, 300 pounds . . . giant muthafucka.

Before I could hang up the phone good, valet was opening my door.

"Where you want me to put it?" he asked as I stepped out the whip, pulling my fitted low. "Here go a bill. You know what to do with it."

With Quet and Torrey in stride, we made it to the back of the club, the entrance for the VIP. A red carpet, surrounded by paparazzi, decorated the ground. A velvet rope headed the red carpet where the $200 VIP fee was collected. Cameras flashed as a host of media outlets did live interviews with the city's "who's who" that came out to celebrate with us.

"Yo Chino!" I heard someone yell over all the commotion. I looked to my right and saw Ced. He was towering over everyone as he headed in my direction.

"What's up fam?" I said, giving him dap. "I was just about to call and tell you where I was."

"You didn't have to call me, I already had an eye on you. That's what you pay me for." Ced informed me seriously.

About that time Travis, Ju Ju, Vick, Roc, A.K., Redman, Reece and O walked up. Everybody was fresh from head to toe.

"What's up fellas?" I asked as I passed out the VIP bands.

"Ayo, Chino Dolla," a voice called out from a group of people.

"What's up Jason?" Jason was a member of the Bad Boy staff and was one of the cooler dudes who worked there.

"I want you to walk the red carpet with Kevin Lyles, y'all two together will represent both sides of the Yung Joc movement," he said.

"Cool," I said, understanding what he meant.

Time seemed like it was moving hyperspeed. We bounced from one camera flash to another, one question to the next until we made it into the club.

The inside of Visions was humongous. It wasn't all the way packed yet. That made it easier for us to slide through the club and mingle. Rick Ross's song "Hustlin" vibrated through the club as we passed jiggling asses and bouncing titties with every step.

Just as we set out to find our VIP section I heard my name called by a female voice, "Chauncey! Chauncey!!"

Then I felt my arm being grabbed, so I spun around only to see the most unexpected person in the whole world: my ex-girlfriend.

Made up and looking her absolute best in a little white skirt and low cut light green top. She gave me a winning smile.

"Tell these hoes you wit me tonight," she said, while on my heels.

"Look, how about you leave me now like you left me then," I said after coming to a complete stop and walked off. Ced heard the conversation and held her back asking her politely to leave.

I was in a new place with my life and feeling wonderful. All the long hours had come to this and I was moving on. It felt bittersweet to see her. I knew now she'd go back and see how all my hard work was indeed to better myself and her but now there was no "her."

"Where's Joc and them?" asked Reece.

At that moment it seemed the club had gotten super crowded. Then we saw Joc, Block, Biggs and a host of others make their way in from a side door. They were weaving their way through and me and Joc caught eyes as he nodded in the direction of the section they had for us to party in. People were starting to file in fast.

"Look," I said to everybody. "Let's make our way to the VIP section they got for us . . . before it gets too packed."

When I made it over to our VIP, I saw a barricade was set up to separate the dance floor from us. Ced lifted me up like a baby and placed me on the other side, then he stepped over. Our section was up a few stairs in the back of the club overlooking the dance floor. In our section, Joc had everything you could think of to drink: Patron, Rose', Grey Goose. . . .whatever. I saw his mom, wife, Ms. S, Ms. B, Mike, Elvis,

Chris and some more of our people. Plus everyone that was with me now had the whole family there.

Everybody except Nitti . . .

"What's up," I said, making my way over to Joc and embracing him.

"Just taking it all in," he told me. "Sometimes it's hard to believe, after all we've been through."

I spoke to his mom, wife and everyone else: Out of my peripheral, I saw Torrey and Quet hollering at Reece and O. I wasn't sure what they were discussing, but I could tell my cousins from Cali weren't feeling it.

When the time rolled around for Joc to perform, they brought two mics, and Joc gave me one to pump up the crowd.

"*New Joc City* baby," I screamed into the mic. "MasterMind, Block Ent., Bad Boy, it's only the beginning."

About that time, the crowd started screaming and cameras started flashing in my face. P. Diddy stepped over the rail in front of me and posted up with us in front of the sea of people.

The energy of the party escalated times ten. Bottles were being popped and blunts circulated like we'd won a championship game. The DJ had started playing Joc's album. When "It's Goin Down" came on the whole club went ape shit crazy. Then as the first verse ended, the intensity amplified just as Joc brought the hook in. At this point, it was like the whole crowd went into a trance and was doing the motorcycle dance.

"Yeah muthafuckas!! This is Block E-N-T . . . this how we do!" Block yelled as he stood on a table. "We run this bitch!"

From a crowded place in the VIP my attention was drawn to him as he ranted obnoxiously all out of character. With his fitted pulled low and feeling himself, Block continued on as I saw my crew, who were behind him, give each other looks as Block kept his back to them.

"Watch out nigga. You got 'cho ass all in my face," O called out, tapping Block at the same time.

"Well nigga you need to move then," Block said as he turned with an arrogant look.

"You see it's crowded in here but since you wanna get fly, we'll see what's up," O said.

Block dismissed O with the wave of his hand and kept on with his antics. Right then O departed and made it toward me.

"Man, fuck that nigga!" He said.

I could see O was steaming mad. Reece came at that moment as well.

"What's up Chino?" he asked. "Aye O, what was that all about?"

"Cuz, that nigga Block . . . I'm ready to blaze his ass."

"Chino, what's this shit about that nigga Block fuckin' over you with the deal with Joc's shit? Reece asked. "Torrey and Quet told us MasterMind ain't gettin' no credit on the album."

"Man, I don't know what that nigga did. I was gonna wait to holler at him about it." It was hard to hide my disappointment.

"So it's true?" O asked.

I didn't get a chance to respond.

"After all that work you put in," came Reece. "Cuz, fuck that pussy ass nigga. He done fucked over the wrong one."

They both were upset so I tried to calm them. "Look, I'm sure there's a reason . . ."

"Nah, fuck that Chino," O said violently. "You know that nigga on some shit. He went too far."

I tried to get in another word but it was too late. They both stormed off and left the VIP and club all together.

Nobody but my crew paid any attention to the conversation I'd had with Reece and O. They were California gang bangers and I knew they got hot headed at times, which concerned me. Up until that point, I hadn't really relaxed, and honestly, it was because of this shit with Block. I figured I'd grab me a fine bitch for the night, and that would help take my mind off the issues at hand.

Everything was winding down. We blazed the club, had a good time and partied our asses off. People we didn't know congratulated Joc and the crew for our accomplishments and wished us the best. Tipsy as fuck, I walked out of the club smiling like I was on top of the world. APD was deep to ensure there were no problems.

"Hey you," two voices called simultaneously, sounding like music to my ears.

I turned and saw two of the most beautiful women I'd seen that whole night. Both in form fitting body suits standing at about 5'5" and 150 lbs. looking like Serena and Venus Williams. I could barely speak.

"What's up ladies?" I asked.

I still hadn't pulled anything for the night and was granted more than I wished for when both openly admitted they wanted to be with me for the night. They were African beauties living in Atlanta and looking for a good time.

Right up my alley.

With me in the middle, the three of us, with Quet, Torrey and Ced in tow, maneuvered through a large crowd as we made our way to my Mercedes. The night was perfect and the vibe was festive. Joc walked up on me, to give me one last hug.

"All right bra'," he said smiling at the two women on my arm. "Give me a call in the morning."

"Who said I plan on going to sleep?"

"Listen," he continued in a serious tone. "On some real shit, thanks for everything. Look at me now, this all wouldn't have ever happened without you."

"Just have a good time," I said and patted him on the back. "I'll get at 'chu tomorrow."

Joc spinned off in the direction of his wife and family. Just as he did, I caught sight of someone I hadn't seen in years.

"Toya," I yelled out.

Now when I say fine, I mean Toya was fine as hell. I hadn't seen her since I lived in Lithonia. I used to fuck around with her back then, and seeing her that night made me forget about the two African chicks I had with me.

"Hey Chauncey," she said, smiling.

"What's up, you were in the club?" I asked.

"Yeah," she replied. "I saw you."

"Why didn't you speak?"

"I figured y'all were celebrating and I didn't want to bother you," she said with a shrug.

"Baby girl, you know we go way back. If anybody is welcomed it's you."

She was looking sexy as hell in her heels and short skirt that showed off her long yellow legs that led to an apple bottom and small waist that only made that ass look 3 times bigger.

"What 'chu got going tonight?" I asked while looking into her pretty brown eyes.

"I don't know, probably go back to the crib," she said.

"Shit, why don't you roll wit' me. We're going back to my house and chill out."

"Fuck it, why not," she said while looking at the two African chicks, who both smiled at her.

Fuckin' right!

I told Quet and Torrey to take the Benz and the two chicks and meet me at my crib. I was riding with Toya. Then out of the corner of my eye I saw a tall, dark-skinned figure approaching me from my side, with a fitted hat pulled low on his head. At first I thought it was Block, but then I turned and saw it was my partner Shay.

"Chino! My boy," he called out.

"Shay, what it do?"

"I just wanted to say I like how y'all boys done came up," he said sincerely. "I'm just glad you . . ."

That's when we heard a loud scream pierce through the crowd. The type of sound you only hear in horror movies.

I felt a panic rush stir inside me as my eyes darted side to side. That's when I saw two figures darting in my direction with hats pulled low on their heads and blue bandanas on their faces. Aggressively carrying semi-automatic weapons, both men ran right up on me, Shay, Toya and Ced.

I froze.

"What's up now nigga?"

And the night went silent as everybody ducked and rushed behind the vehicles in the parking lot.

Present Day

"Yard recall! Yard recall! All inmates, return to your housing units for count. This begins yard recall."

The announcement from the control center at the facility blared over the P.A. system. Inmates on the recreation yard dropped what they were doing and made their way to the fence for release back to their units.

For the past two hours, I had sat with Money and Don Twan, explaining aspects of my life and incidents pertaining to my involvement in the music business. I had never sat and got as in-depth as I had just now. So much had transpired that time worked against me.

"Damn," Don Twan said. "A nigga was so lost in the story that I forgot about yard recall."

"Yeah," Money agreed. "Chino, you came a long way. I didn't even know you had a hand in Joc's shit like that."

"Me either," Don Twan said.

I laughed.

"A lot of people don't know," I said.

"Let's go fellas. Back to the housing unit," said an officer working the yard.

All three of us got up.

"So real quick," Money began, "What happened when them niggas ran up on y'all?"

"Yeah," Don Twan chimed in. "Did you get hit up? Or did you let them fools have it and that's how you ended up in here and Joc fell off?"

So many questions came at me. I could see their curiosity.

"You know," I began, "all of your questions, I can't answer just like that. All I can say is a whole lot of shit popped off. Shit that showed me niggas' true loyalty, how money affected people's morals and how no matter the level of success people see you gain, it's worthless if you can't keep it real."

Don Twan and Money stood looking at me confused.

"Nigga you sound like a Chinese fortune cookie," Don Twan finally said.

As the yard began to empty, my partners and I had made it to our unit. "I'll tell y'all what, how about we meet back up tomorrow and I'll finish the story."

To Be continued . . . .

The Betrayal and Deceit At The Top of The World

MASTERMIND PUBLISHING

COMING SOON

2013

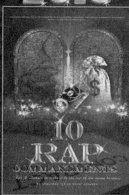

CHINODOLLAR.COM

2014

For publishing and other inquiries:

info@chinodollar.com
CHINODOLLAR.COM INC.
1021 Hardeman Mill Road
Madison, GA 30650
(404) 787-2767

www.chinodollar.com